UFO SIGHTINGS DESK REFERENCE: UNITED STATES OF AMERICA 2001-2015

Frequency-Distribution-Shapes

UFO SIGHTINGS DESK REFERENCE: UNITED STATES OF AMERICA 2001-2015

CHERYL COSTA
LINDA MILLER COSTA

UFO SCHOLAR
an imprint of
DRAGON LADY MEDIA, LLC
SYRACUSE, NEW YORK

2017

We recognize that this is a reference book and we encourage people to use the data for their own research. Please cite this book in your references. If you need custom reports, contact the publisher at reports@cherylcosta.com and arrangements can be made to accommodate your information needs.

Our data was derived from raw reports in the NUFORC (www.nuforc.org) and MUFON (www.mufon.com) databases publically available on the internet. We make no claims to ownership of the original NUFORC and MUFON data and thank them for their generosity to the UFO research community.

First edition 2017
ISBN 13-978-1544219233
ISBN 10-1544219237

Cover art by Susann Snyder, shadoecatart@yahoo.com

Printed by CreateSpace, An Amazon.com Company

Publisher:

Dragon Lady Media, LLC
223 Columbia Avenue
Syracuse, New York 13207
publisher@cherylcosta.com
www.ufoscholar.com

DEDICATION

To Erich von Däniken
For asking 256 questions in his "Chariots of the Gods"

To Dave Singer
Thank you for the introduction to the International Fortean Organization and Charles Fort's "The Book of the Damned"

To our mothers

Jean L. Costa for lovingly explaining a UFO sighting to a fascinated child

Norma Bowes Miller for teaching the importance of independent thinking

When I learned that aliens really do exist, I wasn't too surprised. But what did shock me when I started investigating extraterrestrial reports a decade ago is the extent to which the proof has been hushed up. It isn't just the US government which has kept quiet about alien visits. It would be arrogant of an American like myself to assume that ETs would only choose to visit my country. Indeed, I've heard convincing stories about governments all over the world that know of alien visits - including the British government.

Edgar Mitchell, astronaut

There is no doubt in my mind, after 37 years of study and investigation that the evidence is overwhelming that planet Earth is being visited by intelligently controlled vehicles whose origin is extraterrestrial. There are no acceptable arguments against flying saucer reality, only people who either haven't studied the relevant data or have a strong will not to believe that Earth is at the bottom of the heap sociologically and technologically in our local galactic neighborhood.

Stanton T. Friedman, retired nuclear physicist and professional ufologist

"With our obsession with antagonisms of the moment, we often forget how much unites all the members of humanity. I occasionally think how quickly our differences, worldwide, would vanish if we were facing an alien threat from outside this world."

Former President Ronald Reagan,
while sharing the stage with former Russian leader, Mikhail Gorbachev, 1988.

TABLE OF CONTENTS

FORWARD

Richard Hoffman, MUFON

While sightings of Unidentified Flying Objects or UFOs are nothing new and collections of reports from solid credible citizens have been amassed over the many decades since the late 1940s, much has been learned by the analysis of the data collected. First, we can see that there are periods of heightened activity in certain areas over a short period of time, an event we call a "Flap". These Flaps may be brought about by manmade or natural phenomena or by objects we cannot account for and refer to as unknowns. Next, we learn from reports that the majority of cases are at night. Witnesses can easily see a light moving around on a dark background than a dark object on a light background. Many of us fail to notice the many aircraft moving at 40,000 feet above our heads during the daytime hours. The unfortunate issue about evening sightings is that they provide us the least amount of details about the object(s) and are most often misidentifications of known objects, like aircraft, bolides, and even Chinese lanterns released at many holiday or ceremonial events.

Since I got engaged with this subject at age 13 in 1964, I have investigated nearly a thousand cases and can account for the vast majority as being misidentifications, however, there are a good number (approximately 10%) that seem to defy a logical explanation. It's these head scratchers that, in fact, keep me engaged in this subject and have done this for over five decades. Another motivation by this long-term interest is in knowing that it is a worldwide phenomenon that extends to every culture throughout recorded history. Regardless of where we are, on the ocean, on land or in our atmosphere and in space, they are observed. Knowing that if I apply the same logic that many are explainable, there is still a very large number statistically that would remain unknown after careful investigation has been completed.

UFO statistics have been collected by various governmental projects that continue to validate what I have experienced during my tenure. The US Air Force Projects (Sign, Grudge and Blue Book) had 701 cases that remained as unknowns out of the over 12,000 cases they collected from 1947 until their termination in 1969. The controversial Colorado University study led by Edward Condon, evaluated cases where around 30 percent were classified as unknowns. Even the projects in the UK and other countries have similar statistical outcomes. The Mutual UFO Network, MUFON, a non-governmental organization that is one of the largest independent UFO organizations remaining worldwide has over 70,000 cases reported and shows similar percentages.

I currently work as a defense contractor for the Army Materiel Command at Redstone Arsenal in Huntsville, Alabama. My profession is in the Information Technology field as a Lead Systems Architect. One of my key responsibilities lies in improving the information systems that support the soldiers and the employees engaged in Army business. I have many technology tools that allow me to do better analysis of data and information than we find in the grass roots of ufology. Our antiquated tools barely scratch the surface and the data provided to us is often insufficient as reluctant witnesses come forward with details. Since we are unable to get cooperation from governments in performing open, transparent and objective studies of the UFO phenomena, organizations like MUFON rely on public donations to gain use of capable tools.

Multiple disparate databases exist in ufology with different data elements, some of which are validated by investigations and some that are not. This is a very key consideration in the interpretation of UFO data. Access of the data and information is not always open and fully available to all. The primary concerns about sharing data and information is largely due to personal privacy needs where witnesses will only share if their identities can remain anonymous. MUFON does its best to reassure witnesses that their identities will not be revealed and certain data such as phone numbers, addresses or other personal identity information is scrubbed from public scrutiny.

The National UFO Reporting Center or NUFORC is an organization that takes reports via phone or via an on-line form but does not conduct an investigation of the cases received. Yet another UFO organization that collects UFO reports is NARCAP or the National Aviation Reporting Center on Anomalous Phenomena. This organization, led by Dr. Richard Haines, maintains a database of incidents where an aircraft and a UFO shared the same airspace and aviation safety may have become a factor for concern. It collects reports from pilots, air traffic controllers, radar operators or other aviation professionals. It recently is expanding its reports from the US to now include German and EU countries.

Recognizing that disparate databases abound, the authors of this book, Cheryl and Linda have taken on the arduous task of integrating various databases and other source data in an attempt to document the volume of sightings across the US over the years 2001 - 2015. Their compilation of sighting data extends down to each county in each state allowing us to gain a better understanding of the possible patterns that contribute to witnesses reporting an unknown to an organization. Further, the book answers many frequently asked questions that the reader will find as both informative and humorous. I appreciate the amount of work and dedication it takes to do what they did here. Working in Army Information Technology, generally a contract is let with ample funding and resources available to tackle this type of task. Hats off to Cheryl and Linda for their incredible work in support of ufology.

I encourage the reader to ponder the implications of the numbers shown. Look at the geographies, populations and other key pieces of information such as proximity to military bases or water that also come into play with these phenomena. My hope is that this incredible work can be replicated in other countries so that the true extent of this global phenomena can be fully realized by all. This work serves as the guidebook and sets the standard baseline for all to follow.

Rich Hoffman
MUFON, Director Strategic Projects
Alabama State Director

FORWARD

Dr. Gordon G. Spear, Emeritus, Sonoma State University

The **Desk Reference** is a massive statistical summary of more than 120,000 UFO sighting reports. This document is the kind of resource that UFO researchers have dreamed of having and the public has deserved to be able to consult. Throughout the nearly 70 years that the modern UFO phenomenon has been apparent in our skies and in our consciousness there has never before been available a summary of UFO sightings this large and this complete. Virtually everyone has heard of UFOs, but a satisfactory explanation for this perplexing phenomenon has not yet been developed. A main reason why success has not been achieved is because of the unavailability of a convenient means to access the data. The **Desk Reference** shows that there is a massive amount of UFO data available and provides for the first time a convenient and practical means for researchers of all levels to view summaries of the data and to find the data they would like to analyze.

Government agencies have claimed to have no interest in collecting and studying such data so that civilian organizations and private individuals have felt compelled to engage in such work. This work continues even though it has always required what is politely termed "self-funding" and the individuals engaged in the work must always have a "day job." The UFO phenomenon has continued to amaze us, to inspire some of us, and to frighten some of us. But it has refused to go away. This **Desk Reference** clearly documents that UFOs are still very much alive and continue to be experienced and reported by very large numbers of people. The **Desk Reference** study clearly documents that the number of sighting reports continues to increase at the present time. This is the unavoidable, if somewhat uncomfortable, truth. This is the reality even if governments continue to claim a total lack of interest in a phenomenon that obviously has a profound impact on the security and well-being of all of us who are living on planet Earth.

The reported UFO sightings in the **Desk Reference** are characterized according to the state and county, the month and year, and the appearance of what was sighted. Detailed charts are provided for each state and for the nation as a whole. The raw data, which is the actual sighting descriptions, is available from the web sites of the organizations that compile the data. These organizations are MUFON (Mutual UFO Network) and NUFORC (National UFO Reporting Center). The **Desk Reference** provides the key that is needed to determine how to identify and request the desired UFO sighting data. You cannot ask for it unless you know that it is there and know how it is characterized and organized. The **Desk Reference** is an invaluable resource that can be used to unlock, as it were, the massive archives of the publically available UFO sighting data.

The **Desk Reference** is the first application of Big Data techniques to UFO sightings. This study deals with more than 120,000 sighting incidences and certainly qualifies as Big Data. This parallels the important independent concurrent release of the **Experiencer Research Study.**

This study analyzed more than 4000 individuals who experienced UFO events and responded to a survey consisting of 600 questions.

This too qualifies as Big Data. Taken together, these two studies show that the UFO phenomenon is entering a new arena where modern analysis techniques are being applied to massive quantities of data. These sophisticated contemporary projects will provide a new understanding of the most significant influence on our development as humans that our species has yet encountered. The **Desk Reference** will provide the spark that will ultimately lead to the development of an explanation for one of the most provocative aspects of the 20th and 21st centuries: The UFO Phenomenon.

Dr. Gordon G. Spear
Professor Emeritus
Department of Physics and Astronomy
Sonoma State University

Rohnert Park, California

PREFACE

Cheryl was presenting at the 2015 International Unidentified Flying Objects Congress (IUFOC) held outside Phoenix, Arizona. Based on research from her weekly "New York Skies" column published in SyracuseNewTimes.com, her topic was "200 years of UFOs over New York." Besides talking about interesting stories from sightings from 1790 to the present, she also included statistical sighting numbers for New York State for the years 2000 through 2014. There is no "official" government database of UFO sightings, at least not one available to the citizenry. So the task of collecting data about UFOs sighting has fallen to privately funded and operated civilian organizations like the Mutual UFO Network (MUFON) and the National UFO Reporting Center (NUFORC). The data from the NUFORC & MUFON UFO sightings databases began to become stable around 1999. The compiled numbers made for some interesting bar charts and supported the part of her speech regarding the volume of UFO sightings.

During a pre-banquet mixer she was approached by an astronomy professor from a west coast university. He was doing some archaeoastronomy work related to some ancient stone chambers in the Hudson Valley. He explained that these ancient sites had been geographically mapped down to the latitude and longitude; in fact he joked he even knew their zip codes. Then he asked if she could compile her UFO data for New York down to the county, perhaps the city, and maybe even the zip code level?

This request wasn't an easy one to fulfill.

First off, neither national UFO database had zip code information. NUFORC didn't collect county data, only city and state information. MUFON collected county data but suffered from incomplete or incorrect information being supplied by the individuals reporting the sightings. Finally the NUFORC database was by far the larger database by at least 20%. The typical state had a ratio of 60/40 NUFORC/MUFON data available; therefore there was a lot of county information missing.

But in the end she was intrigued by his project and told him she would help.

Because of the irregularities in the quality and completeness of the data fields, it was determined there was no app or script to do any of this and it was impractical to try and write our own script. In the end it came down to old-school manual Excel spreadsheet editing.

The effort was arduous and took Cheryl months of effort, forcing her to write smart process procedures for scrubbing the data fields and looking up counties for over 6000 records. She figured out how to do it and managed to generate charts for all 62 counties in New York State. The effort produced some eye-opening results. We saw UFO sighting patterns that nobody had ever guessed existed.

Meanwhile, Cheryl began including more statistical charts in her weekly column. We were both surprised by the popularity of the UFO sightings data and the clamor by her readers for more. One evening we were discussing the amazing things that adding county information had done for the NY sighting data. That's when we hatched the idea of doing a nationwide sighting compilation and publishing a book that could be a resource for other UFO researchers. Also, during Linda's career as a science librarian and researcher, she had developed strong beliefs in the power of information, especially statistics, and felt we had an ethical obligation to do what we could to raise awareness of the extent the American public was seeing UFO phenomena.

The United States of America has over 3000 counties. The data from the NUFORC and MUFON UFO sightings databases began to become stable around 1999, therefore we decided to limit the timeframe to 2001 through 2015, making a 15-year sample. We would analyze and compile all 50 states and the District of Columbia, but omit Puerto Rico and other territories. It has taken over a year to do so.

ACKNOWLEDGEMENTS

The authors would like to acknowledge the following persons and organizations for without their data contributions, expert help and encouragement this book would not have been possible:

Dr. Gordon G. Spear, Emeritus Professor of Physics and Astronomy, Sonoma State University, who originally presented Cheryl with the challenge to generate county level UFO data for New York State counties. Something that led to bigger things.

Steven Davenport, Director of the National UFO Reporting Center (NUFORC) and his team for their data and giving the average citizen a place to report what they see.

Jan C. Harzan, Executive Director of the Mutual UFO Network (MUFON) & *Robert Powell*, the Director of Research, *Rich Hoffman* for his great Forward, *Ben Moss*, Virginia MUFON chief investigator, *John Ventre*, Pennsylvania State Director and others at MUFON for all of their help, advice and data.

Alejandro Rojas, Director of Operations at Open Minds Productions.

Steve Bassett, Director of the Paradigm Research Group.

Richard M. Dolan, the master of exopolitics.

Syracuse New Times – Publisher/Owner – *William C. Brod* : Editor-In-Chief - *Bill DeLapp* : Digital Editor – *David Armelino*, former editor *Ty Marshall*, and all the other staff for all of their help.

Tom Conwell, a fellow New York State UFO researcher and writer.

To our muse *Charmaine*.

To the hundreds of thousands of UFO eye witnesses who bravely reported what they observed.

We would also like to thank the many friends, readers, and colleagues who have shown interest in this project, resulting in their encouragement providing us incentive to keep going.

121,036 EYE WITNESS ACCOUNTS

Since 9/11/2001 we've been asked to notify authorities, in the name of protecting us from terrorism, what we see. You are being a good citizen if you dutifully report someone acting oddly in a train station or if you see a suspicious package alone in an airport terminal or public place. The paradox is that the same government agencies, at every level, will laugh you off the phone if you try to report an Unidentified Flying Object (UFO). Do they not remember that it was flying objects that wreaked havoc on 9/11? Why the hypocrisy?

Part of the reason we chose to use the 2001-2015 sample period was firstly, to use crisp numbers that represented 21st century context; and secondly, to illustrate that the magnitude of sighting reports are huge.

From 2001 through 2015 the United States and the District of Columbia reported 121,036 unidentified flying objects (UFOs).

What the number represents are 121,036 eyewitness reports of unidentified flying objects (UFOs) during the sample period.

Are they all of them exotic off world spacecraft? No, of course not; perhaps none are.

So the question is usually raised, just how many are of the exotic nature? Expert investigators usually say about 20% is a good number to use to get a rough estimate for the number of truly special sightings. We prefer to use a much more conservative number for the special sightings, 6% seems comfortable us. Still if we take 6% of 121,036, we get a number of 7262 that might reasonably represent the special, but it's still very sizable. If we divide 7262 x 15 years we get a number of roughly 484 special sightings per year. When you consider that these sightings are something big, bright and amazing--that qualifies as exotic. Something potentially from out of this world, which descends from the sky, in our minds meets the requirements of a majestic event. Consider for a moment that there might be 484 majestic events in the United States each year and yet we hear nothing about it.

Please note that while the 121,036 sum was derived from combining the sighting numbers from the National UFO Reporting Center (NUFORC) and the Mutual UFO Network (MUFON), we acknowledge there are other good databases out there. But for our purposes NUFORC and MUFON seemed to be the largest, well known and most popular, therefore probably receiving the majority of UFO sighting reports. In addition, Cheryl has used them extensively during the three years that Cheryl has written her weekly "New York Skies" newspaper column.
One of the things she has observed over the years was the sincerity of people who just wanted to report what they had witnessed. That's an important word: witnessed. The establishment for years has advanced the notion that only hoaxers and mentally deranged people report UFOs. But UFO researchers suggest that less than 7% of sightings might be attributed to this group of reports. An expert investigator once told us that short of physical evidence, eyewitness

testimony can get you convicted in any court in this country. So the argument boils down to this: If eyewitness testimony is good in a court of law, why isn't it good enough for sightings of Unidentified Flying Objects?

As we stated, from 2001 through 2015; we've complied and tabulated 121,036 eyewitness reports from the two combined national data bases. That's a pretty huge number, but is 121,036 all there is? No it's not; there is the phenomena of what we will refer to as "the Friedman factor." World renowned Nuclear Physicist and UFO researcher Stanton T. Friedman has put forth the notion that only 1 in 10 person actually reports what they see. Every time he gives a presentation at a college or convention, he always asks the large audience "How many have seen a UFO?" Virtually the whole audience raises their hand. Then he asks the audience, how many bothered to report those UFO sightings? The majority of the audience puts their hands down. Time after time, volunteer counters in the audience keep coming up with a value of about 10%, yielding the theory that one in ten persons reports their sightings.

So if we multiply our fifteen year study number of 121,036 reported UFO sightings by 10 we get a number of 1,210,360 probable UFO sightings for our national sample period of 2001-2015. As you can see, those are staggering national UFO sightings numbers to comprehend and a very different story. (Keep in mind there are not necessarily over 1 million UFOs, only 1 million potential people who have seen one.)

Consider that 121,036 divided by 15 years gives an average number of 8069 sightings per year. Multiply that yearly amount by 10x of the Friedman factor and we see a potential of 80,690 UFO sightings per year. That's something worth discussing!

THE TRUTH EMBARGO

Some in the media have been trying hard to paint the UFO advocates as a rabble of smart, silly people, liberally labeling us as UFO true believers and UFO die-hards, and, of course conspiracy theorists. They'd have you believe it's all about little green men. What is silly about being concerned about transparency on the part of the government? It's about the "truth embargo" that's been at the heart of it all. It's about important people like Air Force General Curtis LeMay telling Senator Barry Goldwater in 1964 in regards to UFOs, "Don't ever ask me that question again." It's about General Nathan Twining, head of the U.S. Air Materiel Command (AMC), who wrote a classified letter to Air Force General George Schulgen regarding the "flying discs in the fall of 1947." He said the objects were "real and not visionary or fictitious." During the Paradigm Research Group-sponsored Citizen Hearings on Disclosure (CHD) in Washington, D.C. in 2013, researcher Grant Cameron read from a top secret Canadian government memo that declared UFOs were "the most highly classified subject in the United States."

If all the controversy and discourse about UFOs are simply misidentifications, weather phenomena, hoaxes and crazy people, then why is it so highly classified?

It is not within the scope of this book to recount the history of distortion and lies surrounding the field of Ufology. There are plenty of books and websites you can pursue for further information.

In 2012 the National Geographic organization commissioned a polling study regarding the American people's interest in UFOs, as reported on ABC news. The poll found that 36 percent were solid believers, 47 percent were on the fence and 17 percent flat out didn't believe in the subject. The poll also found that 70 percent believe the government is not sharing what it knows. But what does this mean in term of actual numbers of people?

Well if 70 percent or 218.69 million Americans think that the government is not being forth coming and transparent about this UFO business, isn't it time to present some data?

As we address in the FAQ chapter, we explain why we cannot prove any of this. What we seek to do in this volume is present in an organized, accessible manner, the compiled data of fifteen years of eyewitness reports of individuals in the United States of America who have experienced seeing something in the sky that affected them so strongly they made the effort to say what they have seen. And if the people in power choose to ignore these witnesses, we will not. Almost every county in our country has experienced UFOs. Here is the data. Can they all be wrong?

Sometimes I am a collector of data, and only a collector, and am likely to be gross and miserly, piling up notes, pleased with merely numerically adding to my stores. Other times I have joys, when unexpectedly coming upon an outrageous story that may not be altogether a lie, or upon a macabre little thing that may make some reviewer of my more or less good works mad. But always there is present a feeling of unexplained relations of events that I note, and it is this far-away, haunting, or often taunting, awareness, or suspicion, that keeps me piling on.

Charles Fort, scientist

Skeptics, who flatly deny the existence of any unexplained phenomenon in the name of 'rationalism,' are among the primary contributors to the rejection of science by the public. People are not stupid and they know very well when they have seen something out of the ordinary. When a so-called expert tells them the object must have been the moon or a mirage, he is really teaching the public that science is impotent or unwilling to pursue the study of the unknown.

Jacques Vallee, ufologist

As a scientist I must be mindful of the past; all too often it has happened that matters of great value to science were overlooked because the new phenomenon did not fit the accepted scientific outlook of the time.

J. Allen Hynek, scientific consultant to U.S. Air Force UFO investigations

ANALYSIS OF UFO SIGHTINGS IN THE UNITED STATES: 2001-2015

OBJECTIVES

In this chapter we present some observations and possible explanations for some of the trends and relationships the data reveal. It is not intended to be a comprehensive analysis, but instead gives examples of the types of conundrums inspired by the UFO sighting phenomena. In addition, we pose other questions still to be answered. One of the main purposes of this volume is to provide resource data that will provided incentive and encouragement for other UFO researchers and interested readers to pursue answers.

THE INCREASE IN NUMBER OF UFO SIGHTINGS REPORTED

If we examine the summary of 15 years of UFO sighting reports, the first thing that seems to

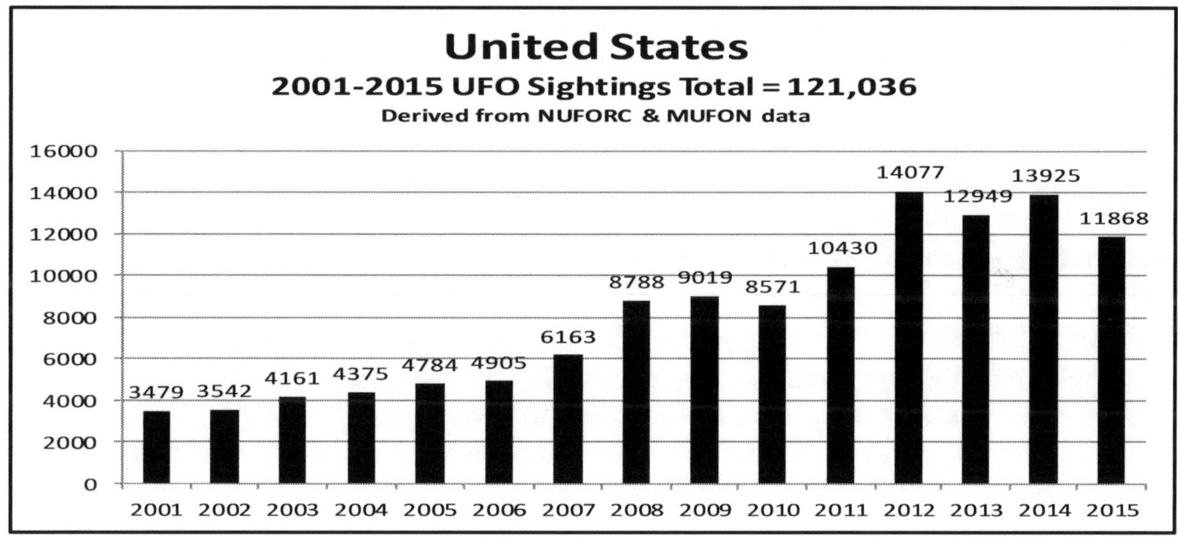

stand out is the upward trend. But we also see jumps in the numbers first in the 2008-2009 timeframe. Many, but not all, state-level summary charts display similar substantial jumps for 2008. This 2008 anomaly puzzled us for a long time. A couple of years ago at a convention, John Ventre of MUFON pointed out that in 2008 a documentary about MUFON was televised nationwide. John attributed the 2008 spike to that television program. The idea being that many more people learned about the existence of MUFON and its mission as well as its website that allows people to report UFO sighting.

So let us look at individual state Michigan as an example to see if this theory could be right.

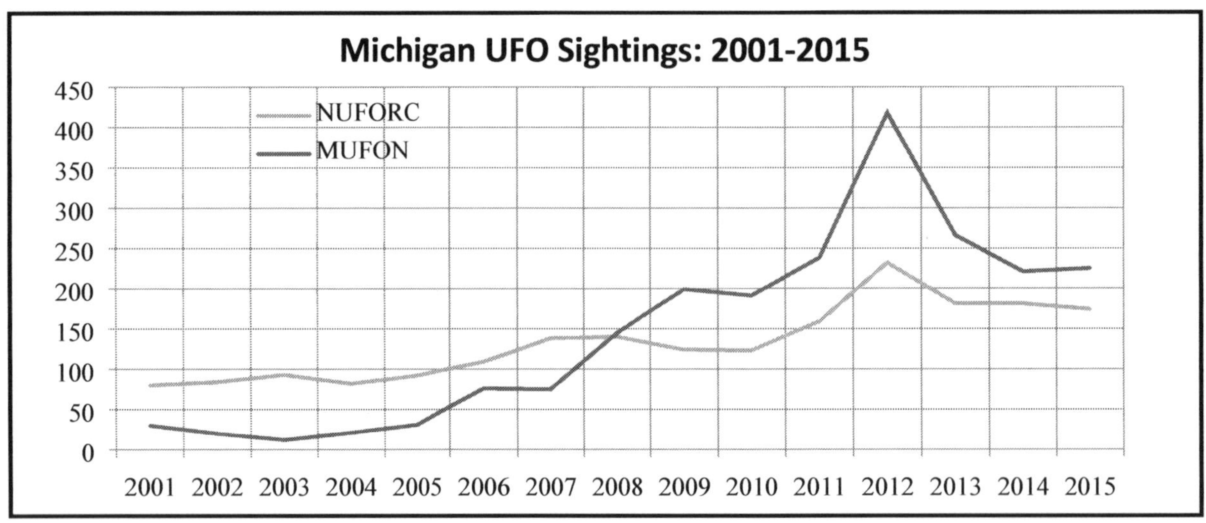

In the Michigan chart above, note that the dark line which represents MUFON reporting data takes a very steep increase around 2008 – 2009. Also note that thereafter, the MUFON baseline continues to be elevated due to the increased knowledge of MUFON's website reporting service. If we look at the NUFORC line in gray we notice that there is a smoother upward trend. Likewise, if we look at the sighting numbers spike associated with 2012, we can clearly see that both reporting services experienced increased sightings reports for the year 2012. A quick generalization can be made: 2012 was the year that the Mayan calendar ended a 5,126 year cycle. Logic suggests that the fascination and interest in this event in the popular imagination motivated more people to report the UFOs they were seeing.

In conclusion, if we look at the above NUFORC & MUFON combined data for the U.S. overall, it's clear to see an overall trend upward in sightings. Part of the trend upward can be attributed to an overall general increase in the amount of UFO sightings. As previously stated, part of this is increase is attributed to increased awareness of the availability of the MUFON web site because of the 2008 television special. Therefore, the 2008 & 2012 spikes are considered artifacts of reporting.

THE TOP TEN STATES FOR UFO SIGHTINGS

Everyone loves a top ten list. It is a handy way to extract meaning from a large data set and present it in a format that is easily understandable. It also adds an element of competition—usually everyone wants to be first! Since part of our mission is to encourage witnesses to report their sightings to NUFORC or MUFON, competition may prove an incentive. Anecdotally, we had a complaint that Nevada has many more sightings than we were presenting. Asked if they reported them, they answered sheepishly, "No." We can only count what is reported! California is the number one state for UFO sightings; it towers above the other nine states in terms of reported sightings. California's number is double the sighting numbers of Florida and

Texas. In addition it has three times the sighting numbers of Washington State, Pennsylvania and New York. Finally, California has nearly four times the sighting numbers of: Arizona, Illinois, Michigan and Ohio.

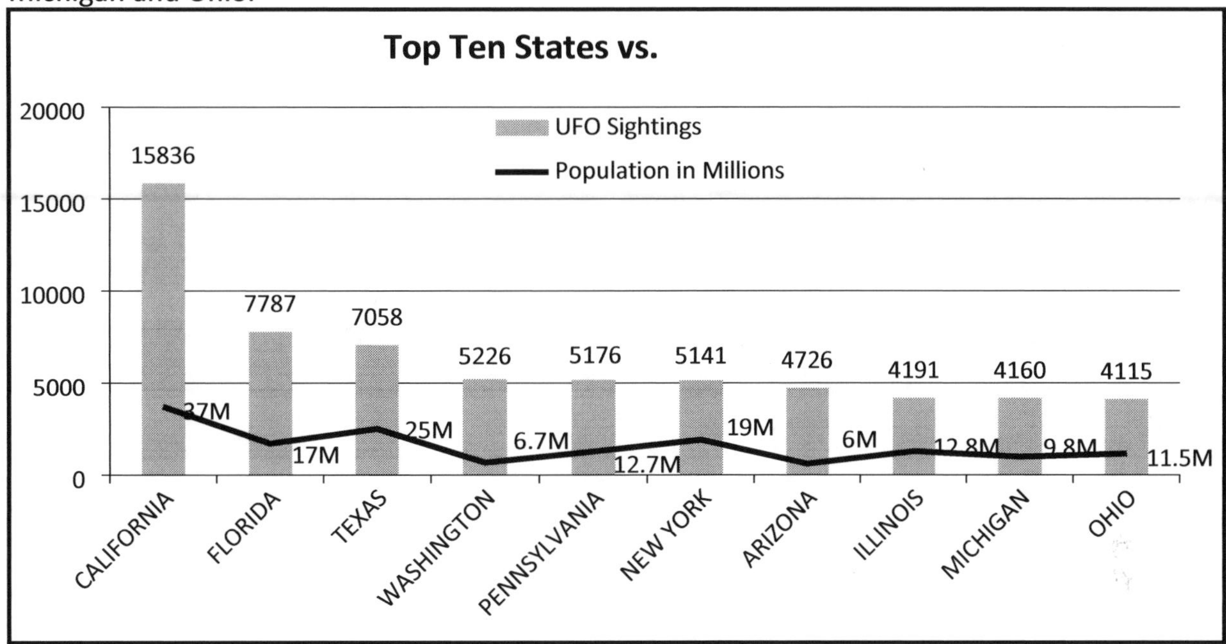

[All population information is from the 2010 census (U.S. Census Bureau, 2010)].

The question most commonly asked: Can all of this be attributed to population? Upon looking at the top 10 list, various people made this judgment that the states involved all had very large populations. They felt that the large populations had a bearing on the number of UFO sightings reported. If we quickly examine the UFO sighting magnitudes versus the population we can clearly see there is no consistent correlation.

While large UFO reports seem to follow centers of population densities like major metropolitan areas, it should be noted that the sighting mysteries seem to be with the out-of-the-way clusters nested in rural areas in various states.

By augmenting the databases with county information, scant sightings near small rural communities suddenly become visible for examination. What is going on in the small rural regions related to the small clusters? The other question to be answered: Why are there places where there are no sightings? Both new or the seasoned investigators will be challenged by these questions.

THE TRUTH IS IN THE SHAPES

The shapes of UFOs that witnesses report are both the most intriguing and most frustrating of the data we report. The United States shapes chart was difficult to build. The NUFORC database has one set of shape standards and MUFON has another. By combining the shapes from both reporting services we felt we preserved the integrity of both services' reports. This artifact is most evident in the existence of both "disk" (MUFON) and "disc" (NUFORC) shapes.

Shapes of UFOS Ranked by Frequency of Reported Observation

UFO Shape	USA Count	Percentage
Light	15491	12.8%
Circle	13840	11.4%
Sphere	12132	10.0%
Unknown	11452	9.5%
Triangle	11066	9.1%
Fireball	8718	7.2%
Other	8203	6.8%
Star-like	5291	4.4%
Oval	5208	4.3%
Disk	3353	2.8%
Disc	3275	2.7%
Cigar	2804	2.3%
Flash	2520	2.1%
Cylinder	2406	2.0%
Formation	2291	1.9%
Diamond	1906	1.6%
Changing	1846	1.5%
Boomerang	1326	1.1%
Chevron	1286	1.1%
Rectangle	1147	0.9%
Egg	1044	0.9%
Teardrop	1014	0.8%
Bullet/Missile	723	0.6%
Cone	677	0.6%
Blimp	509	0.4%
Cross	398	0.3%
Unspecified	327	0.3%
N/A	318	0.3%
Square/Rectangular	226	0.2%
Saturn-like	224	0.2%
Bullet	10	0.0%
Square	5	0.0%
Total	121036	100.0%

Ultimately, how someone decides what to choose as the "shape" of their sighting must often be the most difficult decision of the whole reporting process. UFO sightings are usually seconds, sometimes minutes, and rarely much longer. If you see a triangular craft hovering 10 feet over your house, you are going to be pretty certain what it looks like. Lights is the sky? Is it lights or a fireball? Is it an oval or an egg? Yet one cannot deny that having over 26 different shapes, plus "other, unknown or unspecified" reported is a wide diversity of apparitions.

HOW MANY ARE "REAL"?

In the early days of UFO research there were attempts at devising statistical formulas to account for all the possible things observers might have been misidentified when they were reporting UFO sightings.

One of the early numbers for the unknown or potentially exotic off world craft was about 20%. We have noted such a number referenced in various declassified CIA documents.
Later the United States Air Force's "Project Blue Book" claimed about 23% of sightings as unexplained.

Various contemporary UFO investigators we've met, shared with us numbers ranging from 20%, 7% and as low as 4% for the unexplained.

In this book we have compiled UFO sighting numbers for the United States and individually for all 50 states during the 15 years of 2001-through 2015.
With the very large sample size of 121,036 reported UFO sightings during the sample period we decided to take another approach. We decided to remove certain classes of UFO Shapes from the chart to illustrate a point.

UFO Shapes Table with Vague and Unknown Shapes Removed

UFO Shape	USA Count	Percentage
Light		0.0%
Circle	13840	11.4%
Sphere	12132	10.0%
Unknown		0.0%
Triangle	11066	9.1%
Fireball	8718	7.2%
Other		0.0%
Star-like		0.0%
Oval	5208	4.3%
Disk	3353	2.8%
Disc	3275	2.7%
Cigar	2804	2.3%
Flash		0.0%
Cylinder	2406	2.0%
Formation	2291	1.9%
Diamond	1906	1.6%

UFO Shape	USA Count	Percentage
Changing		0.0%
Boomerang	1326	1.1%
Chevron	1286	1.1%
Rectangle	1147	0.9%
Egg	1044	0.9%
Teardrop	1014	0.8%
Bullet/Missile	723	0.6%
Cone	677	0.6%
Blimp		0.0%
Cross	398	0.3%
Unspecified		0.0%
N/A		0.0%
Square/Rectangular	226	0.2%
Saturn-like	224	0.2%
Bullet	10	0.0%
Square	5	0.0%
Total	75079	62.0%

100-62%=38% Vague and Unknown or 45,957

As illustrated in the above table, see what happens when we take out the obviously vague and hard to pin down shapes: Light, Unknown, Other, Star-like, Flash, Blimp, and Changing. This exercise just removed 38% of the very undefinable sighting shapes or about 45,957 sightings from the 121,036 national UFO sightings for the period.

We kept the shapes that in our opinion couldn't be easily mistaken for conventional aircraft. These shapes are: Circle, Sphere, Triangle, Fireball, Oval, Disk, Disc, Cigar, Cylinder, Formation, Diamond, Boomerang, Chevron, Rectangle, Egg, Teardrop, Bullet/Missile, Cone, Cross, Square/Rectangular, Saturn-like, Bullet, Square.

This list represents 62 % of the total United States sighting shapes of unusual silhouettes or 75079 of 121,036 sightings reported.

So if 75079 UFO sighting reports don't resemble any conventional aircraft, it begs the question. Are these the genuine articles that everybody wants to believe are off world craft or inter-dimensional craft?

UFO Researcher and Nuclear Physicist Stanton T. Friedman, has sampled speaking audiences for years asking how many have persons have seen a UFO. He says the vast majority of the audience responses with their hands up. When asked how many actually reported their sighting the number drops to about 10%.

Let us consider that of those 9 out of 10 persons who didn't report because they figured out that the sighting was something clearly an explainable phenomenon and actually something very ordinary. Perhaps the people who have reported UFO sightings over the years are the people who really saw something extra ordinary and quite literately out of this world.
So let's take the sample period number of 121,036 and multiply it by 10 to accommodate the Friedman factor. We get 1,210,360 possible UFO sightings nationwide, both reported and unreported.

Next let's take the number we derived by filtering out the vague and non-descript sightings, 75079.

Divide 75079 by the Friedman number 1,210,360 and what do we get? 6.2%

So those contemporary exotic sighting numbers originally suggested between 7% and 4% are probably pretty close to the mark. The full truth is anybody's guess until such time as we have full and honest governmental Disclosure about what is really going on.

TIME OF YEAR DISTRIBUTION OF UFO SIGHTINGS: MONTHLY CHARTS

During the generation of the book's charts we decided to provide sightings by month. Several people closely following our book project did not think that monthly data was worth including. As a result, the monthly graphs and tables were among the last items to be generated for the individual states. Amazingly, we found the monthly data illustrated a set of unique patterns that were literally unknown until these charts were developed.

The first pattern was detected came from one of Cheryl's "New York Skies" news columns in which she shared a monthly chart for a recent year in New York State. In essence, the monthly sightings were relatively flat and at a quiescent level during the December through April time frame. Then there was a steep climb in sightings in May and June with a peak season in July and August that began falling off in September and October. With sightings falling off, back to quiescent levels in November and December.

She received mail and texts from her readers telling her "why" the pattern was the way that it was. The principle reason stated by readers was simply the seasonal weather influenced the percentage of people being outside. Upstate winters are notoriously cold and snowy; one doesn't spend a lot of time outdoors walking the dog or taking a smoke. This seasonal pattern made sense for New York State.

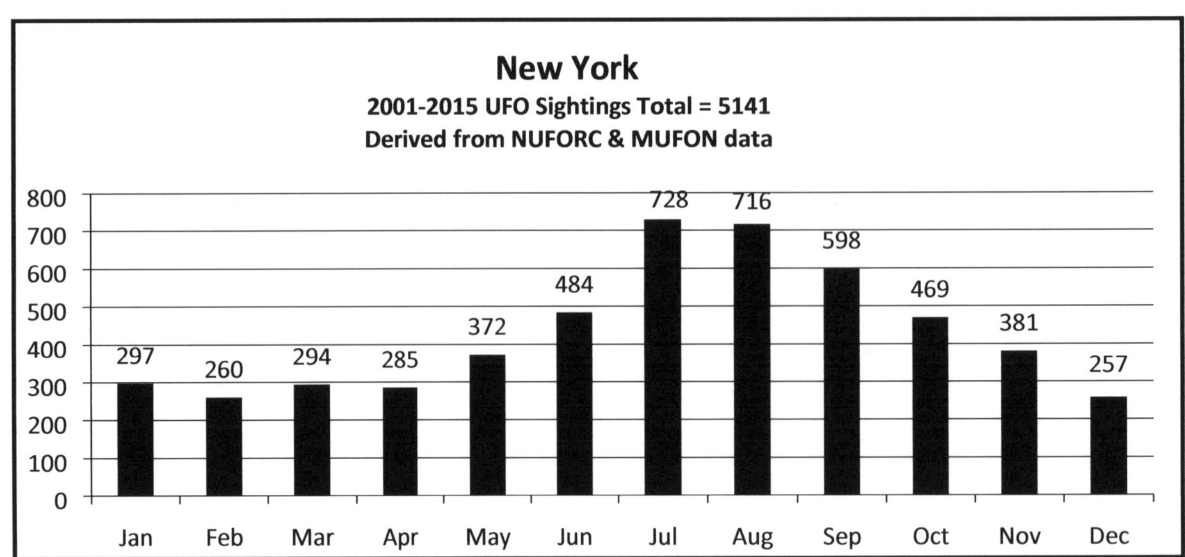

As we started to generate the charts for the other states, as expected, states at northern latitudes from New England across the continental USA to the West Coast all had a similar peak season pattern very much like New York's.

The first surprise was when we began to move to latitudes further south. We noted that the monthly pattern began to change. West Virginia for example clearly represents this flattening pattern of the northern peak season pattern. Note that the peak summer months begin to flatten more in line with the winter and spring seasons.

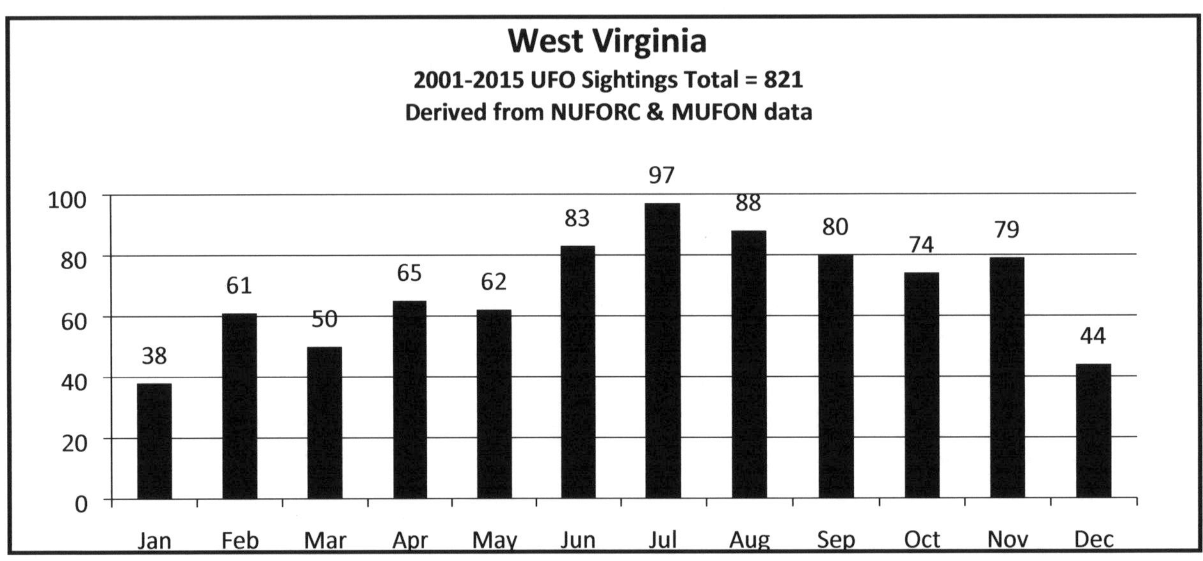

As we moved into the middle latitude states like North Carolina the monthly chart flattened greatly. I found this to be true of most middle latitude states. Although it should be noted that February seems to be the month for the least amount sighting reports. As one observer remarked: "It's the dead of winter."

When we look at the deeper southern states like Florida, another pattern emerges: the monthly chart is relatively flat. The Florida chart is representative of most Deep South states and those of the Southwest. Now many people could easily say: okay the year-round milder weather in the southern states would account for this. We could account for January and December being higher due to the population increase due to seasonal residential shifts by northern snowbird folks.

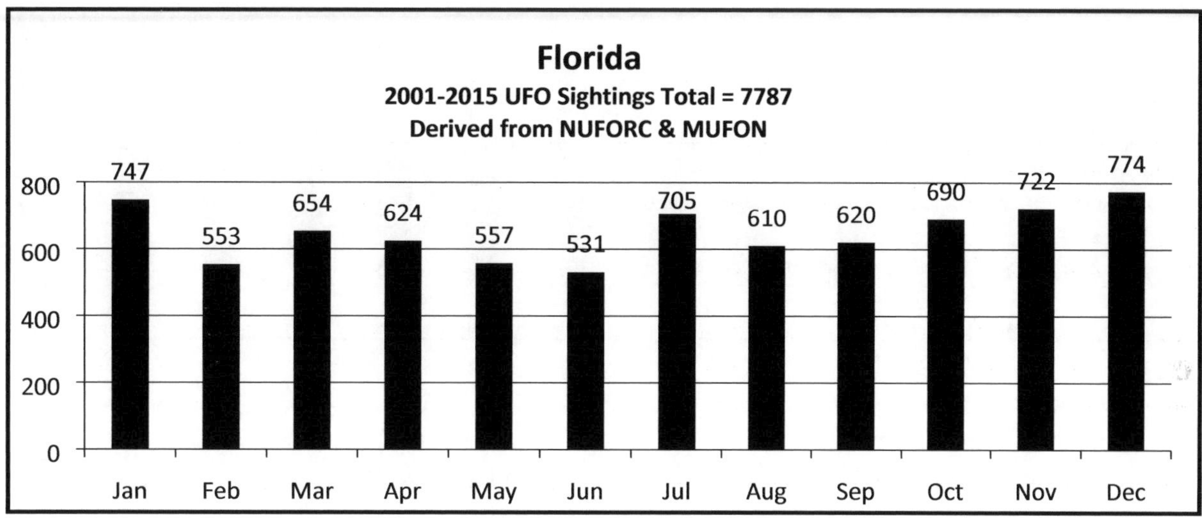

If we examine the monthly graph for Alaska we see something totally unexpected; another pattern. Take note that the sighting numbers bottoms out in what would be the Alaskan summer. Curiously, May, June and July are the lowest sighting numbers for Alaska. The warmer weather theory completely falls apart in terms of Alaska. In examining the phenomenon, we propose that perhaps it's because Alaska is largely in daylight during the May through July time period. In Alaska's the night season March and April and August and September, the sighting levels increase. As Alaska goes into deep winter it is dark most of the time. Traditionally, UFO sightings are mostly seen at night.

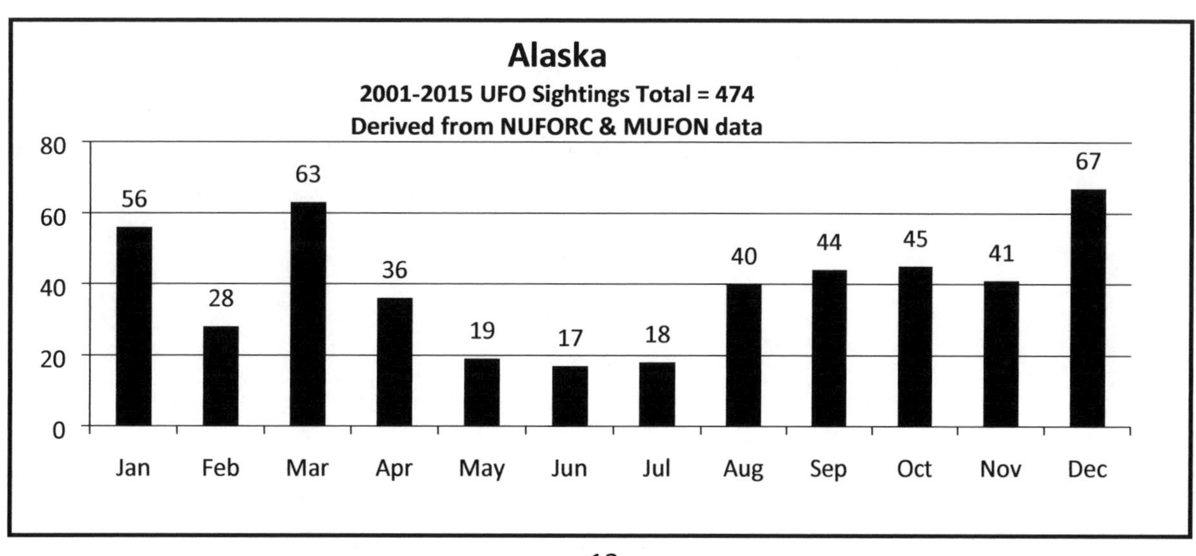

When looking at our only non-continental state, Hawaii, nothing makes any sense except perhaps four seasons of tourist spikes. Maybe someone from Hawaii can figure out what goes on during January December May and August and perhaps even October.

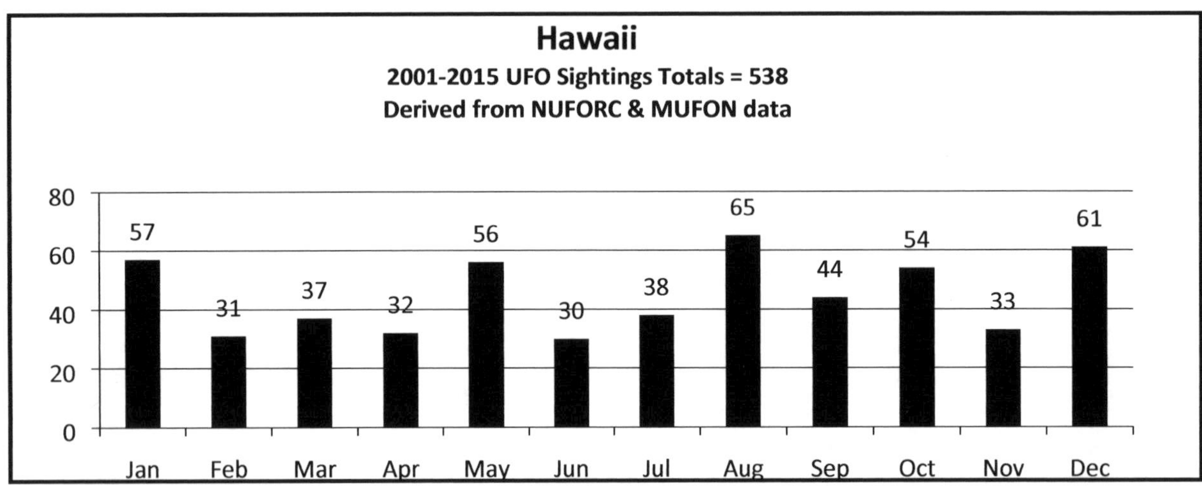

Lastly we had to mention New Mexico. It has the classic deep southern state flatness with the characteristic February dip. But why is there a huge spike in September? Why is this happening in September in New Mexico? Now there is a mystery to be solved!

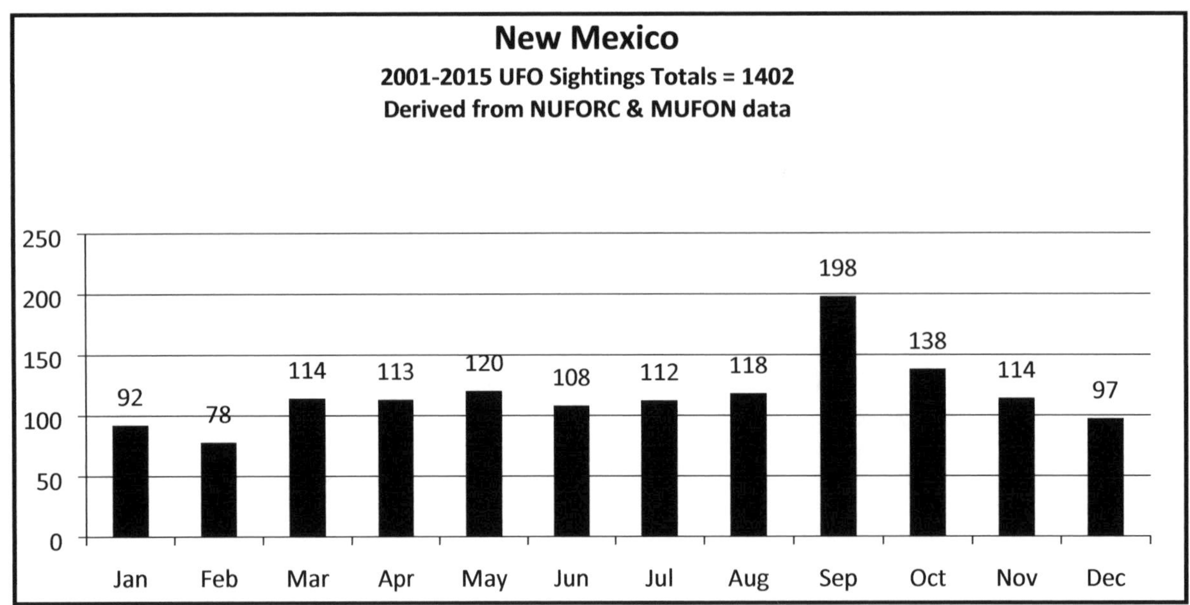

MAPS: U.S. CENSUS REGIONS ANALYSIS

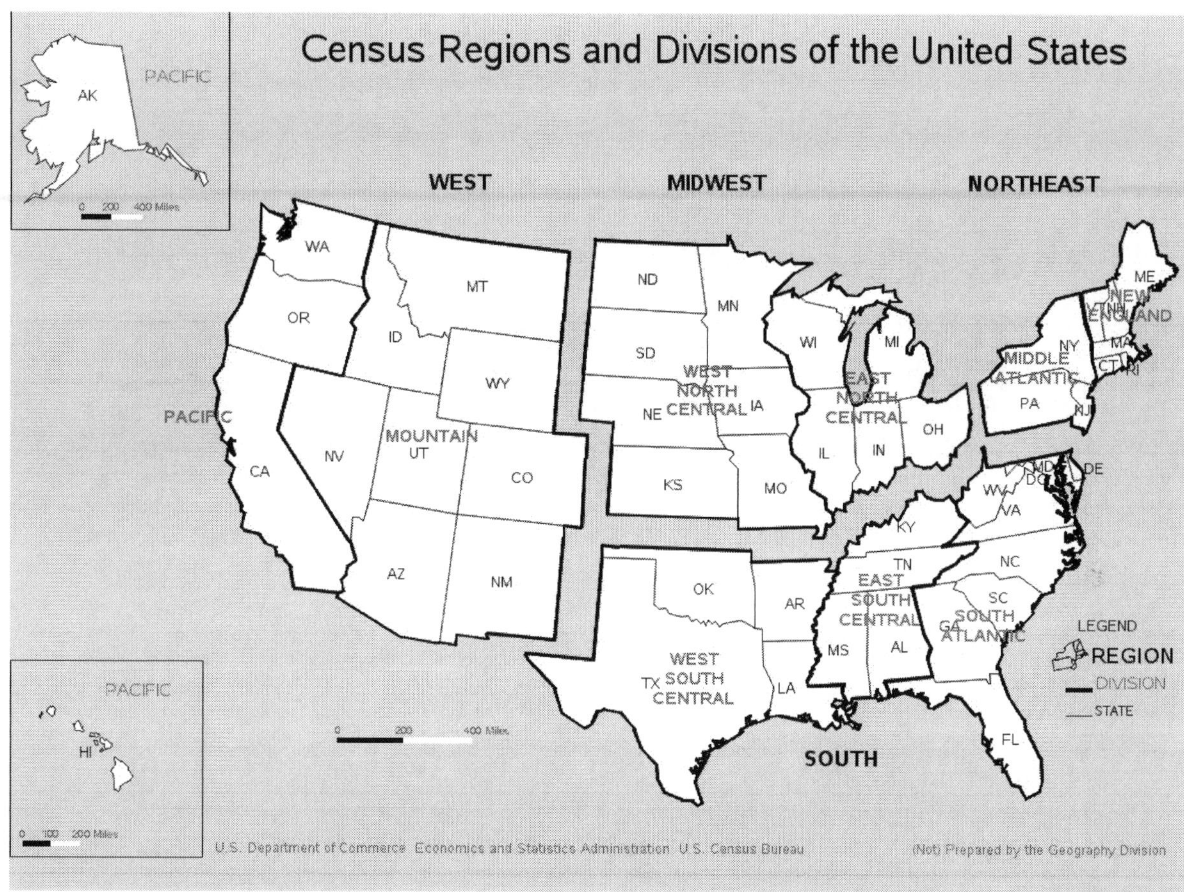

When we started looking at ways to do regional state summaries, we hit a significant snag. There seemed to be a great deal of contention as to what made up a classic regional area. For example one source told us that New York was included in the New England area. Another source insisted that New York was part of the Mid-Atlantic States. Don't even get us started on the South vs. the middle south and the Deep South. In all of these categories we explored there was varied ideas what groups of states were part of what part of the south.

The oil companies looked at the regions one was, other types of agencies looked at it another way. One reference document said that America was broken down by five regions. Although as it turns out the United States Census Department breaks the country down into four regions. After examining other government agencies we noted that they all used Census data and charts, needless to say we decided to fall in line with Census as well. There were several reasons: partly for standard regional maps, and of course for aligning Census population data with our state by state charts. Going forward anyone using our book for analysis will be able to use standard Census tables to make population versus UFO studies.

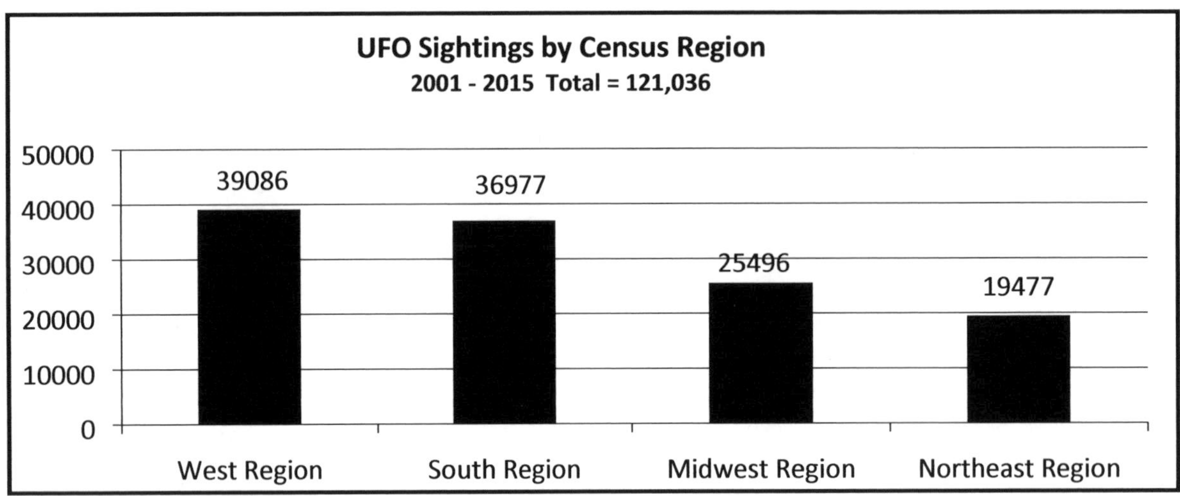

The table below lists a sub total of UFO sightings with each region. In addition also listed are the sight sub totals for each division with in a particular region.

U.S. Census Regions & Divisions	UFO Sighting Summaries	Percentages
Midwest Region	**25496**	**21.06%**
East North Central Division	17361	14.34%
West North Central Division	8135	6.72%
Northeast Region	**19477**	**16.09%**
Middle Atlantic Division	12884	10.64%
New England Division	6593	5.45%
South Region	**36977**	**30.55%**
East South Central Division	5572	4.60%
South Atlantic Division	20854	17.23%
West South Central Division	10551	8.72%
West Region	**39086**	**32.29%**
Mountain Division	13999	11.57%
Pacific Division	25087	20.73%
Grand Total	**121036**	**100.00%**

As we previously stated Census breaks the United States down into four regions as shown above. Within each region are logical sub divisions. Examining the Census map provided it's easy to see what states are parts of each of the sub divisions.

At a glance it readily apparent what regions and divisions had the most UFO Sightings during the sample period. We've also provided four Census regional maps and annotated call-outs for each of the states with their UFO sighting totals for the 15 years sample period of this research 2001 through 2015.

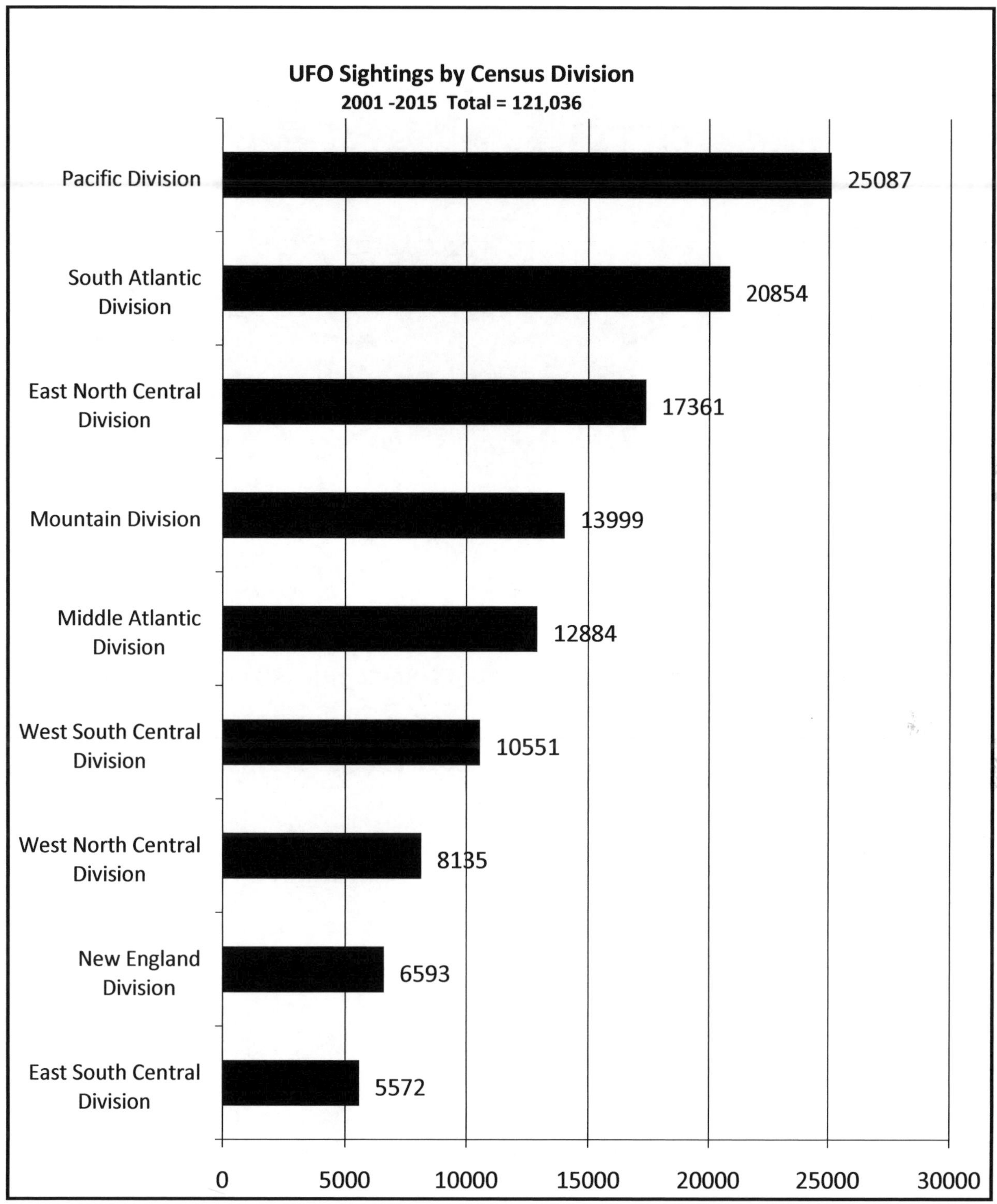

Northeast Region = 19,477 or 16.09% of USA Sightings 2001 - 2015

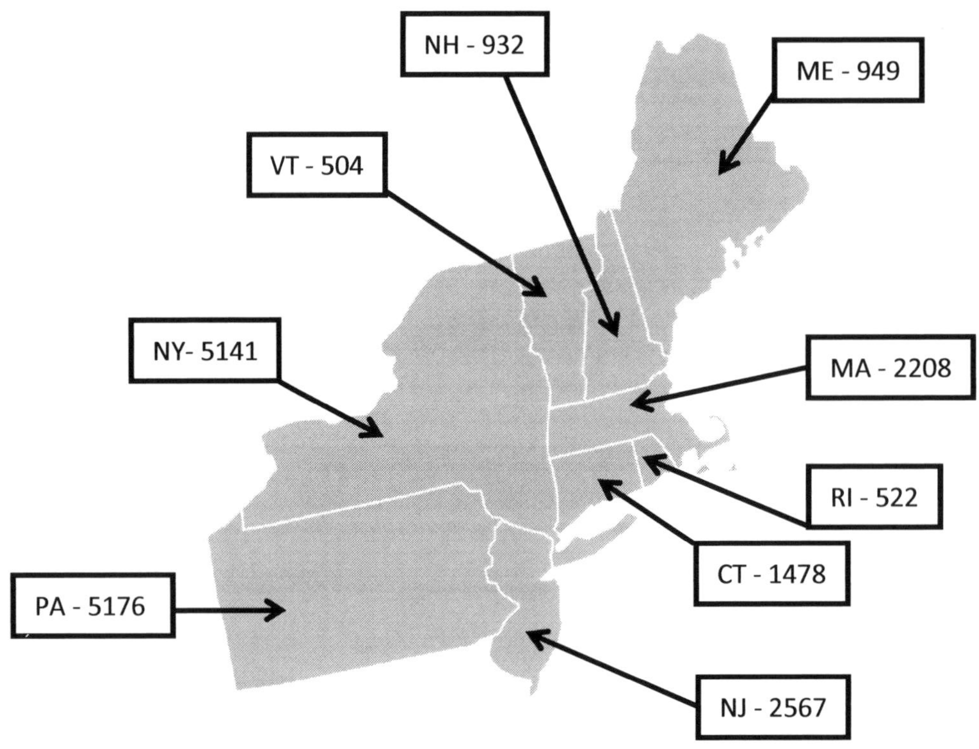

South Region = 36,977 or 30.55% of USA Sightings 2001 - 2015

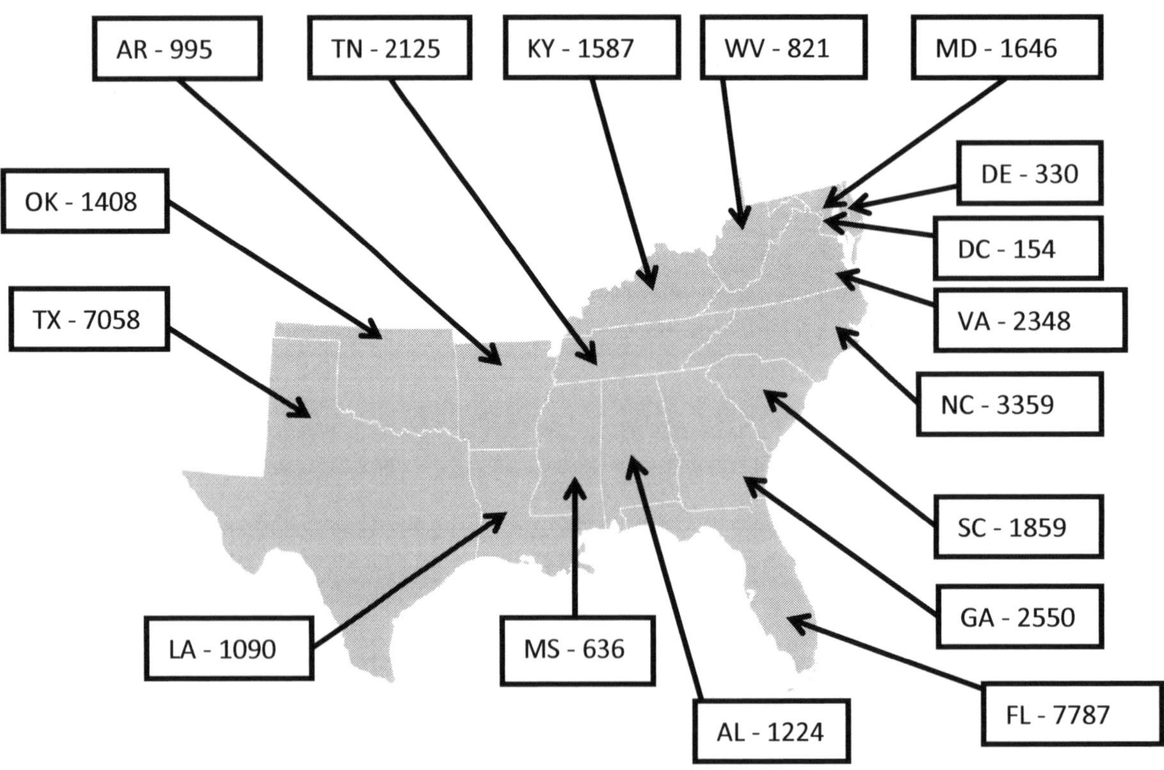

Midwest Region = 25,496 or 21.06% of USA Sightings 2001 - 2015

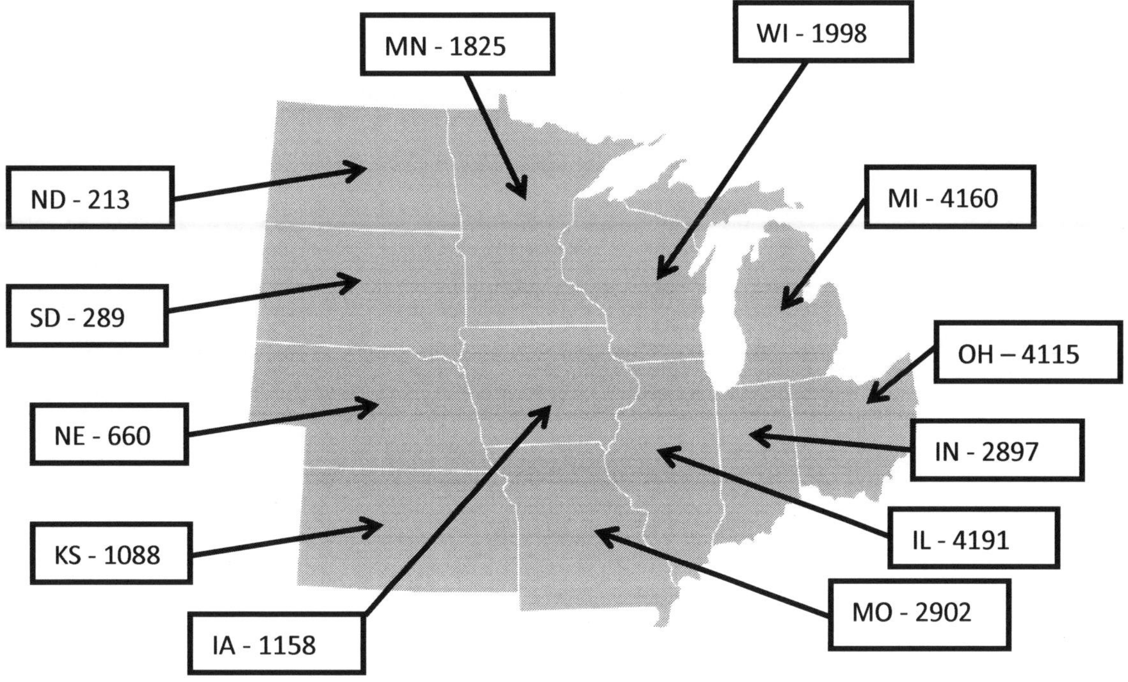

West Region = 39,086 or 32.29% of USA Sightings 2001 - 2015

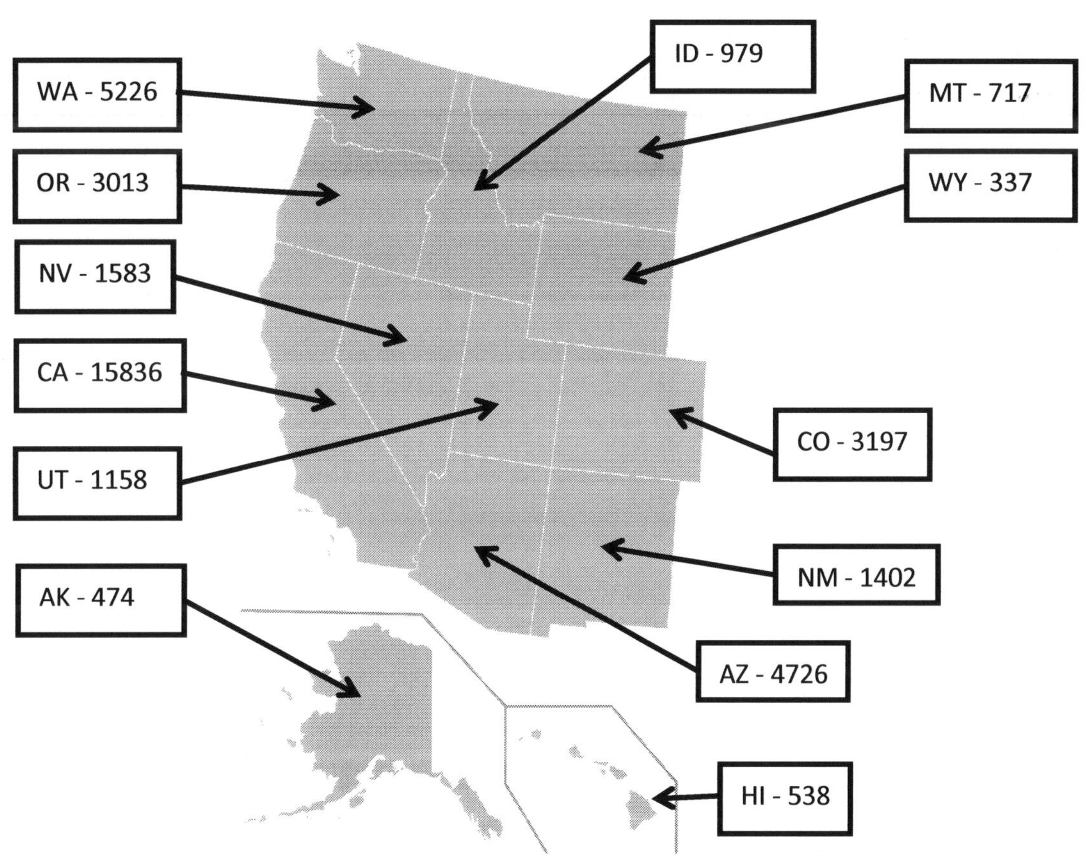

CLOSING THOUGHTS

Investigating of UFOs and their coming and goings isn't just for the experienced investigator. With this book even an armchair investigator and novice can find something to research. All you have to do is ask WHY? Then dig into the data. And let us know what you find!

FAQ/FREQUENTLY ASKED QUESTIONS

This chapter covers the miscellaneous questions that we have been asked during the book writing process. An attempt has been made to organize them for easier access. The sections are:

DISCLOSURE

Why the subject of UFOs is treated the way it is by the news media, scientific establishment, and governments.

Who is the intended audience for this book?

- Anybody interested in the UFO phenomena, seasoned investigators, those interested in becoming investigators. Main stream media writers so they have facts. The academic and scientific community. Finally, the public policy community, so they can see how widespread the UFO sighting phenomena is in the United States.

These can't be official numbers?

- These are not official government numbers. But since 1969, there isn't anybody to call and report such things within the government. The Condon report in 1968, recommended that no government money be spent; taking reports, collection and researching data or funding civilian academic research. For over 70 years, all of the evidential information related to an extraterrestrial presence in the United States has resided with the Unacknowledged Special Access Programs (USAPS) within the Pentagon. While the CIA probably has had its own special access program, it has been the military and intelligence complex that has held onto the lion's share of suppressed information. After all, since the early days of encounters with UFOs, the subject matter has been of defense concern at the highest levels of the Pentagon.
- So what you have is half a dozen private civilian groups of citizen researchers who collect data and do their best to share it.

How come I never hear about these things?

- You never hear about these things because for fifty years there has been a Truth Embargo. Newspapers and the media don't report or discuss the UFO subject matter in a serious way, if at all.

- In 1968 the Condon Report to Congress stated that there is no valid reason for researching UFOs. Further the report suggested that people who report such things are less than credible and perhaps mentally deranged. The Condon Report discouraged scientific research on the topic by both government research agencies and civilian academic institutions. The mainstream media took its cue from the report to down play UFO activity.

Why are you publishing these numbers? Why isn't the government?

- Good question. Please contact the White House, your local Congressperson and/or Senator and ask them.

Do you have any proof of censorship?

- Cheryl: For over three years I've been authoring a weekly UFO column (New York Skies) for the SyracuseNewTimes.com, the web edition of the weekly newspaper Syracuse New Times. Normally my column enjoys international readership and receives many thousands of page views weekly. Of course I said normally, there are certain weeks that if I mention certain topics like military jets chasing UFOS, or topics like the Truth Embargo or writing congress for Disclosure; on those weeks you almost can't find my articles on Google. It's been consistent that these topics guarantee that internet visibility of my column tanks to virtually nothing. Yes the word is CENSORSHIP. The Snowden papers have told all of us that certain government agencies have their fingers into Google and other search engines. Ask yourself this: If the topic of UFOs is so silly, so fringe and so stupid; why do certain topics regarding it get censored? The topic of UFOs is not just about lights in the sky, it's about serious lies down here on the ground!

Isn't there any proof of government interest in UFOs?

- During the final production of this book, the New York Times published an article on 18 January 2017 about the National Archives publishing a website of declassified CIA documents spanning from the 1940s to the 1990s, a total of 930,000 documents. A portion of those documents were related to Unidentified Flying Objects. See https://www.cia.gov/news-information/blog/2016/take-a-peek-into-our-x-files.html. On the menu page there is one groups of links given an X-Files theme: "Top 5 CIA Documents Scully Would Love to Get Her Hands On." Of particular interest is item # 3: "Memorandum to the CIA Director on Flying Saucers, 2 October 1952." It's a declassified Memorandum from the Assistant Director of the Office of Scientific Intelligence (OSI), which discusses in an executive summary, deep concerns about the "SUBJECT: Flying Saucers."

What would you like to see this book accomplish?

- We want to destigmatize the topic of UFO sightings. A problem/mystery cannot be solved by the scientific method if people are afraid to even talk about it because of fear of ridicule or professional career suicide. Since 9/11 citizens have been asked to report anything strange, yet when they see unidentified flying objects they are at the best ignored, and at the worst shamed, for trying to report to authorities what they have seen. Perhaps congressional representation will take finally take an interest when presented with data about their home districts. If nothing else, people will know they are not alone when they see strange things in the night skies.

EVIDENCE/PROOF

Points about the validity of the data.

All these numbers you list, they can't all be real?

- Are they all off world vehicles? No, perhaps only a small percentage, like under 6% are of fantastic origin, but if you look at the sheer size of the overall numbers, that still keeps the possibility open statistically. That is why we are reporting them. Are they all real eye witness reports? Absolutely!

Aren't these all reported by kooks and nuts?

- The Condon report and popular prejudice would have you believe that. Statistically speaking it's estimated that less than 2% of sighting report might be by mentally deranged persons. As a journalist, experience has been that most people just feel a civic duty to report what they've seen. We have found that UFO sighting experiences are handed down within families as heirloom stories.

Are all these sightings vetted?

- Only a small percentage. To vet all of them would require an army of volunteer investigators, since the government is not willing to take responsibility. If you feel that a better job of vetting should be done, why not sign-up with MUFON and get trained as an investigator? If you are a fan of Crime Scene Investigation shows, you'd love doing UFO field investigations.

Can you prove it?

- We get this remark a lot. "You can't prove what they really are." Likewise, you can't prove that they aren't! We can only share the data from 121,036 eye witness reports. While science follows different standards than the law, we note that short of solid CSI evidence, eye witness testimony can get you convicted in any court in the country.

Aren't these all just military planes?

- Military aircraft can probably explain a percentage of the unidentified sightings. They don't explain craft that exhibit performance characteristics far beyond that of traditional aircraft, such as the ability to run silently, hover vertically, and change directions on a dime.

Is 120,000+ UFO sightings in the last 15 years all there is? (The Friedman factor)

- World-renowned Nuclear Physicist and UFO researcher Stanton T. Friedman has put forth the notion that only 1-in-10 people actually report what they see. Every time he gives a presentation at a college or convention, he always asks the audience, "How many have seen a UFO?" A massive amount of hands go up, usually most of the audience. Then he asks, "How many bothered to report those UFO sightings?" Most of the hands go down. Time after time, the audience keeps coming up with a value of about 10 percent who actually report what they see.

- So if we multiply our fifteen year UFO sightings total of 121,036 by 10 we get 1,210,000 or an average of about 80,000 a year. Both numbers are staggering but the data seems to support it. Do note that we are talking sightings, not vehicles.

NUMBERS

These include questions about the major content of the book, the data.

How many UFOs do we get in an average year?

- Averaged out from 2001 through 2015, the United States has averaged about 8000 reported UFO sightings. Of course this doesn't cover the high percentage of UFO sightings that witnesses fail to report.

Why didn't you put the cities in here?

- Several reasons, first the city data was very messy; spelling errors, letter case irregularities, punctuation problems and other problems made publishing the cities too difficult for this first reporting effort. In addition, the average state had about 4% of the witness records failing to list a city.
- We plan to publish a state by state county and city UFO sighting compilation as a companion Desk Reference.

Have you checked these numbers against air routes?

- We have not. We encourage anyone who wishes to investigate the correlation of UFO sightings and air routes to search for information on "victor airways," which are the low altitude routes defined in the U.S. and Canada. Unfortunately, most UFO sighting reports don't give enough information that would support that sort of comparison.

Do you have latitude and longitude for all these sightings?

- In the over 121,000 UFO sighting records we have touched during the compiling of this book we remember less than 25 records where the latitude and longitude were reported.

Are these numbers legit?

- These numbers were carefully derived from the combined UFO reporting databases of the National UFO Reporting Center (NUFORC) and the Mutual UFO Network (MUFON). We cannot address the "legitimacy" of these databases. We do believe that the people who made the effort to report their sightings did so in good faith.

Why does California have so many?

- Nobody knows for sure. If we assume that the amount of UFO activity is constant; then factors such as great sighting weather and size of population may play a strong role.

Why didn't you include Puerto Rico and other U.S. territories?

- We made a conscious decision to report only the formally recognized states and the District of Columbia. In addition, the quantities were very small.

Why didn't you include other countries?

- We plan to include Puerto Rico and other U.S. territories and the world's countries in an International UFO Sighting desk reference. There were concerns about keeping the size of the volume manageable.

Why is county data such a big deal?

- If we look at the UFO sighting numbers for any state, on first glance all the serious activity focuses on major population centers. Sightings in small communities tend to get ignored because they don't add up to anything. Cheryl discovered in her weekly journalism research that many UFO sighting reports come from small rural places. Some of these places aren't much more than a general store and a volunteer fire department at a cross road. By inserting county level information, suddenly we start seeing previously unknown clusters. Clusters identification opens the door to a different kind of investigation research. Why is that cluster there, in that rural area?
- Example: In New York State, ufologists knew that Erie County was a very high sighting region. In fact this knowledge helped foster a term, "The Lake Erie effect." When Cheryl generated her first county level data charts for New York State, it quickly became evident that another county had a similar volume of UFO reports: Monroe County, which is on Lake Ontario.

Seems to me they congregate around high population areas?

- This is one of those cause and effect scenarios. Do we get lots of UFO reports because there are lots of people there to see them? Or do we get UFO reports because the UFOs are interested in our population centers where there are concentrated numbers of humans? Yet one of the mysteries of the data is that there seem to be are surprising clusters of reports in some rural areas. We hope users of this volume will investigate.

I'm from Nevada. We have got more UFOs than you have listed here!

- If they weren't reported to NUFORC or MUFON then they can't be counted.

Can we have access to your database?

- Not at this time. Of course the raw reports are available from NUFORC and MUFON.
- We are happy to run specialized reports for serious investigators upon request, with a reasonable service charge. Contact us at: reports@cherylcosta.com.

Did you leave anything out?

- Yes, a small percentage of sightings record had either hacker damage or were corrupt for other reasons. When we encountered data corruption we deleted the record. In addition, occasionally we find reports from veterans reporting sightings from Germany and the Middle-east. These sightings were not in the international database but were usually reported in their home state's data. We removed these sightings in order to keep the home state's data as clean as possible.
- We estimate that about .02% of the overall data was lost to corruptions or location report errors.

Who are the people who report these sightings?

- At the 2016 MUFON International convention, Cheryl was chatting with a senior MUFON investigator. We concluded that late night dog walkers and folks outside for a smoke reported the most UFO sightings.

Why is "unknown" listed in all the county charts?

- Each state's records had an average of 2.5% to 4% where the reporting person did not list a city or town. Sometimes the City field was blank, sometimes the reporting person would indicate fear or a personal security concerns. Sometimes a Highway mille Maker was given, in these cases we could usually connect it with a county. If zip codes or Latitude and Longitude were used, again we could connect that with a county. All unspecified city fields were labeled as such and designated to the unknown county.

BOOK PUBLICATION PROCESS

Questions about the creation of this book.

Why a book of UFO statistics?

- Because Ufology has been sadly lacking for compiled data to support scientific inquiry.
- Because the general public has been largely left in the dark about the magnitude of UFO activity due to the Truth Embargo.
- A personal effort to help bring about official disclosure.

Why didn't you go back farther in time with the data?

- All data reported prior to the early 1990s was pretty much done via telephone calls to answering machines, faxes, and newspaper clippings mailed to the collecting organization. In the 1990s access to the internet was growing, by the late 90s web access was becoming common place and the UFO reporting services were installing web interfaces for ease of report filing. The data much before 1999 was very unstable. By 1999-2000 the reporting level were leveling off with an upward trend. From an editorial context it was decided that the book with be a study of 21st century UFO sighting data, with a crisp 15 year sample period.

Why did you just use MUFON and NUFORC? There are other databases.

- Those are the largest databases, and Cheryl was most familiar with working with these two from her newspaper column research.

What intrigued you the most while writing this book?

- Cheryl: it was the constant little surprises examining the data. It seemed that just as you'd get a handle on something, it all changed.
- Linda: it was the diversity of shapes reported. We don't have that much diversity among automobile designs!

Why doesn't this book have sightings?

- Both NUFORC and MUFON allow public access to sighting data so we didn't see the need. Our focus was on illuminating the magnitude of UFO sightings in the United States overall, the individual states, and at the county level. None of this information has ever been presented and published this way before, as far as we can determine.

How long did it take you to do this?

- Just about every weekend for about 14 months.

While aren't you publishing the data electronically?

- This work has been designed to be a Reference Book, and we feel the charts and tables don't format well on electronic reading devices.
- Also Cheryl previously had a collection of her plays published in book form, five years later the publisher asked if it was ok to make it available electronically. Within two weeks the work was available for FREE on a pirate web site. We may publish digitally in the future, but right now we are staying in print format. Any creator of digital copies will be prosecuted to the fullest extent of the law.

Why is your cover so boring?

- We wanted to avoid the classic trap of pop culture silliness. Our book involves serious data researched by citizen scientists. We gave it a cover that resembled those typical of institutional scientific reports. Many flying saucer reports over the years contained hand drawn renderings by the witnesses. Therefore we commissioned local artist Susann Snyder to draw and ink something reminiscent of that look

Why didn't you use maps with little flying saucers in this book?

- It is not an illustrated children's book.

AUTHORS

Personal and strange questions the authors have received.

What makes you qualified to do this?

- Cheryl Costa has been writing a UFO column for Syracuse New Times for over three years. In addition she has a writing degree, has worked as a security analyst, and currently does data crunching work for an international bank. Linda Miller Costa has a library science master's degree and has worked for universities, scientific research and publishing organizations, and government science libraries; and has published on science topics.

Is this your hobby?

- Cheryl is a newspaper columnist who writes about the UFO topic matter weekly. This book and the research involved was an endeavor in deep research to support her on-going writing. As an avocational citizen scientist Cheryl had questions she wanted answered and that took serious inquisitive research.
- Linda was exposed to the topic of UFOs while growing up in the 1960s. As an adult, she was introduced to the International Fortean Society, which had conferences presenting speakers on the type of phenomena explored by Charles Fort. As a librarian, she is curious about everything. She has a day job in a college library.

Why did you write this book?

- Originally this was a research project that was supposed to be Cheryl's master's degree work. The graduate program leadership and advisors told Cheryl that such research was problematic and would meet with great academic resistance. Cheryl withdrew from the graduate program and continued her research.
- Linda had scientific publishing experience and had been functioning as an editor of the New York Skies column. She volunteered to coauthor and publish the book as a Dragon Lady Media, LLC product. Additionally, she is outraged that the scientific establishment has neglected their responsibilities to research and peer review such an important scientific issue that could affect the inhabitants and environment of our planet. Shame on them!

Do you personally investigate some of these sightings?

- Cheryl: No! I'm a middle-aged lady, I don't like stomping around in farmer's fields with barbed wire, ticks and plenty of cow paddies. I prefer to do my research in a library or on a computer.

Do you know what kind of propulsion systems they are using?

- We haven't a clue. But we suspect that it would make about as much sense to us as trying to explain a Boeing 757 engine to a Stone Age person.

Aren't you afraid of being called crazy?

- We did the serious research and compiled the data to reveal some unknown truths. We feel true craziness is not being willing to examine our data and consider the implications and possibilities.
- Linda has a B.A. in Psychology and is confident having an open mind is not the same as insanity.

Have you personally seen any UFOs?

- Yes plenty of them. Chery's first was in the mid-1960s. Linda's first was several years ago over the St. Lawrence River.

Have you ever met an alien?

- Cheryl: I'm told they walk among us. I have wondered who or what I may have sat next to on the subway. The question you should ask yourself: Have you ridden on a bus or a train with one, or perhaps sat next to an off worlder at your favorite pub?

Do you believe in life on other worlds?

- Recent scientific data produced by the Kepler Telescope has revealed that there are trillions upon trillions of planets in our galaxy. Statistically this suggests that some portion of those worlds probably support life. Our spiritual beliefs hold that the Universe is teeming with life.

Have you been abducted by aliens?

- We can neither confirm nor deny such activity. If they have abducted us, too bad they didn't give us free dental while they were at it.

Are you afraid of the Men in Black?

- Not really. But we did take steps to protect our data and the book as it progressed. Less from fear of the Men in Black and more from a concern for data thief or computer crash. We also have promises from several neutral parties to investigate if we disappear suddenly.

Do you have a tinfoil hat?

- No, but we have some nice fedoras.

HOW TO USE THIS BOOK

The data section starts with summary charts and tables covering the whole United States of America, including the District of Columbia. The individual state data is presented in separate chapters, arranged in alphabetical order by name of state.

ELEMENTS

- Name of state
- UFO Rank/USA: this presents that state's rank as a ratio to the overall number of entities ranked (50 states plus District of Columbia) number 1 having the highest number of UFO sightings.
- Bar graph of state's UFO sightings by year.
- Side by side tables listing the Top Ten Counties ranked by number of UFOs and the Top Ten Shapes ranked in order, including the percentage of the total number of shapes counted for that state. Note that NUFORC and MUFON use slightly different nomenclature for the UFO shapes, the most notable example being NUFORC uses "disc" and MUFON uses "disk." To preserve the integrity of the data we chose not to combine them, leaving that decision to the reader.
- UFO Shapes: a table of the UFO shapes reported having been seen in that state, listed by year. The shapes are in alphabetical order, and only those shapes reported for that state were included. This results in some states having longer lists of shapes than others.
- UFOs by County: a table of that state's counties, in alphabetical order, broken down by year. If a county is missing from the list, it's because no UFO sightings were logged in either the NUFORC or MUFON databases for the 2001-2015 sample period. This table will be the most rewarding for those looking to do cluster analysis of sightings.
- UFOs by Month: presents a bar graph of total sightings for the states by month of year. We present some theories about this data in the Analysis chapter.
- Distribution of Sightings between Databases: There are some who have said that the NUFORC and MUFON databases duplicate each other. We have not found this to be true, and present this table for each state to show what percentage of that state's sightings came from which database. This in another area ripe for data analysis to see whether there are preferences between the two for reporters in various geographic regions.
- State Demographic Information: for the convenience of our users, we have included 2010 U.S. Census Bureau information on the population and area of each state.
- Bonus charts: these are unique charts that were included as illustrations of other types of presentation of the data that are possible. Only a few states have them.

Please note that in the interest of keeping this volume a reasonable size, we have not included all the possible permutations of the data in our database. If you wish customized reports such as UFO Shapes by County, or UFO sightings by city, please contact at us at reports@cherylcosta.com and we will try to accommodate your requests.

UNITED STATES 50 STATES & DISTRICT OF COLUMBIA

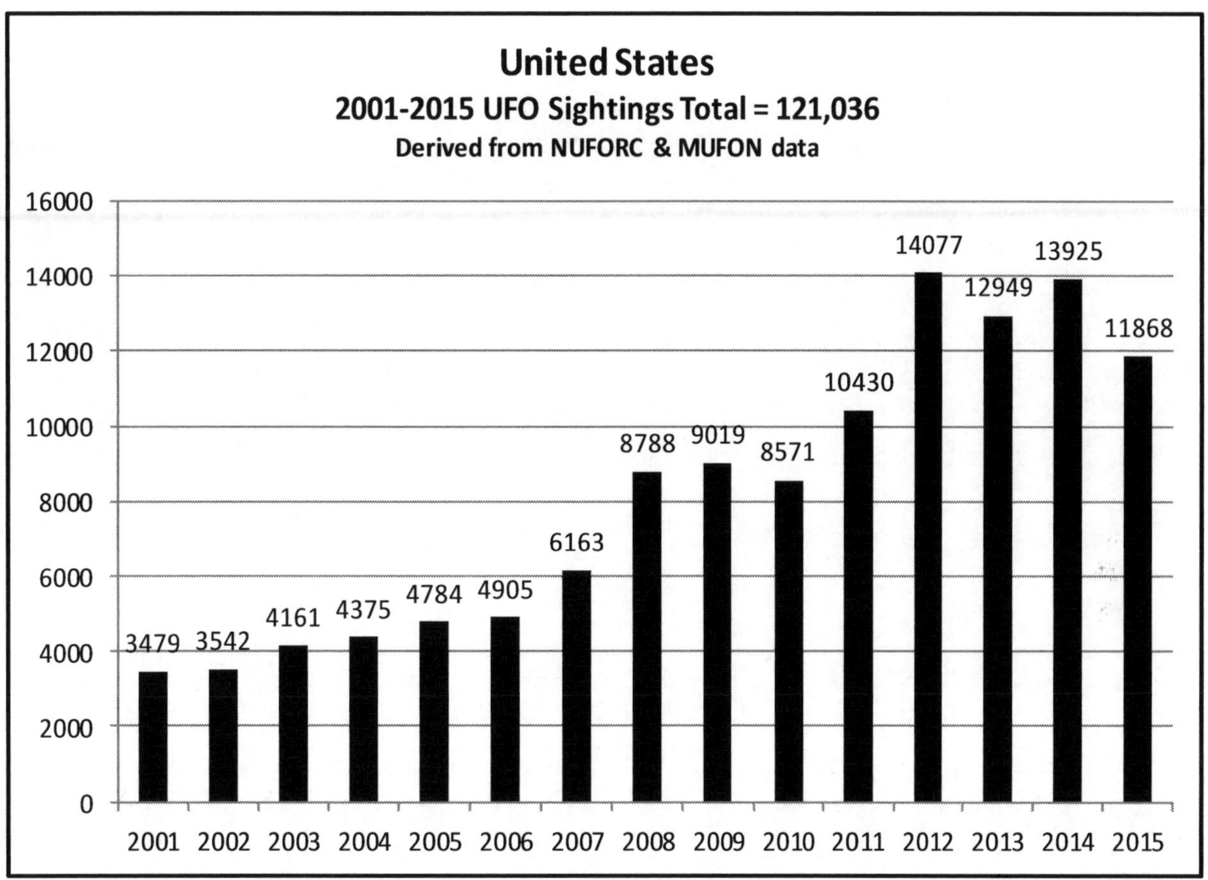

TOP TEN STATES		RANK	TOP TEN SHAPES		
CALIFORNIA	15836	1	Light	15491	12.80%
FLORIDA	7787	2	Circle	13840	11.43%
TEXAS	7058	3	Sphere	12132	10.02%
WASHINGTON	5226	4	Unknown	11452	9.46%
PENNSYLVANIA	5176	5	Triangle	11066	9.14%
NEW YORK	5141	6	Fireball	8718	7.20%
ARIZONA	4726	7	Other	8203	6.78%
ILLINOIS	4191	8	Star-like	5291	4.37%
MICHIGAN	4160	9	Oval	5208	4.30%
OHIO	4115	10	Disk	3353	2.77%

UFO SHAPES: UNITED STATES

UFO Shape	2001	2002	2003	2004	2005	2006	2007	2008	2009	2010	2011	2012	2013	2014	2015	Total
Blimp	6	9	6	5	11	20	40	64	39	43	72	66	56	32	40	509
Boomerang	14	12	22	19	25	41	65	115	134	135	157	171	152	138	126	1326
Bullet/Missile	7	8	5	10	15	29	42	85	79	85	86	90	84	49	59	733
Changing	79	93	97	121	121	110	98	142	109	120	108	170	146	182	150	1846
Chevron	50	63	52	55	47	56	70	108	80	97	114	129	114	118	133	1286
Cigar	92	76	99	84	125	145	203	295	243	239	248	282	236	235	202	2804
Circle	256	269	343	340	356	472	620	918	1106	1038	1291	2008	1803	1685	1335	13840
Cone	22	20	15	16	22	23	34	38	108	43	47	81	76	61	71	677
Cross	8	11	15	15	9	15	12	39	34	43	32	47	53	36	29	398
Cylinder	63	76	92	78	80	86	130	168	156	148	190	299	298	281	261	2406
Diamond	69	58	58	62	70	74	105	139	155	139	172	209	214	202	180	1906
Disc (NUFORC)	41	58	77	58	83	138	188	328	326	255	321	395	302	353	352	3275
Disk (MUFON)	184	200	227	264	236	221	242	282	196	202	201	227	210	261	200	3353
Egg	47	47	41	51	45	51	57	94	77	74	86	116	84	112	62	1044
Fireball	195	170	184	191	214	254	273	424	426	582	837	1514	1390	1217	847	8718
Flash	43	65	67	68	92	112	120	236	264	221	238	275	279	226	214	2520
Formation	106	80	110	132	115	102	116	153	128	101	161	216	277	296	198	2291
Light	632	601	720	847	846	700	910	990	1067	928	1117	1523	1503	1716	1391	15491
N/A		2		2	1	3	6	6	8	6	10	8	19	120	127	318
Other	261	295	345	354	370	388	442	612	641	602	618	738	754	937	846	8203
Oval	191	152	229	192	179	225	289	411	361	350	444	612	516	577	480	5208
Rectangle	56	43	44	45	56	72	80	83	75	63	80	123	94	122	111	1147
Saturn-like	2	3	3	2	8	7	11	32	21	30	21	14	24	27	19	224
Sphere	227	245	283	304	301	344	455	657	755	763	1035	1649	1652	1871	1591	12132
Square												1			4	5
Sq/Rectangle		1		1		2		2	2	1	1	6	12	47	151	226
Star-like	17	12	25	24	77	137	221	536	621	585	629	646	514	620	627	5291
Teardrop	32	39	48	39	48	49	68	77	78	76	88	103	72	109	88	1014
Triangle	395	364	433	481	495	482	606	846	821	795	1005	1129	1002	1161	1051	11066
Unknown	366	443	495	491	722	525	644	879	884	823	1003	1200	977	1100	900	11452
Unspecified	39	24	20	24	13	19	13	25	19	23	21	19	24	26	18	327
Total	**3500**	**3539**	**4155**	**4375**	**4782**	**4902**	**6160**	**8784**	**9013**	**8610**	**10433**	**14066**	**12937**	**13917**	**11863**	**121036**

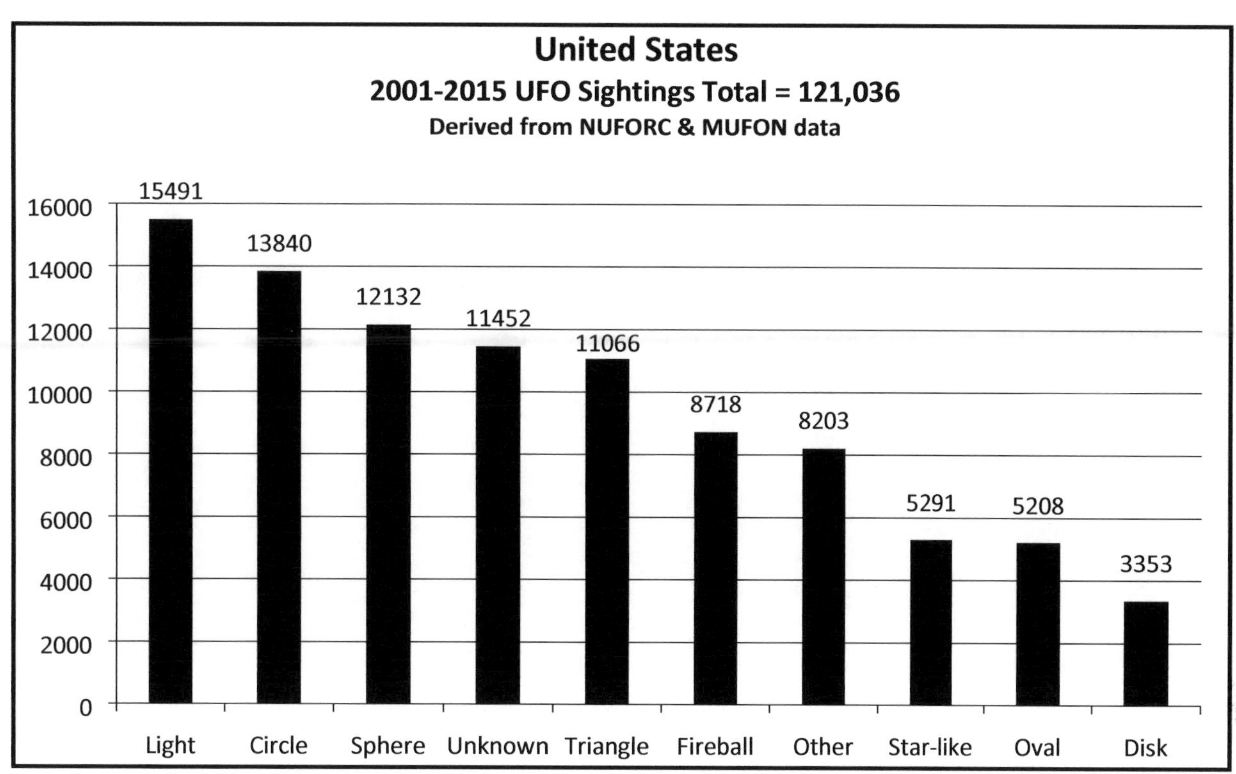

STATE UFO SIGHTINGS: RANKINGS AND DISTRIBUTION BETWEEN DATABASES

Rank	State	MUFON	NUFORC	Total	MUFON%	NUFORC%
1	CALIFORNIA	6576	9260	15836	42%	58%
2	FLORIDA	3186	4601	7787	41%	59%
3	TEXAS *	3656	3402	7058	52%	48%
4	WASHINGTON	1362	3864	5226	26%	74%
5	PENNSYLVANIA	2446	2730	5176	47%	53%
6	NEW YORK	1978	3163	5141	38%	62%
7	ARIZONA	2069	2657	4726	44%	56%
8	ILLINOIS	1609	2582	4191	38%	62%
9	MICHIGAN*	2168	1992	4160	52%	48%
10	OHIO	1713	2402	4115	42%	58%
11	NORTH CAROLINA	1300	2059	3359	39%	61%
12	COLORADO	1586	1611	3197	50%	50%
13	OREGON	1155	1858	3013	38%	62%
14	MISSOURI	1405	1497	2902	48%	52%
15	INDIANA*	1501	1396	2897	52%	48%
16	NEW JERSEY	1042	1525	2567	41%	59%
17	GEORGIA	1109	1441	2550	43%	57%
18	VIRGINIA	857	1491	2348	36%	64%

Rank	State	MUFON	NUFORC	Total	MUFON%	NUFORC%
19	MASSACHUSETTS	750	1458	2208	34%	66%
20	TENNESSEE	886	1239	2125	42%	58%
21	WISCONSIN	673	1325	1998	34%	66%
22	SOUTH CAROLINA	543	1316	1859	29%	71%
23	MINNESOTA	678	1147	1825	37%	63%
24	MARYLAND	654	992	1646	40%	60%
25	KENTUCKY	699	888	1587	44%	56%
26	NEVADA	705	878	1583	45%	55%
27	CONNECTICUT	474	1004	1478	32%	68%
28	OKLAHOMA	623	785	1408	44%	56%
29	NEW MEXICO	597	805	1402	43%	57%
30	ALABAMA	517	707	1224	42%	58%
31	IOWA	447	711	1158	39%	61%
32	UTAH	440	718	1158	38%	62%
33	LOUISIANA	469	621	1090	43%	57%
34	KANSAS	460	628	1088	42%	58%
35	ARKANSAS	396	599	995	40%	60%
36	IDAHO	344	635	979	35%	65%
37	MAINE	343	606	949	36%	64%
38	NEW HAMPSHIRE	328	604	932	35%	65%
39	WEST VIRGINIA	320	501	821	39%	61%
40	NEBRASKA	267	393	660	40%	60%
41	MISSISSIPPI	238	398	636	37%	63%
42	MONTANA	90	527	617	15%	85%
43	HAWAII	164	374	538	30%	70%
44	RHODE ISLAND	197	325	522	38%	62%
45	VERMONT	139	365	504	28%	72%
46	ALASKA	138	336	474	29%	71%
47	WYOMING	142	195	337	42%	58%
48	DELAWARE	114	216	330	35%	65%
49	SOUTH DAKOTA	90	199	289	31%	69%
50	NORTH DAKOTA	94	119	213	44%	56%
51	DISTRICT OF COLUMBIA	53	101	154	34%	66%
	TOTALS	**49790**	**71246**	**121036**	**41%**	**59%**

* States that the majority of sightings were in the MUFON database.

STATE UFO SIGHTINGS BY YEAR (Alphabetical order)

	2001	2002	2003	2004	2005	2006	2007	2008	2009	2010	2011	2012	2013	2014	2015	TOTAL
AL	16	28	53	35	53	58	74	78	79	67	81	122	149	212	119	1224
AK	20	12	17	12	28	16	24	15	31	30	36	59	66	58	50	474
AZ	140	137	151	215	255	195	269	326	388	298	391	491	465	534	471	4726
AR	42	33	64	38	48	36	51	81	68	96	103	97	93	63	82	995
CA	433	487	668	636	690	774	855	1206	1205	1124	1323	1584	1464	1814	1573	15836
CO	116	92	106	117	122	169	187	242	294	190	273	296	308	357	328	3197
CT	42	27	43	49	43	39	83	88	125	108	135	224	192	154	126	1478
DE	5	10	5	9	14	10	14	16	23	19	29	48	24	54	50	330
DC	6	12	3	13	4	7	7	17	16	17	10	18	4	8	12	154
FL	171	188	236	238	310	337	371	534	518	504	666	867	964	1040	843	7787
GA	57	51	79	89	92	106	142	174	181	210	223	274	251	356	265	2550
HI	16	16	13	19	20	19	31	30	34	44	33	49	75	100	39	538
ID	31	25	34	25	38	45	34	43	58	65	75	104	135	132	135	979
IL	157	114	109	233	232	184	266	318	279	359	416	509	366	318	331	4191
IN	52	55	105	135	123	118	154	323	239	261	265	323	284	267	193	2897
IA	41	30	46	42	54	33	69	74	78	81	101	178	134	103	94	1158
KS	35	31	31	40	54	45	61	58	81	103	114	131	103	112	89	1088
KY	35	37	45	51	80	62	80	119	107	115	182	163	189	176	146	1587
LA	20	29	38	46	38	35	51	86	109	80	88	95	105	163	107	1090
ME	28	34	40	20	30	40	47	48	69	60	77	147	133	85	91	949
MD	47	61	40	48	53	44	72	121	109	106	143	189	200	220	193	1646
MA	54	60	72	73	74	78	103	155	150	163	175	244	296	276	235	2208
MI	110	104	105	103	123	185	213	285	323	314	397	650	447	402	399	4160
MN	59	37	57	83	88	90	87	100	116	114	157	238	201	175	223	1825
MS	25	18	23	27	26	28	33	41	41	35	43	73	64	78	81	636
MO	74	74	78	89	87	94	141	170	202	250	374	440	268	319	242	2902
MT	18	21	19	27	29	26	20	19	33	32	48	74	51	60	140	617
NE	20	20	34	39	16	32	49	31	58	71	68	71	54	42	55	660
NV	61	51	56	58	80	70	91	139	115	105	108	156	112	193	188	1583
NH	22	25	30	22	47	21	43	59	59	55	61	128	108	147	105	932
NJ	81	72	88	91	110	100	101	159	240	178	195	285	293	311	263	2567
NM	33	56	55	48	39	81	80	114	112	97	81	124	143	194	145	1402
NY	184	183	188	203	193	176	243	336	402	326	441	663	497	564	542	5141
NC	73	76	94	88	134	153	159	214	196	225	336	443	377	447	344	3359
ND	7	4	12	9	6	13	8	17	15	13	31	16	19	16	27	213
OH	125	114	148	155	120	143	180	242	308	274	281	498	624	477	426	4115
OK	59	43	62	40	55	52	48	97	99	97	122	186	161	159	128	1408
OR	131	113	105	103	132	109	182	184	193	196	223	333	300	373	336	3013
PA	84	156	118	152	137	161	207	488	479	387	439	661	611	614	482	5176
RI	13	7	17	23	21	19	26	31	37	42	34	86	58	51	57	522

	2001	2002	2003	2004	2005	2006	2007	2008	2009	2010	2011	2012	2013	2014	2015	TOTAL
SC	26	35	72	52	65	44	102	89	103	90	188	271	215	359	148	1859
SD	6	9	10	15	11	9	18	11	20	23	20	37	32	34	34	289
TN	53	62	62	89	64	93	91	168	167	165	200	243	226	229	213	2125
TX	165	210	229	222	259	301	385	909	606	584	618	709	647	698	516	7058
UT	27	54	46	26	39	39	59	54	68	74	99	156	140	141	136	1158
VT	12	17	10	11	20	18	28	25	44	27	29	69	87	51	56	504
VA	74	81	75	66	87	87	112	162	168	145	191	271	322	262	245	2348
WA	232	225	266	259	218	218	260	299	359	374	423	608	501	556	428	5226
WV	24	33	22	25	30	22	42	50	68	39	63	100	99	114	90	821
WI	98	53	72	60	80	57	91	113	131	117	187	244	265	221	209	1998
WY	19	20	10	7	13	14	19	30	16	22	34	32	27	36	38	337
Total	**3479**	**3542**	**4161**	**4375**	**4784**	**4905**	**6163**	**8788**	**9019**	**8571**	**10430**	**14077**	**12949**	**13925**	**11868**	**121036**

MONTHLY DISTRIBUTION OF UFO SIGHTINGS BY STATE

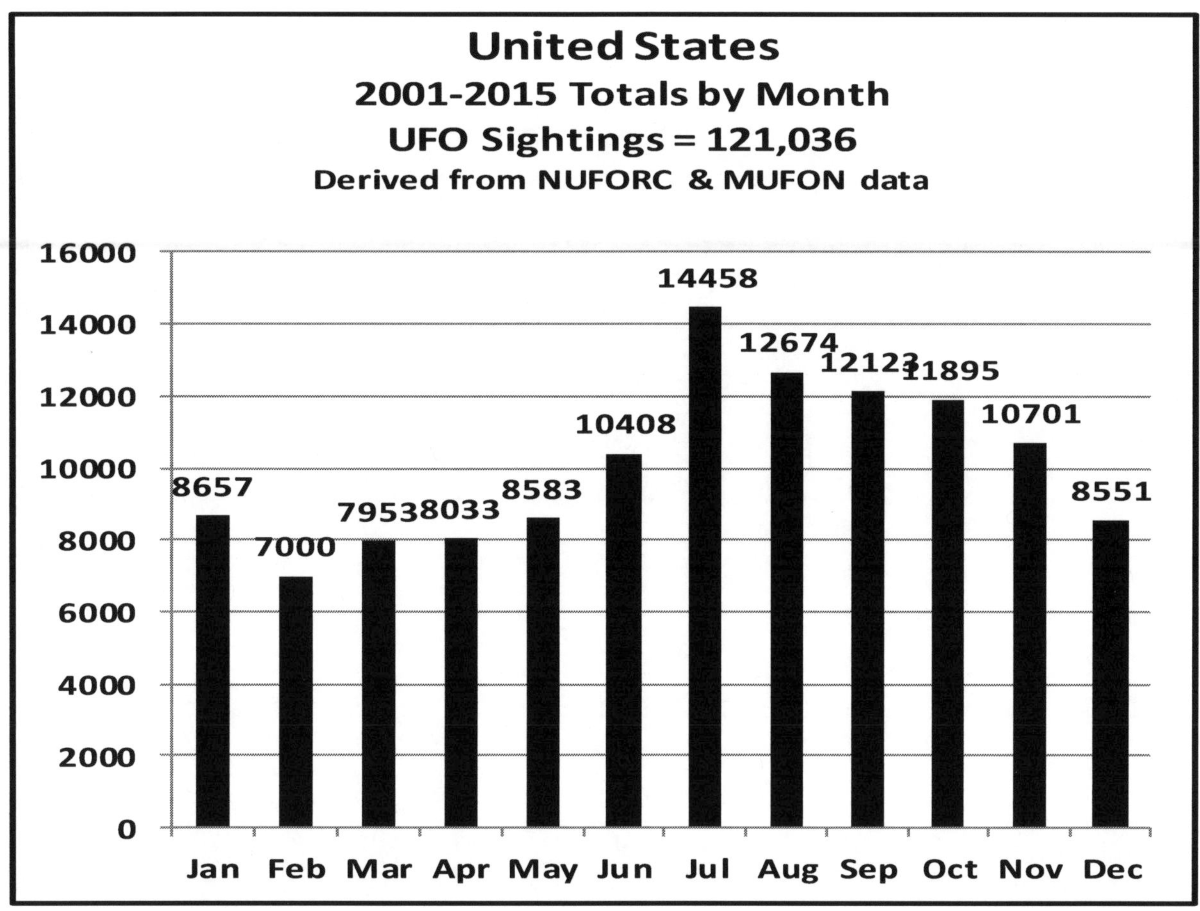

State	Jan	Feb	Mar	Apr	May	Jun	Jul	Aug	Sep	Oct	Nov	Dec	Total
Alabama	93	69	80	113	98	100	136	93	95	125	131	91	1224
Alaska	56	28	63	36	19	17	18	40	44	45	41	67	474
Arizona	385	327	433	383	398	389	350	359	463	448	488	303	4726
Arkansas	82	52	67	78	72	79	119	80	80	117	92	77	995
California	1360	1071	1137	1090	1071	1271	1597	1490	1433	1453	1586	1277	15836
Colorado	212	158	170	187	223	303	364	288	376	387	291	238	3197
Connecticut	116	80	121	87	83	137	176	171	167	126	126	88	1478
Delaware	23	12	13	16	29	25	38	54	27	35	33	25	330
D. of Colombia	17	6	10	8	15	11	28	12	8	9	7	23	154
Florida	747	553	654	624	557	531	705	610	620	690	722	774	7787
Georgia	240	158	174	187	216	185	210	192	234	276	271	207	2550
Hawaii	57	31	37	32	56	30	38	65	44	54	33	61	538
Idaho	54	57	56	74	76	98	137	114	94	87	66	66	979
Illinois	271	199	216	214	311	402	611	514	472	486	290	205	4191
Indiana	142	145	216	240	179	293	463	304	293	287	173	162	2897

State	Jan	Feb	Mar	Apr	May	Jun	Jul	Aug	Sep	Oct	Nov	Dec	Total
Iowa	66	48	73	76	87	116	161	129	109	122	106	65	1158
Kansas	65	69	53	57	62	125	134	98	116	135	93	81	1088
Kentucky	95	83	98	136	105	141	251	157	150	145	136	90	1587
Louisiana	94	73	71	71	77	85	105	104	94	118	103	95	1090
Maine	68	41	60	54	42	72	101	171	109	89	85	57	949
Maryland	132	99	94	107	112	119	165	163	156	186	158	155	1646
Massachusetts	137	101	147	132	156	151	243	281	293	188	222	157	2208
Michigan	178	179	220	238	264	393	686	550	488	376	342	246	4160
Minnesota	86	69	104	131	152	151	253	284	168	161	151	115	1825
Mississippi	72	31	42	49	47	55	49	54	46	64	74	53	636
Missouri	178	126	173	171	237	309	438	278	236	338	247	171	2902
Montana	44	40	44	27	38	68	86	67	51	45	65	42	617
Nebraska	20	29	38	34	44	58	102	70	80	82	69	34	660
Nevada	102	98	100	146	132	152	161	170	162	148	120	92	1583
New Hampshire	59	59	52	55	50	78	96	112	137	83	86	65	932
New Jersey	174	151	167	166	163	237	319	317	278	222	217	156	2567
New Mexico	92	78	114	113	120	108	112	118	198	138	114	97	1402
New York	297	260	294	285	372	484	728	716	598	469	381	257	5141
North Carolina	261	177	232	229	246	326	362	292	323	321	318	272	3359
North Dakota	12	5	9	21	11	22	34	42	22	13	13	9	213
Ohio	198	164	241	244	299	364	623	450	494	456	365	217	4115
Oklahoma	95	69	69	87	118	108	198	142	126	153	135	108	1408
Oregon	197	185	193	187	226	259	434	389	329	234	192	188	3013
Pennsylvania	330	260	285	317	355	457	756	571	552	473	452	368	5176
Rhode Island	36	33	26	22	39	37	69	64	68	54	46	28	522
South Carolina	141	102	86	85	128	217	213	163	188	225	157	154	1859
South Dakota	21	17	12	8	24	25	46	33	22	31	29	21	289
Tennessee	138	141	126	170	144	177	190	210	208	251	228	142	2125
Texas	644	505	478	480	481	532	689	623	642	836	647	501	7058
Utah	98	75	79	70	84	112	129	127	93	115	95	81	1158
Vermont	41	37	24	39	43	30	40	55	60	39	55	41	504
Virginia	156	164	190	121	199	192	220	190	216	250	239	211	2348
Washington	314	316	321	349	300	473	857	706	510	419	335	326	5226
West Virginia	38	61	50	65	62	83	97	88	80	74	79	44	821
Wisconsin	103	87	122	101	146	183	280	259	234	181	174	128	1998
Wyoming	20	22	19	21	15	38	41	45	37	36	23	20	337
Totals	**8657**	**7000**	**7953**	**8033**	**8583**	**10408**	**14458**	**12674**	**12123**	**11895**	**10701**	**8551**	**121036**

TOP US COUNTIES FOR UFO SIGHTINGS

PO#	County	State	UFOs
1	Los Angeles	CA	3212
2	Maricopa	AZ	2019
3	Cook	IL	1431
4	San Diego	CA	1393
5	King	WA	1393
6	Orange	CA	1271
7	Essex	MA	984
8	Riverside	CA	958
9	Clark	NV	940
10	San Bernardino	CA	836
11	Harris	TX	794
12	Horry	SC	627
13	Multnomah	OR	621
14	Miami-Dade	FL	619
15	Broward	FL	590
16	Jackson	MO	584
17	Palm Beach	FL	575
18	Sacramento	CA	571
19	Santa Clara	CA	569
20	Snohomish	WA	555
21	Suffolk	NY	554
22	Tarrant	TX	537
23	Alameda	CA	518
24	Wayne	MI	501
25	Orange	FL	489
26	Allegheny	PA	477
27	Dallas	TX	473
28	Pierce	WA	473
29	Travis	TX	466
30	Contra Costa	CA	445
31	Oakland	MI	435
32	Ventura	CA	429
33	New York	NY	426
34	Hillsborough	FL	425
35	Salt Lake	UT	424
36	Pinellas	FL	423
37	Denver	CO	415
38	Saint Louis	MO	413
39	Bucks	PA	397
40	Franklin	OH	392
41	New Haven	CT	389
42	Bernalillo	NM	385
43	Fresno	CA	379
44	Bexar	TX	376
45	Cuyahoga	OH	354

46	El Paso	CO	353
47	Erie	NY	352
48	Hennepin	MN	341
49	Philadelphia	PA	336
50	Macomb	MI	333
51	San Francisco	CA	327
52	Brevard	FL	323
53	Lane	OR	323
54	Arapahoe	CO	322
55	Sonoma	CA	321
56	DuPage	IL	321
57	Lee	FL	314
58	Clark	WA	305
59	Hartford	CT	304
60	Marion	IN	303
61	Fairfield	CT	302
62	Kern	CA	299
63	Fulton	GA	299
64	Ada	ID	297
65	Sarasota	FL	289
66	Will	IL	283
67	Montgomery	PA	282
68	Washoe	NV	279
69	Nassau	NY	276
70	Wake	NC	276
71	Mecklenburg	NC	272
72	Tulsa	OK	271
73	Boulder	CO	267
74	Jefferson	CO	263
75	Oklahoma	OK	260
76	Duval	FL	259
77	Pima	AZ	256
78	Lake	IL	254
79	Providence	RI	254
80	Stanislaus	CA	251
81	Washington	OR	249
82	Ocean	NJ	249
83	Monmouth	NJ	248
84	Davidson	TN	244
85	Larimer	CO	243
86	Spokane	WA	241
87	Collin	TX	240
88	Santa Barbara	CA	238
89	Monroe	NY	236
90	Johnson	KS	236
91	Kent	MI	233
92	Kitsap	WA	232
93	Pasco	FL	231

94	Volusia	FL	231
95	Douglas	NE	230
96	Unknown	FL	228
97	Kings	NY	225
98	Honolulu	HI	225
99	New Hanover	NC	224

"I believe that these extra-terrestrial vehicles and their crews are visiting this planet from other planets... Most astronauts were reluctant to discuss UFOs." "I did have occasion in 1951 to have two days of observation of many flights of them, of different sizes, flying in fighter formation, generally from east to west over Europe."
Major Gordon Cooper (NASA astronaut) to the United Nations

"If I become President, I'll make every piece of information this country has about UFO sightings available to the public and scientists. I am convinced that UFOs exist because I have seen one."
Former President Jimmy Carter (during his Presidential campaign).

"In the firm belief that the American public deserves a better explanation than that thus far given by the Air Force, I strongly recommend that there be a committee investigation of the UFO phenomena. I think we owe it to the people to establish credibility regarding UFOs, and to produce the greatest possible enlightenment of the subject."
Former President Gerald Ford (during his years as a US Congressman).

ALABAMA

UFO RANK 49/51

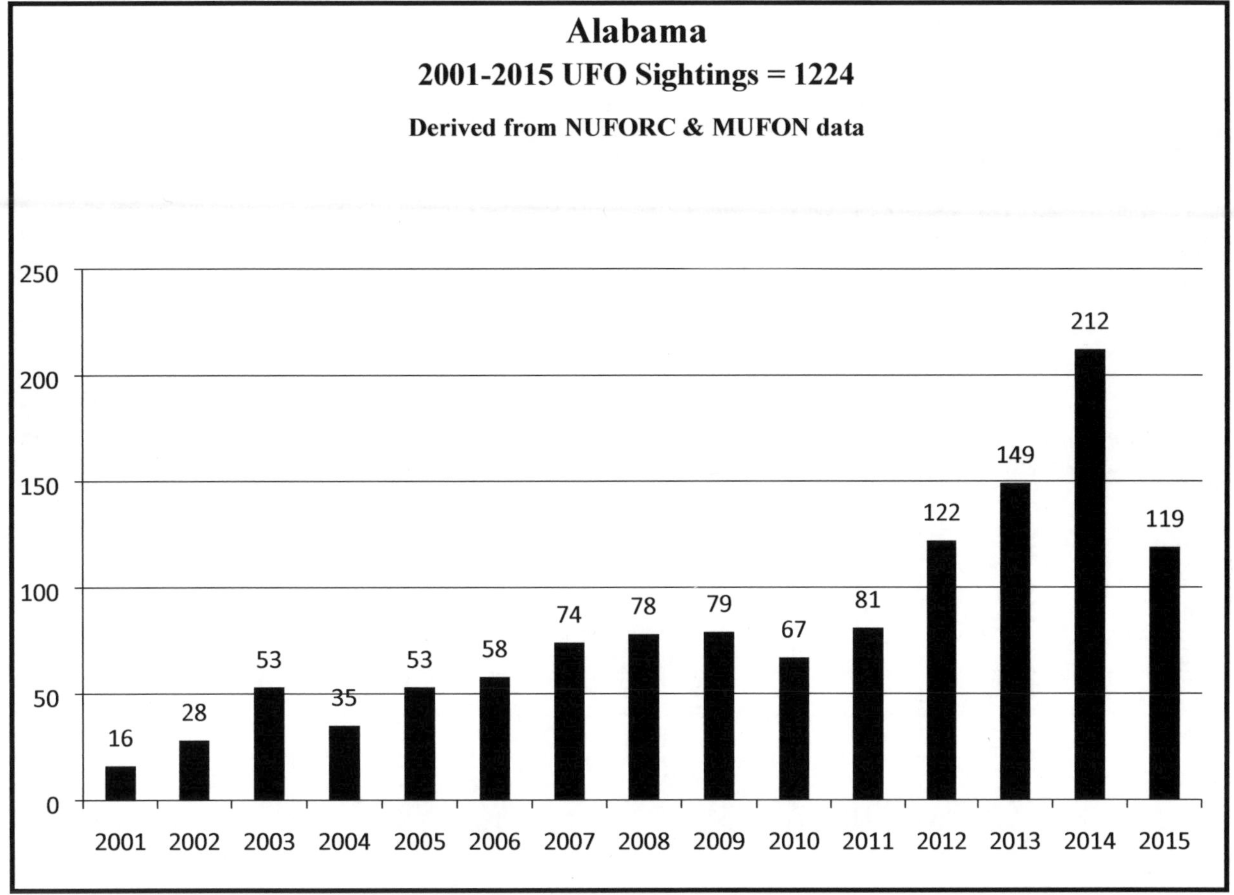

TOP TEN COUNTIES		RANK	TOP TEN SHAPES		
Jefferson	180	1	Light	178	14.54%
Madison	102	2	Unknown	125	10.21%
Baldwin	97	3	Circle	122	9.97%
Mobile	91	4	Sphere	122	9.97%
Limestone	50	5	Triangle	112	9.15%
Shelby	49	6	Other	84	6.86%
Unknown	48	7	Fireball	69	5.64%
Calhoun	40	8	Star-like	68	5.56%
Etowah	34	9	Oval	43	3.51%
Montgomery	33	10	Disc	39	3.19%

UFO SHAPES: ALABAMA

UFO Shapes	2001	2002	2003	2004	2005	2006	2007	2008	2009	2010	2011	2012	2013	2014	2015	Total
Blimp							1	1	1							7
Boomerang				2		1		2		1	1		3	1		11
Bullet/Missile							1			2	1	3	1	2	1	11
Changing		1	1		2		3	1	1			2	2	2		15
Chevron		2	1	2			1	2	1	2		1	1	2	3	18
Cigar				1				6	4	1		4	4	3	1	24
Circle	3	3	1	4	6	6	7	7	8	7	17	15	16	14	8	122
Cone			1	1									1			3
Cross											1	1		4	1	7
Cylinder			3				2	1	7	2		5	6	6	2	34
Diamond			2	1			2	4	2	2	2	2	2	1	2	22
Disc		1			1	1		4	6	3	2	5	1	10	5	39
Disk		2	4		2	1	6	3	1				2	3		24
Egg			2			2		1		4	1	1	2	3		16
Fireball	2		1	1	1	6	4	3	2	1	6	9	13	9	11	69
Flash	1				1	1			1	2	1	3	6	6	1	23
Formation	1		1			1				1			3	12	1	20
Light	3	5	6	7	6	6	12	7	7	4	9	23	18	33	32	178
N/A										1			1	1	4	7
Other	3	3	6	1	2	4	7	4	10	5	4	5	10	15	5	84
Oval	1		7	1	5	3	1	5		2	3	4	4	6	1	43
Rectangle			1	1	1			1	1			1				6
Saturn-like			1												1	2
Sphere	1	1	2	3	4	7	3	9	7	7	10	15	18	26	9	122
Sq/Rect															4	4
Star-like						6	5	1	5	8	5	7	9	14	8	68
Teardrop						1		2		2	1	2				8
Triangle	1	5	9	6	9	3	11	7	7	4	5	7	13	14	11	112
Unknown		5	4	4	13	9	8	7	8	6	11	7	12	23	8	125
Total	**16**	**28**	**53**	**35**	**53**	**58**	**74**	**78**	**79**	**67**	**81**	**122**	**149**	**212**	**119**	**1224**

UFOS BY COUNTY: ALABAMA

Counties	2001	2002	2003	2004	2005	2006	2007	2008	2009	2010	2011	2012	2013	2014	2015	Total
Autauga						1	1	1	2			1	2		2	10
Baldwin	1	2		6	3	2	10	5	3	2	6	11	20	15		97
Barbour										1	2	1	1			5
Bibb						2						1		5		8
Blount							1				1	3	4	2		11
Butler						1				1		1			2	5
Calhoun		1	1	1			3	4	1	7	5	5	6	5	1	40
Chambers	1						1	5	2	1				6	1	17
Cherokee		1		1		1				2		2			4	11
Chilton				1				1		1					2	5
Choctaw												1			1	2
Clarke					1		1					1				3
Cleburne					2	1								2	1	6
Coffee		1	2	1	1								1		1	7
Colbert			2		1			2		1	2	2		3	6	19
Coosa													2	1		3
Covington			3	1		2	1	1	1			4		2	2	17
Crenshaw										1		1	1	1		4
Cullman			5	1	3	2		1		2		2	4	2	2	24
Dale	1						1	1	1	2	2		1	1	1	11
Dallas										1		4				5
De Kalb	2		1		1			1	3		1		1	4	2	16
Elmore	1				1		4		1		1		1	3	1	13
Escambia		1				1			1			1	3	3		10
Etowah			1	2	1	1	3	2		4	1	2	4	12	1	34
Franklin						1			1	1		1		3		7
Geneva									1					5	2	8
Greene											1					1
Hale			2									2	1			5
Henry				1	1						2			3		7
Houston			1	2			1	2	4		2	1	1	4	4	22
Jackson							1	5					1	2	1	10
Jefferson	1	4	8	7	8	11	12	13	13	5	8	19	25	33	13	180
Lauderdale			1			1		2		4		1	8	4	7	28
Lawrence			1	1		1										3
Lee		1	1		3	2	2	2	4			1	2	3	5	26
Limestone	2	1	3			4	6	3	2	5	5	3	8	7	1	50
Lowndes			1													1

Counties	2001	2002	2003	2004	2005	2006	2007	2008	2009	2010	2011	2012	2013	2014	2015	Total
Madison		1	3	2	10	9	6	2	11	6	8	7	15	14	8	102
Marengo												2			1	3
Marion	2	1							1		2		1	1	1	9
Marshall	1	3			1		1	1		1	3		1	2	2	16
Mobile	1	5	6	1	2	4	7	5	4	3	6	9	7	23	8	91
Monroe												1				1
Montgomery				1	4	4	2	2	4	3	2	3	1	4	3	33
Morgan				1				1	2			3		5		12
Perry												2				2
Pickens						1						2				3
Pike			1							1		1		1		4
Randolph												1	3		1	5
Russell								1	2			3	1	4	1	12
Saint Clair		1	1		1		1	2	2	1	3	2	1	4	2	21
Shelby	2	1	1	1	2		1	2	1	4	4	4	11	8	7	49
Sullivan											1					1
Sumter								1								1
Talladega		1			1			2	2		1		2	2	1	12
Tallapoosa			2		1				1						2	6
Tucaloosa	1		1	1	1		1	3	2	1	2		4	5	3	25
Unknown			3	2	4	4	5	2	6	2	4	6	2	4	4	48
Walker			2	1			2	1	1	4	1	4	2	2		20
Washington						2					2			1	1	6
Wilcox		3														3
Winston								2			3	1	1	1		8
Total	**16**	**28**	**53**	**35**	**53**	**58**	**74**	**78**	**79**	**67**	**81**	**122**	**149**	**212**	**119**	**1224**

If a county is missing from the list, it's because no UFO sightings were logged in either the NUFORC or MUFON databases for the 2001-2015 sample period.

UFOS BY MONTH: ALABAMA

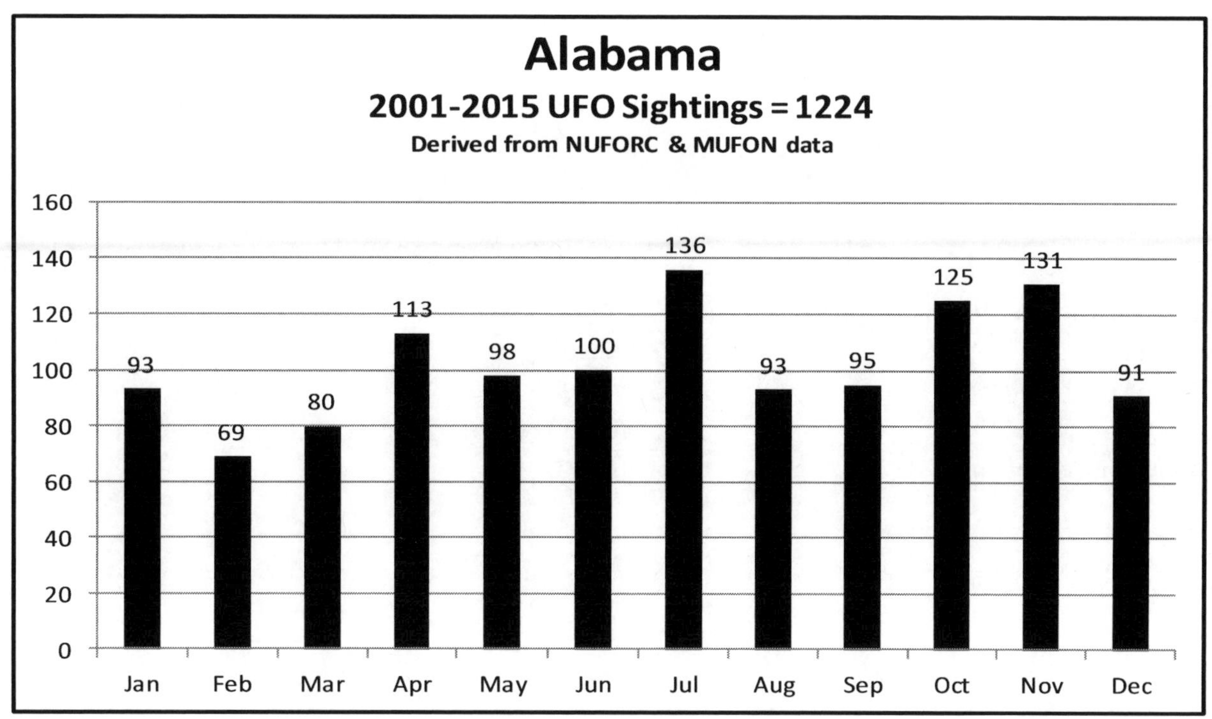

Years	Jan	Feb	Mar	Apr	May	Jun	Jul	Aug	Sep	Oct	Nov	Dec	Total
2001		1	1	4	3	1		1	1	2	1	1	16
2002	1	3	5	2	1	2	5	1	2	1	3	2	28
2003	6	2	1	2	1	9	4	1	3	10	13	1	53
2004	1	3	2	4	4	2	3	4	3	2	4	3	35
2005	4	2	4	4	4	5	2	6	3	8	6	5	53
2006	3	6	4	1	2	3	3	8	1	6	17	4	58
2007	5	5	3	14	5	11	9	3	3	4	3	9	74
2008	7	2	5	11	4	7	8	6	4	12	9	3	78
2009	4	11	6	5	8	2	9	8	13	4	7	2	79
2010	1		3	1	4	5	22	4	6	10	6	5	67
2011	7	4	5	7	8	3	9	6	8	16	5	3	81
2012	10	7	9	11	11	9	8	9	9	11	11	17	122
2013	10	5	16	16	12	11	17	10	14	10	11	17	149
2014	17	12	14	24	27	20	27	18	13	13	16	11	212
2015	17	6	2	7	4	10	10	8	12	16	19	8	119
Total	**93**	**69**	**80**	**113**	**98**	**100**	**136**	**93**	**95**	**125**	**131**	**91**	**1224**

Distribution of Sightings between Databases: Alabama

Source Database	Count	Percent
MUFON	517	42.24%
NUFORC	707	57.76%
Total	1224	100.00%

State Demographic Information: Alabama

2010 US Census Statistics	
Population	4,779,736.00
Area in Square Miles	52,420.07
Land Area Sq. Miles	50,645.33
Population/Square mile	94.40

ALASKA UFO RANK 46/51

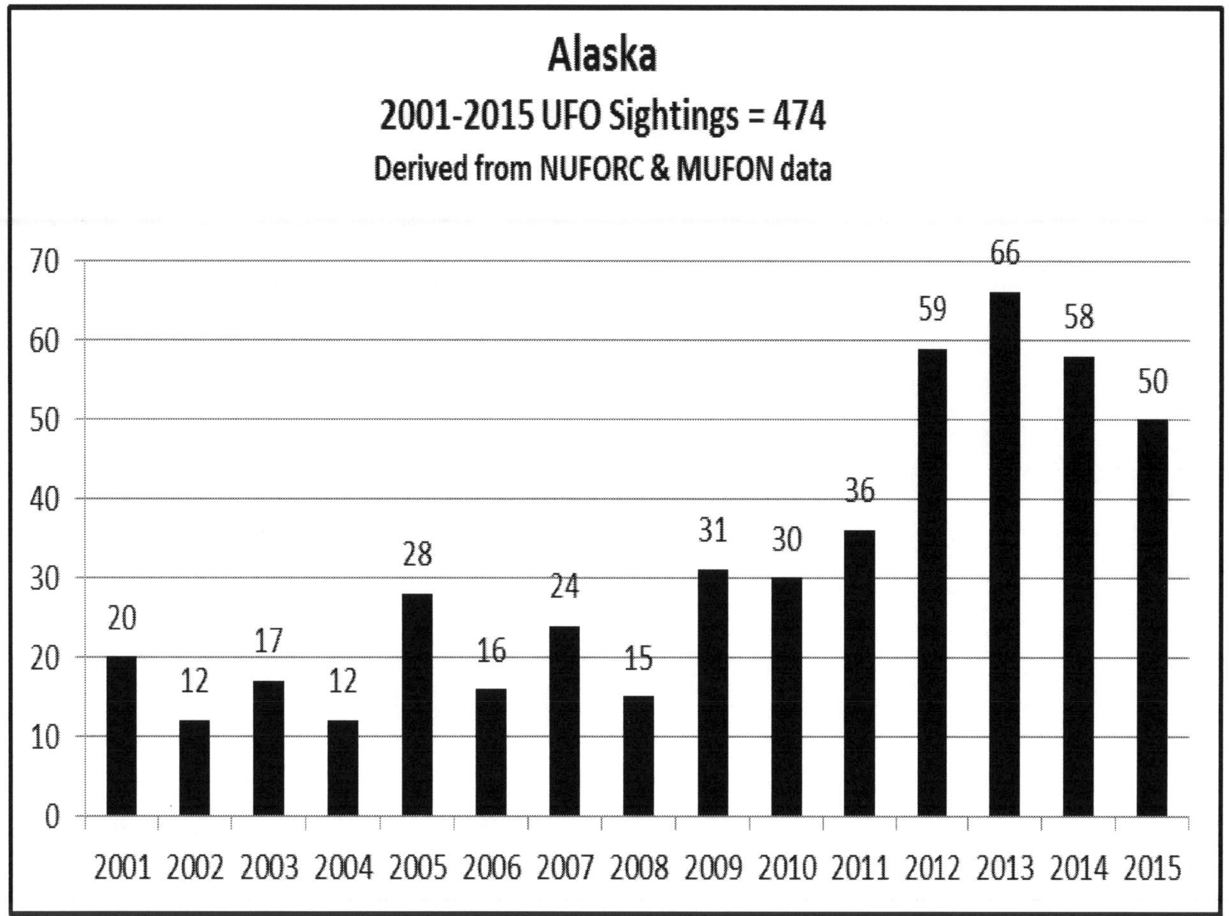

TOP TEN COUNTIES		RANK	TOP TEN SHAPES		
Anchorage	138	**1**	Other	37	7.81%
Fairbanks North Star	77	**2**	Oval	29	6.12%
Matanuska Susitna	70	**3**	Disk	28	5.91%
Kenai Peninsula	47	**4**	Fireball	28	5.91%
Unknown	30	**5**	Star-like	18	3.80%
Ketchikan Gateway	16	**6**	Light	92	19.41%
Juneau	13	**7**	Circle	48	10.13%
Bethel	10	**8**	Unknown	45	9.49%
Yukon Koyukuk	8	**9**	Triangle	39	8.23%
Valdez Cordova	7	**10**	Sphere	38	8.02%

UFO SHAPES: ALASKA

UFO Shapes	2001	2002	2003	2004	2005	2006	2007	2008	2009	2010	2011	2012	2013	2014	2015	Total
Boomerang						1	1		1					1		4
Changing			1	1		1								2		5
Chevron										1			1		1	3
Cigar								1	1	1				1		4
Circle	1		2	2	1	2	3	1	4	6	7	3	9	4	3	48
Cone										2						2
Cylinder			1				1					1	2	1	2	8
Diamond			1									1	2	1	2	7
Disc					1		3	1		2				1	2	10
Disk	2	1	1		2	3	1	2	3	1		2	3	1	6	28
Egg	1	1												1		3
Fireball	2	1				1	2	1	1	1	1	5	7	2	4	28
Flash			1		1							3	3	2	1	11
Formation							1		1	1		1	1			5
Light	4	2	3	5	6	2	1	4	4	3	6	21	14	10	7	92
N/A															1	1
Other	2	2	3		6	1	1	1	3		2	2	5	5	4	37
Oval		1	1	1	1	2			2	1	2	4	4	6	4	29
Rectangle	1				1									2	1	5
Saturn-like							1									1
Sphere	2		2	2	1	2			2	6	6	7	3	4	1	38
Star-like							1	1	1		3	3	2	3	4	18
Teardrop								1			1					2
Triangle	5	1			3	1	4		4	1	5	3	3	8	1	39
Unknown		3	1	1	5		4	2	4	3	3	3	7	3	6	45
Bullet/Missile										1						1
Total	**20**	**12**	**17**	**12**	**28**	**16**	**24**	**15**	**31**	**30**	**36**	**59**	**66**	**58**	**50**	**474**

UFO BY COUNTY: ALASKA

Counties	2001	2002	2003	2004	2005	2006	2007	2008	2009	2010	2011	2012	2013	2014	2015	Total
Alakanuk														2		2
Aleutians West		1		1												2
Anchorage	3	2	7	3	4	7	5	8	5	8	5	25	18	20	18	138
Bethel		1				1		1	2			2	1	1	1	10
Bland										1						1
Denali									1					1		2
Fairbanks North Star	3	2	3	4	10	5	3	2	4		8	7	16	4	6	77
Haines			1		1					1		1		1		5
Juneau		1			1			1	1	2	2	1			4	13
Kenai Peninsula	4		2	1	2		3		3	5	10	4	3	7	3	47
Ketchikan Gateway	1			1						2		4	2	5	1	16
Kodiak Island								1					3	1		5
Lake And Peninsula	1		1													2
Matanuska Susitna	3	1	1	1	4	2	3		5	5	5	7	12	12	9	70
Nome			1			1					2	2				6
North Slope		1			1				2			1				5
Northwest Arctic		1													1	2
Petersburg					1											1
Prince Wales Ketchikan										2		1			1	4
Sitka					1		1		1						2	5
Skagway Hoonah Angoon										2			1			3
Southeast Fairbanks		1						1	1			1	1		1	6
Unknown		1			2		6	1	4	2	3	2	4	2	3	30
Valdez Cordova	1				1		2		1				1	1		7
Wade Hampton											1					1
Wrangell Petersburg	3			1			1									5
Yakutat			1													1

Counties	2001	2002	2003	2004	2005	2006	2007	2008	2009	2010	2011	2012	2013	2014	2015	Total
Yukon Koyukuk	1								1			1	4	1		8
Total	20	12	17	12	28	16	24	15	31	30	36	59	66	58	50	474

If a county is missing from the list, it's because no UFO sightings were logged in either the NUFORC or MUFON databases for the 2001-2015 sample period.

UFOS BY MONTH: ALASKA

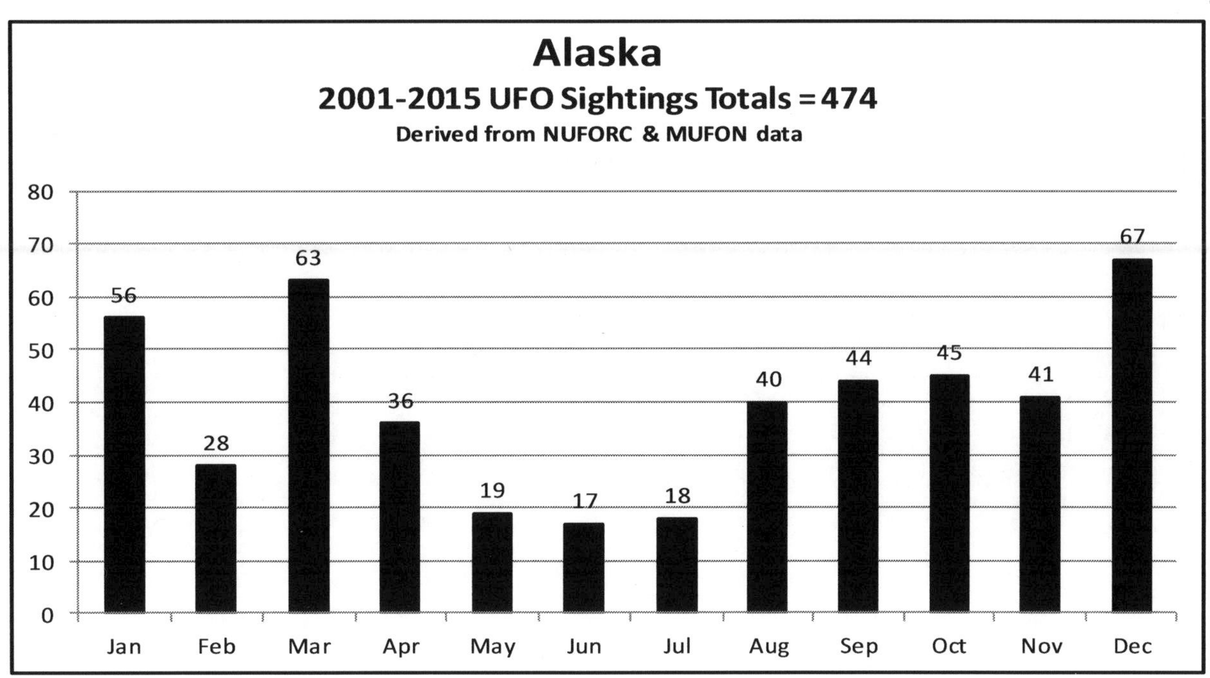

Years	Jan	Feb	Mar	Apr	May	Jun	Jul	Aug	Sep	Oct	Nov	Dec	Total
2001		1	1	4	3	1		1	1	2	1	1	16
2002	1	3	5	2	1	2	5	1	2	1	3	2	28
2003	6	2	1	2	1	9	4	1	3	10	13	1	53
2004	1	3	2	4	4	2	3	4	3	2	4	3	35
2005	4	2	4	4	4	5	2	6	3	8	6	5	53
2006	3	6	4	1	2	3	3	8	1	6	17	4	58
2007	5	5	3	14	5	11	9	3	3	4	3	9	74
2008	7	2	5	11	4	7	8	6	4	12	9	3	78
2009	4	11	6	5	8	2	9	8	13	4	7	2	79
2010	1		3	1	4	5	22	4	6	10	6	5	67
2011	7	4	5	7	8	3	9	6	8	16	5	3	81
2012	10	7	9	11	11	9	8	9	9	11	11	17	122
2013	10	5	16	16	12	11	17	10	14	10	11	17	149
2014	17	12	14	24	27	20	27	18	13	13	16	11	212
2015	17	6	2	7	4	10	10	8	12	16	19	8	119
Total	**93**	**69**	**80**	**113**	**98**	**100**	**136**	**93**	**95**	**125**	**131**	**91**	**1224**

Distribution of Sightings between Databases: Alaska

Source Database	Count	Percent
MUFON	138	29.11%
NUFORC	336	70.89%
Total	474	100.00%

State Demographic Information: Alaska

2010 US Census Statistics	
Population	710,231.00
Area in Square Miles	665,384.04
Land Area Sq. Miles	570,640.95
Population/Square mile	1.20

ARIZONA UFO RANK 7/51

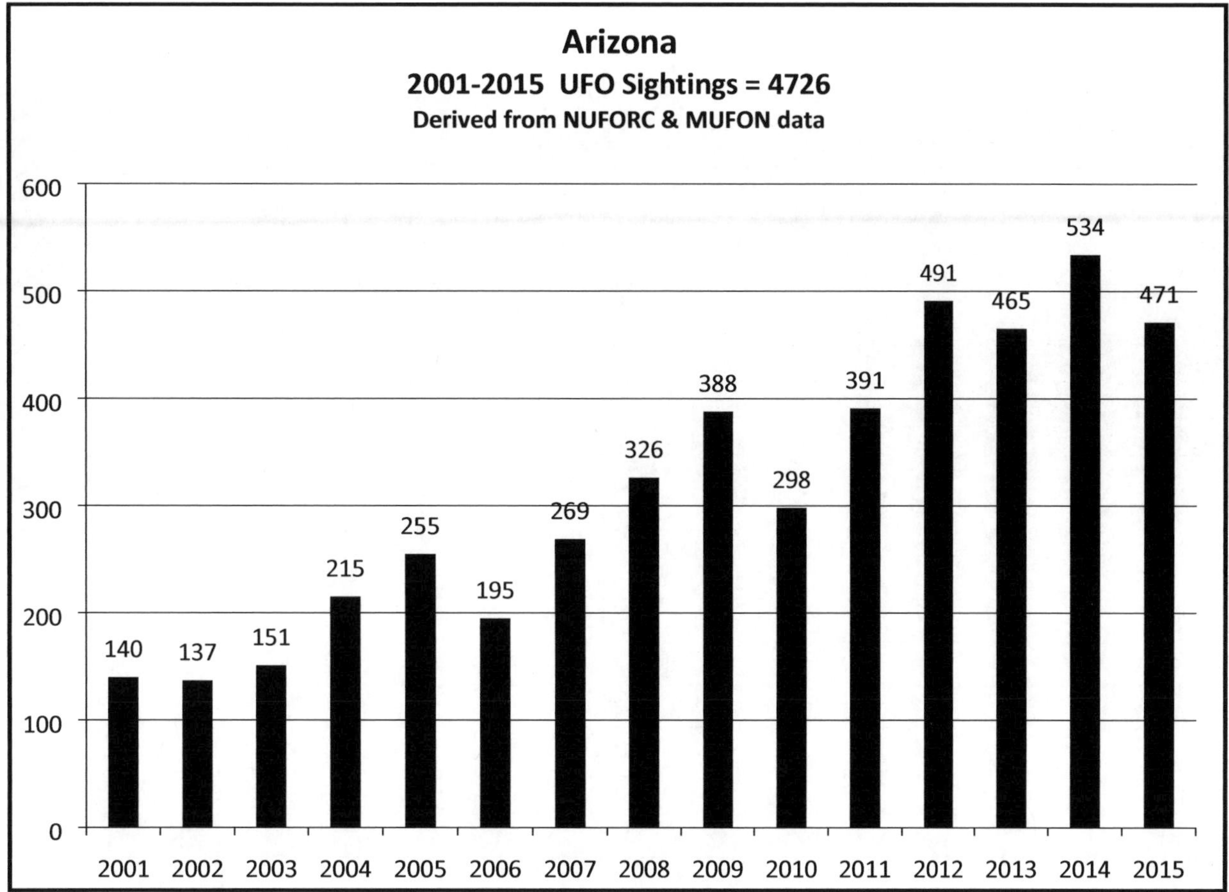

TOP TEN COUNTIES		RANK	TOP TEN SHAPES		
Maricopa	2523	**1**	Light	627	13.27%
2523	578	**2**	Circle	525	11.11%
Pima	365	**3**	Sphere	502	10.62%
Yavapai	297	**4**	Unknown	476	10.07%
Mohave	280	**5**	Other	345	7.30%
Unknown	140	**6**	Triangle	332	7.02%
Yuma	102	**7**	Fireball	322	6.81%
Coconino	89	**8**	Oval	190	4.02%
Navajo	74	**9**	Star-like	187	3.96%
Cochise	71	**10**	Disc	179	3.79%

UFO SHAPES: ARIZONA

UFO Shapes	2001	2002	2003	2004	2005	2006	2007	2008	2009	2010	2011	2012	2013	2014	2015	Total
Blimp	1	1			1		1	1	4	2	2	1		2	2	18
Boomerang		2	1	1	2	3	3	5	11	8	3	14	7	6	1	67
Bullet/Missile					1	4	2	5	4	2	4	1	4	3	1	31
Changing	4	1		9	6	8	5	6	2	6	6	12	5	10	9	89
Chevron	3	2	1	2	1	4	1	3	4	2	2	3	6	3	5	42
Cigar	5	2	6	6	5	4	7	10	6	10	8	13	8	7	9	106
Circle	9	13	12	14	8	22	26	30	58	44	58	72	64	54	41	525
Cone			1		2			1	4	1	4	2	3	1	4	23
Cross			1	1				1	2	2	1	1	3	1	1	14
Cylinder	1	5	4	4	2	5	8	6	7	4	7	7	14	13	7	94
Diamond	2	4	4	1	4	1	1	5	5	4	5	4	2	8	8	58
Disc	1		3	3	10	5	29	16	26	9	16	19	9	19	14	179
Disk	10	4	8	18	17	9	7	8	12	8	8	6	5	8	8	136
Egg	3	3	2	2	3			1	5	3	3	4	4	7	2	42
Fireball	5	6	8	11	13	11	11	12	14	19	25	41	61	57	28	322
Flash	1	2	4		2	4	1	6	16	8	13	7	10	7	12	93
Formation	7	4	4	10	15	8	6	12	3	5	9	4	15	13	11	126
Light	29	29	23	54	59	31	29	32	46	21	25	50	51	68	80	627
N/A							1		1					4	4	10
Other	8	14	11	16	16	15	23	31	17	23	36	25	24	52	34	345
Oval	9	8	9	8	6	5	6	12	12	15	24	17	20	23	16	190
Rectangle	1	3		1	2	5	3	1	2	2	2	6	4	5	4	41
Saturn-like							1			1	1	1	1			5
Sphere	3	7	14	21	17	13	33	29	35	26	39	78	53	68	66	502
Star-like	1			1	2	2	3	25	25	24	24	13	22	21	24	187
Teardrop	1		1	2	4	1	4	3	7	4	3	5	3	3	5	46
Triangle	17	10	14	15	34	15	19	35	22	15	26	32	19	27	32	332
Unknown	19	17	20	15	23	20	39	30	38	30	37	53	48	44	43	476
Total	**140**	**137**	**151**	**215**	**255**	**195**	**269**	**326**	**388**	**298**	**391**	**491**	**465**	**534**	**471**	**4726**

UFOS BY COUNTY: ARIZONA

Counties	2001	2002	2003	2004	2005	2006	2007	2008	2009	2010	2011	2012	2013	2014	2015	Total
Apache	1	2	2	3	5	2	6	2	6	2	3	4	3	3	3	47
Cochise	2	2	4	2	7	3	4	6	5	2	11	8	3	6	6	71
Coconino	8	6	8	3	6	4	3	10	4	4	7	6	8	5	7	89
Gila	1	4	4	1	4	2	4	1	6	6	8	2	4	4	4	55
Graham			1	1	2		1	2		1	1	3	3		1	16
Greenlee											2			1	1	4
La Paz	4	4	3	4	4		5	4	4	2	6	10	1	7	4	62
Maricopa	89	71	64	136	137	109	133	146	197	158	166	288	256	313	260	2523
Mohave	7	8	7	10	8	6	16	24	32	22	44	31	25	26	31	297
Navajo	1	2	4	5	2	3	7	8	4	7	5	9	5	6	6	74
Pima	14	18	23	22	30	31	29	49	58	29	44	46	52	72	61	578
Pinal	2	4	7	7	12	10	10	26	22	20	25	21	38	44	32	280
Santa Cruz	1	1	1			2			3	3	2	2	5	1	2	23
Unknown	1	5	3	2	11	4	20	13	10	6	16	13	13	8	15	140
Yavapai	8	8	14	16	20	15	27	26	29	20	44	36	41	31	30	365
Yuma	1	2	6	3	7	4	4	9	8	16	7	12	8	7	8	102
Total	**140**	**137**	**151**	**215**	**255**	**195**	**269**	**326**	**388**	**298**	**391**	**491**	**465**	**534**	**471**	**4726**

If a county is missing from the list, it's because no UFO sightings were logged in either the NUFORC or MUFON databases for the 2001-2015 sample period.

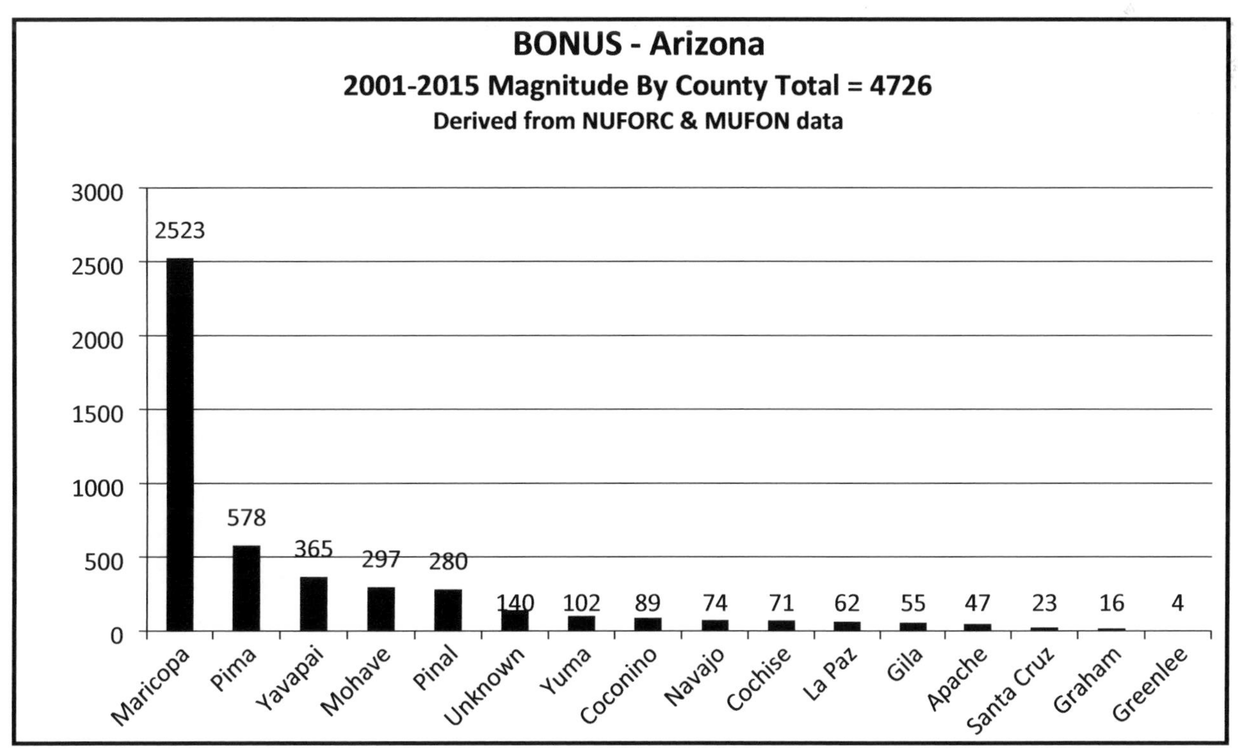

UFOS BY MONTH: ARIZONA

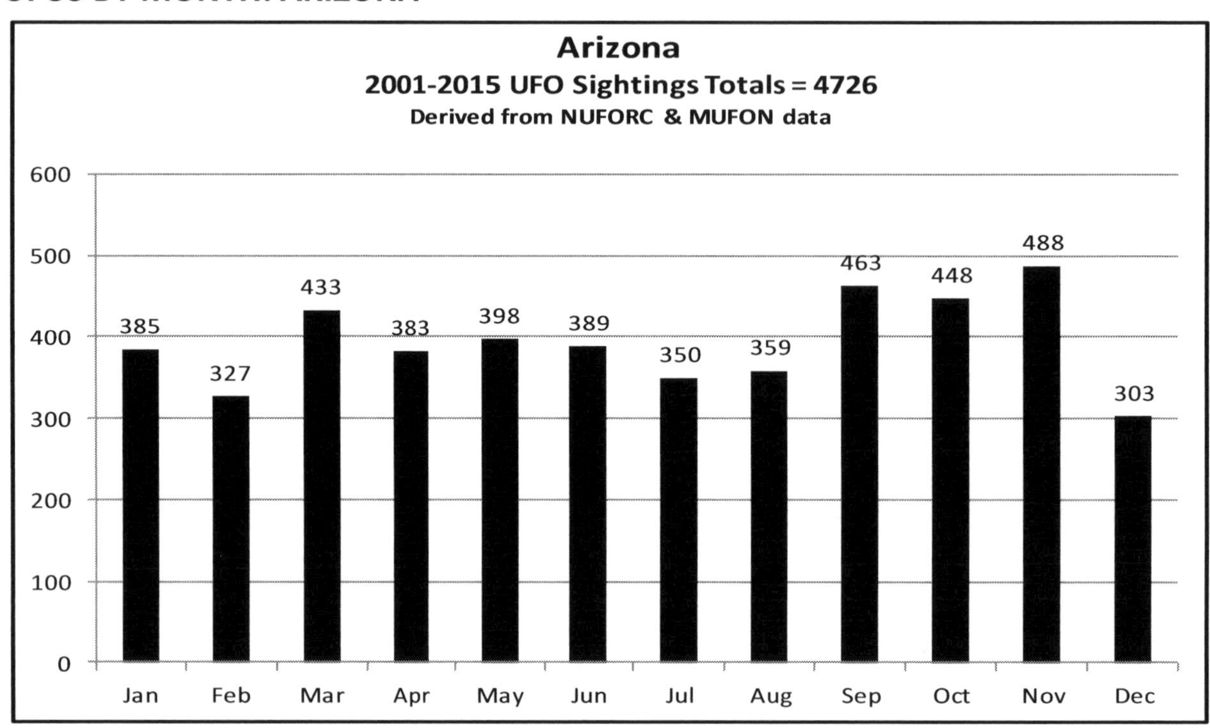

Years	Jan	Feb	Mar	Apr	May	Jun	Jul	Aug	Sep	Oct	Nov	Dec	Total
2001	13	13	19	9	10	11	13	14	13	11	10	4	140
2002	9	14	19	10	7	16	9	10	12	12	13	6	137
2003	10	8	7	9	14	14	11	25	15	13	16	9	151
2004	14	13	15	27	27	32	23	15	15	13	10	11	215
2005	14	13	19	18	19	25	18	11	44	35	28	11	255
2006	12	12	12	13	14	13	22	15	14	25	28	15	195
2007	20	28	24	14	15	19	17	23	17	13	60	19	269
2008	13	19	30	47	20	30	35	21	24	28	38	21	326
2009	26	38	43	29	51	48	32	27	41	18	21	14	388
2010	10	14	19	35	37	29	14	21	26	36	37	20	298
2011	35	25	40	23	19	24	21	34	55	52	40	23	391
2012	46	38	55	27	42	35	40	43	39	56	36	34	491
2013	46	14	38	31	44	34	26	37	54	46	42	53	465
2014	71	39	46	52	45	36	31	25	48	52	42	47	534
2015	46	39	47	39	34	23	38	38	46	38	67	16	471
Total	**385**	**327**	**433**	**383**	**398**	**389**	**350**	**359**	**463**	**448**	**488**	**303**	**4726**

Distribution of Sightings between Databases: Arizona

Source Database	Count	Percent
MUFON	396	39.80%
NUFORC	599	60.20%
Total	995	100.00%

State Demographic Information: Arizona

2010 US Census Statistics	
Population	6,392,017.00
Area in Square Miles	113,990.30
Land in Sq. Miles	113.990.08
Population /Square Mile	56.30

ARKANSAS

UFO RANK 35/51

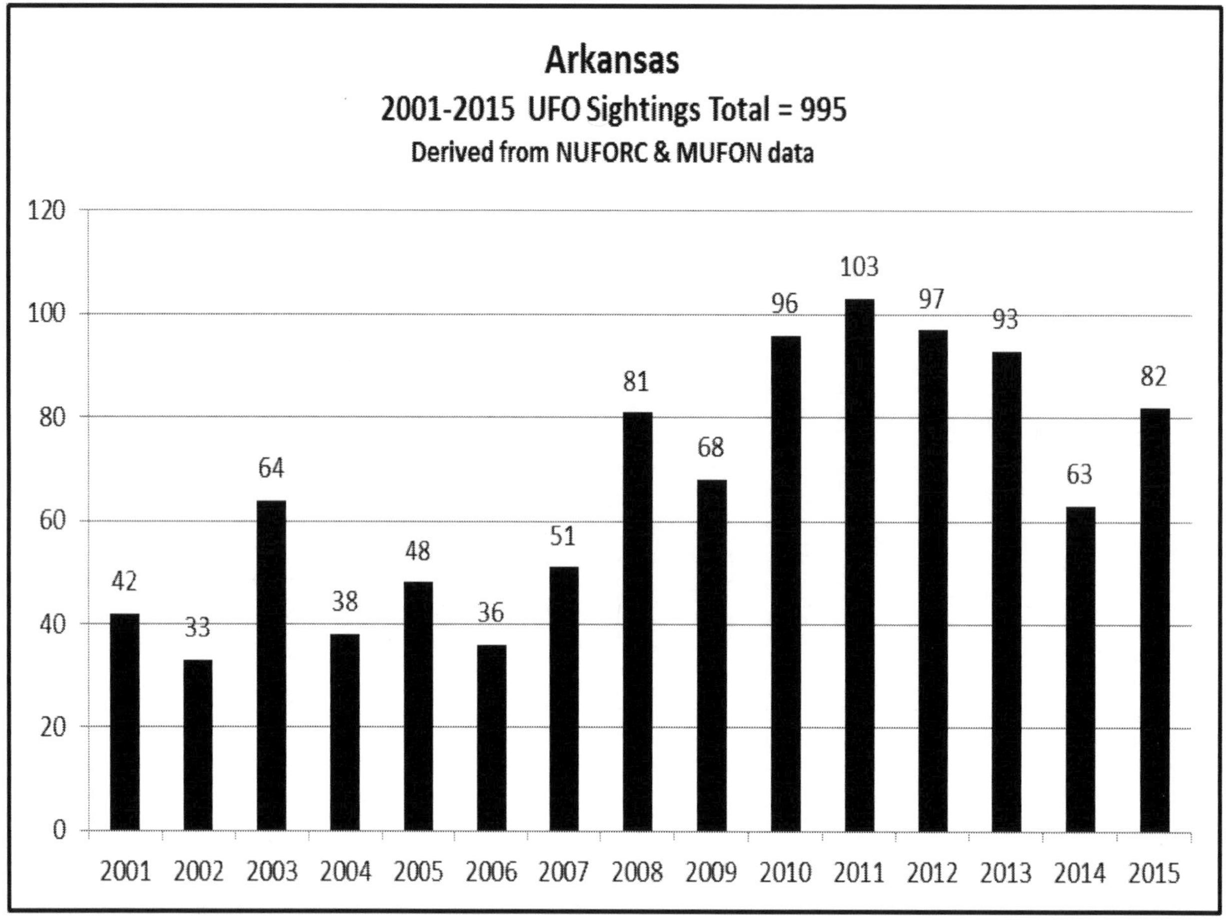

TOP TEN COUNTIES		RANK	TOP TEN SHAPES		
Washington	92	1	Light	135	13.57%
Benton	89	2	Circle	118	11.86%
Pulaski	88	3	Triangle	116	11.66%
Faulkner	48	4	Unknown	110	11.06%
Sebastian	47	5	Sphere	82	8.24%
Pope	36	6	Other	61	6.13%
Garland	35	7	Oval	50	5.03%
Saline	34	8	Star-like	50	5.03%
Unknown	32	9	Fireball	36	3.62%
Baxter	28	10	Cigar	30	3.02%

UFO SHAPES: ARKANSAS

UFO Shapes	2001	2002	2003	2004	2005	2006	2007	2008	2009	2010	2011	2012	2013	2014	2015	Total
Blimp								1							1	2
Boomerang							1		1			1	1	2	1	7
Bullet/Missile								1		2	1	2			1	7
Changing	1	1	1	4	3	1	1	3				1				16
Chevron		2				2	2		1	1		1	2	2	1	14
Cigar	2		3	1	2	1	1	3	3	8	1	1	2	1	1	30
Circle	2	4	5	1	3	2	6	13	4	14	9	19	15	11	10	118
Cone	1												1	1		3
Cross					1	1		1			1					4
Cylinder	2		1	3				4	1	2	1	2	1	3	1	21
Diamond	2	1	1					1	2	1	1		1	1	1	12
Disc							1	3	4	2	5	1	1	1	4	22
Disk	2	2	1	2	2	2	2	2		3	4	2	2	1	2	29
Egg	1	1					1		3	1		1	1			9
Fireball	1	2			1	2	1	3	3	1	8	4	5	2	3	36
Flash		2			2	2	1	1	6	3	2	1	4	1	1	26
Formation	1		3					2		1	1		3	1		12
Light	4	5	15	10	7	6	15	5	7	13	8	13	9	7	11	135
Other	8	1	5	1	1	1	1	3	3	4	8	9	9		7	61
Oval	2	1	4	1	4	5	2	3	3	2	8	5	4	4	2	50
Rectangle					1		1	1		1		2	1		1	8
Saturn-like								1			1					2
Sphere	3	4	5	2	4	2	3	3	3	7	13	7	9	3	14	82
Sq/Rect												1				1
Star-like				1			4	9	2	11	9	4	3	4	3	50
Teardrop			2		4						1	2	2	1		12
Triangle	4	2	15	7	5	4	3	8	7	8	13	11	8	8	13	116
Unknown	6	5	3	5	8	5	5	10	15	11	8	7	9	9	4	110
Total	**42**	**33**	**64**	**38**	**48**	**36**	**51**	**81**	**68**	**96**	**103**	**97**	**93**	**63**	**82**	**995**

UFOS BY COUNTY: ARKANSAS

Counties	2001	2002	2003	2004	2005	2006	2007	2008	2009	2010	2011	2012	2013	2014	2015	Total
Ashley											1					1
Baxter	3		1		1	1	3	1	2		1	4	6	2	3	28
Benton	4		1		9	3	6	2	11	13	11	9	5	6	9	89
Boone					1			3		1	3	1		1		10
Bradley															2	2
Calhoun	1											1				2
Carroll	1		2		2		2		2	3	4	1	1	2		20
Chicot						1						2				3
Clark								1			1			2		4
Clay		1	2						1							4
Cleburne	1	2	1				1	1		1	3	2		1		13
Columbia			1				1			1	2				1	6
Conway	3		1				1		1				1			7
Craighead	1	1	2		1		1		2	1	2	1	2	1	1	16
Crawford			3	2	3	1		4	2	4		1	3	2		25
Crittenden			1	1				3		2	1	3	1	2	1	15
Cross						1						1				2
Dallas							1						2			3
Desha										1				1		2
Drew													2	1		3
Faulkner			3		1		1	4	1		8	10	12	1	7	48
Franklin			1							1			1			3
Fulton		1				1				1				1		4
Garland	2		6	1	1			5	1	6	1	2	2	4	4	35
Grant			1													1
Greene				1	1			1	1	1				2	1	8
Hempstead	1			1	1				2	1						6
Hot Spring		1		1			1			1	1	1			1	7
Howard												2				2
Independence			1	3				2		1	1			1		9
Izard	1															1
Jackson		1	1				1									3
Jefferson	1		1	1				1	2	1		2	2	1		12
Johnson	1			3	4							2	4	1		15
Lafayette							1			1			1	1		4
Lawrence	1		1					3			1	2	2	1		11
Lincoln							1								1	2

If a county is missing from the list, it's because no UFO sightings were logged in either the NUFORC or MUFON databases for the 2001-2015 sample period.

UFOS BY MONTH: ARKANSAS

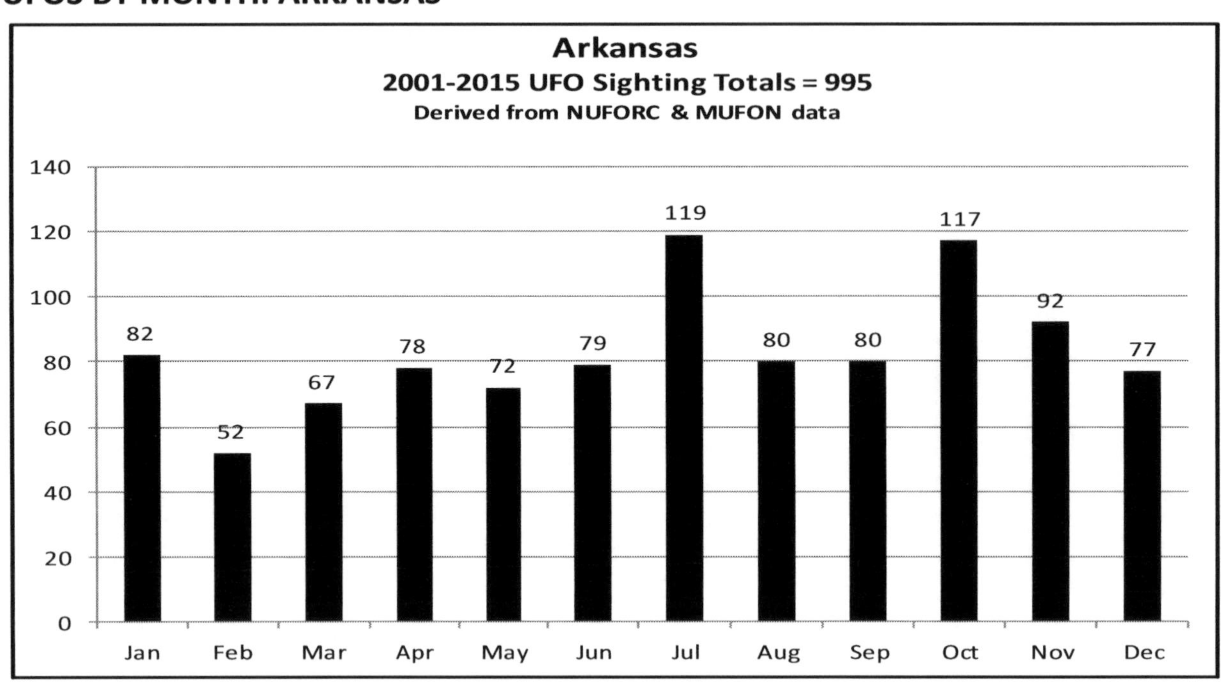

Years	Jan	Feb	Mar	Apr	May	Jun	Jul	Aug	Sep	Oct	Nov	Dec	Total
2001	2	2	9	3		4	2	3	2	8	4	3	42
2002	3	1		6	3	4	3	3	2	1	3	4	33
2003	7		3	3	4	2	7	4	10	14	8	2	64
2004		2	3	6	4	2	4	1	3	6	4	3	38
2005		5	5	11		3	5	4	5	7	1	2	48
2006	2	3	4	3	7		3	3	1	3	3	4	36
2007	7	3	2	2	4	1	5	11	4	6	4	2	51
2008	5	3	4	9	6	6	5	2	1	16	15	9	81
2009	5	8	5	3	4	10	8	7	7	2	4	5	68
2010	13	3	8	6	8	13	15	8	3	10	4	5	96
2011	11	6	2	5	4	10	19	4	16	14	6	6	103
2012	12	10	5	7	9	9	3	7	5	5	11	14	97
2013	2	4	6	4	3	9	20	7	10	12	9	7	93
2014	9		3	2	8	1	9	10	3	3	9	6	63
2015	4	2	8	8	8	5	11	6	8	10	7	5	82
Total	**82**	**52**	**67**	**78**	**72**	**79**	**119**	**80**	**80**	**117**	**92**	**77**	**995**

Distribution of Sightings between Databases: Arkansas

Source Database	Count	Percent
MUFON	396	39.80%
NUFORC	599	60.20%
Total	995	100.00%

State Demographic Information: Arkansas

2010 US Census Statistics	
Population	2,915,918.00
Area in Square Miles	53,178.55
Land Area Sq. Miles	52.035.48
Population/Square mile	56.00

CALIFORNIA UFO RANK 1/51

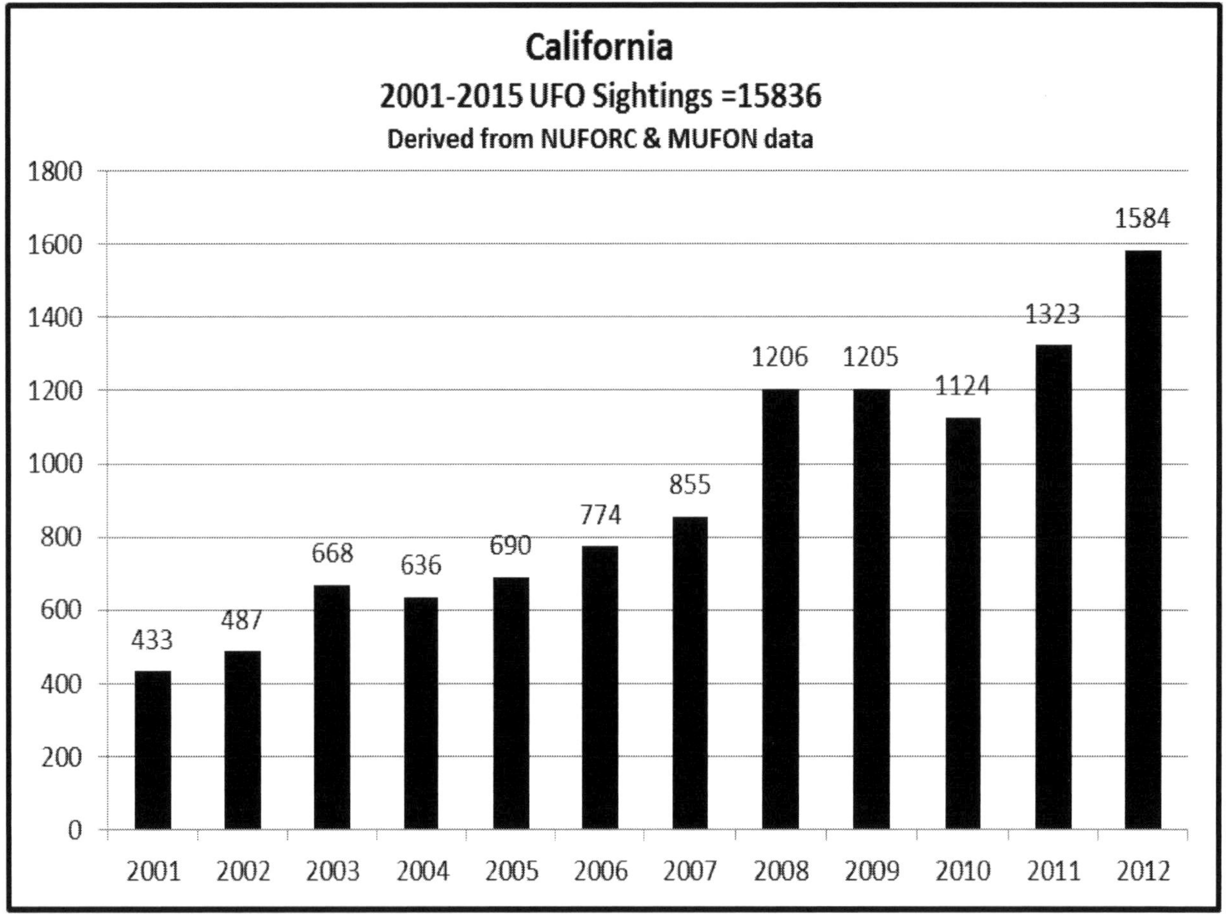

TOP TEN COUNTIES		RANK	TOP TEN SHAPES		
Los Angeles	3212	1	Light	2012	12.71%
San Diego	1393	2	Sphere	1652	10.43%
Orange	1271	3	Circle	1638	10.34%
Riverside	958	4	Triangle	1454	9.18%
San Bernardino	836	5	Unknown	1436	9.07%
Santa Clara	569	6	Other	1158	7.31%
Alameda	518	7	Fireball	1085	6.85%
Contra Costa	445	8	Disc	902	5.70%
Ventura	429	9	Star-like	848	5.35%
Fresno	379	10	Oval	714	4.51%

UFO SHAPES: CALIFORNIA

UFO Shapes	2001	2002	2003	2004	2005	2006	2007	2008	2009	2010	2011	2012	2013	2014	2015	Total
Blimp			1		1	1	1	1	3	1		6		3	4	22
Boomerang		2	5	1	3	3	6	13	17	10	8	9	8	19	22	126
Bullet/Missile			1	3	3	4	2	13	13	7	11	12	15	7	15	106
Changing	12	27	16	20	15	21	12	30	20	18	17	27	19	25	26	305
Chevron	8	13	10	9	10	11	12	18	10	13	23	14	15	17	17	200
Cigar	10	12	10	9	5	23	24	28	31	25	18	32	25	33	20	305
Circle	36	36	72	53	53	96	102	131	125	108	104	174	155	222	171	1638
Cone	4	5	2	3		1	5	6	6	7	6	4	13	13	18	93
Cross	4		2	2	1	2	2	3	2	6	3	4	7	4	7	49
Cylinder	8	8	9	7	8	11	20	21	21	19	29	39	36	37	32	305
Diamond	8	10	13	9	15	20	10	17	21	18	21	28	28	35	20	273
Disc	33	30	46	50	45	52	50	79	78	57	77	84	61	93	67	902
Egg	6	3	7	13	7	9	15	19	7	8	6	10	8	17	10	145
Fireball	30	25	48	29	37	44	41	69	48	73	92	163	142	127	117	1085
Flash	2	6	8	11	10	13	20	30	37	34	36	37	41	27	30	342
Formation	7	13	15	17	18	16	24	27	27	17	18	26	30	29	14	298
Light	89	80	133	116	112	118	111	141	172	122	139	151	159	183	186	2012
Other	38	39	45	54	52	57	67	77	85	93	92	82	83	148	146	1158
Oval	19	16	27	27	27	35	41	58	49	59	60	96	71	64	65	714
Rectangle	6	7	5	7	3	8	10	20	14	4	12	15	8	17	11	147
Saturn-like				1	2	1	2	5	3	6	5	5	6	5	3	44
Sphere	31	38	41	44	55	56	80	102	96	101	121	190	213	288	196	1652
Sq/Rect													2	13	24	39
Star-like	2	1	2	1	21	15	40	76	100	78	125	108	88	106	85	848
Teardrop	4	4	5	5	5	6	7	8	10	16	10	15	10	18	15	138
Triangle	39	54	64	82	66	71	78	124	112	119	166	124	115	117	123	1454
Unknown	37	58	81	63	116	80	73	90	98	105	124	129	106	147	129	1436
Total	**433**	**487**	**668**	**636**	**690**	**774**	**855**	**1206**	**1205**	**1124**	**1323**	**1584**	**1464**	**1814**	**1573**	**15836**

UFOS BY COUNTY: CALIFORNIA

Counties	2001	2002	2003	2004	2005	2006	2007	2008	2009	2010	2011	2012	2013	2014	2015	Total
Alameda	14	25	31	34	18	19	38	36	45	33	36	52	40	45	52	518
Alpine	1			2							1	1		1		6
Amador	2	1			1	1	1	1	1	2		2	4		3	19
Butte	3	4	6	2	8	2	10	2	9	10	11	15	13	11	8	114
Calaveras		3	4		9	2	2		5	4		1	3	1	3	37
Colusa					4	1	1	1		2	1		1	1	1	13
Contra Costa	10	17	18	21	25	21	26	27	26	35	29	66	41	43	40	445
Del Norte	4		1	2		2	3			3	2	1	2	4	4	28
El Dorado	5	1	4	7	3	11	6	6	5	5	6	9	10	11	3	92
Fresno	10	6	14	15	23	18	22	26	32	28	39	29	36	54	27	379
Glenn							1					1		1		3
Humboldt	5	3	7	6	5	8	3	12	11	11	13	14	6	10	13	127
Imperial	2	3	2	2	3	6	3	7	3	2	7	12	8	7	7	74
Inyo	2	4		3	1	3	5	3	5	1	5	9	3	2	2	48
Kern	8	11	10	21	18	17	16	20	13	25	30	21	19	34	36	299
Kings	4	6	6	3	4	2	2	2	4	3	2	2	2	4	5	51
Klamath			1							1	1	1	1		1	6
Lake	4	2	3	1	3		6	1	2	4	6	6	8	8	7	61
Lassen	1	1	1	2	2	1	1	1	1		1	3	4	1	3	23
Los Angeles	96	101	162	137	137	176	159	282	252	242	242	285	275	336	330	3212
Madera		2		2	2	1	3	1	4	2	5	4	4	9	7	46
Marin	4	4	6	8	6	10	9	5	11	7	8	13	21	22	17	151
Mariposa	1			1				1			1					4
Mendocino	1	3	2	6	3	7	2	15	9	12	14	4	9	13	14	114
Merced		1	5	4	2	4	2	3	1	12	7	25	12	26	4	108
Modoc	1	1	1		2	1				1			3		4	14
Mono	2		3	1	3	5	3	2	2	4	2	3		3		33
Monterey	5	6	4	9	2	6	13	8	11	20	21	30	15	23	15	188
Napa	2	4	6	2	4	6	2	8	2	4	6	6	14	6	5	77
Nassau															1	1
Nevada	2	5	3	3	3	3	3	5	11	5	7	6	7	10	7	80
Orange	25	20	37	45	49	62	92	116	98	82	81	137	129	183	115	1271
Placer	6	4	8	9	5	10	8	12	13	14	19	31	26	18	30	213
Plumas	4		2	1	1		4	3	4	1		4		4	6	34
Riverside	19	19	25	32	31	40	41	82	79	63	93	82	99	131	122	958
Sacramento	16	14	23	16	23	28	30	44	36	36	51	63	79	60	52	571
San Benito		2		2	2	5	5	1	3	1	2	3	6	10	3	45
San Bernardino	30	29	37	30	38	33	31	57	69	58	83	94	53	92	102	836
San Diego	36	38	73	55	56	66	76	111	121	77	122	124	126	176	136	1393

Counties	2001	2002	2003	2004	2005	2006	2007	2008	2009	2010	2011	2012	2013	2014	2015	Total
San Francisco	8	12	17	13	18	17	22	36	29	27	30	30	28	26	14	327
San Joaquin	5	3	7	3	7	7	7	21	14	27	22	19	19	32	15	208
San Luis Obispo	7	10	7	3	8	6	15	18	12	12	5	9	13	20	28	173
San Mateo	6	3	9	8	13	12	18	13	13	9	16	17	22	12	17	188
Santa Barbara	6	13	14	6	16	10	18	21	17	18	19	18	20	18	24	238
Santa Clara	16	24	35	28	25	23	21	42	53	41	55	49	43	64	50	569
Santa Cruz	6	12	4	8	3	8	13	10	8	11	13	18	15	15	11	155
Shasta	4	6	5	5	7	5	10	4	8	23	18	26	13	17	10	161
Sherman Oaks											2	1				3
Sierra					1					2	2			1		6
Siskiyou		2	5	2	2	5	5	3	4	6	6	3	2	5	6	56
Solano	4	1	8	6	8	7	4	16	10	13	11	18	16	18	22	162
Sonoma	15	13	19	15	11	12	22	16	21	12	23	34	27	47	34	321
Stanislaus	7	6	7	7	17	12	12	14	22	22	21	25	26	29	24	251
Sutter	1	1	1	3	2	2	1	1		3	1	4	8	1	4	33
Tehama	2		2	2	1	2		1		4	5	3	1	5	3	31
Trinity	1							3	3	3			3	2		15
Tulare	4	6		7	10	6	7	3	14	11	17	17	12	14	15	143
Tuolumne	1	4	2	14	5	7	6	3		4	3	7	7	6	2	71
Unknown	4	2	2	7	14	33	30	49	49	21	54	60	65	64	56	510
Ventura	9	29	18	11	22	18	13	21	32	40	36	57	34	47	42	429
Yolo	2		1	2	3	3	1	7	4	1	8	5	7	8	6	58
Yuba				2	1	1	1	3	4	3	2	5	4	3	5	34
Yuma						1				1						2
Total	**433**	**487**	**668**	**636**	**690**	**774**	**855**	**1206**	**1205**	**1124**	**1323**	**1584**	**1464**	**1814**	**1573**	**15836**

If a county is missing from the list, it's because no UFO sightings were logged in either the NUFORC or MUFON databases for the 2001-2015 sample period.

UFOS BY MONTH: CALIFORNIA

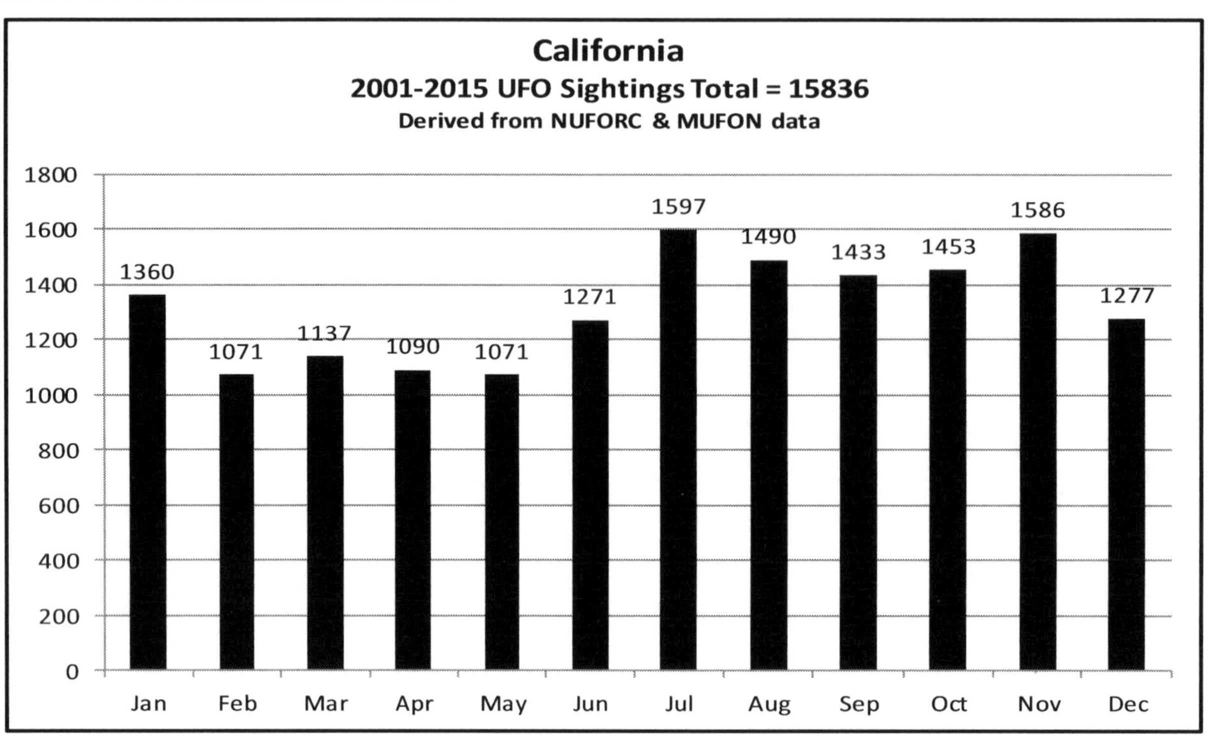

Years	Jan	Feb	Mar	Apr	May	Jun	Jul	Aug	Sep	Oct	Nov	Dec	Total
2001	40	27	34	26	40	39	45	50	35	31	44	22	433
2002	26	26	35	27	52	46	56	43	50	57	36	33	487
2003	71	53	17	40	37	47	57	95	55	68	72	56	668
2004	46	30	63	48	53	52	97	56	57	47	50	37	636
2005	38	34	49	48	46	54	80	58	82	72	86	43	690
2006	47	64	69	49	48	57	73	81	55	67	70	94	774
2007	78	52	77	49	42	76	82	80	70	78	94	77	855
2008	128	99	87	100	67	95	69	90	111	137	126	97	1206
2009	164	95	90	56	70	87	146	117	120	100	89	71	1205
2010	82	58	78	96	84	75	149	103	107	95	116	81	1124
2011	96	112	82	104	94	80	135	141	122	122	104	131	1323
2012	139	92	103	122	121	160	164	146	133	146	120	138	1584
2013	101	99	103	96	115	108	152	150	123	120	117	180	1464
2014	176	135	131	151	126	176	158	170	156	160	127	148	1814
2015	128	95	119	78	76	119	134	110	157	153	335	69	1573
Total	**1360**	**1071**	**1137**	**1090**	**1071**	**1271**	**1597**	**1490**	**1433**	**1453**	**1586**	**1277**	**15836**

Distribution of Sightings between Databases: California

Source Database	Count	Percent
MUFON	6576	41.53%
NUFORC	9260	58.47%
Total	15836	100.00%

State Demographic Information: California

2010 US Census Statistics	
Population	37,253,956.00
Area in Square Miles	163,694.74
Land Area Sq. Miles	1,557,793.22
Population/Square mile	239.10

COLORADO UFO RANK 12/51

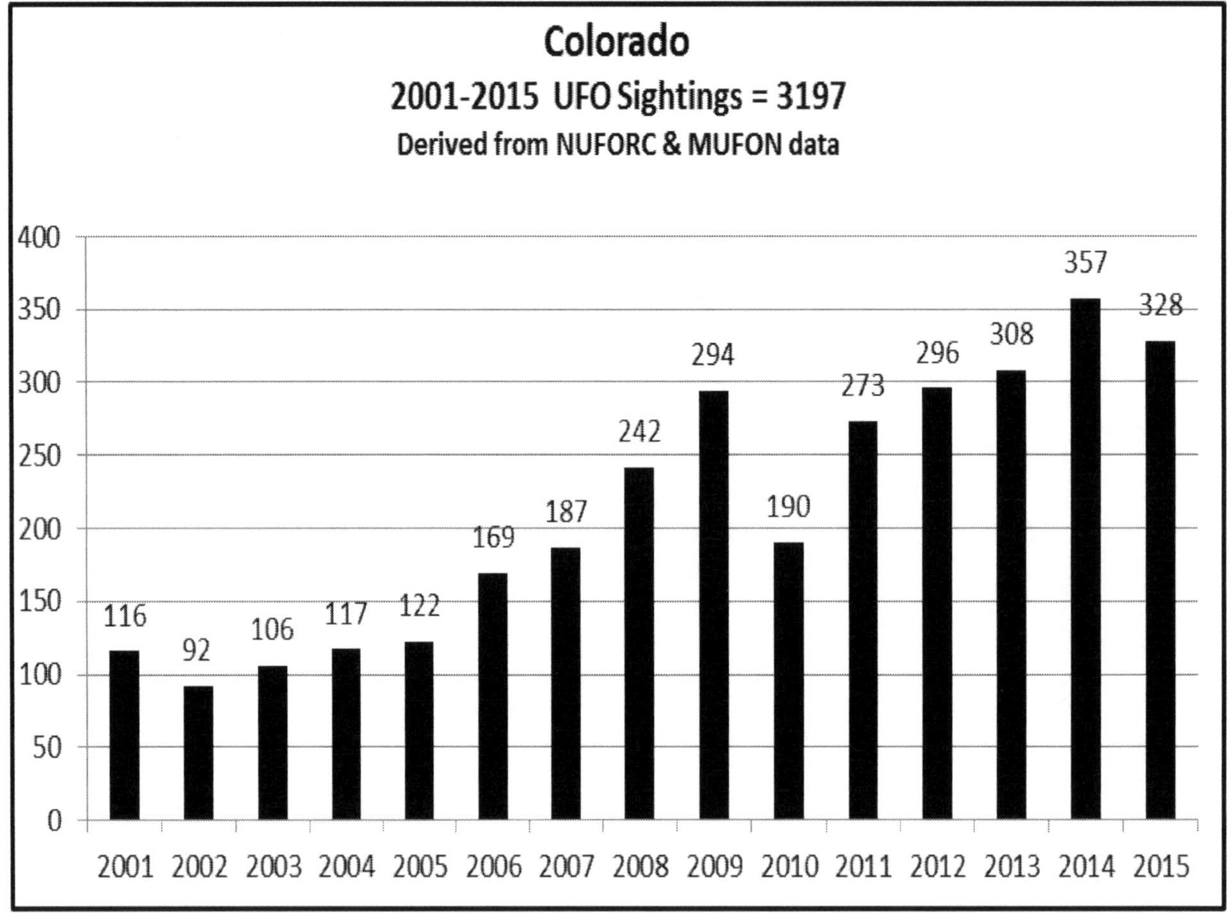

TOP TEN COUNTIES		RANK	TOP TEN SHAPES		
Denver	415	**1**	Sphere	356	11.14%
El Paso	353	**2**	Circle	350	10.95%
Arapahoe	322	**3**	Light	324	10.13%
Boulder	267	**4**	Unknown	311	9.73%
Jefferson	263	**5**	Triangle	291	9.10%
Larimer	243	**6**	Other	235	7.35%
Adams	174	**7**	Star-like	198	6.19%
Unknown	122	**8**	Fireball	157	4.91%
Douglas	115	**9**	Oval	134	4.19%
Weld	106	**10**	Disc	102	3.19%

UFO SHAPES: COLORADO

UFO Shapes	**2001**	**2002**	**2003**	**2004**	**2005**	**2006**	**2007**	**2008**	**2009**	**2010**	**2011**	**2012**	**2013**	**2014**	**2015**	**Total**
Blimp				1	1	1	2	2		1	4	4	1	1		18
Boomerang	1		1	1	3	4	4	2	6	3	7	10	14	4	4	64
Bullet/Missile	1					2	2	3	2	2	6		1	1	1	21
Changing	3	1	1	2	1	4	3	4	1		4	3	7	2	7	43
Chevron	2	2	3	4	1	2	3	4	2	4	7	7	3	7	18	69
Cigar	2	1	2	4	5	5	4	5	12	6	7	10	8	1	3	75
Circle	5	11	5	7	13	10	16	23	45	25	30	42	46	39	33	350
Cone							3	1				1	2	1	3	11
Cross			1				1	1	1	2			1			7
Cylinder	5	5	3	2	3		5	4	1	2	7	7	7	3	7	61
Diamond	2		2	2	1	1	10	4	2	2	9	3	3	2	3	46
Disc	1	2	6	2	3	8	6	10	18	2	2	9	12	5	16	102
Disk	5	3	3	12	6	5	8	6	8	7	8	1	7	8	1	88
Egg	1	2	2		1		3	3	2		1	2	2	6	1	26
Fireball	14	5	1	3	3	8	3	15	14	5	10	20	22	16	18	157
Flash	1	3		3	3	3	6	9	8	8	4	6	4	9	6	73
Formation	4	2	3	5	2	6	2	3	1		6	1	4	11	6	56
Light	13	10	23	11	18	22	17	21	28	17	25	28	23	36	32	324
N/A							1				1		1	7	4	14
Other	6	9	7	8	10	13	19	21	23	12	13	16	21	27	30	235
Oval	6	4	4	8	5	10	2	15	9	8	6	10	15	21	11	134
Rectangle	3	1	2			3	2	1	1		2	3	3	2	5	28
Saturn-like						1				2	2		1	1		7
Sphere	17	6	11	17	8	10	16	14	25	18	30	30	31	77	46	356
Sq/Rect						2							1		6	9
Star-like				3		8	14	24	20	31	23	19	16	19	21	198
Teardrop	1	3	2			4	1	1		1	2	4	1	1	2	23
Triangle	18	15	14	13	11	17	14	25	31	16	25	22	25	23	22	291
Unknown	5	7	10	9	24	20	20	21	34	16	32	38	26	27	22	311
Total	**116**	**92**	**106**	**117**	**122**	**169**	**187**	**242**	**294**	**190**	**273**	**296**	**308**	**357**	**328**	**3197**

UFOS BY COUNTY: COLORADO

Counties	2001	2002	2003	2004	2005	2006	2007	2008	2009	2010	2011	2012	2013	2014	2015	Total
Adams	2	4	6	2	8	10	8	11	20	7	15	13	20	15	33	174
Alamosa			1		1	1	8	1	1			2	2	1	2	20
Arapahoe	11	14	11	16	13	17	14	19	38	16	22	28	23	42	38	322
Archuleta						1		1	1	1			2	2	1	9
Baca				1					1						1	3
Bent			1	1												2
Boulder	11	9	10	16	9	13	12	13	33	12	26	29	27	23	24	267
Broomfield		2						1	4	2	7	7	4	6	5	38
Chaffee	2	1		2				3	4	2		1	3	3	1	22
Cheyenne							1	1						1		3
Clear Creek		1		1		1				1			2	1	1	8
Conejos	1					1			1					1		4
Costilla			1	1			5	1			1					9
Custer		1		2					1				1			5
Davis							1									1
Delta	1		1	1	1		2	1		2	1	3	5	2	1	21
Denver	19	7	7	17	20	28	32	36	43	22	39	28	44	38	35	415
Denver										1						1
Dolores		1		1							1					3
Douglas	10	3	3	3	6	5	4	12	8	5	3	8	18	17	10	115
Eagle	2		4	3	5	4	2	5	8	1	3	3	2	7	1	50
El Paso	9	8	14	10	12	21	22	19	27	23	29	43	33	54	29	353
Elbert	1	2	1						1		1			2	1	9
Fremont	1			1	1	2		4	1	3	3	3	2	3	1	25
Garfield	1	1	2		2		2	2	3	3	1	3	2	6	5	33
Gilpin	1															1
Grand	1	2		1	1			1	1	1	4		3		3	18
Gunnison						3	2	1	7	1	1	2	4	2	1	24
Huerfano	1	1	2	1	1	2		2	1		3		1	3	2	20
Jackson															1	1
Jefferson	13	7	6	10	10	12	12	17	20	16	31	21	28	30	30	263
Kiowa	1							1				1				3
Kit Carson						1	2	1	1			1		1		7
La Plata	1	3	2		1	4	4		3	1	3	4		5	3	34
Lake						1		1		1		1		2	2	8
Larimer	7	3	6	7	12	11	20	22	21	23	25	24	11	22	29	243
Las Animas			1		2		5			1	2			1	1	13

Counties	**2001**	**2002**	**2003**	**2004**	**2005**	**2006**	**2007**	**2008**	**2009**	**2010**	**2011**	**2012**	**2013**	**2014**	**2015**	**Total**
Lincoln								1				2	2	1		6
Logan						1	2	1	1				2		2	9
Mesa		3	6	3	3	2	1	14	5	7	6	16	8	8	6	88
Moffat			1			2	1	1		1		1	3	2		12
Montezuma	1			2		1	2	2	1	2	1	4	1	3		20
Montrose		1		2				2	1	2	1	1	2	1	3	16
Morgan	1	1		1			1			1	1	1			1	8
Otero	1		1	1		1	1		1	1	2			3		12
Ouray	1		1			2	1					2				7
Park		2	1	1		3			3	5	3	3	3	7	1	32
Phillips							1									1
Pikes Peak						1										1
Pitkin					1	2	1	1		1	2		1		3	12
Prowers				1								2			1	4
Pueblo	5	4	5	3	2	4	5	8	11	7	7	10	9	12	8	100
Rio Blanco										1			2		1	4
Rio Grande	3							1							1	5
Routt	1		2		2			1	1		1		3	1	1	13
Saguache					1		1		2	1	1		3		1	10
San Juan			1		1						1	1		1		5
San Miguel		1							2		1		1			5
Sedgwick								1				1		1		3
Summit		3		1		2			3		2	3	2	2	2	20
Teller	1	1	1		1	1		1	1	3	1	3	2	1	3	20
Torrance										1						1
Unknown	2	4	3	1	3	5	9	18	11	8	13	11	14	9	11	122
Washington		1														1
Weld	3	1	5	3	2	4	3	14	2	4	9	10	13	12	21	106
West				1										1		2
Yuma	1				1									2	1	5
Total	**116**	**92**	**106**	**117**	**122**	**169**	**187**	**242**	**294**	**190**	**273**	**296**	**308**	**357**	**328**	**3197**

If a county is missing from the list, it's because no UFO sightings were logged in either the NUFORC or MUFON databases for the 2001-2015 sample period.

UFOS BY MONTH: COLORADO

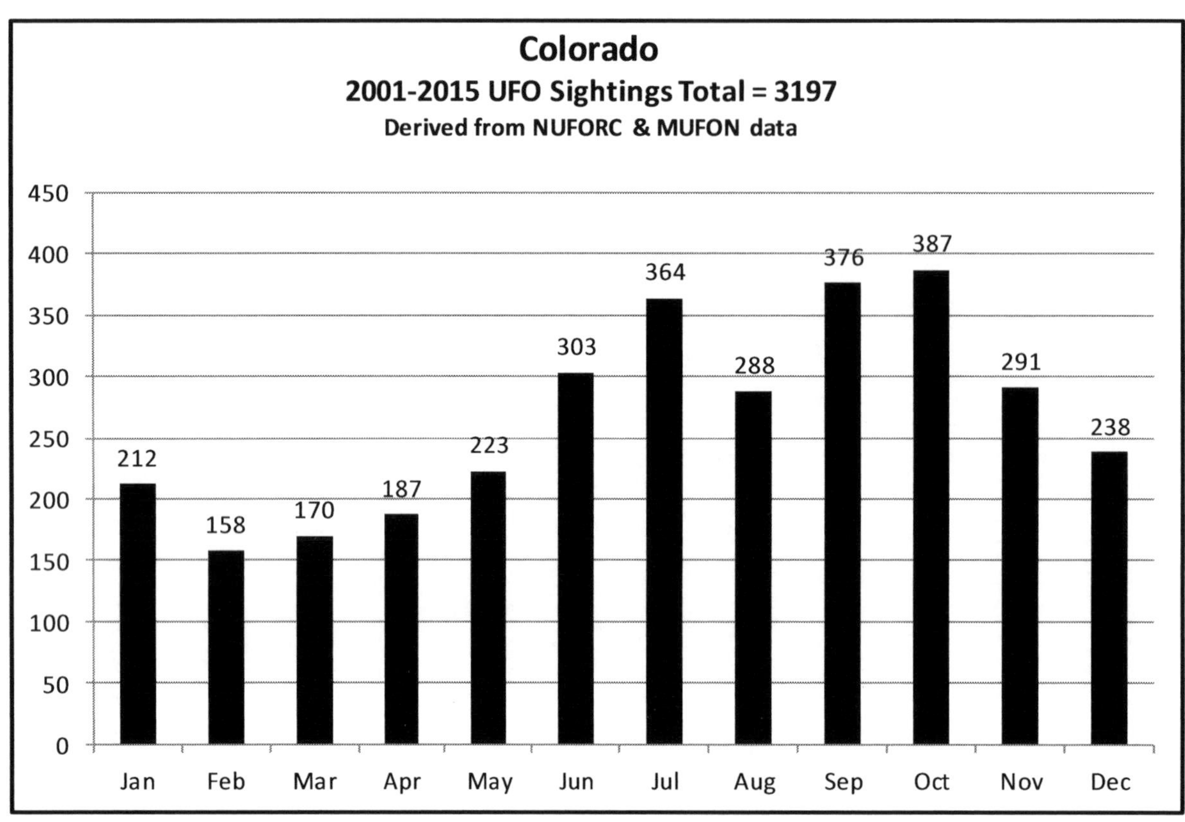

Year	Jan	Feb	Mar	Apr	May	Jun	Jul	Aug	Sep	Oct	Nov	Dec	Total
2001	14	5	3	5	4	12	10	11	21	9	15	7	116
2002	3	8	7	7	3	7	10	11	9	13	8	6	92
2003	9	3	7	3	3	10	11	11	13	15	10	11	106
2004	9	3	16	4	20	8	11	17	12	8	4	5	117
2005	4	11	4	4	9	10	14	12	16	20	10	8	122
2006	6	6	7	13	7	22	11	10	15	36	24	12	169
2007	8	8	13	15	12	23	14	20	23	22	12	17	187
2008	23	18	9	17	22	24	28	15	25	26	19	16	242
2009	19	24	16	23	19	30	37	24	29	17	40	16	294
2010	18	8	6	13	16	18	23	16	29	15	15	13	190
2011	12	9	16	9	28	19	34	30	41	31	17	27	273
2012	21	13	15	25	18	32	27	25	22	37	34	27	296
2013	26	10	15	13	26	29	43	29	31	35	21	30	308
2014	23	17	14	20	16	31	46	33	44	60	25	28	357
2015	17	15	22	16	20	28	45	24	46	43	37	15	328
Total	**212**	**158**	**170**	**187**	**223**	**303**	**364**	**288**	**376**	**387**	**291**	**238**	**3197**

Distribution of Sightings between Databases: Colorado

Source Database	Count	Percent
MUFON	1586	49.61%
NUFORC	1611	50.39%
Total	3197	100.00%

State Demographic Information: Colorado

2010 US Census Statistics	
Population	5,029,196.00
Area in Square Miles	104,093.67
Land Area Sq. Miles	103,641.89
Population/Square mile	48.50

CONNECTICUT UFO RANK 27/51

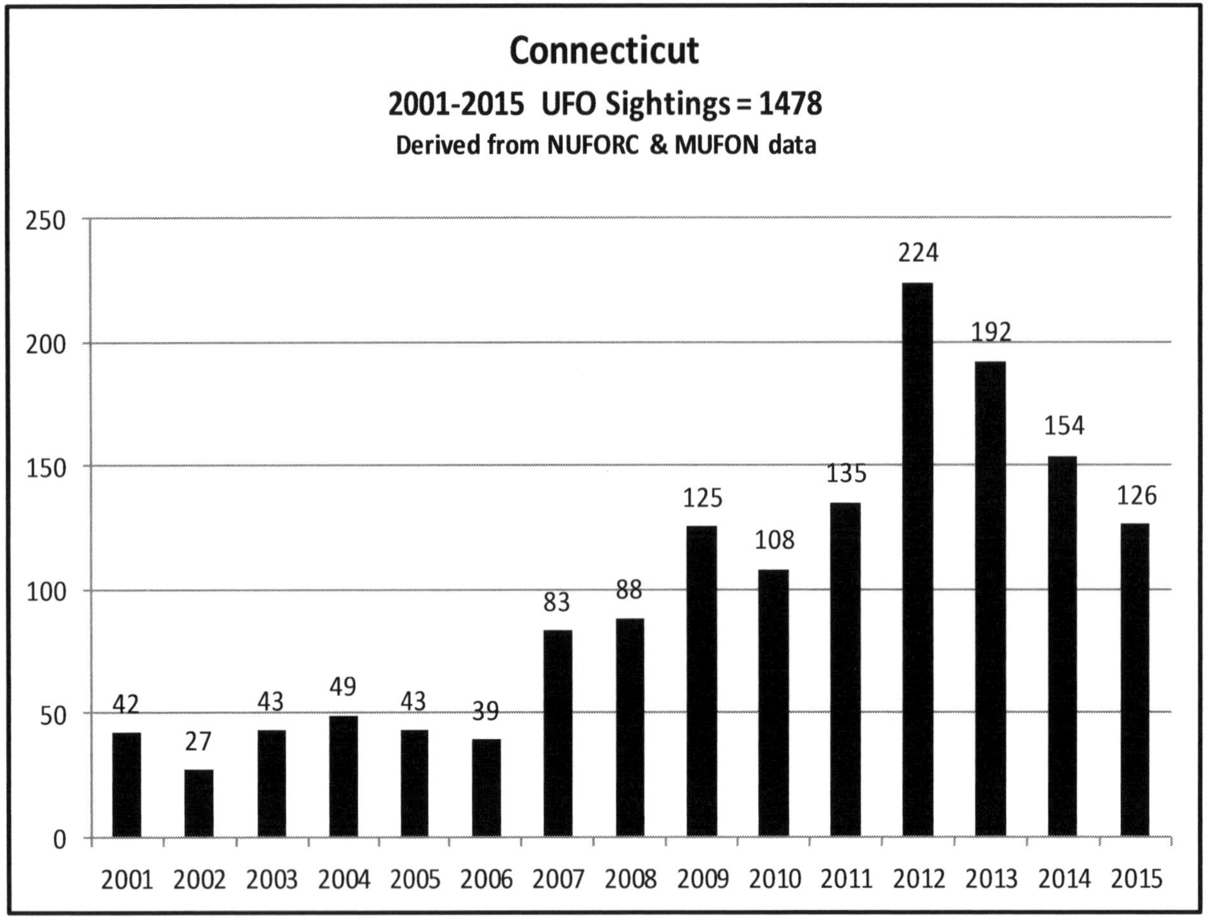

TOP TEN COUNTIES		RANK	TOP TEN SHAPES		
New Haven	389	**1**	Light	188	12.72%
Hartford	304	**2**	Circle	162	10.96%
Fairfield	302	**3**	Fireball	150	10.15%
New London	124	**4**	Unknown	142	9.61%
Litchfield	115	**5**	Sphere	131	8.86%
Middlesex	107	**6**	Triangle	131	8.86%
Tolland	58	**7**	Other	100	6.77%
Windham	56	**8**	Oval	64	4.33%
Unknown	23	**9**	Cigar	50	3.38%
N/A		**10**	Disk	41	2.77%

UFO SHAPES: CONNECTICUT

UFO Shapes	2001	2002	2003	2004	2005	2006	2007	2008	2009	2010	2011	2012	2013	2014	2015	Total
Blimp	1								1	2	1		4	1	1	11
Boomerang	1			2	1					1			1	2		8
Bullet/Missile			1				3	1		1			1	1	1	9
Changing	3					1		1		1	3	2	1	1	2	15
Chevron				1				2	1	2	2	1	3	1		13
Cigar	3		2	2	3	3	4	4	4	8	2	6	3	1	5	50
Circle	2	3	1	4	1	4	11	6	18	8	17	33	24	16	14	162
Cone	1								8				2	1		12
Cross					1			1	1	1		2			1	7
Cylinder		1	2	1	1		1	2	4	2	4	5	3	2	3	31
Diamond			1	1	1	3	1	5	3	5	4	1	5	5	3	38
Disc	1	1		1	1			5	1	2	7	5	5	2	1	32
Disk	1	3	3	2	3	2	2	4	4	1	3	3	6	1	3	41
Egg	2	1	1			1	1	1				3	1		1	12
Fireball	1		2	2	1	3	8	5	9	9	14	39	22	26	9	150
Flash	1	1	1			4	1		2	4	4	4	2	3	3	30
Formation	1						1	2	2		2	6	5	1	1	21
Light	1	4	7	5	10	1	14	12	15	19	16	31	25	13	15	188
Other	5	3	4	6	4	3	4	6	7	7	9	10	10	12	10	100
Oval	3	3	3	3	2	3	6	2	1	3	4	9	10	7	5	64
Rectangle	1		1		2	1	2	2		2	1	3	3	3	2	23
Saturn-like					1											1
Sphere	2	1	2	2		3	5	12	9	3	7	25	17	26	17	131
Sq/Rect													1		1	2
Star-like	1						3		3	11	4	6	1	4	4	37
Teardrop	4					1	3	1	2	1	2		1		1	16
Triangle	2	1	5	8	3	6	4	8	18	9	10	18	12	14	13	131
Unknown	5	5	7	9	8		9	6	12	6	19	12	24	11	10	143
Total	**42**	**27**	**43**	**49**	**43**	**39**	**83**	**88**	**125**	**108**	**135**	**224**	**192**	**154**	**126**	**1478**

UFOS BY COUNTY: CONNECTICUT

Counties	2001	2002	2003	2004	2005	2006	2007	2008	2009	2010	2011	2012	2013	2014	2015	Total
Fairfield	11	3	9	4	6	8	24	22	29	24	29	52	35	23	23	302
Hartford	12	4	12	10	9	10	11	14	23	20	34	44	47	31	23	304
Litchfield	1	4	2	7	9	2	10	6	12	5	6	14	18	10	9	115
Middlesex	2	1	2		2		6	3	15	11	15	14	14	15	7	107
New Haven	11	7	10	15	12	13	13	23	24	22	31	58	56	55	39	389
New London	2	5	2	3	1	2	7	11	13	15	11	17	8	11	16	124
Tolland	1	1	2	3	1	3	4	2	6	5	5	9	5	7	4	58
Unknown	1	2	2	2	1	1		1		2	1	4	3	1	2	23
Windham	1		2	5	2		8	6	3	4	3	12	6	1	3	56
Total	**42**	**27**	**43**	**49**	**43**	**39**	**83**	**88**	**125**	**108**	**135**	**224**	**192**	**154**	**126**	**1478**

If a county is missing from the list, it's because no UFO sightings were logged in either the NUFORC or MUFON databases for the 2001-2015 sample period.

UFOS BY MONTH: CONNECTICUT

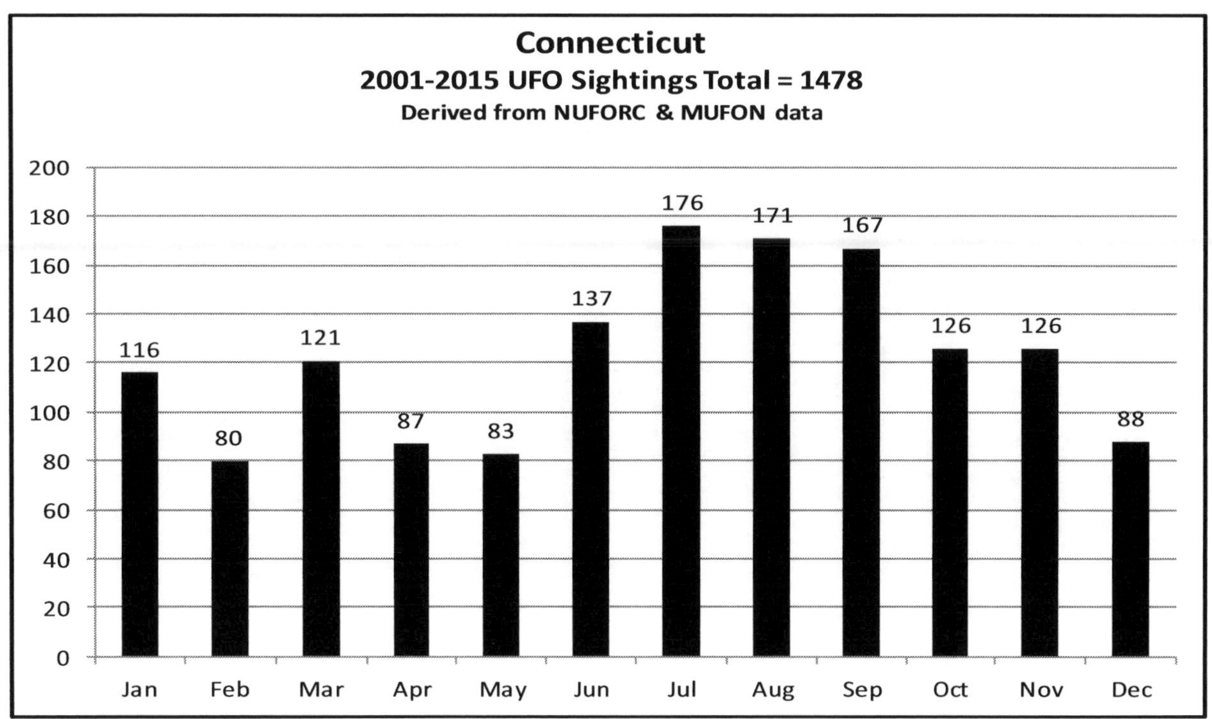

Years	Jan	Feb	Mar	Apr	May	Jun	Jul	Aug	Sep	Oct	Nov	Dec	Total
2001	2	2	4	3	2	6	6	4	6	2	2	3	42
2002		2	3	2	2	4	4	3	1	3		3	27
2003	6	7	5	5	1	4	3	2	1	2	3	4	43
2004	9	4	6	3	2	3	1	11	5	3	2		49
2005	5	2	5	2	2	8	2	3	2	4	6	2	43
2006	3	1	5	3	3	5	2	4	3	3	3	4	39
2007	6	3	12	4	3	8	15	11	13	4	2	2	83
2008	8	4	6	10	6	11	9	12		8	11	3	88
2009	12	12	10	4	4	9	11	17	31	5	2	8	125
2010	8	2	6	6	6	8	18	11	16	9	13	5	108
2011	6	7	11	9	3	14	18	10	9	22	14	12	135
2012	21	10	17	15	9	17	30	19	27	21	26	12	224
2013	8	7	8	7	15	22	32	29	22	13	17	12	192
2014	13	9	8	7	18	8	20	22	16	15	5	13	154
2015	9	8	15	7	7	10	5	13	15	12	20	5	126
Total	**116**	**80**	**121**	**87**	**83**	**137**	**176**	**171**	**167**	**126**	**126**	**88**	**1478**

Distribution of Sightings between Databases: Connecticut

Source Database	Count	Percent
MUFON	474	32.07%
NUFORC	1004	67.93%
Total	1478	100.00%

State Demographic Information: Connecticut

2010 US Census Statistics	
Population	3,574,097.00
Area in Square Miles	5,543.41
Land Area Sq. Miles	4,842.36
Population/Square mile	738.10

DELAWARE UFO RANK 48/51

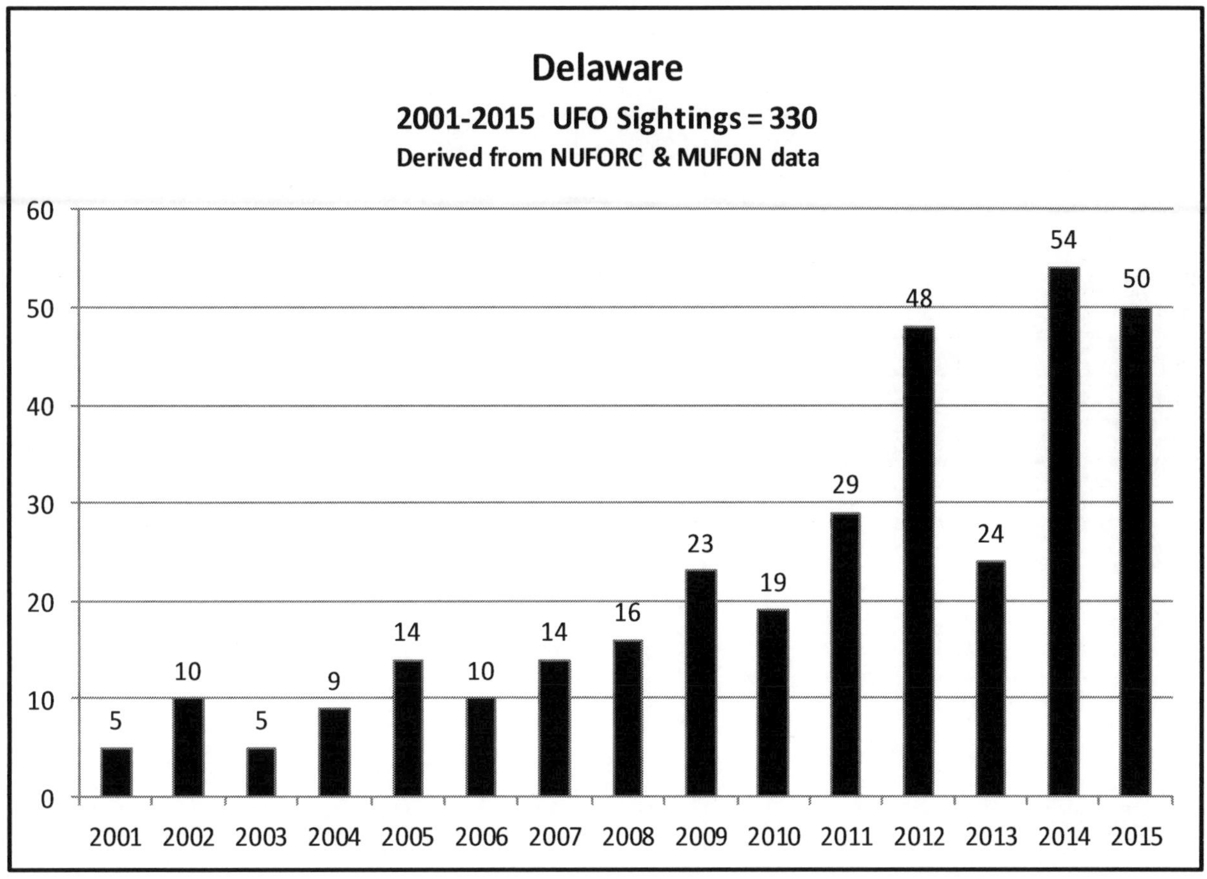

TOP TEN COUNTIES		RANK
New Castle	157	1
Sussex	105	2
Kent	53	3
Unknown	13	4
Chesapeake City	1	5
Chester	1	6
NA		7
NA		8
NA		9
NA		10

RANK	TOP TEN SHAPES		
1	Circle	53	15.28%
2	Light	41	12.06%
3	Triangle	36	12.06%
4	Unknown	33	10.19%
5	Sphere	28	8.04%
6	Other	24	7.77%
7	Fireball	21	5.90%
8	Disc	13	5.36%
9	Star-like	13	3.49%
10	Oval	11	3.49%

UFO SHAPES: DELAWARE

UFO Shapes	2001	2002	2003	2004	2005	2006	2007	2008	2009	2010	2011	2012	2013	2014	2015	Total
Blimp									1				1	1		3
Boomerang															1	1
Bullet/Missile		1													1	2
Changing								1	2	1	1					5
Chevron				1										1		2
Cigar										2	1			2	1	6
Circle	1	1		3		1	2	2	2	4	5	5	6	9	12	53
Cone									1						1	2
Cylinder								1		1						2
Diamond					1						2			1	2	6
Disc		1		1						2	3	3	1	1	1	13
Egg	1												2			3
Fireball			1				1	1	1		2	5	2	7	1	21
Flash				1							1	2		2		6
Formation	1		1									4		2	1	9
Light	1	2	1	1	5	2	3	1	1	4	1	5	2	5	7	41
Other				1	1	1		4	3	1	2	3	4		4	24
Oval								1			1	1		5	3	11
Rectangle									1			1		2		4
Saturn-like								1								1
Sphere				1	1	2	2	3		3	3	7	3	1	2	28
Sq/Rect															3	3
Star-like					1				7		2	1		1	1	13
Teardrop												1		1		2
Triangle		4	1		2	3	2	1	2	1	2	6		5	7	36
Unknown	1	1	1		3	1	4		2		3	4	3	8	2	33
Total	**5**	**10**	**5**	**9**	**14**	**10**	**14**	**16**	**23**	**19**	**29**	**48**	**24**	**54**	**50**	**330**

UFOS BY COUNTY: DELAWARE

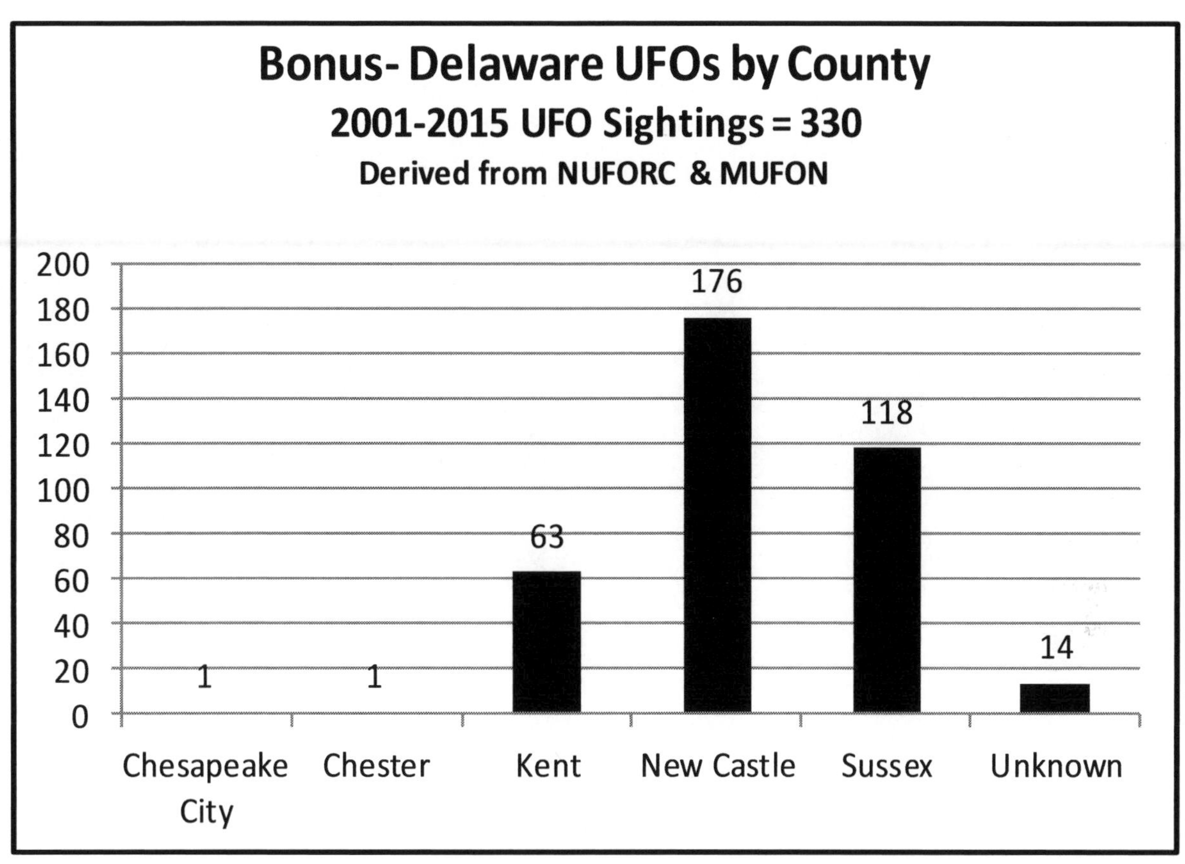

Counties	2001	2002	2003	2004	2005	2006	2007	2008	2009	2010	2011	2012	2013	2014	2015	Total
Chesapeake City												1				1
Chester										1						1
Kent	1	3			3	1	3	4	4	2	8	10	2	4	8	53
New Castle	2	1	4	4	8	5	9	5	13	11	10	22	8	28	27	157
Sussex	2	6	1	5	3	4	2	6	5	5	8	15	11	20	12	105
Unknown								1	1		3		3	2	3	13
Total	**5**	**10**	**5**	**9**	**14**	**10**	**14**	**16**	**23**	**19**	**29**	**48**	**24**	**54**	**50**	**330**

If a county is missing from the list, it's because no UFO sightings were logged in either the NUFORC or MUFON databases for the 2001-2015 sample period.

UFOS BY MONTH: DELAWARE

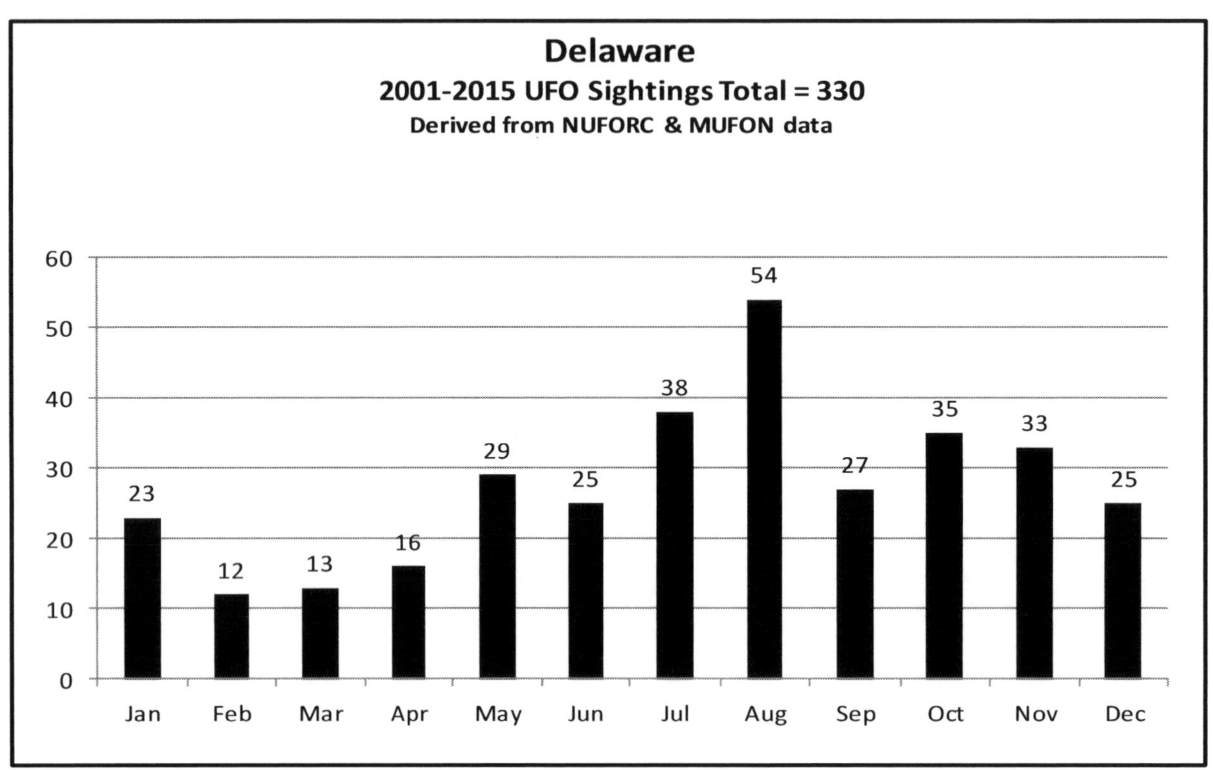

Years	Jan	Feb	Mar	Apr	May	Jun	Jul	Aug	Sep	Oct	Nov	Dec	Total
2001	1					1	2	1					5
2002	1					2		2	2			3	10
2003		1		1	1		2						5
2004	1		2	2		1		2			1		9
2005	1	3		1	1				1	1	3	3	14
2006				1	4	2		1		1	1		10
2007	2					1	1	2		1	4	3	14
2008	1		1		3	1	1	1	2	2	3	1	16
2009	3	2	1	2	5		2	1	4		2	1	23
2010			2			1	4	4	1	5	1	1	19
2011	2		1	2	3	1	4	5	3	3	4	1	29
2012	4	4	1	1	3	7	9	3	3	3	2	8	48
2013	2		3		2	1		8	2	1	3	2	24
2014	3	2		2		4	11	12	3	13	4		54
2015	2		2	4	7	3	2	12	6	5	5	2	50
Total	**23**	**12**	**13**	**16**	**29**	**25**	**38**	**54**	**27**	**35**	**33**	**25**	**330**

BONUS: UFOs by County and Month

Counties	Jan	Feb	Mar	Apr	May	Jun	Jul	Aug	Sep	Oct	Nov	Dec	Total
Chesapeake City				1									1
Chester										1			1
Kent	6	3	3	1	7	9	9	10	8	1	4	2	63
New Castle	9	9	6	10	17	16	18	20	14	25	15	17	176
Sussex	8	2	4	5	7	8	16	25	8	9	19	7	118
Unknown	2			1	2	2	1	2	3	1			14
Total	**25**	**14**	**13**	**18**	**33**	**35**	**44**	**57**	**33**	**37**	**38**	**26**	**373**

BONUS: UFOs by County & City Delaware

Counties & Cities	2001	2002	2003	2004	2005	2006	2007	2008	2009	2010	2011	2012	2013	2014	2015	Total
Chesapeake City												**1**				**1**
Chesapeake City												1				1
Chester										**1**						**1**
Landenberg										1						1
Kent	**1**	**3**			**3**	**1**	**3**	**4**	**4**	**2**	**8**	**10**	**2**	**4**	**8**	**53**
Camden														2		2
Clayton					2			1				1				4
Dover		2			1	1	2	1	3		2	6	1		3	22
Felton								1		1	1			1		4
Frederica												1				1
Harrington									1		4			1		6
Hartly												1	1		1	3
Magnolia															1	1
Sandtown															1	1
Smyrna	1	1					1	1			1				2	7
Viola												1				1
(Hwy DE-1 N)										1						1
New Castle	**2**	**1**	**4**	**4**	**8**	**5**	**9**	**5**	**13**	**11**	**10**	**22**	**8**	**28**	**27**	**157**
Bear			1				1	1	1	2		3	3	1	3	16
Bellefonte												1				1
Christiana															1	1

Counties & Cities	2001	2002	2003	2004	2005	2006	2007	2008	2009	2010	2011	2012	2013	2014	2015	Total
Claymont		1					1				2				1	5
Deerfield															1	1
Delaware City										1						1
Elsmere			1	2							1	2		1	1	8
Glasgow												1				1
Hockessin	1				1			1	1	1				1		6
Middletown			1				1		1		2	1	1	3	2	12
New Castle				1			1						2		4	8
Newark					5	1	5		8	2	3	8	2	4	4	42
North Star															1	1
Orlando			1													1
Pike Creek															2	2
St. Georges									1							1
Stanton															1	1
Townsend														3	1	4
Wilmington	1			1	2	4		3	1	5	2	6		15	5	45
Sussex	**2**	**6**	**1**	**5**	**3**	**4**	**2**	**6**	**5**	**5**	**8**	**15**	**11**	**20**	**12**	**105**
Bethany Beach											2	3	1	2	2	10
Bridgeville								1						2	1	4
Broadkill											1					1
Dagsboro									1							1
(DE Hwy 113)								1								1
Dewey										1						1
Dewey Beach		1							2					1		4
Ellendale											1			1		2
Fenwick Island						1								1		2
Frankford	1	1														2
Georgetown													1			1
Laurel													1		1	2
Lewes					3		2		1			4	4	1		15
Lincoln								1				2				3
Long Neck										1				1		2

Counties & Cities	2001	2002	2003	2004	2005	2006	2007	2008	2009	2010	2011	2012	2013	2014	2015	Total
Milford			1			1		1			1	2		1	1	8
Millsboro								1			1		2	3	4	11
Milton				1											1	2
Ocean View				1								1	1			3
Rehoboth Beach	1	1		1		1		1	1	2	1	3	1	2	1	16
Seaford		2		2		1					1			1		7
Selbyville															1	1
Slaughter Beach		1														1
South Bethany Beach										1				4		5
Unknown								1	1		3		3	2	3	13
Unspecified								1	1		3		3	2	3	13
Total	**5**	**10**	**5**	**9**	**14**	**10**	**14**	**16**	**23**	**19**	**29**	**48**	**24**	**54**	**50**	**330**

Distribution of Sightings between Databases: Delaware

Database	Count	Percentage
MUFON	114	34.55%
NUFORC	216	65.45%
Total	330	100.00%

State Demographic Information: Delaware

2010 US Census Statistics	
Population	897,934.00
Area in Square Miles	2,488.72
Land Area Sq. Miles	1,948.54
Population/Square mile	460.80

DISTRICT OF COLUMBIA UFO RANK 51/51

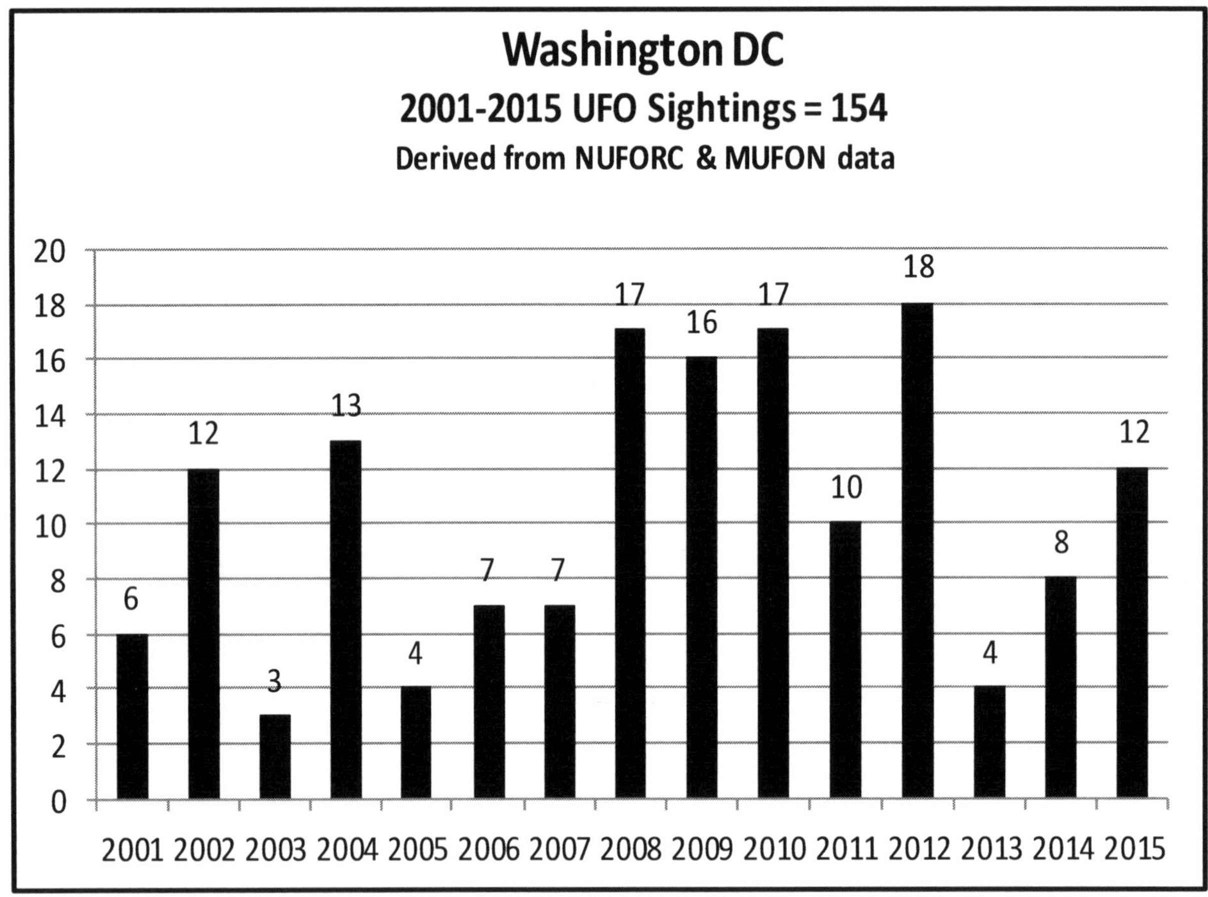

TOP TEN COUNTIES		RANK	TOP TEN SHAPES		
Washington	154	1	Light	20	13.42%
NA		2	Sphere	18	12.08%
NA		3	Other	14	9.40%
NA		4	Circle	13	8.72%
NA		5	Fireball	11	7.38%
NA		6	Triangle	11	7.38%
NA		7	Unknown	10	6.71%
NA		8	Disk	7	4.70%
NA		9	Cigar	6	4.03%
NA		10	Cylinder	6	4.03%

UFO SHAPES: WASHINGTON, DC

UFO Shapes	2001	2002	2003	2004	2005	2006	2007	2008	2009	2010	2011	2012	2013	2014	2015	Total
Changing		2										1			1	4
Chevron			1												1	2
Cigar				1			1		4							6
Circle	1	1		1						2	1	3	2	1	1	13
Cone															1	1
Cross								1								1
Cylinder		1				1		1			3					6
Diamond						1										1
Disc					1				1			1				3
Disk		1		1	1			2		1	1					7
Egg								2								2
Fireball	3	1		1			1		3	1		1				11
Flash				1						1				1		3
Formation					1	1								2		4
Light		2	2	3	1	1		1		2	1	4		3		20
Other				3			1	3	2	1		2			2	14
Oval	1					1		1		1					1	5
Rectangle		1														1
Sphere		1					1	1	2	4	1	3	1	1	3	18
Star-like								1							1	2
Triangle	1	1				2	1	1		1	1	1	1		1	11
Unknown				1			2	2	1	1	1	2				10
Bullet/Missile								1								1
Blimp									2							2
Boomerang										1						1
Total	**6**	**11**	**3**	**12**	**4**	**7**	**7**	**17**	**15**	**16**	**9**	**18**	**4**	**8**	**12**	**149**

UFOS BY COUNTY: WASHINGTON, DC

The District	2001	2002	2003	2004	2005	2006	2007	2008	2009	2010	2011	2012	2013	2014	2015	Total
Washington, DC	6	12	3	13	4	7	7	17	16	17	10	18	4	8	12	154
Total	**6**	**12**	**3**	**13**	**4**	**7**	**7**	**17**	**16**	**17**	**10**	**18**	**4**	**8**	**12**	**154**

UFOS BY MONTH: DISTRICT OF COLUMBIA

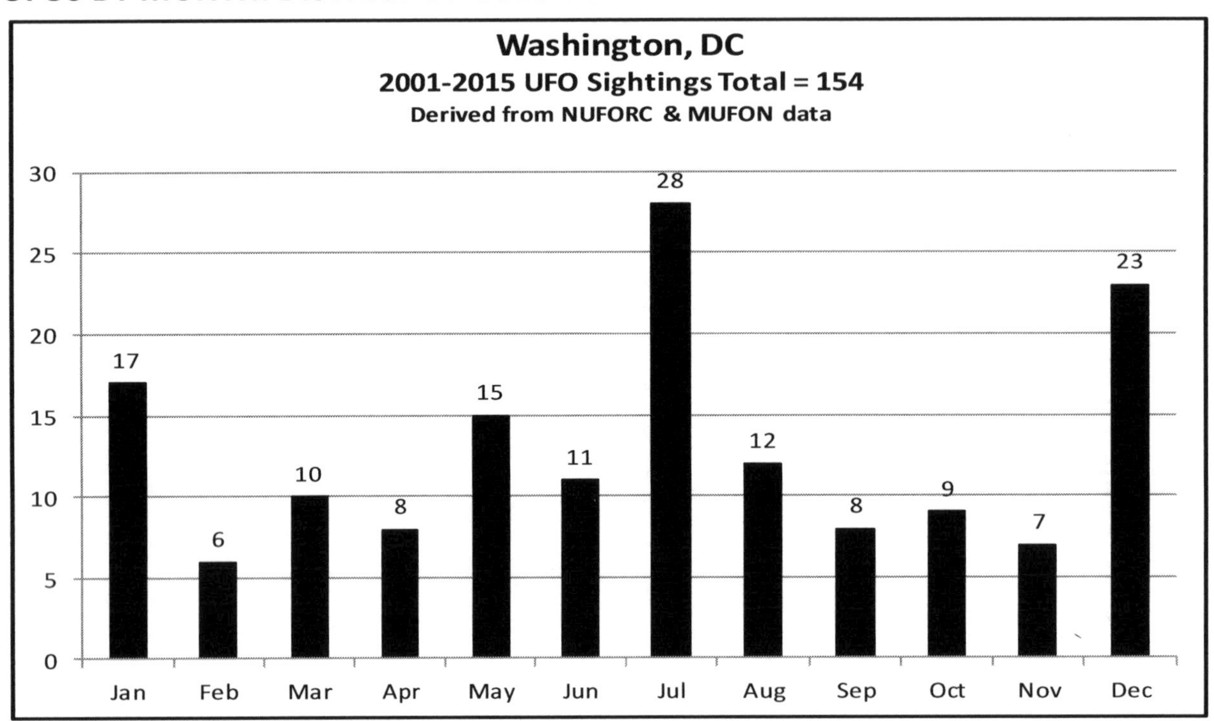

Year	Jan	Feb	Mar	Apr	May	Jun	Jul	Aug	Sep	Oct	Nov	Dec	Total
2001					2		2		1			1	6
2002						2	6	1	1		1	1	12
2003	1						1				1		3
2004			2		4		1	1	1	1		3	13
2005					1		2					1	4
2006		1		2	1				1		1	1	7
2007	1		1	2					1	2			7
2008	2		1	1	1	3	1	2	1	1	2	2	17
2009	7		1		3			2				3	16
2010		1	1	1	1	1	6	1	1	1	1	2	17
2011	1	2			1	1	3					2	10
2012	2		1	2	1	1	4	1		2		4	18
2013			1				1	1				1	4
2014	1	1				1	1	1		1		2	8
2015	2	1	2			2		2	1	1	1		12
Total	**17**	**6**	**10**	**8**	**15**	**11**	**28**	**12**	**8**	**9**	**7**	**23**	**154**

Distribution of Sightings between Databases: District of Columbia

Database	Count	Percentage
MUFON	53	31.42%
NUFORC	101	65.58%
Total	154	100.00%

State Demographic Information: District of Columbia

2010 US Census Statistics	
Population	601,723.00
Area in Square Miles	68.34
Land Area Sq. Miles	61.05
Population/Square mile	9,856.20

FLORIDA

UFO RANK 2/51

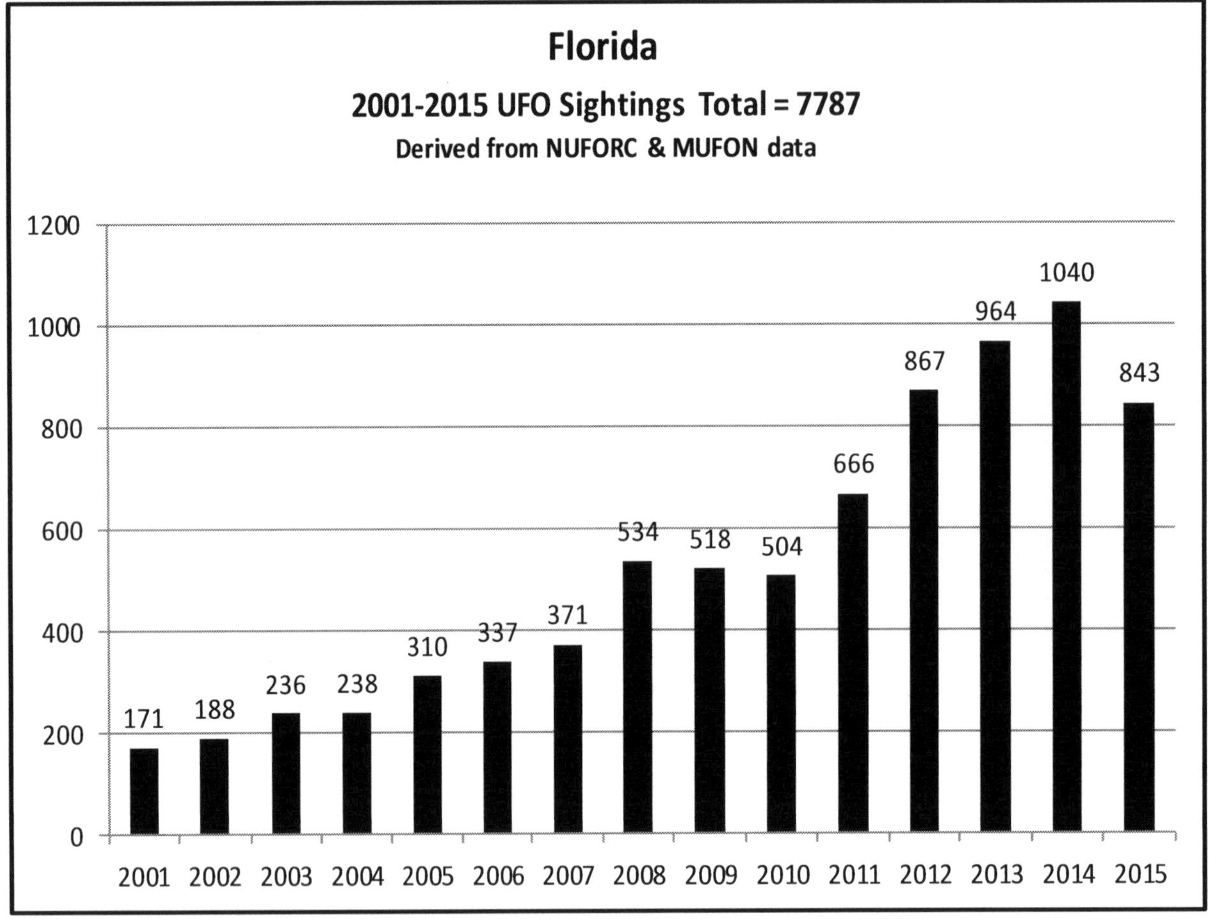

TOP TEN COUNTIES		RANK	TOP TEN SHAPES		
Miami-Dade	619	**1**	Light	901	11.57%
Broward	590	**2**	Sphere	882	11.33%
Palm Beach	575	**3**	Unknown	765	9.82%
Orange	489	**4**	Circle	726	9.32%
Hillsborough	425	**5**	Fireball	718	9.22%
Pinellas	423	**6**	Triangle	665	8.54%
Brevard	323	**7**	Other	492	6.32%
Lee	314	**8**	Oval	424	5.44%
Sarasota	289	**9**	Star-like	358	4.60%
Duval	259	**10**	Disk	246	3.16%

UFO SHAPES: FLORIDA

UFO Shapes	2001	2002	2003	2004	2005	2006	2007	2008	2009	2010	2011	2012	2013	2014	2015	Total
Blimp			1							1		1	1	3	4	11
Boomer-ang	2	1	2		2	2	3	3	6	5	9	4	8	16	10	73
Bullet /Missile	1					2	1	8	15	8	4	8	4	1	5	57
Changing	2	2	5	8	4	9	6	16	9	8	10	9	8	8	8	112
Chevron	4	2	4	3	4		4	5	3	3	7	18	5	7	11	80
Cigar	1		9	7	7	5	10	11	18	8	10	7	10	10	14	127
Circle	15	14	14	13	19	25	25	36	35	43	56	93	90	138	110	726
Cone	3		1				3	4	5	4	5	7	2	3	4	41
Cross				5	1	1		2		2		1	5	1	3	21
Cylinder	1	5	7	8	7	13	10	10	9	13	10	26	24	23	19	185
Diamond	2	2	3	4	3	6	6	7	9	6	12	11	18	7	13	109
Disc	1	4	3		2	11	5	26	16	21	19	19	21	19	20	187
Disk	13	12	17	14	16	18	24	20	9	9	16	16	16	29	17	246
Egg	2	3		4	2	5	4	8	7	6	10	9	4	8	7	79
Fireball	9	9	13	7	19	18	17	29	23	37	54	137	145	123	78	718
Flash		6	4	4	5	5	7	14	16	21	23	25	43	18	14	205
Formation	4	7	6	7	13	10	4	8	7	5	11	9	15	19	12	137
Light	25	35	27	45	56	37	64	48	54	48	62	79	108	129	84	901
N/A						2				1	1			9	10	23
Other	18	10	20	24	26	22	18	34	35	34	41	42	55	66	47	492
Oval	10	11	20	14	16	15	32	30	33	27	35	45	40	57	39	424
Rectangle	5	2	5	2	4	4	5	6	6	5	8	3	5	8	7	75
Saturn -like								1	3	2			3		2	11
Sphere	15	24	14	19	16	35	26	45	53	48	66	130	143	121	127	882
Sq/Rect														3	9	12
Star-like			2	2	2	13	10	31	37	43	46	42	50	37	43	358
Teardrop	2		3		6	2	3	4	4	5	9	4	5	11	7	65
Triangle	17	19	27	18	27	31	42	66	50	42	77	54	55	79	61	665
Unknown	19	20	29	30	53	46	42	62	56	49	65	68	81	87	58	765
Total	**171**	**188**	**236**	**238**	**310**	**337**	**371**	**534**	**518**	**504**	**666**	**867**	**964**	**1040**	**843**	**7787**

UFOS BY COUNTY: FLORIDA

Counties	2001	2002	2003	2004	2005	2006	2007	2008	2009	2010	2011	2012	2013	2014	2015	Total
Alachua	4	1	6	3	6	4	3	7	12	8	11	15	8	11	7	106
Baker										1	1		1	1		4
Bay	1	5	7	4	4	18	9	8	4	11	6	11	14	22	18	142
Bradford			1	1				3	2	1	1	1	2	2	1	15
Brevard	11	7	8	5	14	14	16	21	26	30	29	32	32	42	36	323
Broward	14	17	13	15	22	17	19	50	37	28	48	68	76	109	57	590
Calhoun			1			1										2
Charlotte	4	4	2	5	1	1	5	4	8	8	3	13	23	9	9	99
Chester												1				1
Citrus			2	1	3	2		8	1		2	2	9	2	9	41
Clay	1	1	1	1	1	1	3	6	1	5	1	2	5	9	10	48
Collier	2	6	1	5	4	5	2	11	7	16	15	18	21	27	12	152
Columbia			2	1	1		3	1		2		1		1	2	14
DeSoto							3	1			1	3	3	1	1	13
Dixie									1	1		1	1			4
Duval	3	10	12	6	11	9	16	22	18	12	27	23	28	41	21	259
Escambia	4	5	9	2	5	9	6	7	17	9	10	15	13	9	4	124
Flagler	2	1	3	2	2	3	6	5	4	1	4	7	6	5	4	55
Franklin				2	1	1	3	4	4		2	2	3	5	4	31
Gadsden	2	1					1		2	1		1	2			10
Gilchrist										3	1				1	5
Glades		2				1						1		1		5
Gulf			1			1		1	2			2		2	1	10
Hamilton						1				1					1	3
Hardee				1		1					1		1		1	5
Hendry	1					1			1					4	1	8
Hernando		2	2	3	2	1	2	3	5	4	7	8	5	5	6	55
Highlands	1	1		2	4	1	3	2	4	1		4	5	5	6	39
Hillsborough	5	7	15	9	16	16	16	31	50	34	38	43	40	54	51	425
Holmes	1				1		1		1			2				6
Indian River	1	4	1	2	2	3	5	4	7	3	6	12	12	12	18	92
Jackson	1	1					1		1	1	2	1				8
Jefferson											1					1
Lafayette					1	1		2	9	3			1			17
Lake	3	4	2	3	4	5	4	8	1	6	9	5	16	21	14	105
Lee	5	9	7	7	10	11	12	22	9	22	14	34	69	45	38	314
Leon	5	2	4	1	2	4	8	8	5	5	6	6	2	4	11	73
Levy		1	4				2		2		4	4	1		1	19

Counties	2001	2002	2003	2004	2005	2006	2007	2008	2009	2010	2011	2012	2013	2014	2015	Total
Liberty													1			1
Madison															1	1
Manatee	5	4	2	4	2	8	4	6	9	10	16	19	12	14	9	124
Marion	4	5	2	5	5	2	8	8	6	11	12	16	12	13	9	118
Martin	1		2	2	3		3	15	2	5	6	8	15	15	7	84
Miami-Dade	16	9	27	16	35	21	25	38	55	44	61	62	70	75	65	619
Monroe	2	3	2	4	5	5	1	6	5	6	8	15	15	11	7	95
Nassau	2	2		1	1	1	2	3		1	3	1	1		2	20
Okaloosa	1	4	10	6	6	5	5	12	6	12	11	6	6	5	5	100
Okeechobee	1	1			3	2	1	1	2	1		3	6	1	3	25
Orange	9	10	14	17	14	19	26	42	23	22	47	66	70	60	50	489
Osceola		4	1	4	4	4	7	5	6	5	8	9	7	8	19	91
Palm Beach	13	8	9	19	29	48	27	24	39	33	43	55	84	93	51	575
Pasco	1	2	4	11	11	7	9	21	13	26	13	27	35	23	28	231
Pinellas	10	7	11	15	14	7	23	18	24	30	54	51	55	48	56	423
Polk	2	13	1	8	9	9	16	11	6	7	7	29	32	29	35	214
Putnam	1	1		1	1	1	2	1	1	1			1	2	2	15
Santa Rosa	3		8	1	11	9	5	8	6	6	2	15	6	2	5	87
Sarasota	11	7	11	10	8	5	12	8	15	17	42	41	38	28	36	289
Seminole	1	4	7	13	5	10	10	5	5	8	10	21	19	26	16	160
St. Johns	1	2	1	5	2	7	11	8	7	6	11	17	9	14	10	111
St. Lucie	1	2	3	5	3	7	7	6	10	6	11	12	21	31	15	140
Sumter		2					1	4		2	2		2	6	1	20
Suwannee	1	1				1	1	2	1	3	2	1	1	1	2	17
Taylor	2										1	2	1	1	2	9
Union			1									1				2
Unknown	1		4	2	7	20	9	23	18	11	29	16	21	36	31	228
Volusia	11	6	9	6	11	6	4	17	15	9	14	31	23	42	27	231
Wakulla				1	2	1			1		1	1	1	1	2	11
Walton			3	1	1		3	2	2	5	2	4	1	6	2	32
Washington					1			1								2
Total	**171**	**188**	**236**	**238**	**310**	**337**	**371**	**534**	**518**	**504**	**666**	**867**	**964**	**1040**	**843**	**7787**

If a county is missing from the list, it's because no UFO sightings were logged in either the NUFORC or MUFON databases for the 2001-2015 sample period.

UFOS BY MONTH: FLORIDA

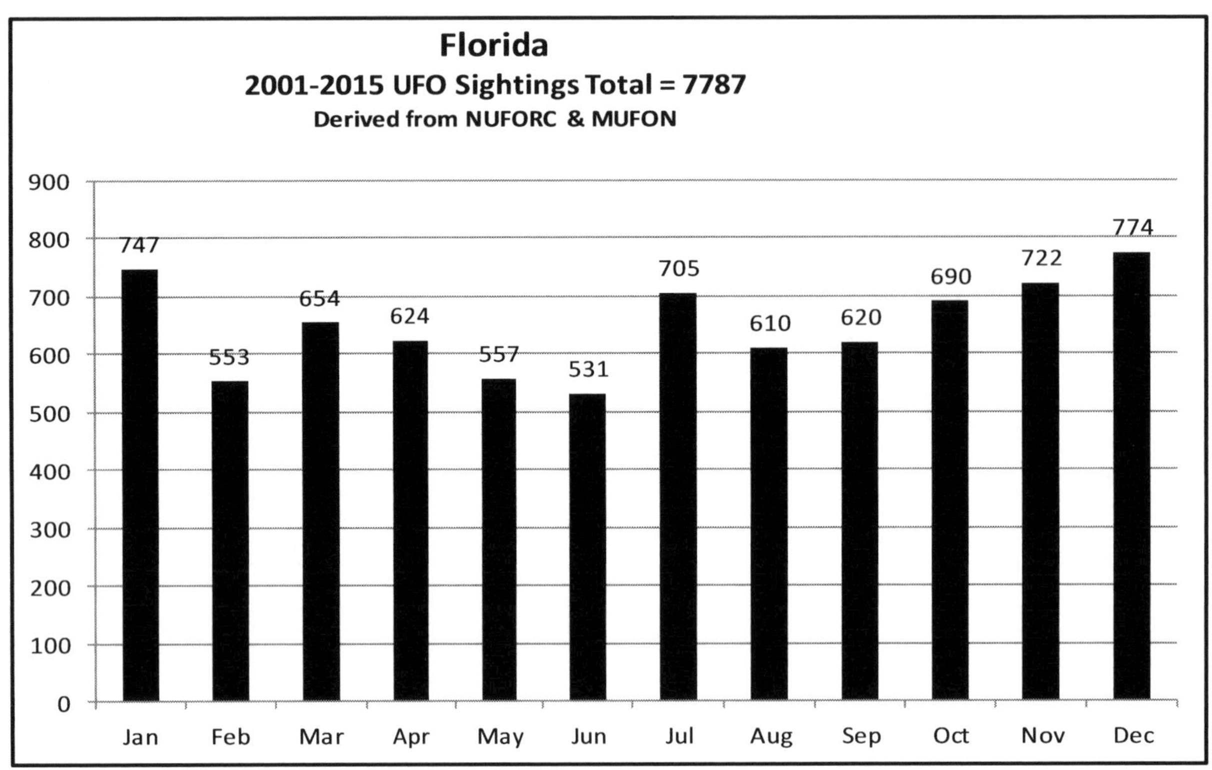

Year	Jan	Feb	Mar	Apr	May	Jun	Jul	Aug	Sep	Oct	Nov	Dec	Total
2001	12	8	10	12	11	30	23	9	17	13	19	7	171
2002	18	23	14	11	11	18	15	17	13	18	10	20	188
2003	15	22	14	16	15	13	17	30	25	25	30	14	236
2004	12	16	28	32	25	18	23	15	17	16	17	19	238
2005	18	17	33	38	16	28	19	17	36	29	40	19	310
2006	22	15	23	16	26	37	34	26	34	46	33	25	337
2007	36	22	27	30	24	21	33	25	32	27	42	52	371
2008	50	40	54	55	45	34	40	37	48	35	50	46	534
2009	61	46	49	50	30	34	45	38	47	42	45	31	518
2010	37	40	49	34	51	26	44	30	38	52	49	54	504
2011	60	33	38	35	27	26	75	64	60	76	76	96	666
2012	113	57	80	73	42	50	77	49	57	53	91	125	867
2013	94	47	62	43	79	41	91	118	55	96	83	155	964
2014	105	98	102	121	76	70	78	80	67	91	73	79	1040
2015	94	69	71	58	79	85	91	55	74	71	64	32	843
Total	**747**	**553**	**654**	**624**	**557**	**531**	**705**	**610**	**620**	**690**	**722**	**774**	**7787**

Distribution of Sightings between Databases: Florida

Database	Count	Percentage
MUFON	1109	43.49%
NUFORC	1441	56.51%
Total	2550	100.00%

State Demographic Information: Florida

2010 US Census Statistics	
Population	17,801,310.00
Area in Square Miles	65,757.70
Land Area Sq. Miles	53,624.76
Population/Square mile	350.60

GEORGIA

UFO RANK 17/51

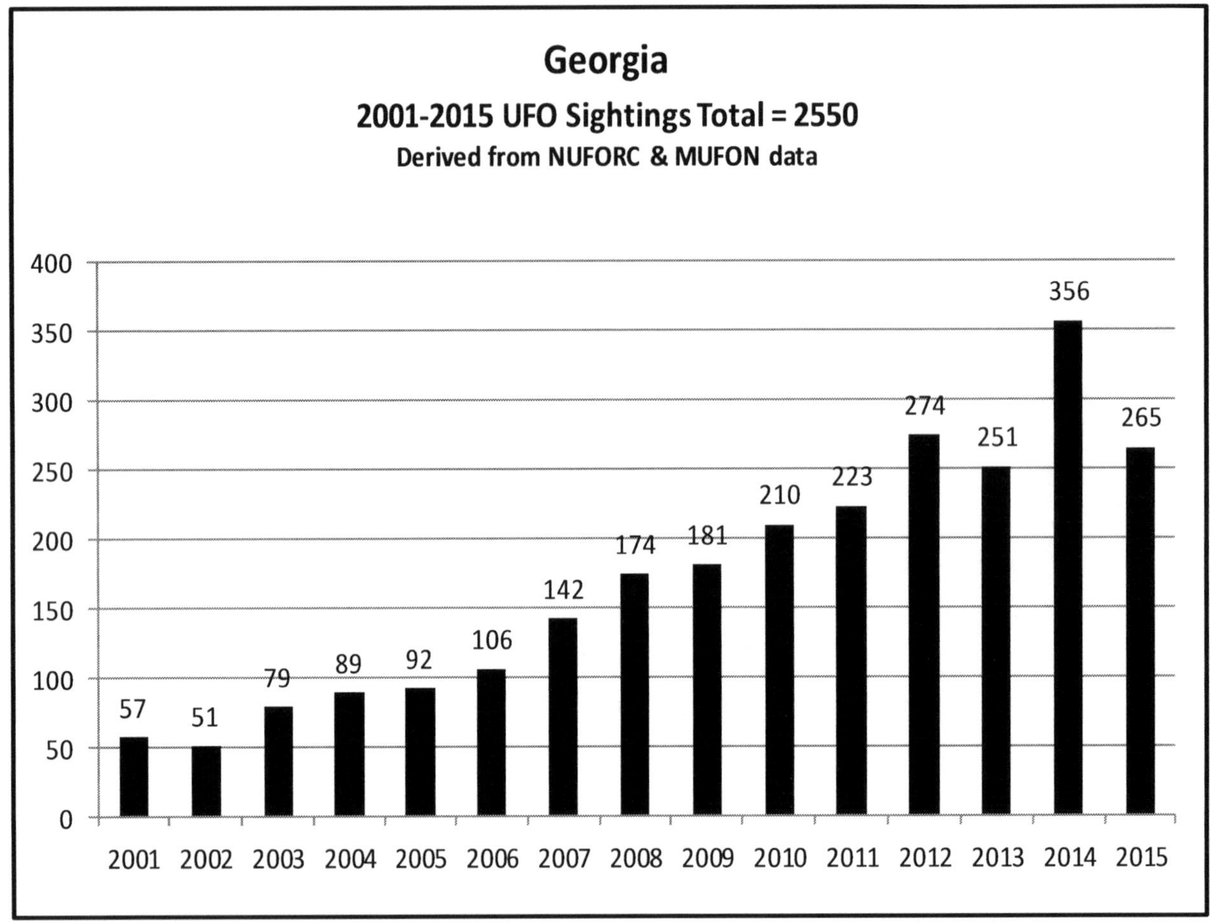

TOP TEN COUNTIES		RANK
Fulton	299	1
Gwinnett	201	2
Cobb	160	3
DeKalb	94	4
Chatham	83	5
Richmond	74	6
Unknown	66	7
Hall	63	8
Cherokee	62	9
Forsyth	59	10

TOP TEN SHAPES		
Circle	320	12.55%
Light	288	11.29%
Sphere	239	9.37%
Other	198	7.76%
Fireball	180	7.06%
Oval	126	4.94%
Star-like	118	4.63%
Disc	73	2.86%
Cigar	70	2.75%
Disk	70	2.75%

UFO SHAPES: GEORGIA

UFO Shapes	2001	2002	2003	2004	2005	2006	2007	2008	2009	2010	2011	2012	2013	2014	2015	Total
Blimp						1	1	1	1	5	3			1	1	14
Boomerang					1	1	2	1	5	5	5	4	6	1	2	33
Bullet/Missile						2	1		2	1	3	2			1	12
Changing	3		3	4	3		2	5	1	1		2	2	10	1	37
Chevron	1		1			1	1	2	1	3	2	1	2	1	5	21
Cigar		2	1	2	3	4	6	7	3	8	7	5	4	14	4	70
Circle	3	7	6	7	8	14	16	13	31	35	29	46	36	44	25	320
Cone				2	1					1	3			3	3	13
Cross				1	2	1			1		1	1	1	3	1	12
Cylinder	1	1	4	1	2		4	3		7	3	6	9	4	6	51
Diamond	1	3		1	1	1	2	2	3	3	5	5	2	3	5	37
Disc			2		1	1	2	10	13	8	7	11	4	5	9	73
Disk	3	2	5	4	3	2	5	11	4	4	5	3	5	9	5	70
Egg		1	2	1	1	3		1	1	3	2	1	4	3		23
Fireball	1	1	6	1	1	8	10	10	8	9	15	24	35	24	27	180
Flash	1	1	2	1		1	8	5	9	3	5	5	3	4	7	55
Formation	1		2	1	1	1	3	3	1	1	3		4	12	11	44
Light	11	12	9	17	13	22	24	24	17	13	14	24	24	42	22	288
N/A													1	2	3	6
Other	6	2	8	5	7	9	9	15	12	19	9	22	22	26	27	198
Oval	5	1	3	7	1	3	6	6	8	10	15	8	18	15	20	126
Rectangle	2		1		2	1	1	2	3	3	3	2		3		23
Saturn-like								1						1		2
Sphere	4	6	5	10	9	7	10	9	14	20	27	32	21	41	24	239
Sq/Rect												1	1	4	3	9
Star-like	1			2	3	4	4	7	13	16	16	16	10	15	11	118
Teardrop			2	1	2		1	4	1	1	2	1		1	2	18
Triangle	6	4	5	13	14	6	13	15	15	16	15	27	19	35	18	221
Unknown	7	8	12	8	13	13	11	17	14	15	24	25	18	30	22	237
Total	**57**	**51**	**79**	**89**	**92**	**106**	**142**	**174**	**181**	**210**	**223**	**274**	**251**	**356**	**265**	**2550**

UFOS BY COUNTY: GEORGIA

Counties	2001	2002	2003	2004	2005	2006	2007	2008	2009	2010	2011	2012	2013	2014	2015	Total
Atkinson									1			1				2
Augusta								1								1
Bacon										1	1			1	1	4
Baldwin		1				2		1			3				1	8
Banks						1								1		2
Barrow						1	1	2	2	6	1	4	1	5	4	27
Bartow		1			2	1	3	4	3	4	3	3	5	5	3	37
Ben Hill						2		2								4
Berrien								3	1					2	1	7
Bibb	2	1	1				1	2		1	5	1		4	1	19
Bleckley		1							1		1					3
Brantley			2			2		1		1			1		1	8
Brooks		1						1						1		3
Bryan			1				1	1				1			1	5
Bulloch	1					2	3	2	4	1	1	6			3	23
Burke				1				1	1		1		1			5
Butts	1	1				1						1				4
Camden		1		1			3	1	1	3	2	6	1	2	4	25
Candler									1		1					2
Carroll	2						4	1	3	5	1	5	3	5	3	32
Catoosa			1				2	1	1	2	2	1	1	5	3	19
Chatham	3	1	2	4	3		5	7	4	3	14	6	4	14	13	83
Chatta-hoochee		1														1
Chattooga											1	2		1	1	5
Cherokee		1	3	3	3	3		3	7	4	4	8	9	4	10	62
Clarke	1		1		2	2		5	2	1	2	2	5	4	4	31
Clay					1					1						2
Clayton	1	2	1	2		1				1	2		2	3		15
Cobb	3	3	5	8	8	3	5	11	11	11	13	22	14	24	19	160
Coffee				2			2		1	1	2	1	1			10
Colquitt	1		1		1	1		2		1	1	4	3	1	1	17
Columbia				2	3				2	1	3	4	7	3	3	28
Cook								1	1			1	2			5
Coweta					2		1		1	5	3	4	3	6	5	30
Crawford													1			1
Crisp												1	2		1	4
Dade						2			1			2				5

Costas' UFO Sightings Desk Reference: USA 2001-2015

Counties	2001	2002	2003	2004	2005	2006	2007	2008	2009	2010	2011	2012	2013	2014	2015	Total
Dawson		1				1	2	2	1				1	4	2	14
Decatur			2												1	3
DeKalb	2		3	3	7	5	10	3	4	6	9	5	10	9	18	94
Dodge		1														1
Dooly														3	1	4
Dougherty								2	1	3	3	2	1	1	1	14
Douglas			4	4	2		2		4		2		1	2		21
Echols							1			1		1				3
Effingham	1							1	2	1	1	3				9
Emanuel								1		1		3			2	7
Evans								1	1	1				2		5
Fannin			1			2	2	2	2	2	1	4		2		18
Fayette	2			1	1		5	2	1	2	2	1	5	4	3	29
Floyd			3			2	4	1	2	4	2	4	8	2	3	35
Forsyth				2		1	2	1	2	8	2	7	15	13	6	59
Franklin		1	1	1			1	1								5
Fulton	11	7	14	10	10	8	14	26	31	31	18	28	31	36	24	299
Gilmer		1									1		1	1		4
Glascock								1		1	2	1				5
Glynn		1			4			1	3	4	5	3	3	1	2	27
Gordon			1	1	1		1	1	1	2	1	3	1	4	5	22
Grady						1	1		1							3
Greene										2			1	2		5
Greenest								1								1
Gwinnett	10	6	2	9	6	8	8	14	8	12	12	23	20	40	23	201
Habersham					1		1	1	2		2	1		2		10
Hall		1	1	5	2	3	4	4	3	5	9	3	6	8	9	63
Hancock															1	1
Haralson						2		1	1	1	1			3	1	10
Harris				1			1	1	2	2	1	1	1		1	11
Hart							1	1	1	1		1	2	1		8
Heard									1	1			2			4
Henry	1	1	2	2	3		5	2	4		3	8	6	11	3	51
Houston	2		1		1	5	2	1	3	1	4	1	4	4	2	31
Irwin	1				1		1									3
Jackson			1		1	1	2	1	2	1	2	4	1	4	3	23
Jasper	1									1					1	3
Jefferson	1	1	1			1	1			2		2	2	3	3	17
Jenkins												1		2		3

Counties	2001	2002	2003	2004	2005	2006	2007	2008	2009	2010	2011	2012	2013	2014	2015	Total
Johnson					1						1			1	1	4
Jones			1	1					1							3
Lamar								2						1	2	5
Lanier														1		1
Laurens			1		1	1	1	8	1			2	2	3	1	21
Lee			1			2		4	2			1	1	1		12
Liberty	1			1	1		3			5	4	2	1		1	19
Lincoln				1								2			1	4
Long											1	1				2
Lowndes	1				1	2	1	1	5	1		3	4	2	1	22
Lumpkin			1			1					1		1	4		8
Macon								1								1
Madison								1	2		2	1			1	7
Marion								1								1
McDuffie			1							1			1		1	4
McIntosh			1													1
Meriwethe r	1		7						1				1		1	11
Miller								1						1		2
Mitchell							1		1		1					3
Monroe						1	1						2		1	5
Montgom-ery										2						2
Morgan							1	2		2	2			1		8
Murray				1					1					1		3
Muscogee				2	3	5	7	3	3	2	3	2	2	2	4	38
Newton				1	2		2		4	3	3	1	3	1	1	21
Oconee								1			1	3		4		9
Oglethorpe									1				1			2
Paulding			2			3			1	3	1	3	3	5	3	24
Peach						1	1	2						2	1	7
Pickens							1			4	2	2		1	2	12
Pierce	1	1		1			1			1	1	1	1	1	2	11
Pike				1		3		1	2	1		3		4		15
Polk					1				1	1	1	1	3		1	9
Pulaski											1			2	1	4
Putnam						1	1					1			1	4
Rabun							1	2	1	1			2	1	1	9
Randolph												1		1		2
Richmond	1	2	2	5		6	1	7	6	3	5	8	8	12	8	74

Counties	2001	2002	2003	2004	2005	2006	2007	2008	2009	2010	2011	2012	2013	2014	2015	Total
Rockdale		1	2	2	1		1	1	2	4	2	4		5	3	28
Screven					2	2	1				1					6
Spalding	1				1		1				2	2		2	2	11
Stephens							1	1						1		3
Stewart															1	1
Sumter			1		2						2	1	2			8
Talbot		1										2		1		4
Taliaferro												1				1
Tattnall					1					2						3
Telfair											1					1
Thomas		1						1				1		1	1	5
Tift							1			1	2	1	2		1	8
Toombs										2	1	1				4
Towns				1					1		1		1	1		5
Troup		1		1		1			3		7	2	2	5	2	24
Turner			1				1		1		1	1			1	6
Twiggs					1				1			2				4
Union	2				2	2	1		1	2	4			1	1	16
Unknown	1	3	1		3	4	1	2	2	4	7	8	5	13	12	66
Upson									1	1				1		3
Walker			1		2					3	3	1	3	1		14
Walton	1	1		2		2	2	1	3	2	2	3	7	6	3	35
Ware				1	1	2	4	1				2	2	1	1	15
Warren										1	1					2
Washing-ton				2	1	1				3		2	2	2		13
Wayne							1			1	1	2		1		6
White		2	1	2			1	2	1	1	1	2		1	1	15
Whitfield		1		2		2	1	2		4	3	1	1	4	1	22
Wilcox														2	1	3
Worth		1									1	1				3
Total	**57**	**51**	**79**	**89**	**92**	**106**	**142**	**174**	**181**	**210**	**223**	**274**	**251**	**356**	**265**	**2550**

If a county is missing from the list, it's because no UFO sightings were logged in either the NUFORC or MUFON databases for the 2001-2015 sample period.

UFOS BY MONTH: GEORGIA

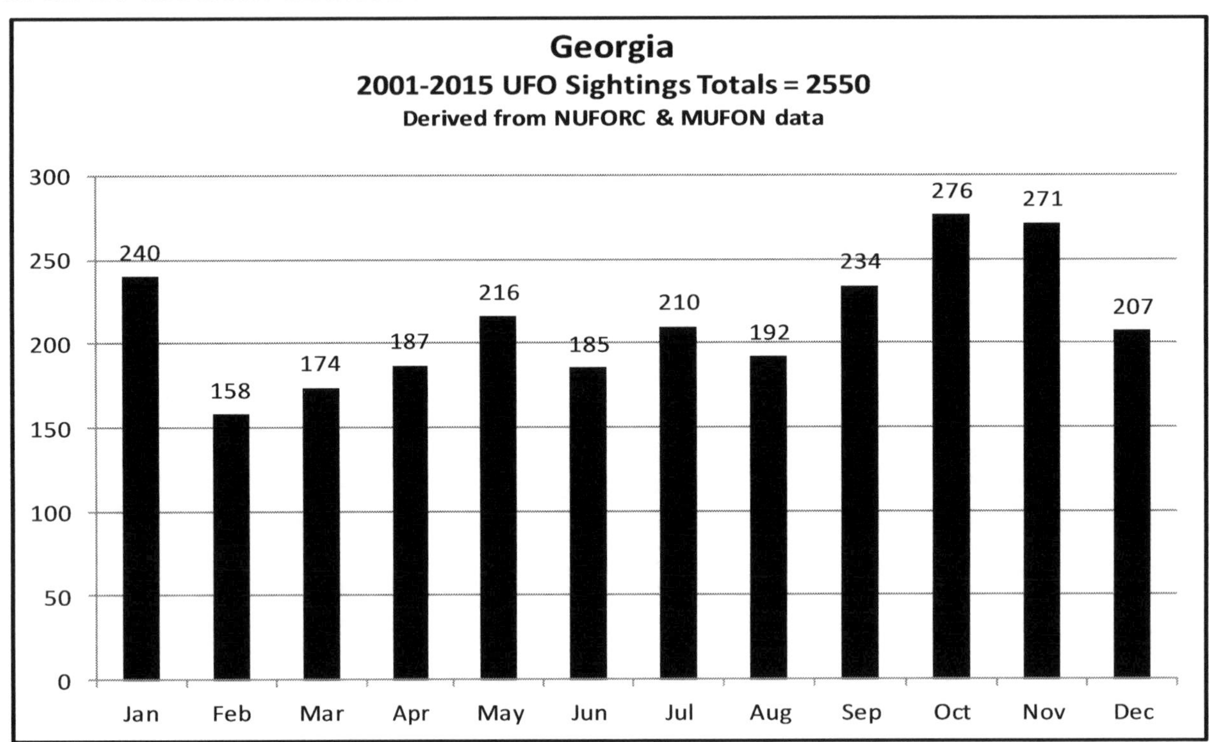

Year	Jan	Feb	Mar	Apr	May	Jun	Jul	Aug	Sep	Oct	Nov	Dec	Total
2001	3	2	6	3	3	10	1	3	12	5	6	3	57
2002	2	4	4	1	4	8	6	6	4	7	2	3	51
2003	6	5		8	3	8	2	7	7	10	12	11	79
2004	9	6	16	11	8	6	7	8	5	5	3	5	89
2005	6	7	3	9	6	6	5	9	16	5	12	8	92
2006	2	3	5	7	2	5	11	7	7	17	27	13	106
2007	9	8	8	8	12	11	4	8	16	16	27	15	142
2008	24	12	13	13	13	12	16	11	11	12	22	15	174
2009	26	18	21	16	17	15	8	10	15	14	16	5	181
2010	17	8	12	21	20	13	16	11	20	41	19	12	210
2011	18	9	17	17	15	7	24	20	16	31	24	25	223
2012	35	19	15	26	31	17	20	15	23	18	26	29	274
2013	21	16	13	10	19	21	17	26	31	27	25	25	251
2014	39	22	21	28	40	19	44	33	19	38	26	27	356
2015	23	19	20	9	23	27	29	18	32	30	24	11	265
Total	**240**	**158**	**174**	**187**	**216**	**185**	**210**	**192**	**234**	**276**	**271**	**207**	**2550**

Distribution of Sightings between Databases: Georgia

Database	Count	Percentage
MUFON	1109	43.49%
NUFORC	1441	56.51%
Total	2550	100.00%

State Demographic Information: Georgia

2010 US Census Statistics	
Population	9,687,653.00
Area in Square Miles	59,425.15
Land Area Sq. Miles	57,513.49
Population/Square mile	168.40

HAWAII

UFO RANK 43/51

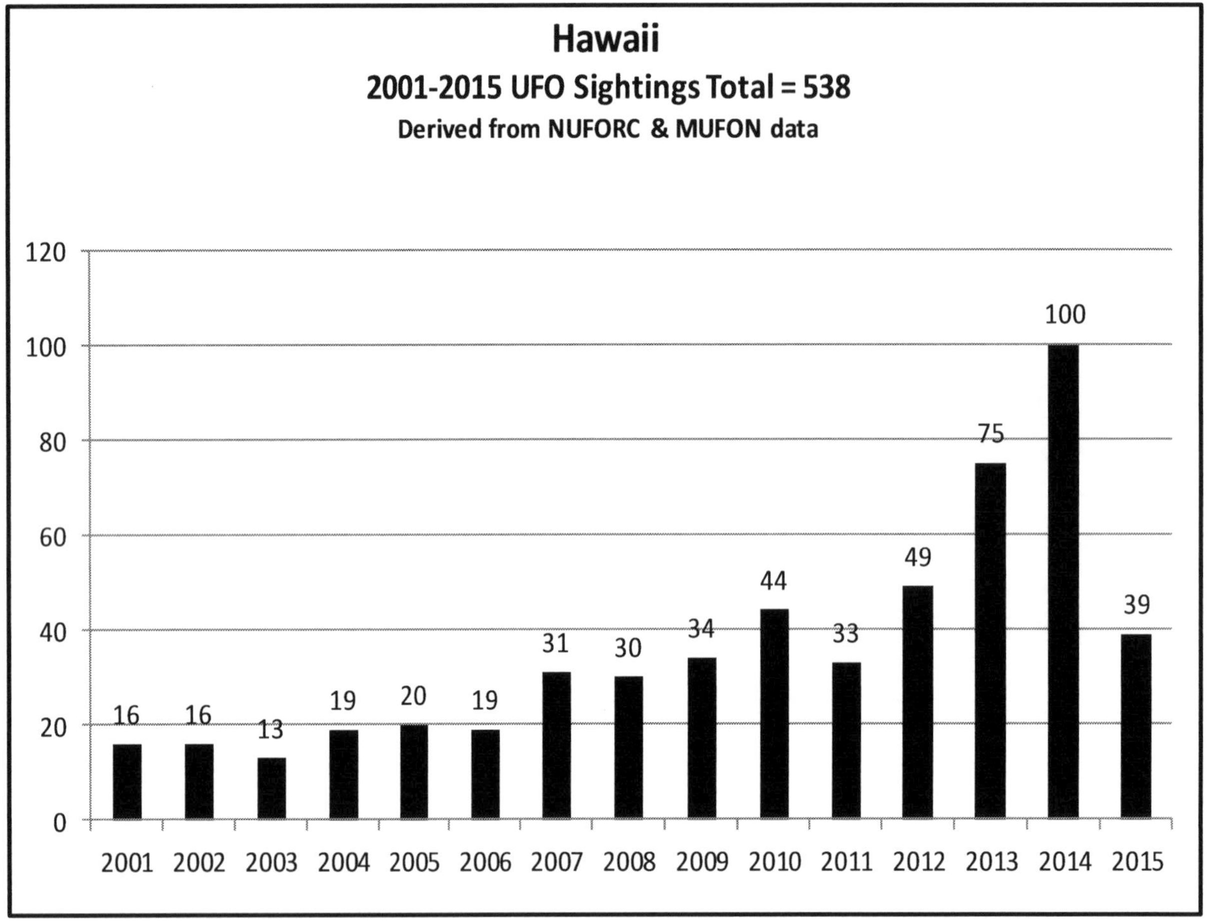

TOP TEN COUNTIES		RANK	TOP TEN SHAPES		
Hawaii	99	**1**	Light	116	21.56%
Honolulu	225	**2**	Sphere	63	11.71%
Kauai	57	**3**	Circle	56	10.41%
Keauhou	1	**4**	Unknown	48	8.92%
Maui	123	**5**	Fireball	44	8.18%
Oahu	2	**6**	Other	37	6.88%
Unknown	31	**7**	Triangle	24	4.46%
NA		**8**	Star-like	21	3.90%
NA		**9**	Disc	18	3.35%
NA		**10**	Oval	17	3.16%

UFO SHAPES: HAWAII

UFO SHAPES	2001	2002	2003	2004	2005	2006	2007	2008	2009	2010	2011	2012	2013	2014	2015	Total
Blimp											1				1	2
Bullet/Missile						1	1									2
Changing		1			2		1			1			1	2		8
Chevron								1		1				1		3
Cigar					1			1		1				1	1	5
Circle	2	4	3	3			3	1	7	3	4	10	5	10	1	56
Cone			1									3		2	1	7
Cross				1												1
Cylinder							2	1		2	1		2	1		9
Diamond					1						1	2	1	1		6
Disc	1			1		2	2	2	1	1	2		5	1		18
Disk	2	1		2	1	2				3				2	1	14
Egg						2			1			1	1			5
Fireball	1	1	1		1		3	1		1		9	16	7	3	44
Flash			1	1	2		2	1		2	1	1	3	1	1	16
Formation								1		1		2		1	2	7
Light	2	3		3	5	2	8	9	3	12	4	12	15	30	8	116
N/A											1				2	3
Other	2		2	3		1	2	3	4		5	1	4	7	3	37
Oval		1		1	1				3	1	1	3	3	3		17
Rectangle							1						1		1	3
Sphere	2	3	4	1	1	3	1	1	3	8	3	3	11	14	5	63
Sq/Rect														1		1
Star-like	1					1	1	3	3	1	2	1	2	5	1	21
Teardrop															1	1
Triangle	2	1		1	2			1	1	5	4		2	3	2	24
Unknown	1	1	1	2	3	5	3	4	8	1	3	1	3	7	5	48
Boomerang							1									1
Total	**16**	**16**	**13**	**19**	**20**	**19**	**31**	**30**	**34**	**44**	**33**	**49**	**75**	**100**	**39**	**538**

UFOS BY COUNTY: HAWAII

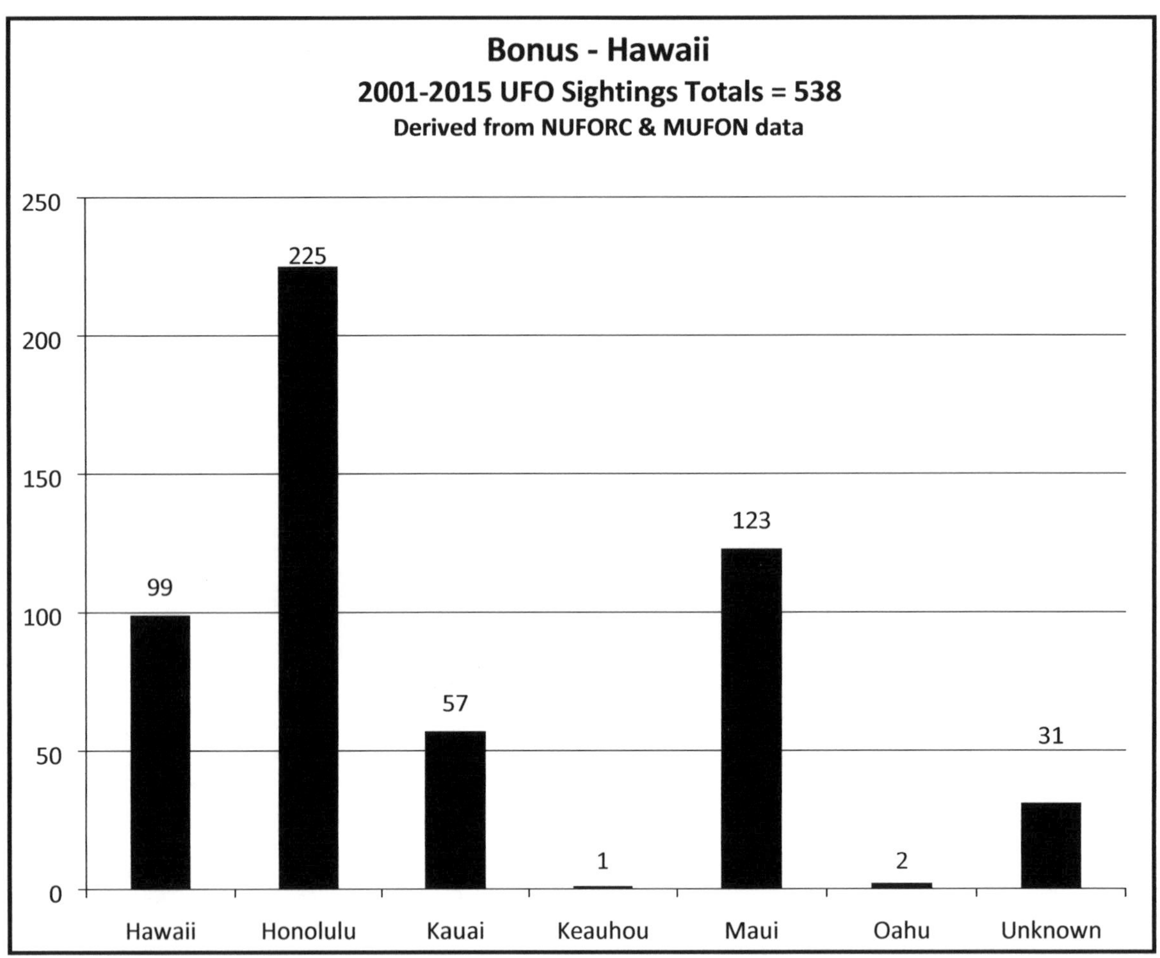

Counties	2001	2002	2003	2004	2005	2006	2007	2008	2009	2010	2011	2012	2013	2014	2015	Total
Hawaii	4	4	2	2	5	2	3	8	3	8	7	7	20	13	11	99
Honolulu	6	4	5	10	10	6	15	11	21	21	14	16	21	48	17	225
Kauai	3	1	1		1	5	3	5	5	3	1	5	11	9	4	57
Keauhou							1									1
Maui	3	6	4	7	3	3	6	4	5	8	4	17	22	25	6	123
Oahu		1								1						2
Unknown			1		1	3	3	2		3	7	4	1	5	1	31
Total	**16**	**16**	**13**	**19**	**20**	**19**	**31**	**30**	**34**	**44**	**33**	**49**	**75**	**100**	**39**	**538**

If a county is missing from the list, it's because no UFO sightings were logged in either the NUFORC or MUFON databases for the 2001-2015 sample period.

UFOS BY MONTH: HAWAII

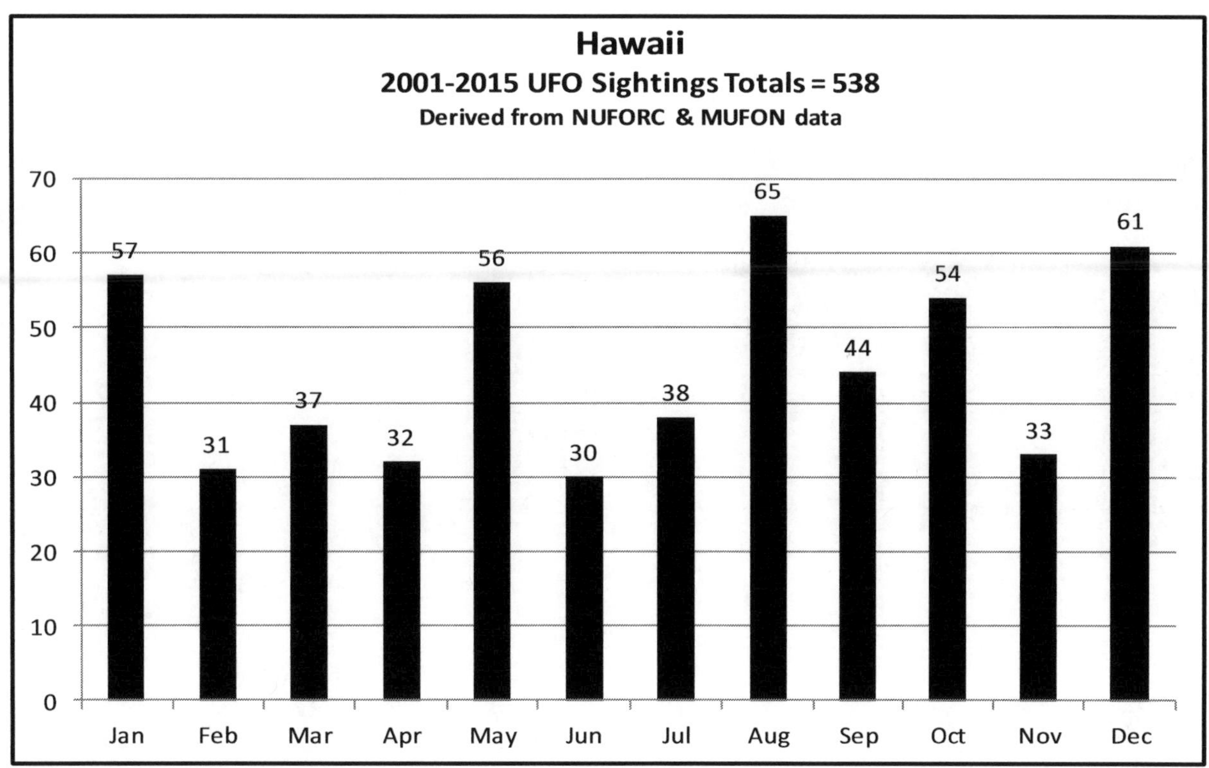

Year	Jan	Feb	Mar	Apr	May	Jun	Jul	Aug	Sep	Oct	Nov	Dec	Total
2001	4			1		3	2		1		2	3	16
2002	4			3	2	1		3	2		1		16
2003			1			2	1		3	1	3	2	13
2004	4	1	1		1	1	1		2	3		5	19
2005	3	1	1	1	3		2	4	2	1	1	1	20
2006		1	2	1	1	1	2	1	4	2	2	2	19
2007	3	2	2	4	5	2		3	2	2	3	3	31
2008	2	2	2	6	3	1	2	2	1	6	1	2	30
2009	3	4	1		1	1	2	7	3	8	1	3	34
2010	5	4	5	2	5		2	5	4	2	4	6	44
2011		2	2		1	4	3	9	1	7		4	33
2012	5	1	1	6	5	2	5	9	2	1	3	9	49
2013	7	4	7	3	7	7	6	8	2	5	5	14	75
2014	11	9	8	4	22	3	4	10	12	8	3	6	100
2015	6		4	1		2	6	4	3	8	4	1	39
Total	**57**	**31**	**37**	**32**	**56**	**30**	**38**	**65**	**44**	**54**	**33**	**61**	**538**

Distribution of Sightings between Databases: Hawaii

Database	Count	Percentage
MUFON	164	30.48%
NUFORC	374	69.52%
Total	538	100.00%

State Demographic Information: Hawaii

2010 US Census Statistics	
Population	1,360,301.00
Area in Square Miles	10,931.72
Land Area Sq. Miles	6,422.63
Population/Square mile	211.80

IDAHO UFO RANK 36/51

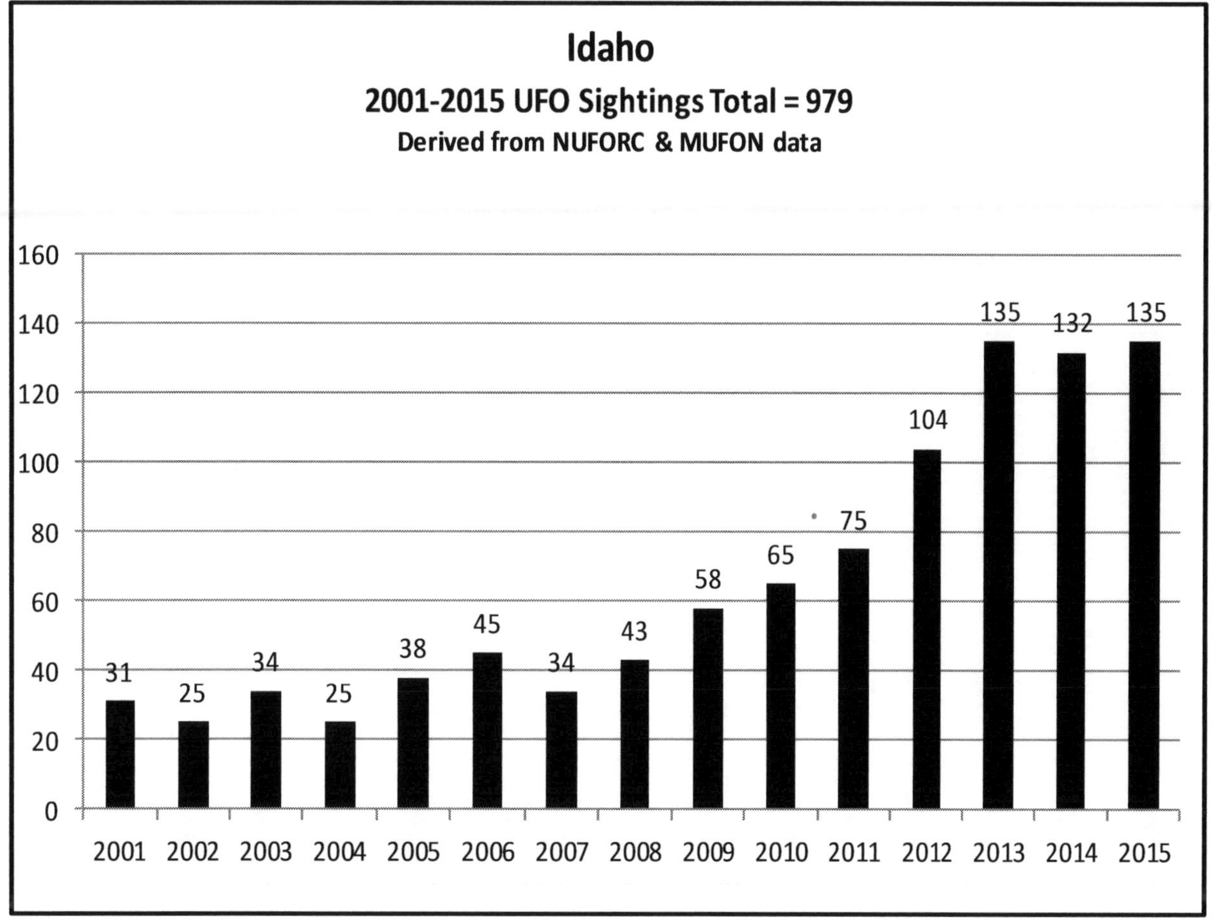

TOP TEN COUNTIES		RANK	TOP TEN SHAPES		
Ada	297	1	Light	170	17.36%
Kootenai	120	2	Sphere	100	10.21%
Canyon	84	3	Circle	99	10.11%
Twin Falls	54	4	Unknown	93	9.50%
Bonneville	37	5	Triangle	79	8.07%
Bonner	32	6	Other	65	6.64%
Bannock	29	7	Fireball	64	6.54%
Unknown	29	8	Star-like	44	4.49%
Latah	26	9	Disc	30	3.06%
Elmore	21	10	Oval	30	3.06%

UFO SHAPES: IDAHO

UFO Shapes	2001	2002	2003	2004	2005	2006	2007	2008	2009	2010	2011	2012	2013	2014	2015	Total
Blimp													1			1
Boomerang				1		1			1	2	4	1				10
Bullet/Missile		1					1	1	1			1		1	2	8
Changing	3	2		1		1	1	1		3		1	2	2	3	20
Chevron				1	1			1			1	1	3	2	1	11
Cigar		1	2		2	4	2		2	3	2		3	2	1	24
Circle	2	4	1		3	3	6	3	6	4	5	13	18	18	13	99
Cone		2						1				2	1		2	8
Cross								1	2		1		2	1		7
Cylinder	1			2					1	2		2	1	1	3	13
Diamond	2				1			1	1	1	1	1	2	2	1	13
Disc	1		1		4		3	4	2	1	3	1	3	2	5	30
Disk	2		1	1	5	2	2		1	3	2	1	3	2	4	29
Egg					1	1		1				2			1	6
Fireball	1		1		1	3	1	1	3	4	6	9	13	11	10	64
Flash			1			1		2	1	2		4	3	1		15
Formation	1	1	1	3	1			1	1				5	2	3	19
Light	7	4	6	6	6	4	6	6	9	10	15	13	25	26	27	170
N/A															2	2
Other	2	1	2	1	4	4	2	3	6	5	3	8	7	10	7	65
Oval	2		2	2	2		2	1			3	5	4	4	3	30
Rectangle						2			1		1		3	1	1	9
Saturn-like					1									1		2
Sphere		3	3	1	2	2	1	2	2	4	9	15	15	20	21	100
Sq/Rect													2		1	3
Star-like	1					1	3	5	7	6	4	7	3	2	5	44
Teardrop		1	1										1	2		5
Triangle		2	7	3	2	13	1	2	5	9	9	6	7	8	5	79
Unknown	6	3	5	3	2	3	3	6	6	6	6	11	8	11	14	93
Total	**31**	**25**	**34**	**25**	**38**	**45**	**34**	**43**	**58**	**65**	**75**	**104**	**135**	**132**	**135**	**979**

UFOS BY COUNTY: IDAHO

Counties	2001	2002	2003	2004	2005	2006	2007	2008	2009	2010	2011	2012	2013	2014	2015	Total
Ada	5	2	10	6	11	13	6	6	18	19	27	35	46	41	52	297
Adams							1		1							2
Bannock	1	1	2	2	1	2		4		3	3	5	4		1	29
Bear Lake									2					1	2	5
Benewah			1		1	1	1		1	1	1		3		2	12
Bingham	1			1	1					1		2				6
Blaine	2				1	2					1	2	3	3		14
Boise		2								1		1	1	1	1	7
Bonner	1	1	5	1	1		5	1		1	2	2	4	4	4	32
Bonneville	2				3	6	2	1		1	5	3	6	7	1	37
Boundary												1		1		2
Butte		1	1					1		1					1	5
Camas						1							1	1	1	4
Canyon	1	2		1	3	3	1	4	3	6	10	10	11	13	16	84
Caribou										1						1
Cassia			1		1		1	2		1	2			3		11
Clearwater	1			1				1							2	5
Custer					1			2	2		1		1	1		8
Elmore						1			1	2	4	1	1	2	9	21
Franklin					1				1			1			1	4
Fremont				1						2		1		1		5
Gem					1	1			1		2	3	1	1		10
Gonzales															1	1
Gooding	1								1	2	1	1		2		8
Idaho		1	4		1		1	2					2			11
Jefferson							1	1				1	1	2	1	7
Jerome	1						2					3		1	2	9
Kootenai	2	4	1	5	4	1	7	9	17	8	6	14	20	16	6	120
Latah	2				1	2	1	1	1		1	1	6	4	6	26
Lemhi		1			1	1	1		1	1		1			1	8
Lewis												1	1	1	1	4
Lincoln						1					1		1		1	4
Madison	1					1		2				1	3	1		9
Minidoka						2						1	1	1	1	6
Nez Perce	3		1	1		1	1	1		2	3	2	1	1	3	20
Oneida												1	1	1		3
Owyhee			4	3			1			1					2	11

Counties	**2001**	**2002**	**2003**	**2004**	**2005**	**2006**	**2007**	**2008**	**2009**	**2010**	**2011**	**2012**	**2013**	**2014**	**2015**	**Total**
Payette	2				2					1			3	2	1	11
Power			1										1			2
Shoshone					1	1	1							2		5
Teton	1									1	2				1	5
Twin Falls		1	2	2	2	2	1	3	2	2	1	8	7	12	9	54
Unknown		5				2		2	4	3	1	1	3	4	4	29
Valley	3	2	1	1						1		1	1	1	2	13
Washington	1	2				1			2	3	1		1	1		12
Total	**31**	**25**	**34**	**25**	**38**	**45**	**34**	**43**	**58**	**65**	**75**	**104**	**135**	**132**	**135**	**979**

If a county is missing from the list, it's because no UFO sightings were logged in either the NUFORC or MUFON databases for the 2001-2015 sample period.

UFOS BY MONTH: IDAHO

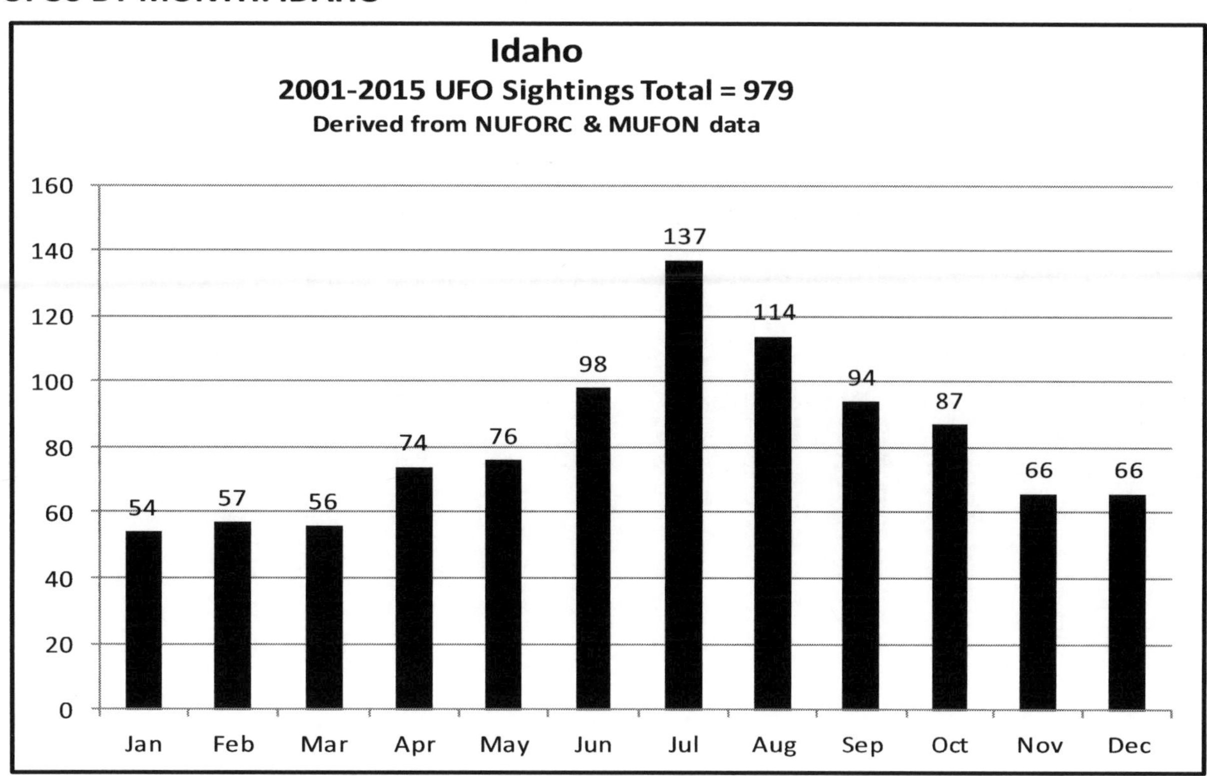

Year	Jan	Feb	Mar	Apr	May	Jun	Jul	Aug	Sep	Oct	Nov	Dec	Total
2001	4	2	3	4	1	2	4	6	2	2	1		31
2002		4		2	3		4	3	2	5	2		25
2003	2	6	1	1	2	2	5	3	1	5	3	3	34
2004		1		2	3	3	8	2	2	3	1		25
2005	1	2	5	2	3	4	7	1	4	5	3	1	38
2006	1	2	5	4	6	12	8	3	1			3	45
2007			1			6	9	7	6	1	3	1	34
2008		3	5	2	4	1	8	10	6	2	1	1	43
2009	5	1	2	2	3	12	6	3	15	3	3	3	58
2010	2	3	2	8	6	3	16	11	5	3	4	2	65
2011	6	1	3	4	7	3	4	18	11	4	3	11	75
2012	10	7	4	10	3	15	17	10	1	4	10	13	104
2013	4	2	8	9	5	17	14	17	9	19	13	18	135
2014	6	10	8	13	16	6	20	13	17	12	4	7	132
2015	13	13	9	11	14	12	7	7	12	19	15	3	135
Total	**54**	**57**	**56**	**74**	**76**	**98**	**137**	**114**	**94**	**87**	**66**	**66**	**979**

Distribution of Sightings between Databases: Idaho

Database	Count	Percentage
MUFON	344	35.14%
NUFORC	635	64.86%
Total	979	100.00%

State Demographic Information: Idaho

2010 US Census Statistics	
Population	1,567,582.00
Area in Square Miles	83,568.95
Land Area Sq. Miles	82,643.12
Population/Square mile	19.00

ILLINOIS

UFO RANK 8/51

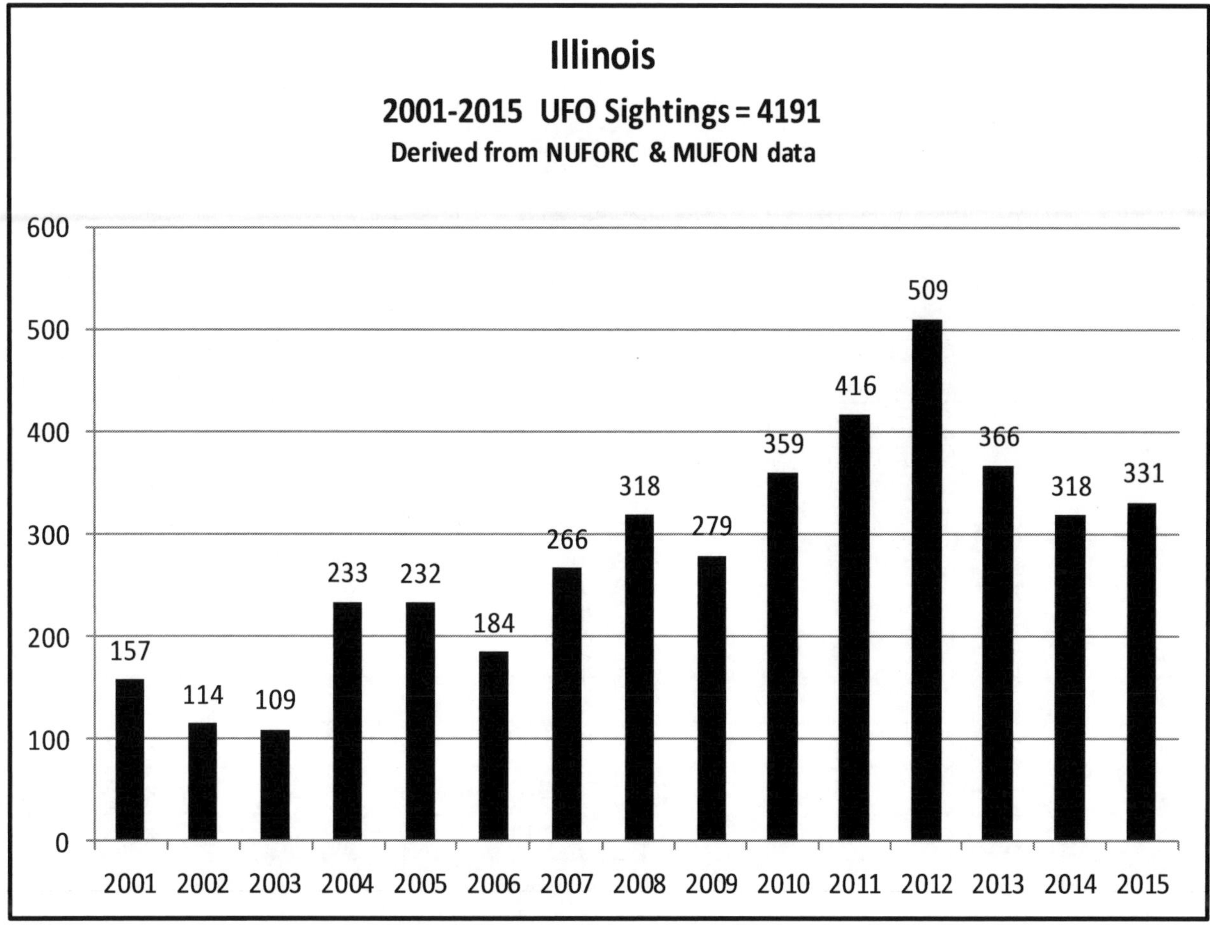

TOP TEN COUNTIES		RANK	TOP TEN SHAPES		
Cook	1431	1	Light	571	13.62%
DuPage	321	2	Circle	537	12.81%
Will	283	3	Triangle	451	10.76%
Lake	254	4	Unknown	383	9.14%
Winnebago	145	5	Sphere	374	8.92%
Kane	136	6	Fireball	317	7.56%
McHenry	124	7	Other	232	5.54%
Unknown	112	8	Oval	181	4.32%
Madison	93	9	Star-like	166	3.96%
Saint Clair	93	10	Disc	117	2.79%

UFO SHAPES: ILLINOIS

UFO Shapes	2001	2002	2003	2004	2005	2006	2007	2008	2009	2010	2011	2012	2013	2014	2015	Total
Blimp							6	1	1	3	2	2	3			18
Boomerang					1	1	3	5	5	9	3	6	3	3	2	41
Bullet/Missile				1	1		4	4	4	2	2		5	2	1	26
Changing	2	3	1	3	9	7	2	5	2	1	6	7	4	3	4	59
Chevron	3	3	2			1	4	4	2	4	4	3	3	2	7	42
Cigar	4	1	5	4	6	4	4	12	4	4	7	14	5	6	1	81
Circle	12	7	8	25	22	16	32	36	41	52	65	90	67	31	33	537
Cone						1	1	1	1	1	4	2	4			15
Cross			1			1	1	1	1	1	1	1		1	3	12
Cylinder	1	1	3	1	3	4	3	6	1	4	9	9	8	3	3	59
Diamond	2	6	1	2	2	3	5	4	2	7	8	10	4	5	5	66
Disc	4	3	2		2	6	5	11	7	11	7	24	13	8	14	117
Disk	5	6	6	5	5	8	19	14	3	6	9	9	6	4	4	109
Egg	3	2	1	2			3	6	5	9	2	5	1	4	1	44
Fireball	9	7	3	7	10	8	4	15	18	36	48	47	39	34	32	317
Flash	2	2	2	4	9	4	5	8	6	7	4	4	9	6	6	78
Formation	8	1	2	16	12	4	11	2	5	3	4	10	12	5	7	102
Light	35	18	14	74	56	25	36	32	30	42	46	54	15	43	51	571
N/A								2						3	5	10
Other	13	11	12	16	13	10	11	11	13	24	18	22	31	12	15	232
Oval	8	7	8	5	4	14	9	13	12	10	14	26	18	18	15	181
Rectangle	4	1		1	1	8	4	2	2	5	4	7	1	1	2	43
Saturn-like	1						1		2	1			1	1		7
Sphere	14	5	6	5	11	10	16	23	21	27	46	55	38	50	47	374
Sq/Rect												2	2	2	7	13
Star-like			1	1	2	6	13	18	23	16	22	16	15	17	16	166
Teardrop		3	1		2	2	3	5	5	1	3	3	3	5	1	37
Triangle	17	11	19	29	30	22	35	38	32	39	45	52	29	28	25	451
Unknown	10	16	11	32	31	19	26	39	31	34	33	29	27	21	24	383
Total	**157**	**114**	**109**	**233**	**232**	**184**	**266**	**318**	**279**	**359**	**416**	**509**	**366**	**318**	**331**	**4191**

UFOS BY COUNTY: ILLINOIS

Counties	2001	2002	2003	2004	2005	2006	2007	2008	2009	2010	2011	2012	2013	2014	2015	Total
Adams								3		2	7	3	1		5	21
Alexander						1										1
Bond									1			1		1		3
Boone			1		1	1	1		2	1	1	2		1		11
Bureau			1			1	5		1	3	2	3			1	17
Carroll	1															1
Cass	1				2	2						1		1		7
Champaign		10	1	1	1	4	1		6	1	4	2	1	2	2	36
Christian	1	2			1			1	1						1	7
Clark		1				1							1			3
Clay										1					1	2
Clinton	1	3					1		2					3	1	11
Coles		1	1	1	1		3	1	1	3	2	1		2	1	18
Cook	35	32	26	158	128	55	98	126	92	121	115	147	101	92	105	1431
Crawford					2			1							1	4
Cumberland	1	1													1	3
DeKalb			1			1		1	3	2	4	4	7	2	5	30
Dewitt				1							1				1	3
Douglas	1			1							1					3
DuPage	14	2	12	11	17	16	31	27	20	33	22	33	25	28	30	321
Edwards								4								4
Effingham				2					1	1	1	1		1		7
Fayette											1	1	1		1	4
Ford				1								1	2			4
Franklin	1	1	4				1	1		1	1	2	2	1	2	17
Fulton	1			1	1	3	1			1	1	3		3	1	16
Gallatin										1	3	1				5
Greene		2				1	1		1			1				6
Grundy			2					1	1	2	9	7	2	3	1	28
Hancock					1		3									4
Hardin			1											3		4
Henderson														1		1
Henry				1	1	1	1			2	3	3				12
Iroquois	3					1			2	1	7		1	1		16
Jackson		1	2	1		4	3		3	1	1	4	4	4	3	31
Jasper					2					2			1	1		6
Jefferson	1	1	1	1				1	2	1	1	2		5	2	18

Counties	2001	2002	2003	2004	2005	2006	2007	2008	2009	2010	2011	2012	2013	2014	2015	Total
Jersey			1								1			1		3
Jo Daviess			1	1					1	2					1	6
Johnson			1			1						3	1		1	7
Kane	2	2	7		3	12	6	17	7	20	10	13	14	11	12	136
Kankakee		1	1		2		1	1	3	6	5	8	5	1	2	36
Kendall				1	1	3	1	2	2	1	6	10	6	2	6	41
Knox	1	4			2		1	5	5	1		4		3	1	27
La Salle		3				4	1	4	2	4	4	6	1	2	7	38
Lake	5	8	6	5	7	11	20	22	15	17	34	33	37	21	13	254
LaSalle			1					1								2
Lawrence			1						1			1				3
Lee			1				1	4	1	2	2	3	1		2	17
Livingston		1		2		2				1	1	1		1		9
Logan							1	1		1	1	1		2		7
Macon		3		1	2	1	1	2		3	6	13	3	4	1	40
Macoupin							1	1		1	3	1		3		10
Madison	6	3	2	1	4	3	3	2	7	9	11	10	15	7	10	93
Marion	2	1	1		2	3		1	3		2	2			3	20
Marshall		1			1					1	1	1		2		7
Mason	1						2	4				2				9
Massac												1	2	3		6
McDonough				2		1			2		2	4		1		12
McHenry	3	3	4	1	4	2	4	12	9	9	21	14	14	9	15	124
Mclean	5	2	1	3		4	6	4	4	3	5	10	10	3	5	65
Menard		1					1		3			1	1	1	1	9
Mercer						1				1	1	3	1			7
Monroe	1	1					1		1				1	1		6
Montgom-ery	2	1					1			1	2	1		1	2	11
Morgan		1	1		1	1				3		2		2	1	12
Moultrie		1					1			1			1		1	5
Ogle		1	2			2	1	1	3			2	1	1	3	17
Peoria	1	2		5	2		3	5	2	6	3	12	4	6	5	56
Piatt				1						1	2	1		1		6
Pike		1				1	1		1	1	2			1		8
Pope												1				1
Posen					1											1
Pulaski					1							2		1		4
Putnam							1									1

Costas' UFO Sightings Desk Reference: USA 2001-2015

Counties	**2001**	**2002**	**2003**	**2004**	**2005**	**2006**	**2007**	**2008**	**2009**	**2010**	**2011**	**2012**	**2013**	**2014**	**2015**	**Total**
Randolph		1		1	1			2	1		2					8
Richland												3			2	5
Rock Island			3	1	6	2	1	4	2	2	6	5	5	4	2	43
Saint Clair	1	3	3	2	5	8	2	9	10	16	7	7	8	4	8	93
Saline			3		3	1	1		6	3	3	4	3	3	2	32
Sangamon			2	1	2	2	8	6	2	3	6	13	15	4	8	72
Schuyler				1					1							2
Scott									1							1
Shelby		1					2	1		3	1	1		2		11
St Clair							1									1
Stark						1										1
Stephenson		1			1		3	1	1	2	1		1		1	12
Tazewell		1	1	1	2		3	4	2	3	2	6	6	4	4	39
Union												1		1	5	7
Unknown	1		1	2	2	2	7	8	11	9	18	10	15	18	8	112
Vermilion	1					4	1	1				5	3	2	3	20
Wabash	1				1		1									3
Warren	1				1											2
Washington	1		1	1			1						1			5
Wayne						2		2						4	1	9
White												1				1
Whiteside			3	1			1		2	2	1	5	1	1	5	22
Will	11	2	4	9	11	15	16	17	24	25	39	40	32	22	16	283
Williamson	2			1		1	4		1	1	1	6		1	1	19
Winnebago	48	7	4	6	4	1	5	7	4	14	16	12	9	1	7	145
Woodford				3	2	1				1	1	1		1	1	11
Total	**157**	**114**	**109**	**233**	**232**	**184**	**266**	**318**	**279**	**359**	**416**	**509**	**366**	**318**	**331**	**4191**

If a county is missing from the list, it's because no UFO sightings were logged in either the NUFORC or MUFON databases for the 2001-2015 sample period.

UFOS BY MONTH: ILLINOIS

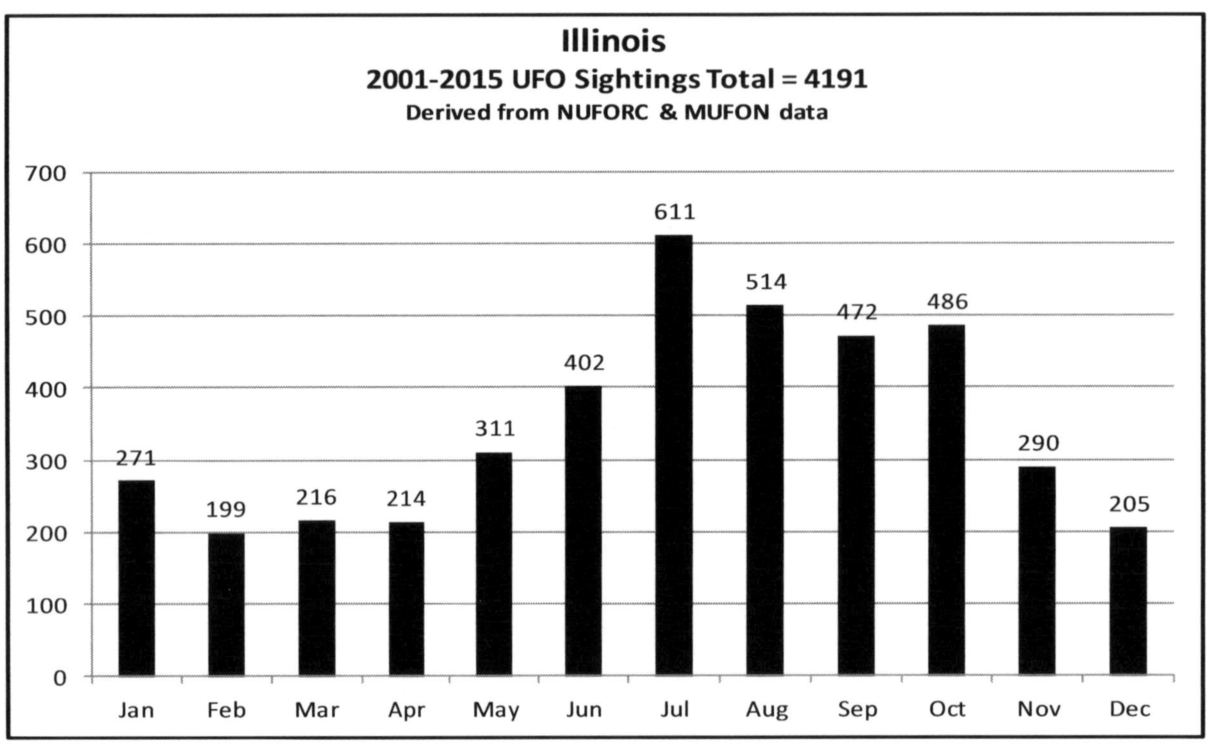

Year	Jan	Feb	Mar	Apr	May	Jun	Jul	Aug	Sep	Oct	Nov	Dec	Total
2001	34	7	12	7	11	14	15	20	14	8	8	7	157
2002	9	16	5	6	11	7	7	15	12	11	11	4	114
2003	7	4	3	1	4	14	20	9	9	11	14	13	109
2004	6	4	1	7	11	14	12	58	14	91	8	7	233
2005	13	6	10	5	6	23	17	18	57	50	16	11	232
2006	7	11	5	13	13	16	24	19	18	19	21	18	184
2007	26	18	12	18	21	27	39	30	25	23	16	11	266
2008	25	17	8	27	14	33	40	54	31	32	27	10	318
2009	16	20	25	11	25	25	40	31	30	15	25	16	279
2010	6	7	23	16	35	33	76	40	42	38	24	19	359
2011	15	19	15	19	36	48	78	51	44	45	27	19	416
2012	39	23	33	25	41	58	72	58	62	35	31	32	509
2013	24	20	18	24	34	38	57	46	33	31	22	19	366
2014	22	16	15	14	34	29	50	32	35	39	20	12	318
2015	22	11	31	21	15	23	64	33	46	38	20	7	331
Total	**271**	**199**	**216**	**214**	**311**	**402**	**611**	**514**	**472**	**486**	**290**	**205**	**4191**

State Demographic Information: Illinois

Database	Count	Percentage
MUFON	1609	38.39%
NUFORC	2582	61.61%
Total	4191	100.00%

Distribution of Sightings between Databases: Illinois

2010 US Census Statistics	
Population	12,830,632.00
Area in Square Miles	57,913.55
Land Area Sq. Miles	55,518.93
Population/Square mile	231.10

INDIANA

UFO RANK 15/51

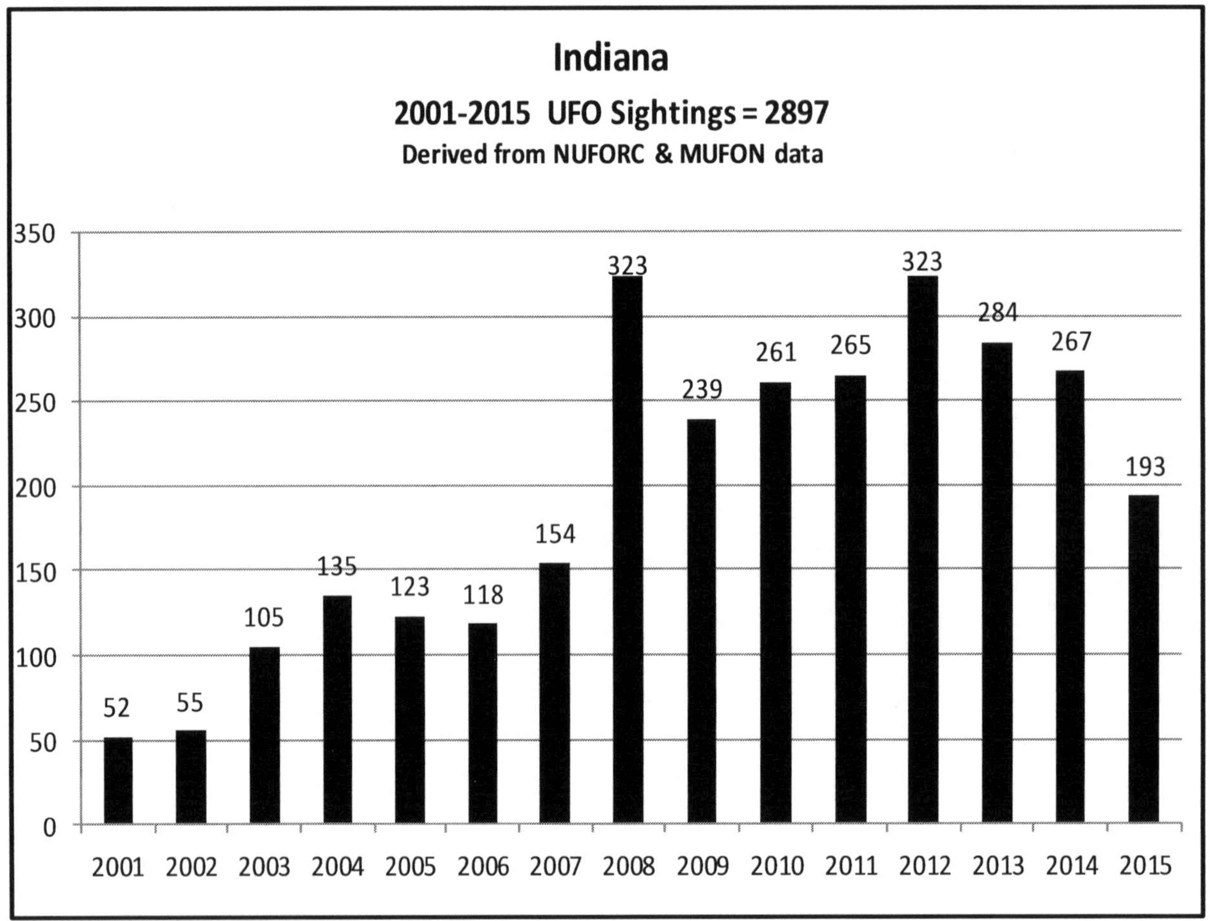

TOP TEN COUNTIES		RANK	TOP TEN SHAPES		
Marion	303	1	Circle	322	11.11%
Lake	166	2	Light	309	10.67%
Allen	136	3	Sphere	293	10.11%
Hamilton	127	4	Unknown	290	10.01%
St Joseph	127	5	Triangle	282	9.73%
Howard	99	6	Fireball	230	7.94%
Tippecanoe	98	7	Other	178	6.14%
Unknown	95	8	Star-like	172	5.94%
Johnson	69	9	Oval	124	4.28%
Vanderburgh	68	10	Cigar	107	3.69%

UFO SHAPES: INDIANA

UFO Shapes	2001	2002	2003	2004	2005	2006	2007	2008	2009	2010	2011	2012	2013	2014	2015	Total
Blimp			1			1	3	3	1	2	5		3	2	1	22
Boomerang	1	1	2			1	4	7	3	4	4	5	2	3	4	41
Bullet/Missile				1				2	1	1		1	1	2	5	14
Changing		1	2	2	3	3	1	1	1	4		1	3	2		24
Chevron				1	3		1	3	3	1		4	6	2	2	26
Cigar		1		1	2	5	5	14	6	14	20	20	11	4	4	107
Circle	3	7	14	11	9	7	16	38	30	29	32	36	36	30	24	322
Cone					1		2	1	1	1			1	1	1	9
Cross				1				4				1		1	1	8
Cylinder	1		3	1	2	1	4	2	3	4	2	6	13	6	10	58
Diamond	1		2	1	2	1		2	6	1	3	5	7	2		33
Disc	1	1	4	4		5	3	11	10	8	8	6	6	8	8	83
Disk	4	4	5	12	5	5	5	8	5	5	3	5	9	6	5	86
Egg		1	1			1		1	3	2	1	3	2		1	16
Fireball	2	5		6	8	10	18	21	19	22	24	36	28	24	7	230
Flash	1	2	1	6	4	2	5	11	9	1	2	7	5	5	8	69
Formation	1		2	5	3	2	2	7	3	2	4	5	5	9		50
Light	8	9	22	25	16	11	27	29	15	18	18	30	31	32	18	309
N/A						1					1	3		1	3	9
Other	4	3	14	7	8	12	11	27	21	14	13	8	11	12	13	178
Oval	8	4	7	5	4	6	4	15	9	11	12	15	10	8	6	124
Rectangle	2			2	2		3	2	1	1	1	2	4	1		21
Sphere	3	2	8	13	12	8	8	12	25	28	37	38	36	35	28	293
Sq/Rect															2	2
Star-like					5	6	9	23	20	25	21	21	10	17	15	172
Teardrop			1	1		1	1		1	6	2	2		2		17
Triangle	5	5	7	11	16	14	10	39	21	33	23	25	22	32	19	282
Unknown	7	9	9	18	18	15	12	40	22	23	29	38	22	20	8	290
Saturn-like				1						1						2
Total	**52**	**55**	**105**	**135**	**123**	**118**	**154**	**323**	**239**	**261**	**265**	**323**	**284**	**267**	**193**	**2897**

UFOS BY COUNTY: INDIANA

Counties	2001	2002	2003	2004	2005	2006	2007	2008	2009	2010	2011	2012	2013	2014	2015	Total
Adams	1				1		1	3	3	1	1	1	1			13
Allen	2	2	1	6	6	2	7	6	8	11	11	15	18	27	14	136
Bartholomew	1		2		1	3		1	2	5	1	2	4	2	1	25
Benton		2					1	1			1			1		6
Blackford								1			2		1		2	6
Boone	1		1	1	2		2	3	1	7	2		6	1	1	28
Brown		1					1	2		1	1			2	1	9
Carroll				2		1						3			1	7
Cass			1	9	1	1		5	1	4	3	2		2	2	31
Clark		1		2	2	5	5	2	2	5	4	9	6	6	4	53
Clay			1		1	1	1	1	2	2	4	2	1	3	1	20
Clinton	1	2	3		2	2	2	1	1	1		2		1		18
Crawford											2		1			3
Daviess				1	1	1				2	1					6
De Kalb			1					2			3			2		8
Dearborn			1	2				1	1	1	1	6	1	1		15
Decatur				1		2	1	3	1	4	3	3		2	1	21
DeKalb								1			1	2		1		5
Delaware		1	2		3	7	5	5	5	2	8	6	6	5	3	58
Dubois			1		1		2	3					3		1	11
Elkhart			1		1	1	4	7	2	4	12	9	13	2	8	64
Fayette					1			2	2	3	1	8	2			19
Floyd	1					1		3	2	6	1	4	5	3	1	27
Fountain	1			2								1		1	1	6
Franklin							2		2	1						5
Fulton	1			4		1				2			1	1	1	11
Gibson	1		1	2	3			2	3	2		3	1	1		19
Grant			2	2	1	1		2	1	3	1	3	6	2	2	26
Greene		1			1				1	2	4	1	2	1		13
Hamilton	1	3	2	6	5	3	7	19	24	5	8	13	14	11	6	127
Hancock		2		1		2	2	9	6		4	6	4	5	4	45
Harrison			2		3	1		8	4	2	2	2	2	3	2	31
Hendricks	1			3	5		3	4	5	3	4	6	5	6	3	48
Henry	1	1	2		2						2		1	3	3	15
Howard		1	2	4	7	6	5	35	16	5	5	7		3	3	99
Huntington		1	2	4			1	1	1			3	2	2	1	18
Jackson	1		2				1	1		1	1	1	2		1	11

Counties	2001	2002	2003	2004	2005	2006	2007	2008	2009	2010	2011	2012	2013	2014	2015	Total
Jasper				1		3	3		1	1	1	2		2	1	15
Jay				1	1				1				1			4
Jefferson		1	1	1				1	1		1	1	1	3	1	12
Jennings				1								1				2
Johnson				1	2	4	3	11	4	4	7	7	10	10	6	69
Knot				1												1
Knox	1	1	1	1	2			1	4	7	6	3	2		3	32
Kosciusko		2	1		1		1	4	1	4	1	2	3	1	2	23
La Porte	1					2	1			3	10	9	4	5		35
Lagrange			1				2	2	1	3	1	1	1		1	13
Lake	2	5	8	7	3	11	10	20	11	23	17	21	10	9	9	166
La Porte	2	2	1		4	2	2	2	6	8	12	12	2	1	4	60
Lawrence	1	1	1	1	3					2	2	2	2		4	19
Madison	2		2		2	2	2	6	4	1	5	9	2	2	2	41
Manitowoc													1			1
Marion	1	9	16	14	8	12	12	33	19	29	24	29	45	27	25	303
Marshall	1			2		2	1	4		7		7		1		25
Martin							2		3	1						6
Miami		1	2	2	5	3	3	12	5	2		1	3	1		40
Monroe	5	1	2	2	1	3	2	6	2	6	2	3	1	4		40
Montgomery			1	1						2		1		2	1	8
Morgan		1	2	2	2			1	1	1	1	4	4	4	1	24
Newton				1		2		1								4
Noble	1		2	1	1		2		3	2		4	1		1	18
Ohio		2						1				1				4
Orange							1	3	2				3			9
Owen		2	1				1	2					2			8
Parke				1			1		2			2	1	1		8
Perry	1								1	1						3
Pike	1															1
Porter	1		2	2	1	2	2	4	3	4	8	12	4	11	8	64
Posey		1		1	1	1	4			1			2	1		12
Pulaski				2	1		1	1			1					6
Putnam	1	1	4		1		1	2	4	1	3	2	6		4	30
Randolph				1	1				1	1	2	1	1	1		9
Ripley						1		3		3	3	2	3	1	1	17
Rush				2					1	1			3	3		10
Scott			1					1	2	1	1			1	1	8
Shelby							2	1	1	2	1	4	1	2	2	16

Counties	**2001**	**2002**	**2003**	**2004**	**2005**	**2006**	**2007**	**2008**	**2009**	**2010**	**2011**	**2012**	**2013**	**2014**	**2015**	**Total**
Spencer								1		2	1	1			1	6
St. Joseph	4	1	4	5	5	6	11	10	11	7	15	16	13	15	9	132
St. Charles					1											1
Starke			2		3		1					1	1		2	10
Steuben	1		2	1	2		2	1	3		2	1		3		18
Sullivan											1		3		1	5
Switzerland							1				1	1				3
Tippecanoe	2	1	5	8	4	10	3	9	11	9	6	2	13	12	3	98
Tipton			1		2		1	4	2	1				1	1	13
Union							1	1		3	1	2		1	1	10
Unknown	1	1		2	4	5	8	11	10	4	12	9	6	14	8	95
Vanderburgh	3	1	3	2	1		2	10	5	5	5	8	5	9	9	68
Vermillion	1					1						2	1		1	6
Vigo	3		3	8	6	1	3	7	9	7	3	4		5	3	62
Wabash			1	1	1		1	3	2	3	3	2	1	2	2	22
Warren								1								1
Warrick			3	1		1	2	3		3	1	4	5	3		26
Washington	1				1	1	2	1		2	4	1	1	4	2	20
Wayne		1	1			1	1		1	1	1	4	1	2	1	15
Wells									2	3	1		1			7
White		1	1	6	1	1	2	3	3	4	2	2	2			28
Whitley	1	1			2		1	2		1	3		4	3	4	22
Total	**52**	**55**	**105**	**135**	**123**	**118**	**154**	**323**	**239**	**261**	**265**	**323**	**284**	**267**	**193**	**2897**

If a county is missing from the list, it's because no UFO sightings were logged in either the NUFORC or MUFON databases for the 2001-2015 sample period.

UFOS BY MONTH: INDIANA

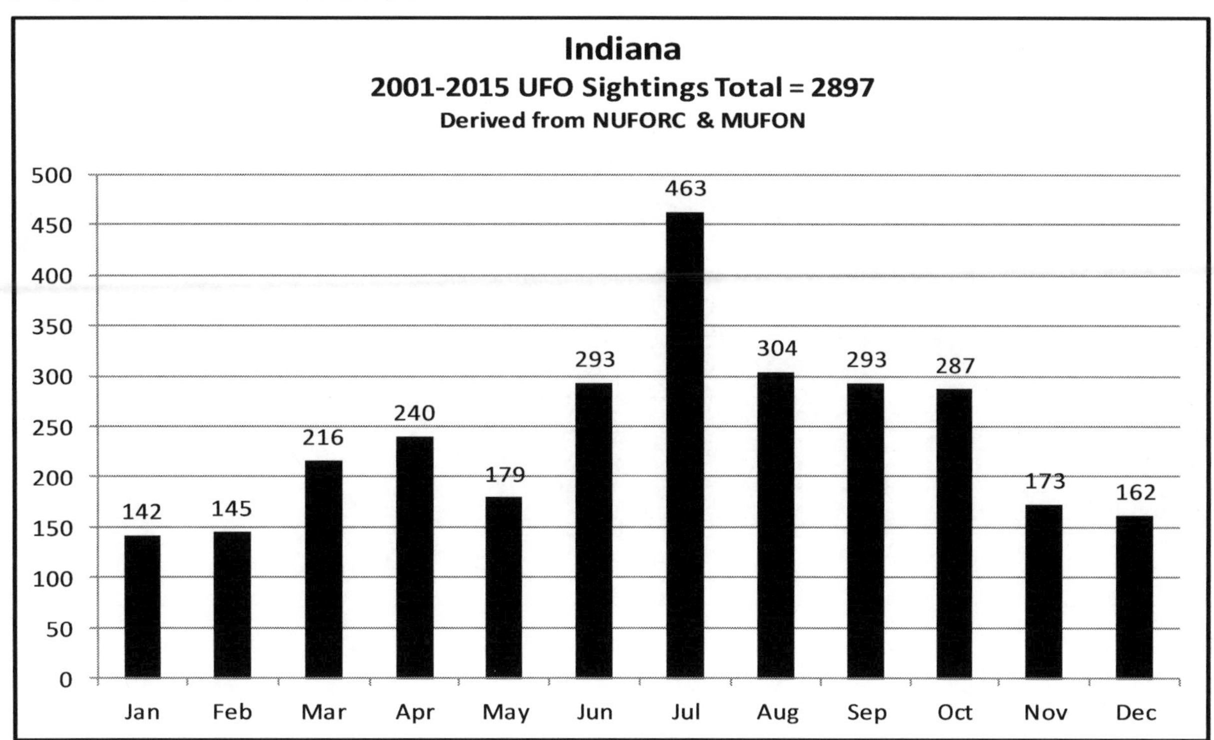

Year	Jan	Feb	Mar	Apr	May	Jun	Jul	Aug	Sep	Oct	Nov	Dec	Total
2001	5	5	3	5	4	3	6	5	11	1	3	1	52
2002	3	1	1	1	3	2	5	13	8	11	3	4	55
2003	7	5	5	7	4	8	8	10	12	19	4	16	105
2004	6	15	9	32	6	7	8	10	11	12	8	11	135
2005	4	8	15	12	8	10	15	16	7	15	9	4	123
2006	4	7	17	13	7	9	8	18	5	7	6	17	118
2007	9	9	6	6	19	28	23	18	15	10	7	4	154
2008	21	6	32	49	13	23	56	31	26	28	20	18	323
2009	17	25	20	13	13	15	54	27	21	16	12	6	239
2010	6	4	24	18	9	34	58	29	18	28	24	9	261
2011	8	5	12	18	12	35	57	35	23	33	14	13	265
2012	16	15	27	25	21	41	43	30	39	22	17	27	323
2013	14	13	16	17	18	34	48	35	31	32	14	12	284
2014	11	20	16	13	24	24	45	15	37	31	15	16	267
2015	11	7	13	11	18	20	29	12	29	22	17	4	193
Total	**142**	**145**	**216**	**240**	**179**	**293**	**463**	**304**	**293**	**287**	**173**	**162**	**2897**

Distribution of Sightings between Databases: Indiana

Database	Count	Percentage
MUFON	1501	51.81%
NUFORC	1396	48.19%
Total	2897	100.00%

State Demographic Information: Indiana

2010 US Census Statistics	
Population	6,483,802.00
Area in Square Miles	36,419.55
Land Area Sq. Miles	35,826.11
Population/Square mile	181.00

IOWA

UFO RANK 31/51

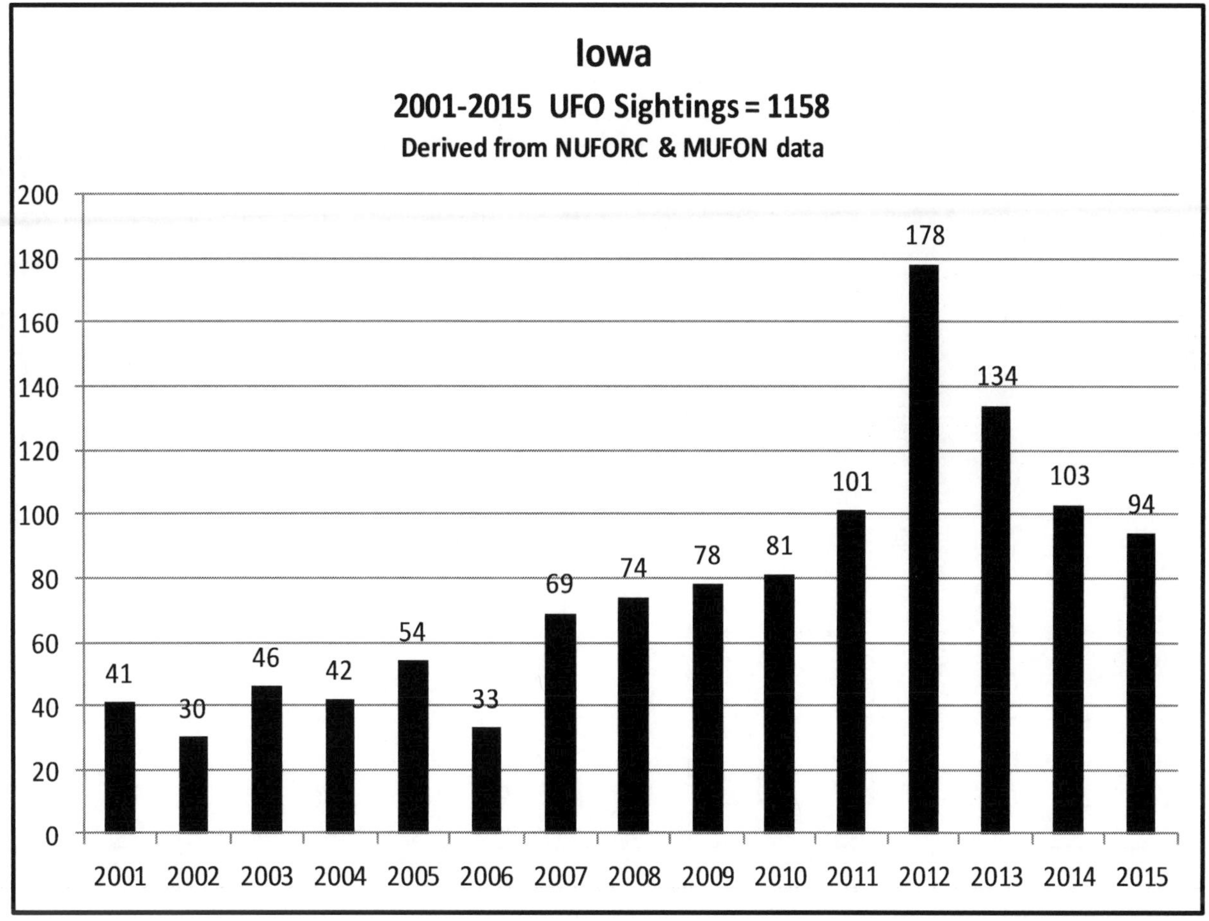

TOP TEN COUNTIES		RANK	TOP TEN SHAPES		
Polk	192	1	Light	179	15.46%
Linn	109	2	Triangle	144	12.44%
Black Hawk	64	3	Circle	119	10.28%
Johnson	51	4	Unknown	115	9.93%
Scott	48	5	Sphere	101	8.72%
Woodbury	41	6	Fireball	71	6.13%
Pottawattamie	37	7	Other	70	6.04%
Dubuque	36	8	Oval	58	5.01%
Story	34	9	Star-like	49	4.23%
Unknown	29	10	Disc	28	2.42%

UFO SHAPES: IOWA

UFO Shapes	**2001**	**2002**	**2003**	**2004**	**2005**	**2006**	**2007**	**2008**	**2009**	**2010**	**2011**	**2012**	**2013**	**2014**	**2015**	**Total**
Blimp							1	1			2	1	1	1		7
Boomerang	1				1			1	1		1		3	1		9
Bullet/Missile									2	3	2	1	1			9
Changing		2	3	2	1		2		1	2		3	3			19
Chevron	1			1	2		4	1			2	1		3		15
Cigar			2		2	2	1			1	1	6	2	4		21
Circle	2	1	1		3	2	6	3	8	8	19	25	24	11	6	119
Cone		2								1	2	3		1	1	10
Cylinder						1		2	1	1	1	5	1	6	2	20
Diamond							1		1	3		5	2	1	3	16
Disc	3	1	3				2	4	1	2	3	3		2	4	28
Disk	1	2	1	2	4	1		2		3	1	3		5	2	27
Egg							1			1	2	3		1		8
Fireball	2		1	3	7		1	5	4	5	5	15	7	9	7	71
Flash						1	1	1	4	2		3	2		1	15
Formation	1	1	4		1		2		1		2	4	5	1	2	24
Light	8	8	5	9	9	11	12	8	12	14	12	25	25	10	11	179
N/A														1	1	2
Other	3	2	2	1	2	1	8	5	7	5	7	7	6	6	8	70
Oval	2	3	5	3		3	2	5	3	4	3	6	9	5	5	58
Rectangle	2			1	1	1			1			1				7
Saturn-like								1			1					2
Sphere	3	1	2		3		3	4	10	8	7	19	10	16	15	101
Sq/Rect															1	1
Star-like			4			1		7	5	7	5	7	5	3	5	49
Teardrop		1	2	1		1		2	2			1	2			12
Triangle	9	2	6	11	14	5	9	10	5	4	15	16	18	8	12	144
Unknown	3	4	5	8	4	3	13	12	9	7	8	15	8	8	8	115
Total	**41**	**30**	**46**	**42**	**54**	**33**	**69**	**74**	**78**	**81**	**101**	**178**	**134**	**103**	**94**	**1158**

UFOS BY COUNTY: IOWA

Counties	2001	2002	2003	2004	2005	2006	2007	2008	2009	2010	2011	2012	2013	2014	2015	Total
Adair						1	1									2
Adams												1				1
Allamakee						1	1			1	1					4
Appanoose			1							1		1			3	6
Audubon										2					1	3
Benton		1		1			1			1		6				10
Black Hawk			3	2	3	4	5	2	3	3	9	9	9	5	7	64
Boone	2				1			1		1			2	1		8
Bremer														2	2	4
Buchanan												3				3
Buena Vista											1	1				2
Butler													2	1		3
Calhoun	2			1			1					1	1			6
Carroll	1		1	1	3		5	1	1			1	2		4	20
Cass	3						1	1								5
Cedar														2	2	4
Cerro Gordo		1			3				3		2	4	2	2		17
Cherokee											1					1
Chickasaw								1							1	2
Clarke					3				1							4
Clay					1		3	2	2	1	1		1		1	12
Clayton	1			1	1											3
Clinton					1		1	2	1			3	3	1		12
Crawford				1		2			1							4
Dubuque													1			1
Dallas			1		3				3	4	5	3	2	2	1	24
Davis			1									1				2
Decatur							1		1	2		1	1			6
Delaware			1												1	2
Des Moines							3	2		1		4		2	1	13
Dickinson	2					1			2	1		1		1		8
Douglas	1			1				1			1					4
Dubuque		1	2		1		1	1	4	5	3	5	3	6	4	36
Emmet				2								1			1	4
Fayette					1				1		1	1	1	1		6

Counties	2001	2002	2003	2004	2005	2006	2007	2008	2009	2010	2011	2012	2013	2014	2015	Total
Floyd						1					1		1	2	2	7
Fremont											1				1	2
Greene											1	1		1		3
Grundy				1				1				2	3	1		8
Hamilton			2			1			1			1	1			6
Hancock						1	1	1			1				1	5
Hardin								1	1				1		1	4
Harrison	1			1					1				1			4
Henry										1		1				2
Howard	1	1											2			4
Humboldt												1	1			2
Ida		1			1						1					3
Iowa											1				1	2
Jackson			1			1								1		3
Jasper						2		1	1	3	1	1			1	10
Jefferson			5				2		3	2	4		1	1		18
Johnson	1	3	2	1	3	2		6		3	6	8	7	6	3	51
Jones		1					1			1		1			1	5
Keokuk														1		1
Kossuth				1		1		1	1							4
Lee				1	1		3		1	2		1		1	2	12
Linn	1	7	4	2	2		6	3	5	10	9	20	17	15	8	109
Louisa				1									1			2
Lucas														1		1
Lyon								1							1	2
Madison	1	5		2		1				1		2	1			13
Mahaska		1			1		1	1			1			2	1	8
Marion			1				2				1	1	1	1	2	9
Marshall			1		1		1	1				2		1		7
Mills			1	1												2
Monona	1		2					1								4
Monroe				1			1					2				4
Montgomery								1				2	1			4
Muscatine	2			1	1	1	1		2		5	3	3	1	3	23
Obrien				1	2	1							1	1	1	7
Osceola													2			2

Counties	**2001**	**2002**	**2003**	**2004**	**2005**	**2006**	**2007**	**2008**	**2009**	**2010**	**2011**	**2012**	**2013**	**2014**	**2015**	**Total**
Page							1		2	2		1	1			7
Palo Alto									2		1		1			4
Plymouth								1		1	1	1				4
Pocahontas		1			1					1		1		2		6
Polk	8	3	10	7	5	4	8	22	8	8	18	38	20	21	12	192
Pottawattamie			3		2		3	2	2	5	1	7	6	2	4	37
Poweshiek													2			2
Ringgold		1														1
Sac					1											1
Scott	1	1	1	1	1	3	4	1	3	4	4	11	8	2	3	48
Shelby											1		1			2
Sioux	1		1	1							2					5
Story	6	1		2			4	2	2		4	7	2	2	2	34
Tama								1			1	2	1		1	6
Taylor									1			1		1		3
Union													2			2
Unknown	1				1	1	3	7	1	3	2	5	1	2	2	29
Van Buren										2						2
Wapello	1			1	3	1	1		6		2	2	1			18
Warren	1	1		1	1				2			1		1	1	9
Washington					1				2	4	2		2	2		13
Wayne															1	1
Webster					2	2		1	4		1	2	4	1	1	18
Winnebago	1				1								1			3
Winneshiek									1	1		2	2	2		8
Woodbury	1		2	4	2	1	2	4	3	4	3	1	3	3	8	41
Worth				1												1
Total	**41**	**30**	**46**	**42**	**54**	**33**	**69**	**74**	**78**	**81**	**101**	**178**	**134**	**103**	**94**	**1158**

If a county is missing from the list, it's because no UFO sightings were logged in either the NUFORC or MUFON databases for the 2001-2015 sample period.

UFOS BY MONTH: IOWA

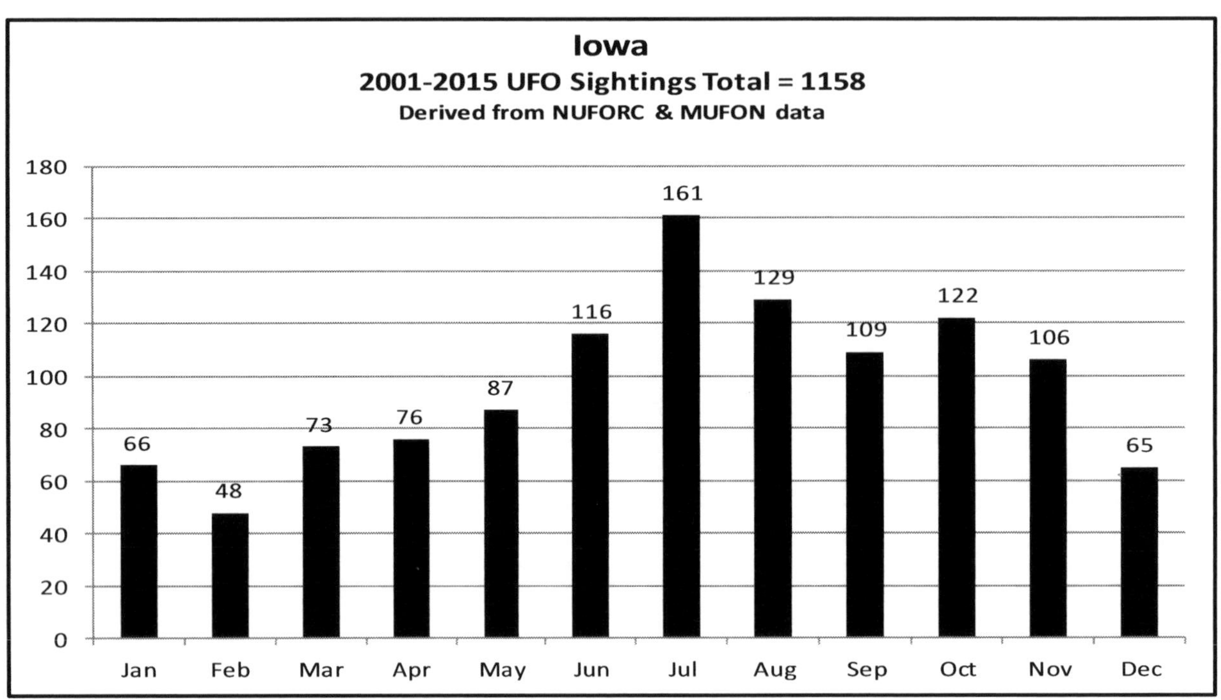

Year	Jan	Feb	Mar	Apr	May	Jun	Jul	Aug	Sep	Oct	Nov	Dec	Total
2001	7	1	1	2	4	3	4	4	3	7		5	41
2002	5	2	4	1		1	2	2	3	3	6	1	30
2003	2	1		5	6	3	6	4	2	10	5	2	46
2004	4	6	2	5	2	7	1	4	3	3	2	3	42
2005		3	5	5	2	6	7	2	10	8	2	4	54
2006		5	1	1	5	2	4	4	3	2	3	3	33
2007	8	6	6	2	3	9	10	5	9	6	3	2	69
2008	9	7	5	4	3	1	9	11	4	8	6	7	74
2009	4	3	7	4	4	3	13	9	12	5	14		78
2010	5	3	2	7	9	8	15	7	8	12	4	1	81
2011	3	1	8	7	11	5	18	12	11	12	6	7	101
2012	5	4	11	13	15	31	20	18	11	14	18	18	178
2013	8	2	7	5	10	21	20	24	8	12	14	3	134
2014	4	3	8	9	9	9	11	11	8	15	11	5	103
2015	2	1	6	6	4	7	21	12	14	5	12	4	94
Total	**66**	**48**	**73**	**76**	**87**	**116**	**161**	**129**	**109**	**122**	**106**	**65**	**1158**

Distribution of Sightings between Databases: Iowa

Database	Count	Percentage
MUFON	447	38.60%
NUFORC	711	61.40%
Total	1158	100.00%

State Demographic Information: Iowa

2010 US Census Statistics	
Population	3,046,355.00
Area in Square Miles	56,272.81
Land Area Sq. Miles	55,587.13
Population/Square mile	54.50

KANSAS

UFO RANK 34/51

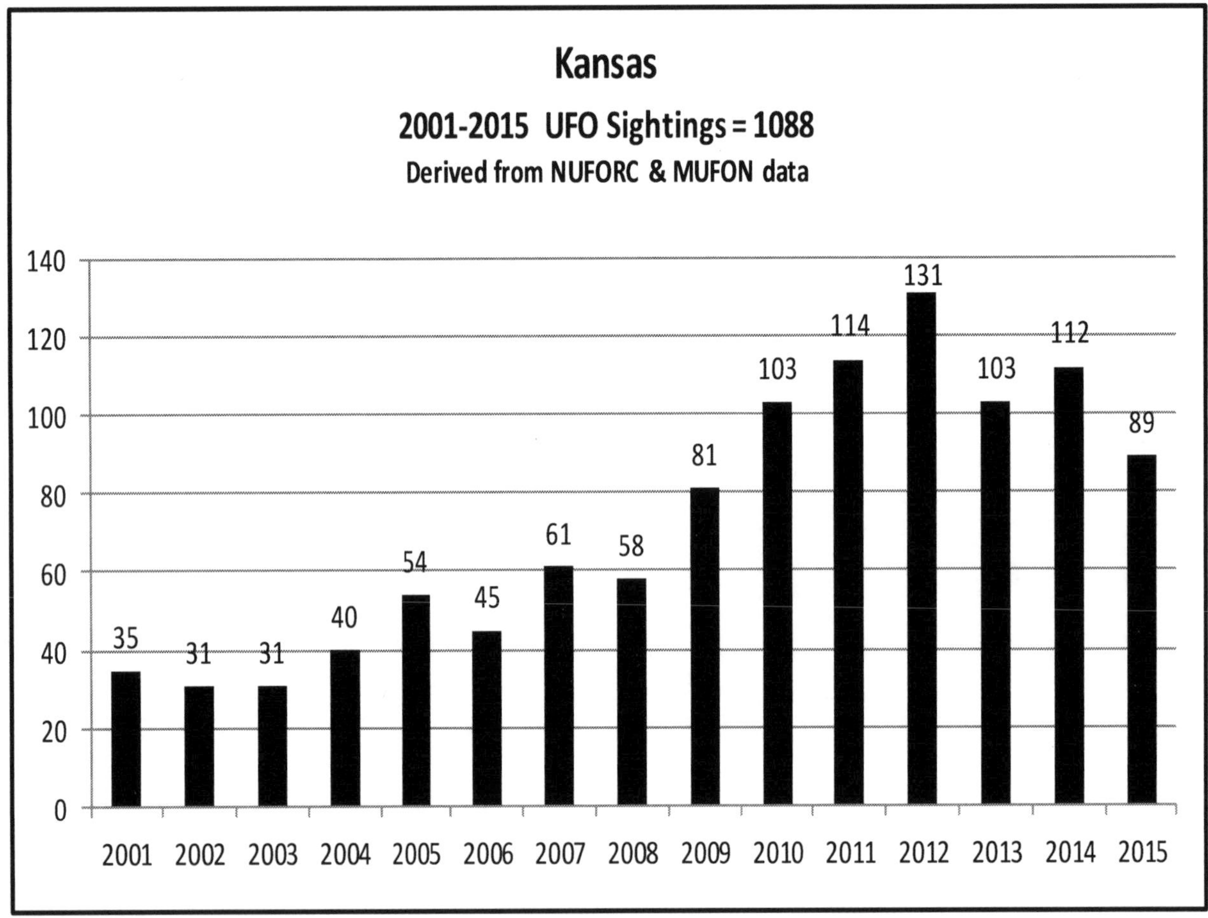

TOP TEN COUNTIES		RANK
Johnson	236	1
Sedgwick	146	2
Wyandotte	64	3
Douglas	61	4
Shawnee	60	5
Unknown	27	6
Leavenworth	32	7
Reno	26	8
Butler	24	9
Saline	60	10

TOP TEN SHAPES		
Light	143	13.14%
Sphere	126	11.58%
Unknown	115	10.57%
Triangle	114	10.48%
Circle	100	9.19%
Other	86	7.90%
Fireball	73	6.71%
Star-like	52	4.78%
Disc	43	3.95%
Oval	38	3.49%

UFO SHAPES: KANSAS

UFO Shapes	2001	2002	2003	2004	2005	2006	2007	2008	2009	2010	2011	2012	2013	2014	2015	Total
Blimp						1					3					4
Boomerang							1	1	1	2	5	5		2	1	18
Bullet/Missile								2							1	3
Changing			2			1	1	1	1			2		1	2	11
Chevron				1					1	1						3
Cigar	1	2	1	1	1			2	4	5	2	3	4	3	2	31
Circle	4	2	1	1	5	2	6	6	10	13	10	16	11	7	6	100
Cone					3								2			5
Cross		1	1	1	1						2	2	3			11
Cylinder	1			1	1	1	1	3	4	1	2	4	2	3	1	25
Diamond						1	1		1	2	1	1		3	1	11
Disc	2		3	4	1		4	4	1	5	6	3	3	3	4	43
Egg	1				1		1	1	2	2	1	1				10
Fireball	3			2	4		3	2	6	9	8	13	11	7	5	73
Flash	1	2	2					5	4	2	1	2	1	1	2	23
Formation	4	1	1	1	1		1	1	1		2	3	1	2	1	20
Light	6	4	2	9	13	9	9	6	12	7	13	14	11	18	10	143
N/A				2									1	2		5
Other	4	3	2	5	3	7	4	3	6	5	8	14	7	7	8	86
Oval		1		2		1	2	1	3	8	4	5	3	2	6	38
Rectangle					2					1			2	2		7
Saturn-like								1								1
Sphere	1	3	3	2	2	2	5	6	9	14	14	15	20	18	12	126
Sq/Rect													1			1
Star-like	1		1		1	1	1	2	4	8	3	11	2	9	8	52
Teardrop		1				1			2	2	2			1		9
Triangle	3	9	5	5	2	9	13	5	5	7	14	7	9	9	12	114
Unknown	3	2	7	3	13	9	8	6	4	9	13	10	9	12	7	115
Total	**35**	**31**	**31**	**40**	**54**	**45**	**61**	**58**	**81**	**103**	**114**	**131**	**103**	**112**	**89**	**1088**

UFOS BY COUNTY: KANSAS

Counties	2001	2002	2003	2004	2005	2006	2007	2008	2009	2010	2011	2012	2013	2014	2015	Total
Allen			1						1	1			1			4
Barber											1					1
Barton			2		3	2	1	1		1	1				1	12
Bourbon							1								1	2
Brown			1						1				1			3
Butler	1	1				1	4		4	1	4	3	1	1	3	24
Chase															1	1
Chautauqua														1		1
Cherokee								2	1		1		1			5
Cheyenne				1												1
Clay		1												1	2	4
Cloud			1							2		1			2	6
Coffey	1		1		2											4
Cowley	1	1		1		1			1	2				1	3	11
Crawford				1			1				1		3	1	3	10
Dickinson			1								1				1	3
Douglas	5	4	2	9	3	1	2	1	5	5	8	2	4	2	8	61
Elk							1						1			2
Ellis						1	1		1	1		1		3		8
Ellsworth															1	1
Finney	2				2		1		1			1				7
Ford							1		1	1	1	3	1			8
Franklin	1				1		1		2		5		1	1	1	13
Geary		1					1			1	2	4	1	1		11
Gove				1								1	1			3
Graham							2		2						1	5
Grant						1			3							4
Gray							2								1	3
Greeley														1		1
Greenwood		1		1			1	2						1	2	8
Hamilton												1				1
Harper						2			1				1			4
Harvey				1		1					1			2		5
Hodgeman									1					2		3
Jackson		1				1										2
Jefferson	1									1		1	1		1	5

Counties	2001	2002	2003	2004	2005	2006	2007	2008	2009	2010	2011	2012	2013	2014	2015	Total
Jewell									2	1					1	4
Johnson	8	3	2	3	13	9	11	12	20	24	25	47	24	25	10	236
Kearny				1							1				2	4
Kingman	1				1	2		2						1	1	8
Labette					3			1		1		1	1			7
Leavenworth		2					1		4	6	2	8	5	3	1	32
Lincoln											1		1			2
Linn			1							1		1				3
Logan									2			1				3
Lyon	1			1	1						3	1		4		11
Marion		1													2	3
Marshall			1					1							2	4
McPherson		1		2		1	1		1		1	2	1	1	4	15
Miami	1			1		1	1		1	1			2	1		9
Mississippi															1	1
Mitchell	1								1							2
Montgomery	2		4					1		1		2	4	1	1	16
Morgan					1											1
Nemaha							1					2	1			4
Neosho		1		1	1	1		1	1	1						7
Nevada					1											1
Osage							1		1	4			1	1		8
Ottawa				1				1			3		1			6
Pawnee					1				1							2
Phillips								2			1		1	1		5
Pottawatomie								1				1				2
Pratt			1	3		1	1	1		2		1	3			13
Rawlins												1				1
Reno		1	1			5	2		2	2	3		1	4	5	26
Rice						1							1			2
Riley		1		1	2	1	1	2	2	1	2	1	1	2	1	18
Rooks						1	1									2
Rush					1											1
Russell					2				1				1	2		6
Saline	1		1	1	1		1	3	1	1	1	6	1	3	1	22
Scott						1								1		2

Counties	2001	2002	2003	2004	2005	2006	2007	2008	2009	2010	2011	2012	2013	2014	2015	Total
Sebastian	1			1		1					3			3		9
Sedgwick	5	4	7	4	5	3	6	12	7	17	14	13	19	17	13	146
Seward									1			2				3
Shawnee		4	1	4	2	3	3	5	2	11	7	4	2	11	1	60
Sheridan												1				1
Sherman	1				1	1				1		2		1		7
Smith													1			1
Stafford														1		1
Stevens														1		1
Sumner							1			1	2	1		1		6
Thomas					1		1			1	1	2		2	1	9
Trego						1										1
Unknown		2	2	1	1		2	4	2	4	5	3	6	1	4	37
Washington											1					1
Wilson														3		3
Woodson									1					1		2
Wyandotte	1	1	1		5	1	6	3	3	6	12	10	7	2	6	64
Total	**35**	**31**	**31**	**40**	**54**	**45**	**61**	**58**	**81**	**103**	**114**	**131**	**103**	**112**	**89**	**1088**

If a county is missing from the list, it's because no UFO sightings were logged in either the NUFORC or MUFON databases for the 2001-2015 sample period.

UFOS BY MONTH: KANSAS

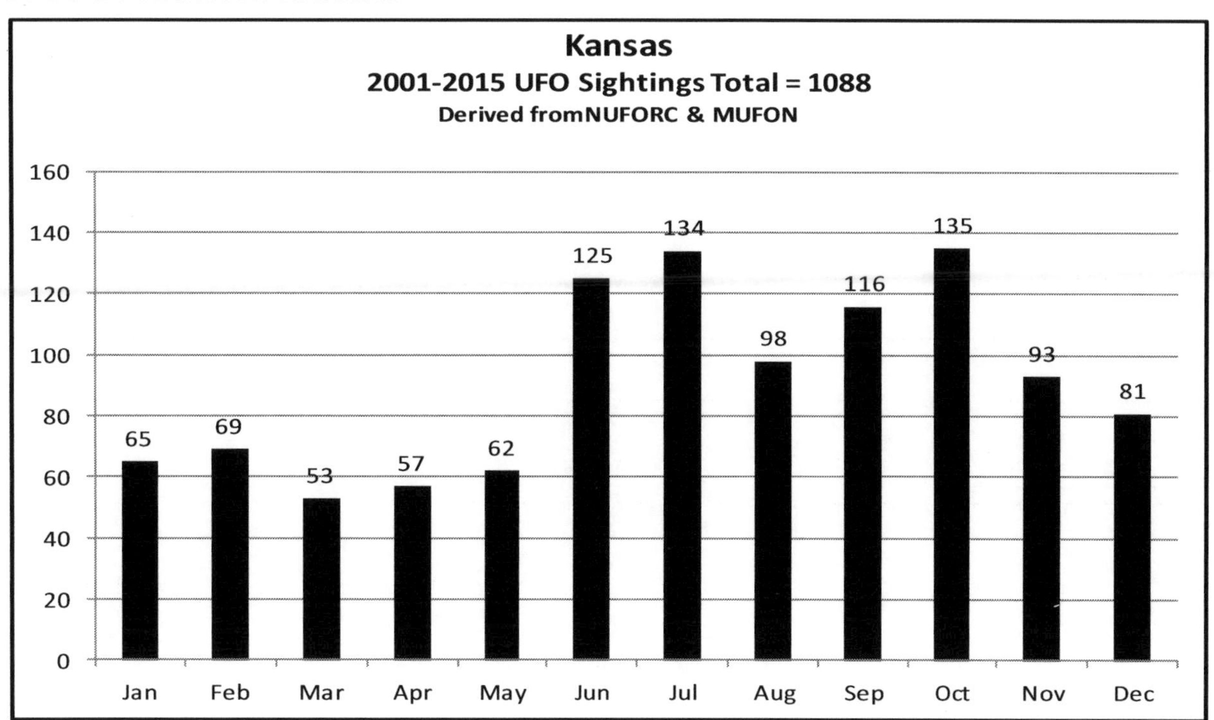

Year	Jan	Feb	Mar	Apr	May	Jun	Jul	Aug	Sep	Oct	Nov	Dec	Total
2001	4	2	2	2	1	2	2	3	3	2	2	10	35
2002		2	1	1	2	3	5	3	6	2	6		31
2003	1	2	3	2	3	2	3	3	4	5	1	2	31
2004	3	3	3	1	2	3	4	4	3	7	2	5	40
2005	1	3	6	4	1	9	5	1	3	8	8	5	54
2006	2	9	3	3	1	5	5	1	2	7	3	4	45
2007	4	4	5	1	6	7	4	3	5	13	5	4	61
2008	3	5	3	4	3	9	3	2	3	10	7	6	58
2009	2	7	1	4	2	12	13	11	7	9	6	7	81
2010	6	10	2	2	1	7	21	14	8	14	13	5	103
2011	7	3	3	9	13	9	11	12	17	19	2	9	114
2012	8	11	8	9	9	17	14	14	14	10	12	5	131
2013	9	3	3	5	6	20	14	8	9	6	9	11	103
2014	11		5	6	7	14	15	13	15	15	9	2	112
2015	4	5	5	4	5	6	15	6	17	8	8	6	89
Total	**65**	**69**	**53**	**57**	**62**	**125**	**134**	**98**	**116**	**135**	**93**	**81**	**1088**

State Demographic Information: Kansas

Database	Count	Percentage
MUFON	460	42.28%
NUFORC	628	57.72%
Total	1088	100.00%

Distribution of Sightings between Databases: Kansas

2010 US Census Statistics	
Population	2,853,118.00
Area in Square Miles	82,278.36
Land Area Sq. Miles	81,758.72
Population/Square mile	34.90

KENTUCKY

UFO RANK 25/51

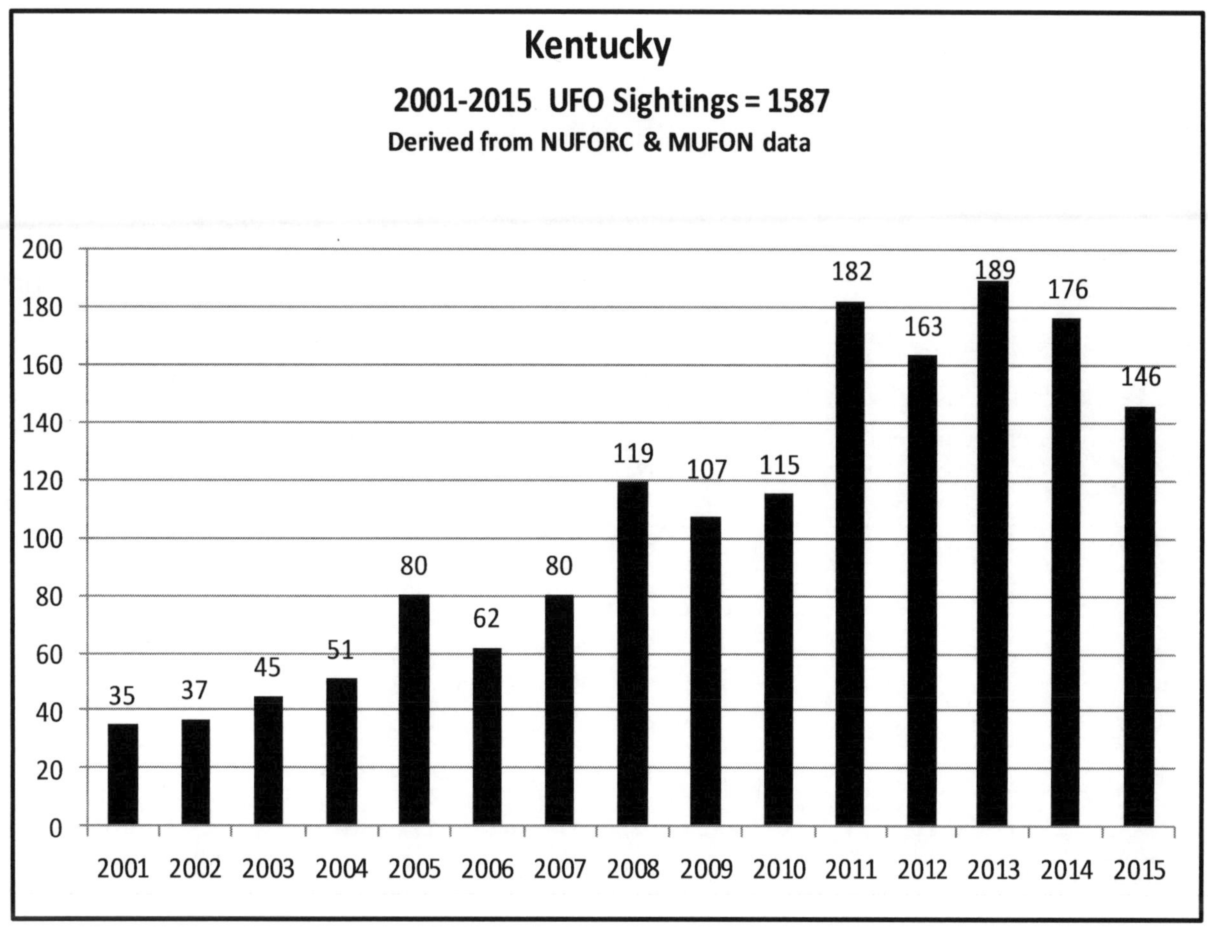

TOP TEN COUNTIES		RANK	TOP TEN SHAPES		
Jefferson	218	1	Circle	187	11.78%
Fayette	108	2	Light	173	10.90%
Boone	58	3	Unknown	170	10.71%
Warren	57	4	Sphere	163	10.27%
Hardin	47	5	Triangle	151	9.51%
Madison	46	6	Fireball	107	6.74%
Kenton	45	7	Other	97	6.11%
Pike	34	8	Star-like	65	4.10%
Campbell	32	9	Cigar	54	3.40%
Unknown	32	10	Disc	52	3.28%

UFO SHAPES: KENTUCKY

UFO SHAPES	2001	2002	2003	2004	2005	2006	2007	2008	2009	2010	2011	2012	2013	2014	2015	Total
Blimp					1				3	1	1	1	3			10
Boomerang				1			1	3		1		4	4	3	1	18
Bullet/Missile			1			1		2	1	2	3	2	1			13
Changing	1	1	3	1	5	6	2	1	4	2	3		1	2		32
Chevron		2			2			1	1	4	3		2	1	3	19
Cigar			1	1	3	5		4	2	1	12	7	11	2	5	54
Circle		2	3	4	6	3	5	10	11	14	31	18	36	28	16	187
Cone				1			1		2	2		1		1		8
Cross			1				1	1	1						2	6
Cylinder		2		1	1	1	2	1	2	4	4	9	4	5	5	41
Diamond	2			5	1	2	1	4		3	3	2	2	3		28
Disc		1		1	4		3	6	4	3	4	4	7	6	9	52
Disk	1	4	2	5	3	7	5	4	4	1	1	4	1	3	2	47
Egg	1	1	1		1				2	2	2	2	1		1	14
Fireball	3		6	1	1	4	2	5	4	9	11	17	20	17	7	107
Flash	1	1					1	2	2	3	2	2	6	2	2	24
Formation		1	1					2				4	1	2	2	13
Light	4	3	8	10	13	8	16	17	14	14	12	11	19	14	10	173
N/A											1			1	1	3
Other	6	4	3	4	4	3	3	9	10	6	7	7	13	10	8	97
Oval	5		2	4	2	3	4	2	6	2	6	5	3	2	6	52
Rectangle	1	1			3	2	1	1	1	1		2	2	3	1	19
Saturn-like								2		1	1				1	5
Sphere	1	1	4	2	3	5	8	6	9	9	21	20	17	22	35	163
Sq/Rect														2	1	3
Star-like					1	1	2	5	5	4	13	14	7	10	3	65
Teardrop					1	1	2				1	1	1	3	3	13
Triangle	7	3	1	4	10	3	13	11	12	10	20	13	15	16	13	151
Unknown	2	10	8	6	15	7	7	20	7	16	20	13	12	18	9	170
Total	**35**	**37**	**45**	**51**	**80**	**62**	**80**	**119**	**107**	**115**	**182**	**163**	**189**	**176**	**146**	**1587**

UFOS BY COUNTY: KENTUCKY

Counties	2001	2002	2003	2004	2005	2006	2007	2008	2009	2010	2011	2012	2013	2014	2015	Total
Adair	1						1		1	1	3			1	1	9
Allen		1		1								2	1	1		6
Anderson							2	1		1	1	1		1		7
Ballard					1	1					1					3
Barren	1								1	1		1		2		6
Bath				1				1				1	1	1	1	6
Bell				1	2	1		1			3	1	1	1		11
Boone	1	1	2	2		1	2	2		3	9	7	12	10	6	58
Bourbon	1	1						1		2		1	1			7
Boyd	1		2	1		1		3	2		11	3	3	3	1	31
Boyle	1			1				3		1		1		4	1	12
Bracken											2		1		1	4
Breathitt			1	1						1	4			1		8
Breckinridge											2		1	1		4
Bullitt		1		2	2		1	3	2	2	2	1		1	5	22
Butler									1							1
Caldwell														1		1
Calloway			3	1	3	2		1	1		2	2	3		2	20
Campbell						2	2		3	1	1	4	8	5	6	32
Carroll							1					2	3			6
Carter					2	1			2		4		3			12
Casey						1				1	1		1		1	5
Christian	1	1	2	1	3		2	1	3	2			2			18
Clark							1	1	2	1	1	2	1	2	3	14
Clay								1			1		1			3
Clinton					1						1					2
Cumberland									1	2	1				2	6
Daviess				2	1	2	1	2	2	2	4	4	3	4	2	29
Edmonson		1									1					2
Elliott			1						1				1			3
Estill												1		2		3
Fayette	4	2	1	4	8	3	3	7	9	8	16	8	15	13	7	108
Fleming			1		3	1	6	2			1	2			1	17
Floyd		1				1			2	1		1	2	2	1	11
Franklin	2			1			3			1	3		3	9	1	23
Fulton												2			1	3
Gallatin									1				1		2	4

Counties	2001	2002	2003	2004	2005	2006	2007	2008	2009	2010	2011	2012	2013	2014	2015	Total
Garrard						2		1		2	3	3	1			12
Grant		1		1		1				2		1		3	6	15
Graves								2		1	1	3	3	4		14
Grayson									1	1	1		3	2	3	11
Green					1						1					2
Greenup			2		3	3	3	1	1	1	1	1		2	2	20
Hamilton				1	2		1		1	1		1				7
Hancock			1													1
Hardin	2		2	1	4	3	2	6	4		6	8	3	4	2	47
Harlan					2				2		1	2	1	2		10
Harrison								1								1
Hart											1				1	2
Henderson	1	1			1	1	2		1		1		2		4	14
Henry			1		1			1			1					4
Hopkins			2	1	2		2	1	1	2		1	1	3	1	17
Jackson		1										1				2
Jefferson	6	9	1	7	10	5	9	17	15	21	19	23	20	30	26	218
Jessamine				1	1			1		1		2	1	1	1	9
Johnson		3				1		1				2	2	2		11
Kenton		2	1	2	3	2	1	3	10	5	2	5	9	7	2	53
Knott		1				1			2		2	1				7
Knox		1	1				1			2	1	1	1			8
Larue			1										1		1	3
Laurel			1	1			1	2	2	3	2		1		1	14
Lawrence		1	1			4			2	1	1	2	2		1	15
Lee															1	1
Leslie						1	2			1	1	1		3		9
Letcher				1	2		1							2	2	8
Lewis	2	1													1	4
Lincoln					1	1	1	2		1	1		3	1		11
Livingston			1		2	2					3			1	1	10
Logan	1						1						2		1	5
Lyon								3	1	2	1		1			8
Madison	2	1	1				1	3	2	2	12	8	5	2	7	46
Magoffin							1						1	1		3
Marion		1			1			1			1		1	1		6
Marshall				1		1	1	1	2	1		3	2	1	2	15
Martin										1		1				2

Counties	2001	2002	2003	2004	2005	2006	2007	2008	2009	2010	2011	2012	2013	2014	2015	Total
Mason		1					2								1	4
McCracken		1	2		2	2		5	3	4	1	4	3	1	1	29
McCreary				1				1	1				1			4
Mclean					1											1
Meade									1	2	1				1	5
Menifee							1	1		1			1			4
Mercer			1	1		1	1		1		6				2	13
Metcalfe					1		1			1		1				4
Monroe						1	2									3
Montgomery				1		1	1	2				1		1	3	10
Morgan		1								1			2			4
Muhlenberg			1				1		1			2	1		1	7
Nelson			2	3	1		1			2	3	1	2	2		17
Ohio				1	1	1						1				4
Oldham						1	1	2		1	1	2	1	1		10
Owen															1	1
Owsley														2		2
Pendleton								1	1				8	1		11
Perry		1				1	1	1		2	3	2	1			12
Pike			1		2	2		2	1	3	3	6	4	9	1	34
Powell	1		1						1		1		1		2	7
Pulaski					1			1		3	2	1	1	4	1	14
Rockcastle							1									1
Rowan			2	1	2		3	4			3	5	1	1		22
Russell	1							2		1	2	5	1		1	13
Saint Louis					1											1
Scott					1				3	1	3	3	5	4	3	23
Shelby			1			1	1			1		1	4	1	1	11
Simpson							1		4		1					6
Spencer						2	1				1			1	3	8
Taylor						1		1	1		3	2	1	1		10
Todd										1	1					2
Trigg	1			1						1		1	2	1		7
Trimble				1							1				1	3
Union					1											1
Unknown					1		2	11	1	1	2	2	2	3	7	32
Warren	5	1	3	5	1	3	3	6	4	4	4	4	8	2	4	57
Wayne					1	1			1	1				2		6

Counties	**2001**	**2002**	**2003**	**2004**	**2005**	**2006**	**2007**	**2008**	**2009**	**2010**	**2011**	**2012**	**2013**	**2014**	**2015**	**Total**
Webster										1			1			2
Whitley			2					1	1	1	1	2	2	2	1	13
Wolfe					1				1		1					3
Woodford							1	1					2			4
Total	**35**	**37**	**45**	**51**	**80**	**62**	**80**	**119**	**107**	**115**	**182**	**163**	**189**	**176**	**146**	**1587**

If a county is missing from the list, it's because no UFO sightings were logged in either the NUFORC or MUFON databases for the 2001-2015 sample period.

UFOS BY MONTH: KENTUCKY

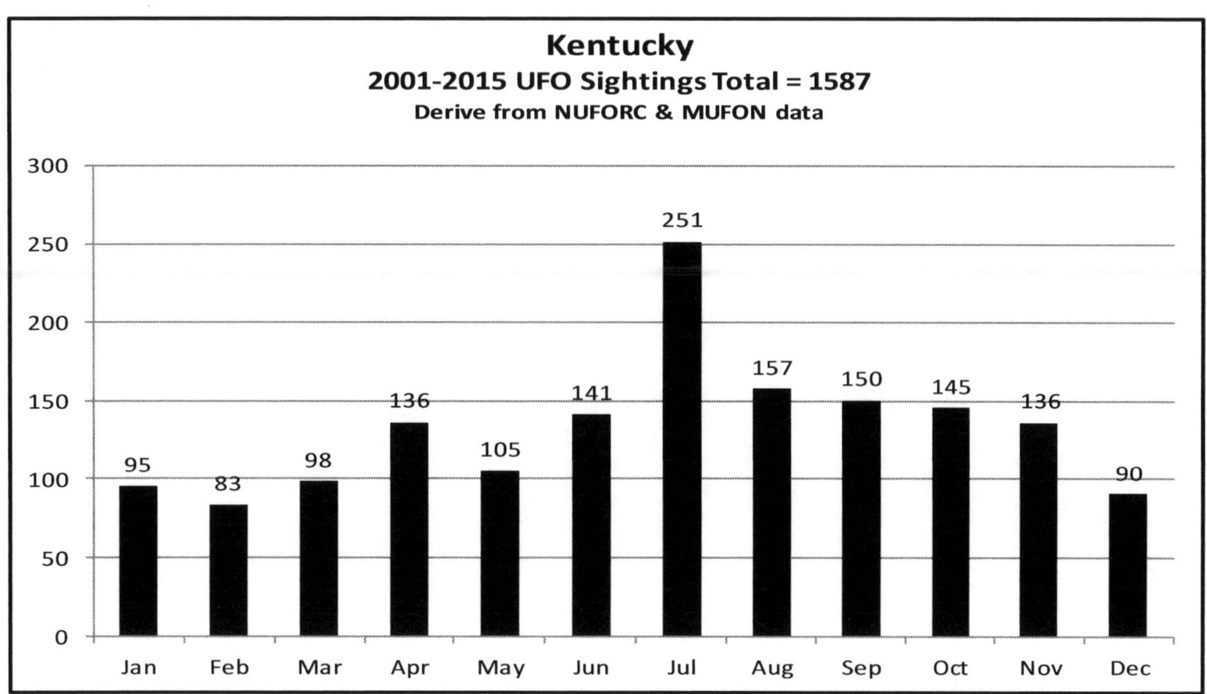

Year	Jan	Feb	Mar	Apr	May	Jun	Jul	Aug	Sep	Oct	Nov	Dec	Total
2001		6	2	1	5	1	1	6	3	5	5		35
2002	7	2	1	3	5	2	4	7	3		2	1	37
2003	2	3	1	4	5	3	3	4	5	3	7	5	45
2004	1	6	7	3	2	4	6	4	5	5	4	4	51
2005	4	4	7	4	5	7	6	9	9	11	8	6	80
2006	1	5	4	4	4	3	7	9	7	1	8	9	62
2007	6	4	6	5	4	13	6	12	6	6	8	4	80
2008	9	1	10	12	3	6	15	13	17	13	10	10	119
2009	11	12	8	8	4	15	16	6	7	6	11	3	107
2010	7		5	6	7	11	24	5	20	15	8	7	115
2011	11	10	7	13	9	16	39	27	11	20	10	9	182
2012	12	11	13	15	16	15	27	10	8	14	13	9	163
2013	7	8	8	21	11	19	34	15	27	18	11	10	189
2014	13	4	11	21	13	12	41	19	15	10	12	5	176
2015	4	7	8	16	12	14	22	11	7	18	19	8	146
Total	**95**	**83**	**98**	**136**	**105**	**141**	**251**	**157**	**150**	**145**	**136**	**90**	**1587**

Distribution of Sightings between Databases: Kentucky

Database	Count	Percentage
MUFON	699	44.04%
NUFORC	888	55.96%
Total	1587	100.00%

State Demographic Information: Kentucky

2010 US Census Statistics	
Population	4,339,367.00
Area in Square Miles	40,407.80
Land Area Sq. Miles	39,486.34
Population/Square mile	109.90

LOUISIANA

UFO RANK 33/51

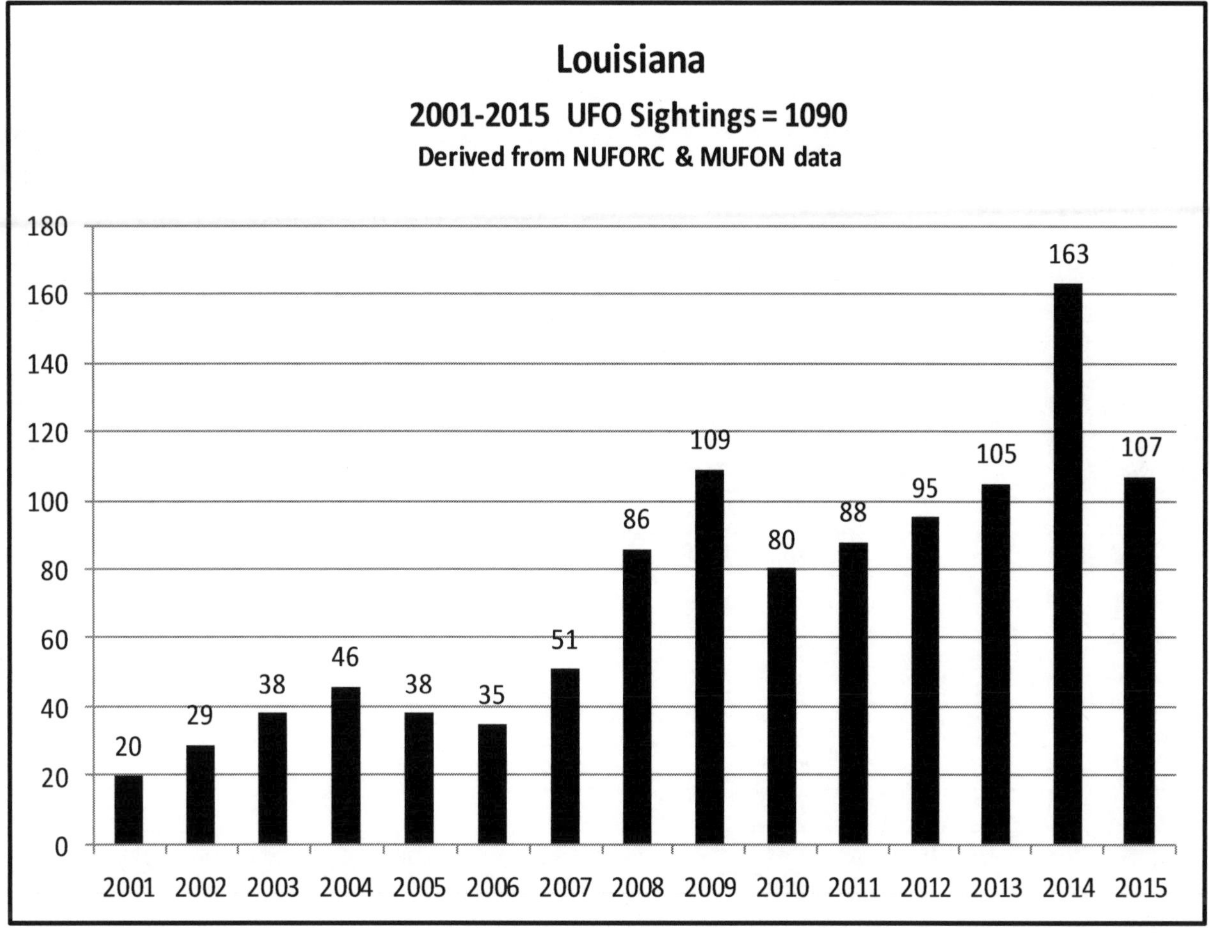

TOP TEN PARISHES		RANK	TOP TEN SHAPES		
East Baton Rouge	88	**1**	Light	142	13.03%
Saint Tammany	83	**2**	Unknown	126	11.56%
Orleans	82	**3**	Triangle	125	11.47%
Calcasieu	81	**4**	Circle	118	10.83%
Jefferson	70	**5**	Sphere	111	10.18%
Unknown	61	**6**	Fireball	73	6.70%
Caddo	54	**7**	Other	58	5.32%
Livingston	47	**8**	Oval	48	4.40%
Lafayette	45	**9**	Star-like	42	3.85%
Bossier	43	**10**	Cigar	31	2.84%

UFO SHAPES: LOUISIANA

UFO Shapes	2001	2002	2003	2004	2005	2006	2007	2008	2009	2010	2011	2012	2013	2014	2015	Total
Blimp							3	1				1	1	1		7
Boomerang			1			1	1		2	1	2	1	3	1		13
Bullet/Missile										5	3	2				10
Changing				1	3		1	1	1			2	2	1	1	13
Chevron			1					1	1	1				1		5
Cigar	3	1	1	1	1		6	2	2	2		3	1	4	4	31
Circle		2	1	5	2	6	2	10	10	10	9	14	16	18	13	118
Cone		1											1	1	1	4
Cross						1			1	1			1			4
Cylinder	2			2	1	1		3	3	3	4	1	1	1	1	23
Diamond							1	2	1	1	1	1	2	2		11
Disc		1				2	3	3	2	1	4	2	4	2	3	27
Disk			2	2	2	2		1	2	2		1	1	6	2	23
Egg								1		1					1	3
Fireball		1		4	4		4	8	8	7	8	6	9	9	5	73
Flash							1	3	1	2		2	5	3	1	18
Formation		1	1	3			2	2	1	1	1	3	2	3	4	24
Light	3	3	9	11	5	7	2	14	13	5	8	12	13	25	12	142
N/A														1	1	2
Other	1	1	3	1	2	3	1	6	3	3	2	3	7	11	11	58
Oval	1	3	2	3	1	2	3		4	5	1	5	4	9	5	48
Rectangle							2		1		1				1	5
Saturn-like										1			3	1		5
Sphere	1	5	6	4	5	1	2	7	16	4	7	9	14	21	9	111
Sq/Rect															2	2
Star-like		1				1	3	4	8	5	4	3	2	7	4	42
Teardrop		1	1	3			1		2	2	3		1	2	1	17
Triangle	8	4	5	4	6	4	3	5	12	11	12	12	7	19	13	125
Unknown	1	4	5	2	6	4	10	12	15	6	18	12	5	14	12	126
Total	**20**	**29**	**38**	**46**	**38**	**35**	**51**	**86**	**109**	**80**	**88**	**95**	**105**	**163**	**107**	**1090**

UFOS BY COUNTY: LOUISIANA

Parishes	2001	2002	2003	2004	2005	2006	2007	2008	2009	2010	2011	2012	2013	2014	2015	Total
Acadia			2	1				2	3	2	3			2	1	16
Allen									1							1
Ascension			1				2	3	7	1	2	3	4	4	1	28
Assumption			1		1		1	1							1	5
Avoyelles		3									1	2	5	1	1	13
Beauregard		1		2				1				1		3		8
Bienville										1		2				3
Bossier	2	5	1		3	1	2	3	4	1	3	3	7	5	3	43
Caddo	2	3	1	1	1	2	3	3	9	4	2	4	1	9	9	54
Calcasieu		2	7	1	7	2		16	17	3	3	5	4	8	6	81
Caldwell	1						1						1			3
Cameron						1	1		1					2		5
Claiborne								1					1			2
De Soto	1		1				1	1							1	5
East Baton Rouge	2	3	1	5		1	7	11	6	12	5	4	5	13	13	88
East Carroll							1									1
East Feliciana			2								1			3		6
Evangeline											1					1
Franklin											1					1
Grant		1	1									2				4
Iberia			1		1	2	1	2				2		1		10
Iberville					1						1				1	3
Jackson						1						2				3
Jefferson			1	5	5		3	4	7	5	4	5	9	11	11	70
Jefferson Davis								2	6	3						11
La Salle	1														1	2
Lafayette		1	1	1	1	1	2	4	2	3	4	3	5	11	6	45
Lafourche			1	1	1	1	1		1		3	5	6	5	2	27
Landry													1			1
Lincoln	1								1	2	1	4	2	2	1	14
Livingston			1		2	3	3	4	2	6	4	5	2	11	4	47
Madison										1						1
Morehouse				1	1			1			2					5
Natchitoches	2	1	2			1					1					7
Orleans	3	3	1	7	4	2		6	3	4	6	9	12	12	10	82
Ouachita		1	1	3		1	2	5	6	4		2	1	4	3	33

Parishes	**2001**	**2002**	**2003**	**2004**	**2005**	**2006**	**2007**	**2008**	**2009**	**2010**	**2011**	**2012**	**2013**	**2014**	**2015**	**Total**
Plaquemines			2					1	2	1			1	2		9
Pointe Coupee						1		1								2
Rapides	1	1	1	5	2	1	2	3	3	3	4		3	1	11	41
Richland									1							1
Sabine		1		1	1								1	2	1	7
Saint Bernard			1	1		1	1			1	3					8
Saint Charles	1			1			4		2			2				10
Saint Helena														1		1
Saint James								1								1
Saint Landry			1			1			1	4		1	1	1		10
Saint Martin								1		1			2	3	1	8
Saint Mary			1	1		1		1	2	2				7	1	16
Saint Tammany	1	1	2	7	1	2	4	2	11	6	7	7	8	16	8	83
St John Baptist						1									1	2
Tangipahoa				1	1	1	2	1	2	2	4	4	4	1	3	26
Terrebonne						3			1	3	1	1	4	6	1	20
Union	1				2				1			1	2	2		9
Unknown		1	2			2	4	3	1	1	18	12	7	6	4	61
Vermilion			1		2					1		1	1	2		8
Vernon									3	2	1			1		7
Washington		1		1			1					3	1	3		10
Webster					1	1	1	1	3		1		1			9
West Baton Rouge	1					1					1					3
West Carroll													1	1		2
West Feliciana							1	1					2	1		5
Winn										1					1	2
Total	**20**	**29**	**38**	**46**	**38**	**35**	**51**	**86**	**109**	**80**	**88**	**95**	**105**	**163**	**107**	**1090**

If a county is missing from the list, it's because no UFO sightings were logged in either the NUFORC or MUFON databases for the 2001-2015 sample period.

UFOS BY MONTH: LOUISIANA

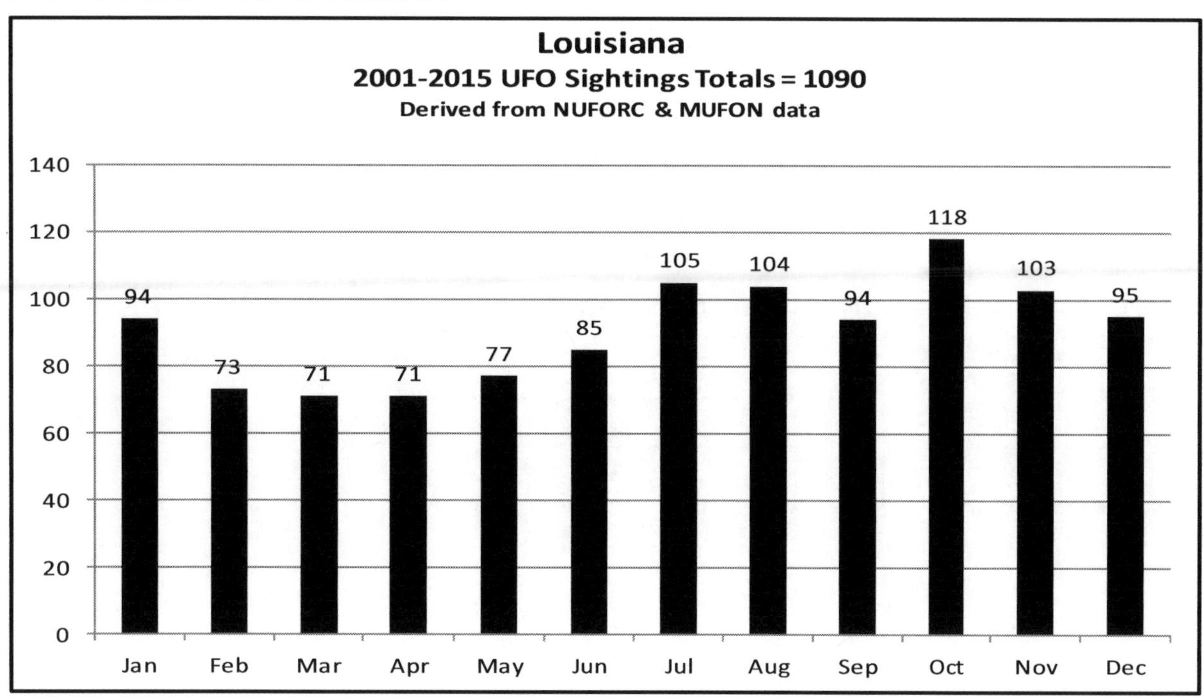

Year	Jan	Feb	Mar	Apr	May	Jun	Jul	Aug	Sep	Oct	Nov	Dec	Total
2001	1	3	1	1	1	1	1		2		5	4	20
2002	3	2	2	1	2	2	4	2		1	6	4	29
2003	4	2	1		3	3	1	4	7	5	5	3	38
2004	5	1	1	8	7	4	4	8	2		2	4	46
2005	1	3	2	2	4	3	3		4	8	4	4	38
2006	1	6	1	4	1	3	3	2	6	3	3	2	35
2007	2	3	7	1		8	5	4	3	9	5	4	51
2008	11	6	6	8	2	5	5	10	4	9	13	7	86
2009	16	12	2	9	8	15	4	15	4	4	5	15	109
2010	3	6	5	5	5	4	12	4	7	15	6	8	80
2011	8	5	11	2	5	7	6	8	9	8	8	11	88
2012	10	3	9	9	6	10	7	8	6	12	8	7	95
2013	4	8	4	7	7	6	13	10	12	14	11	9	105
2014	15	6	8	10	16	5	22	19	20	20	13	9	163
2015	10	7	11	4	10	9	15	10	8	10	9	4	107
Total	**94**	**73**	**71**	**71**	**77**	**85**	**105**	**104**	**94**	**118**	**103**	**95**	**1090**

Distribution of Sightings between Databases: Louisiana

Database	Count	Percentage
MUFON	469	43.03%
NUFORC	621	56.97%
Total	1090	100.00%

State Demographic Information: Louisiana

2010 US Census Statistics	
Population	4,533,372.00
Area in Square Miles	52,378.13
Land Area Sq. Miles	43,203.90
Population/Square mile	104.90

MAINE

UFO RANK 37/51

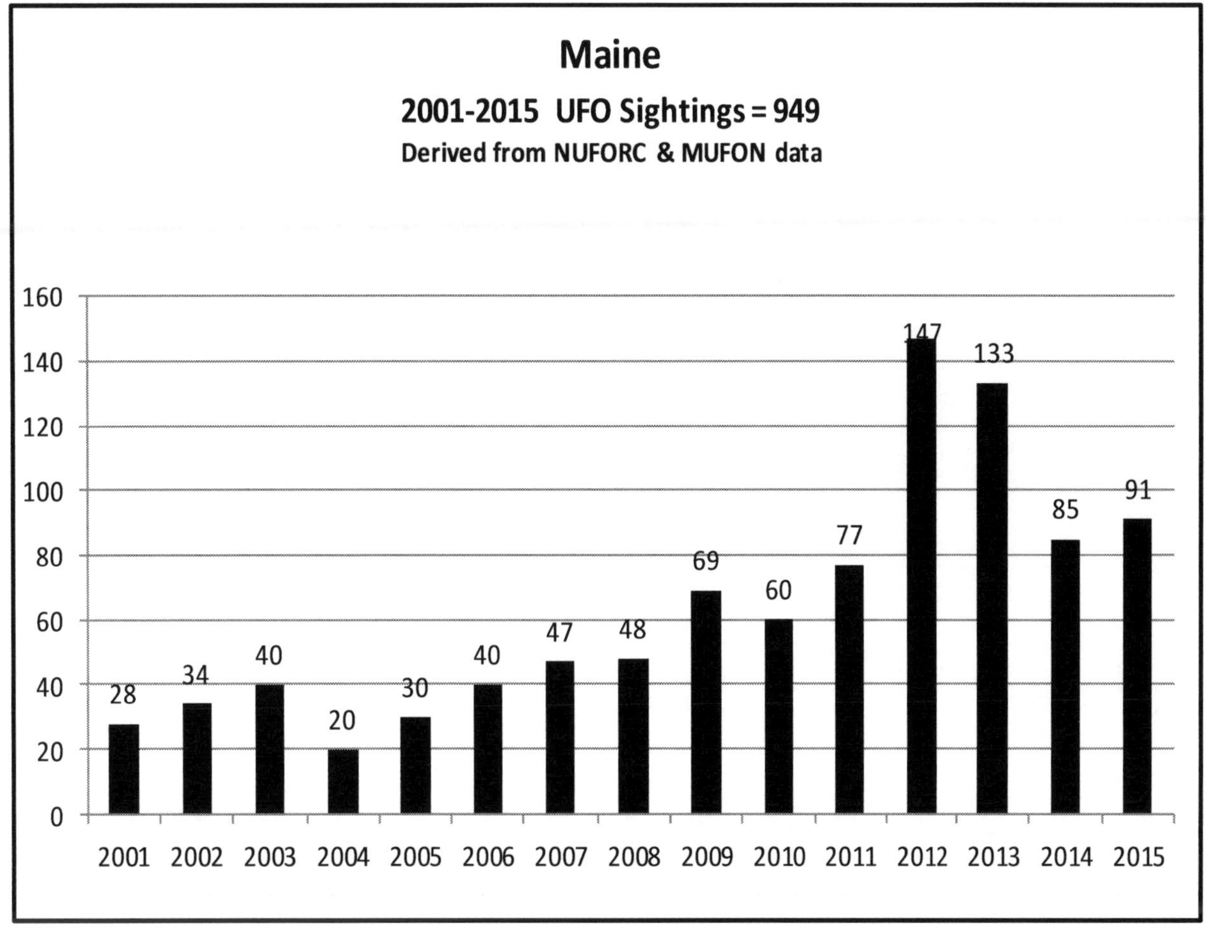

TOP TEN COUNTIES		RANK	TOP TEN SHAPES		
Cumberland	185	**1**	Light	142	14.96%
York	146	**2**	Circle	131	13.80%
Penobscot	117	**3**	Sphere	94	9.91%
Kennebec	80	**4**	Triangle	94	9.91%
Androscoggin	71	**5**	Unknown	86	9.06%
Hancock	48	**6**	Fireball	82	8.64%
Somerset	42	**7**	Other	54	5.69%
Aroostook	35	**8**	Oval	42	4.43%
Waldo	32	**9**	Star-like	38	4.00%
Oxford	30	**10**	Cigar	24	2.53%

UFO SHAPES: MAINE

UFO Shapes	2001	2002	2003	2004	2005	2006	2007	2008	2009	2010	2011	2012	2013	2014	2015	Total
Blimp							1	1							1	3
Boomerang									1	1	1	2	1		1	7
Bullet/Missile										1		1	3			5
Changing	1		2							1		2	1		1	8
Chevron		1							1			1	1	1		5
Cigar	1	3	1		2		2	1	3	2	1	1	3	2	2	24
Circle	1	5	3	2	2	5	7	8	10	9	11	23	20	12	13	131
Circle,Other											1					1
Cone									1						1	2
Cross			2									1	1	1		5
Cylinder		1	1			2	1		1	1	1	1	1	1	3	14
Diamond	1			1			3	1	1	1	2	4	1	1	1	17
Disc			1		1		2	2	1		8	3		3	1	22
Disk		1	1	1	2	2		3		1		3	2	1	2	19
Egg			1								1	1		1		4
Fireball	1	1				2	3	5	2	2	8	17	20	16	5	82
Flash		1	2			1	1	1	3	2		1	5	2	1	20
Formation	1				1		1	1			4		1		1	10
Light	6	7	6	5	7	9	4	4	9	6	13	27	16	8	15	142
N/A														1		1
Other	2	1	5	2	4	1	2	2	7	3	4	7	8	3	3	54
Oval	4				1	2	2		4	3	1	7	7	6	5	42
Rectangle			1				1		2			1	1	1	2	9
Sphere	2	4	4	1	2	3	6	1	7	4	6	15	12	6	21	94
Star-like				1		1	1	6	3	7	4	2	3	6	4	38
Teardrop		1					1	3				2	1	2		10
Triangle	1	1	6	4	3	1	4	5	11	11	5	12	14	9	7	94
Unknown	7	7	4	3	5	11	5	4	2	5	6	13	11	2	1	86
Total	**28**	**34**	**40**	**20**	**30**	**40**	**47**	**48**	**69**	**60**	**77**	**147**	**133**	**85**	**91**	**949**

UFOS BY COUNTY: MAINE

Counties	2001	2002	2003	2004	2005	2006	2007	2008	2009	2010	2011	2012	2013	2014	2015	Total
Androscoggin	7	2	1	3	4	5	4	4	5		6	9	12	3	6	71
Aroostook		1	3			3	1	2	4	2	3	9	3	3	1	35
Cumberland	3	8	9	4	7	8	5	12	12	20	19	26	24	12	16	185
Franklin	2		1				4		1	3	2	2	4	7	1	27
Hancock	2	1			2	1	4	1	8	3	2	6	9	4	5	48
Kennebec	4	3	3		2	3	2	9	7	2	8	16	10	5	6	80
Knox	3		1	1		3	1	2	1	1		4	4	3	4	28
Lincoln	2		3				1			3			3	3	4	19
Oxford	1	4	2	1	3		3	3	3			1	4	4	1	30
Penobscot	1	4	8	3	5	4	5	4	11	4	4	20	16	11	17	117
Piscataquis		1	2	1			1	2	1		1	2	2	3	1	17
Sagadahoc		2					3		2	1	3	5	2	3	1	22
Somerset		5		1	1	2	4	3	2	2	4	7	9		2	42
Strafford										1					1	2
Suffolk							1									1
Unknown	1		2	2		3	2	2	1	1	6		3	1	2	26
Waldo		1		2	1	1	2		2	2	2	8	3	4	4	32
Washington		2					1	2		1	1	5	3	2	4	21
York	2		5	2	5	7	3	2	9	14	16	27	22	17	15	146
Total	**28**	**34**	**40**	**20**	**30**	**40**	**47**	**48**	**69**	**60**	**77**	**147**	**133**	**85**	**91**	**949**

If a county is missing from the list, it's because no UFO sightings were logged in either the NUFORC or MUFON databases for the 2001-2015 sample period.

UFOS BY MONTH: MAINE

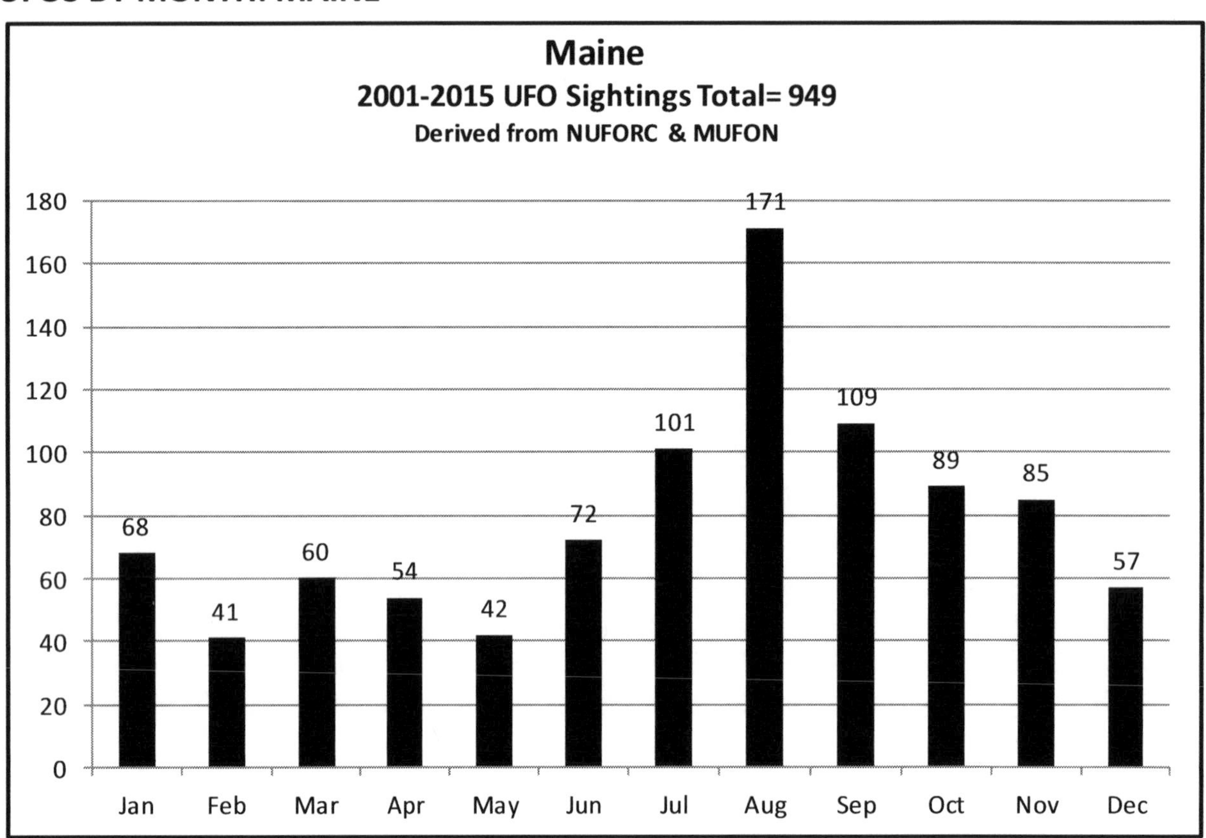

Year	Jan	Feb	Mar	Apr	May	Jun	Jul	Aug	Sep	Oct	Nov	Dec	Total
2001	4				2	2		10	5	4	1		28
2002	1	1	3		2	2	6	10	3	1	3	2	34
2003	3	1	1	4			3	7	3	3	11	4	40
2004	2			2		2	1	4	4	5			20
2005	1		3	5	2	2	7	4	2		2	2	30
2006	4	1	5	1	1	2	1	8	6	5	1	5	40
2007	4	7	3	1	1	3	3	11	2	9	1	2	47
2008	5	1	3	4	2	2	6	7	5	7	3	3	48
2009	5	2	6	5	5	2	4	7	16	1	9	7	69
2010	4	5	7	6	5	4	5	4	4	5	7	4	60
2011	6	1	2	3	3	7	7	22	7	5	6	8	77
2012	8	8	11	9	2	18	16	20	13	14	16	12	147
2013	10	2	7	7	5	8	20	33	19	9	11	2	133
2014	8	7	4	3	4	7	7	10	9	17	5	4	85
2015	3	5	5	4	8	11	15	14	11	4	9	2	91
Total	**68**	**41**	**60**	**54**	**42**	**72**	**101**	**171**	**109**	**89**	**85**	**57**	**949**

Distribution of Sightings between Databases: Maine

Database	Count	Percentage
MUFON	343	36.14%
NUFORC	606	63.86%
Total	949	100.00%

State Demographic Information: Maine

2010 US Census Statistics	
Population	1,328,361.00
Area in Square Miles	35,379.74
Land Area Sq. Miles	30,842.92
Population/Square mile	43.10

MARYLAND

UFO RANK 24/51

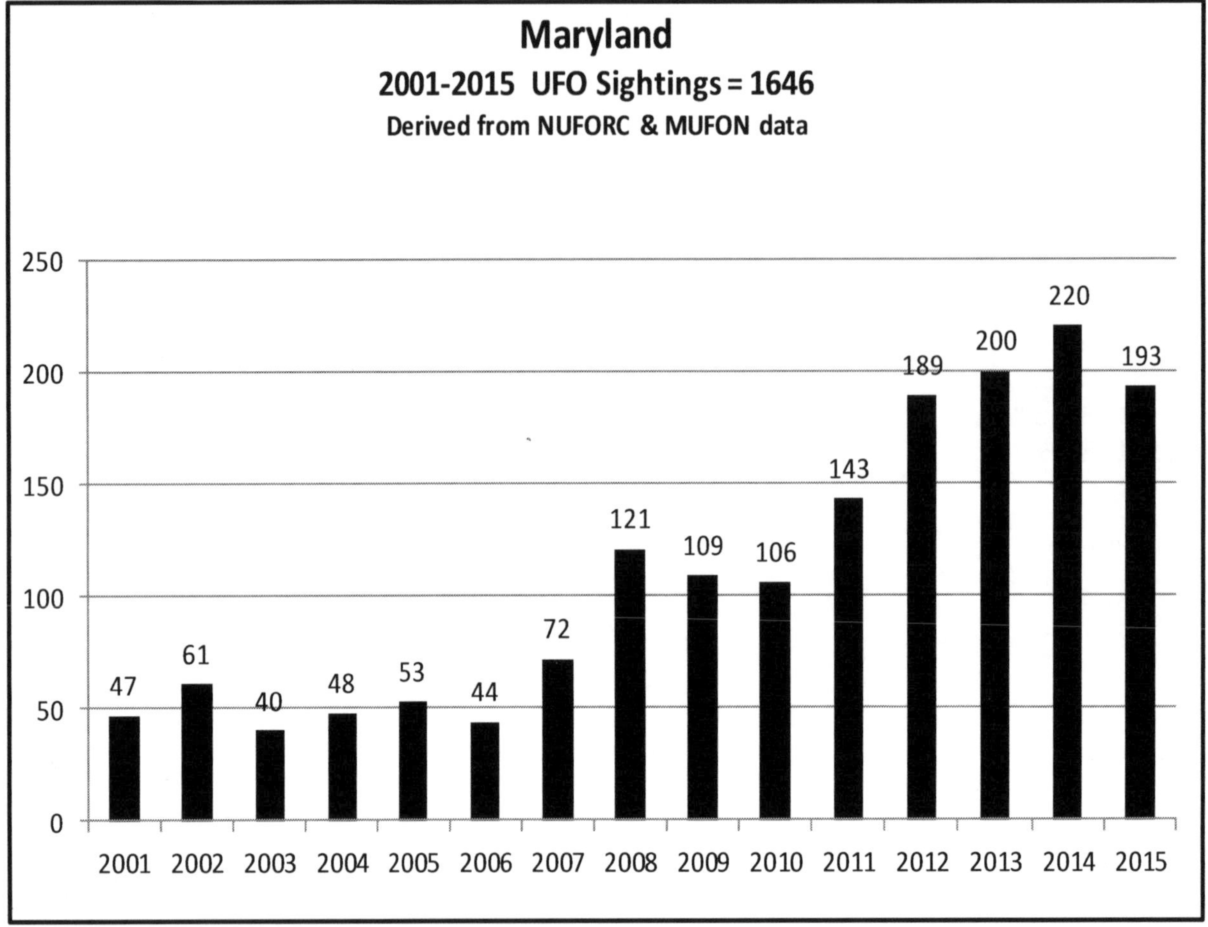

TOP TEN COUNTIES		RANK	TOP TEN SHAPES		
Montgomery	193	**1**	Light	207	12.58%
Anne Arundel	184	**2**	Circle	189	11.48%
Baltimore	177	**3**	Unknown	163	9.90%
Baltimore City	172	**4**	Sphere	156	9.48%
Prince Georges	121	**5**	Triangle	149	9.05%
Harford	98	**6**	Other	119	7.23%
Frederick	97	**7**	Fireball	98	5.95%
Washington	74	**8**	Disc	93	5.65%
Howard	73	**9**	Oval	72	4.37%
Carroll	67	**10**	Star-like	64	3.89%

UFO SHAPES: MARYLAND

UFO Shapes	2001	2002	2003	2004	2005	2006	2007	2008	2009	2010	2011	2012	2013	2014	2015	Total
Blimp					1			1	1		2		1		3	9
Boomerang								1	4	2		3	1	3	3	17
Bullet/Missile										2			1	1		4
Changing	1	1	4	3	1			5	1		2	2	2	4	3	29
Chevron		1	2	2		2	1	2			2	1	3	2	5	23
Cigar	5	1	2	3	1	4	4	3	10	1	6	4	2	7	5	58
Circle	3	3	1	1	3	2	4	10	13	18	18	25	34	32	22	189
Cone	1								5		2	1	1	1		11
Cross											1					1
Cylinder		1			3	2	1	1	2	3	4	3	7	3	9	39
Diamond		2	2		3		2	1	2	1	1	4	2		2	22
Disc	1	3	3	4	6	2	13	8	6	8	4	8	14	9	4	93
Egg	1	1		2		1	1			2	2	1		2	6	19
Egg,Oval											1					1
Fireball	2	3		5	3	3	3	6	2	8	5	12	17	15	14	98
Flash	2	2		2		1	3	1	1	1	6	2	4	2	2	29
Formation	1	2	3		1	1		2	2	1	2	5	6	6	5	37
Light	11	10	5	4	10	7	13	11	8	11	18	22	17	42	18	207
N/A							1			1					2	4
Other	1	3	6	4	5	4	4	11	7	7	9	10	15	14	19	119
Oval	1	4	1	1	1	5	2	4		7	3	10	13	6	14	72
Rectangle	1	2		1			1	1	1	1	1		1	1	3	14
Saturn-like		1												1		2
Sphere	3	5	3	4	2	1	5	11	13	7	15	25	25	22	15	156
Sq/Rect		1												1	2	4
Star-like	1			1	1	2	3	9	7	6	10	7	4	3	10	64
Teardrop		1						5		2			1	2	2	13
Triangle	5	5	4	3	5	2	4	12	10	12	15	25	13	22	12	149
Unknown	7	9	4	8	7	5	7	16	14	5	14	19	16	19	13	163
Total	**47**	**61**	**40**	**48**	**53**	**44**	**72**	**121**	**109**	**106**	**143**	**189**	**200**	**220**	**193**	**1646**

UFOS BY COUNTY: MARYLAND

Counties	2001	2002	2003	2004	2005	2006	2007	2008	2009	2010	2011	2012	2013	2014	2015	Total
Allegany	1			2	1	1	1	2	6	4	2	4	2	5	8	39
Anne Arundel	2	5	3	5	9	7	8	6	8	12	22	23	21	31	22	184
Baltimore	5	5	4	3	1	3	5	7	17	13	15	21	23	23	32	177
Baltimore City	7	11	5	7	11	10	3	21	6	15	12	15	20	8	21	172
Calvert		1			1	1	1	2	2	1	3	1		5		18
Caroline					2			2	3			1	2	1	2	13
Carroll	2	1	2				3	7	9	5	3	8	4	12	11	67
Cecil	3	1	1	1	1		2	4	1	3	6	4	12	3	4	46
Charles		3	1		1		2	3		2	4	2	4	5	1	28
Dorchester			1													1
Frederick	5	2		2		1	6	8	6	5	2	11	18	22	9	97
Garrett	1					1		3	2			1	1			9
Harford	3	6	2	2	2	4	6	7	4	3	18	7	7	17	10	98
Howard	1	2	2	4	3	2	1	1	6	6	5	12	10	12	6	73
Kent			2			2			3	2	2		4	1	2	18
Montgomery	8	6	6	4	10	4	21	18	16	10	14	18	15	19	24	193
Morgan		1														1
Prince Georges	2	8	2	10	5	1	5	9	7	5	15	17	14	14	7	121
Queen Anne		2	2		1		1		1	1	1	5	1	2	7	24
Saint Mary		2		2		2		2	1		5	3	4	5	5	31
Somerset			1	1	1				1	1	1	2	2		1	11
Talbot			1			1			2	2	1			3		10
Unknown	2				1	1	1	7	3	1	3	8	14	3	9	53
Washington	2	1	1	3	1	2	4	6	2	7	3	13	12	11	6	74
Wicomico		1	3		1			3	1	1	5	1	1	6	2	25
Worcester	3	3	1	2	1	1	2	3	2	7	1	12	9	12	4	63
Total	**47**	**61**	**40**	**48**	**53**	**44**	**72**	**121**	**109**	**106**	**143**	**189**	**200**	**220**	**193**	**1646**

If a county is missing from the list, it's because no UFO sightings were logged in either the NUFORC or MUFON databases for the 2001-2015 sample period.

UFOS BY MONTH: MARYLAND

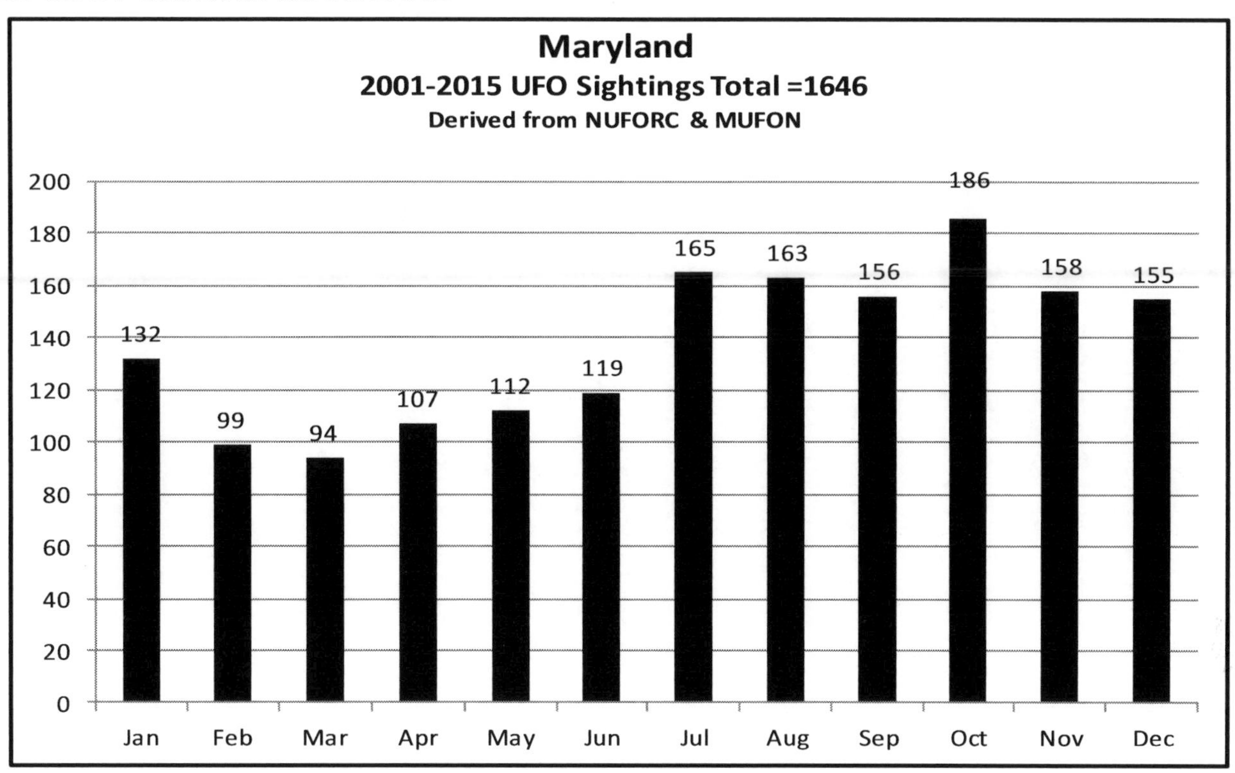

Year	Jan	Feb	Mar	Apr	May	Jun	Jul	Aug	Sep	Oct	Nov	Dec	Total
2001	4	4	2	6	2	4	7	2	4	2	7	3	47
2002	9	7	2	3	3	4	8	9	2	5	4	5	61
2003	5	4	3	1		3	4	1	2	9	3	5	40
2004	4	4	3	3	4	2	5	6	4	3	3	7	48
2005	4	6	3	1	1	4	6	4	5	8	7	4	53
2006	2	2	1	4	3	3	4	5	3	5	4	8	44
2007	8	2	7	6	9	3	9	4	9	3	5	7	72
2008	12	6	5	15	7	11	10	22	4	6	12	11	121
2009	4	10	8	10	6	8	5	9	21	8	11	9	109
2010	9	3	5	7	10	9	17	7	7	12	12	8	106
2011	15	8	8	3	4	14	9	12	9	16	17	28	143
2012	12	5	16	16	8	17	15	15	21	27	14	23	189
2013	12	5	5	12	22	14	17	27	24	24	25	13	200
2014	12	24	14	9	12	14	28	23	24	21	20	19	220
2015	20	9	12	11	21	9	21	17	17	37	14	5	193
Total	**132**	**99**	**94**	**107**	**112**	**119**	**165**	**163**	**156**	**186**	**158**	**155**	**1646**

Distribution of Sightings between Databases: Maryland

Database	Count	Percentage
MUFON	654	39.73%
NUFORC	992	60.27%
Total	1646	100.00%

State Demographic Information: Maryland

2010 US Census Statistics	
Population	5,773,552.00
Area in Square Miles	12,405.93
Land Area Sq. Miles	9,707 .24
Population/Square mile	594.80

MASSACHUSETTS UFO RANK 19/51

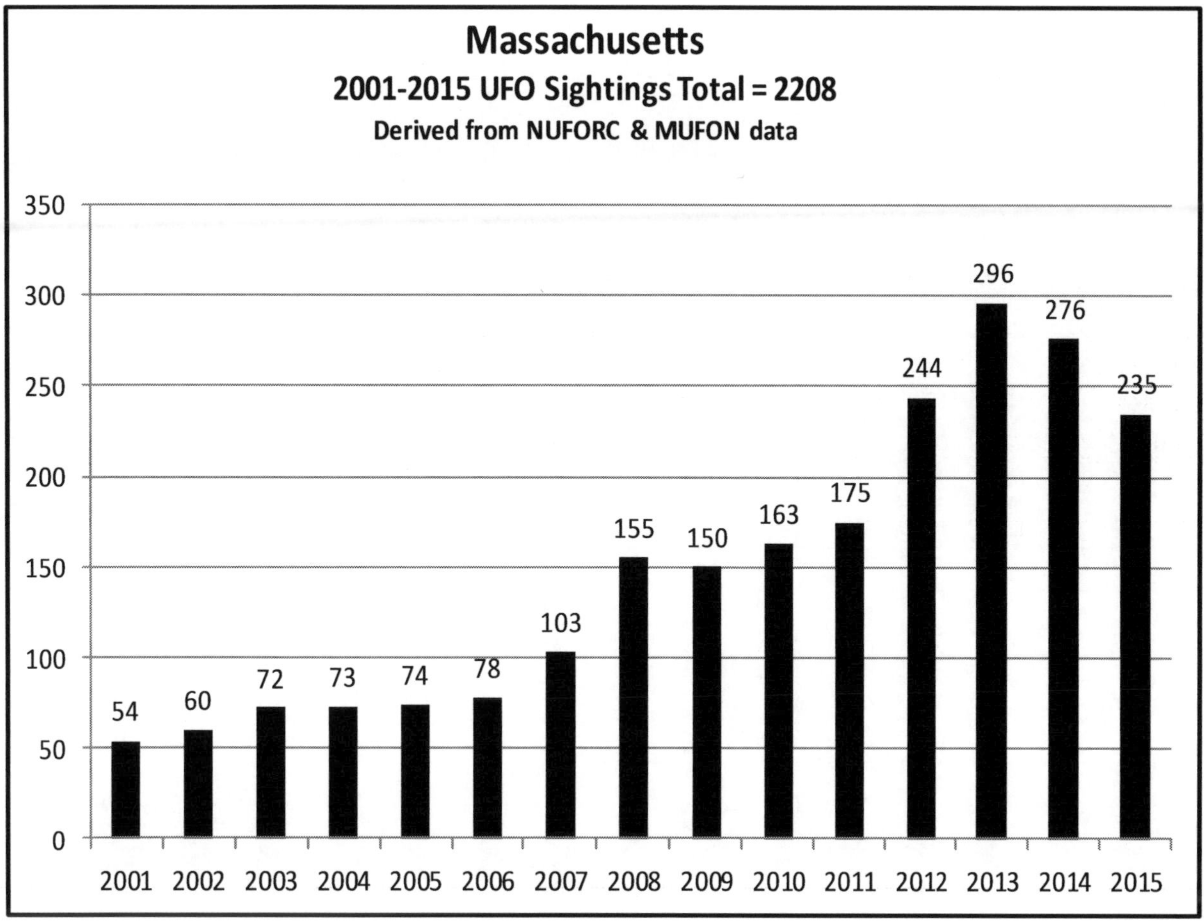

TOP TEN COUNTIES		RANK	TOP TEN SHAPES		
Essex	984	1	Fireball	172	7.79%
Middlesex	198	2	Other	160	7.25%
Worcester	191	3	Oval	119	5.39%
Suffolk	154	4	Disk	69	3.13%
Bristol	134	5	Star-like	60	2.72%
Hampden	119	6	Light	296	13.41%
Barnstable	98	7	Circle	247	11.19%
Plymouth	83	8	Unknown	217	9.83%
Norfolk	78	9	Sphere	198	8.97%
Berkshire	54	10	Triangle	196	8.88%

UFO SHAPES: MASSACHUSETTS

UFO Shapes	2001	2002	2003	2004	2005	2006	2007	2008	2009	2010	2011	2012	2013	2014	2015	Total
Blimp								4		2	2	1	1			10
Boomerang	1		2		1		2	4	3	1	3	3	1	1	1	23
Bullet/Missile								1	1					1	2	5
Changing	2	2	2	3	2	1	2		2	3	1		4	5	3	32
Chevron		1		2	2				1		1	5	4	1	2	19
Cigar	2	1	3	2	4	3	4	5	7	5	1	6	8	3	3	57
Circle	5	1	3	5	6	7	8	13	21	21	20	29	55	30	23	247
Cone						2	1	1	9		2	2	1	3		21
Cross			1			2							1	1		5
Cylinder	4	3	2	1	1	1	2	7		4	3	2	3	6	3	42
Diamond		1	2		1	2	5	5	2	1	6	3	4	12	6	50
Disc		1	1	2	1	2	4	8	3	4	10	4	6	3	2	51
Disk	6	3	3	6	4	5	7	3	2	4	3	6	9	4	4	69
Egg				2	1		3	1	2		2	2	1	5	3	22
Fireball		2	2	3	2	3	5	8	4	12	18	25	28	32	28	172
Flash					1	2	3	6	3	4	6	4	5	2	7	43
Formation	1		4	3		2		3	2	2	4	2	5	7	4	39
Light	10	13	10	14	17	7	12	12	15	24	27	25	40	40	30	296
N/A														5	1	6
Other	4	9	11	4	4	8	14	6	11	6	15	17	14	27	10	160
Oval	2	5	3	5	3	7	6	11	8	5	5	13	13	18	15	119
Rectangle	1		4		2				1	2	1	5	2	3	2	23
Saturn-like														1	1	2
Sphere	6	3	5	6	4	6	6	11	14	13	10	26	32	30	26	198
Sq/Rect											1				1	2
Star-like							3	9	7	10	6	7	7	2	9	60
Teardrop	1	1	3		1			1	2		1	2	4	1	5	22
Triangle	5	7	5	6	6	9	7	13	18	23	11	28	23	14	21	196
Unknown	4	7	6	9	11	9	9	23	12	17	16	27	25	19	23	217
Total	**54**	**60**	**72**	**73**	**74**	**78**	**103**	**155**	**150**	**163**	**175**	**244**	**296**	**276**	**235**	**2208**

UFOS BY COUNTY: MASSACHUSETTS

Counties	**2001**	**2002**	**2003**	**2004**	**2005**	**2006**	**2007**	**2008**	**2009**	**2010**	**2011**	**2012**	**2013**	**2014**	**2015**	**Total**
Barnstable	1	1	4	1		5	3	2	13	10	5	13	15	12	13	98
Berkshire	2		2			2	2	2	2	8	8	9	6	3	8	54
Bristol	1	2	5	4	1	5	9	10	11	12	6	20	14	15	19	134
Dukes		2			1							3		1		7
Essex	25	35	40	33	36	37	46	57	52	69	89	106	140	135	84	984
Franklin			1			1	1	4	3	1	2	3	5	3	2	26
Hampden	7	2	3	4	6	5	7	7	7	6	7	12	16	19	11	119
Hampshire		3	1		1	2	1	1	3	3	2	5	11	5	2	40
Middlesex	7	4	7	11	4	7	6	25	13	10	14	15	29	22	24	198
Norfolk	2		2	1	3	1	5	9	8	11	5	5	8	10	8	78
Plymouth	2	2	1	3	2	3	4	9	8	6	6	13	6	9	9	83
Suffolk	5	6	3	8	11	4	9	10	14	10	13	16	14	12	19	154
Unknown					1			3	1	2	2	4	8	7	12	40
Worcester	2	3	3	8	8	6	10	16	15	15	15	20	24	22	24	191
York											1			1		2
Total	**54**	**60**	**72**	**73**	**74**	**78**	**103**	**155**	**150**	**163**	**175**	**244**	**296**	**276**	**235**	**2208**

If a county is missing from the list, it's because no UFO sightings were logged in either the NUFORC or MUFON databases for the 2001-2015 sample period.

UFOS BY MONTH: MASSACHUSETTS

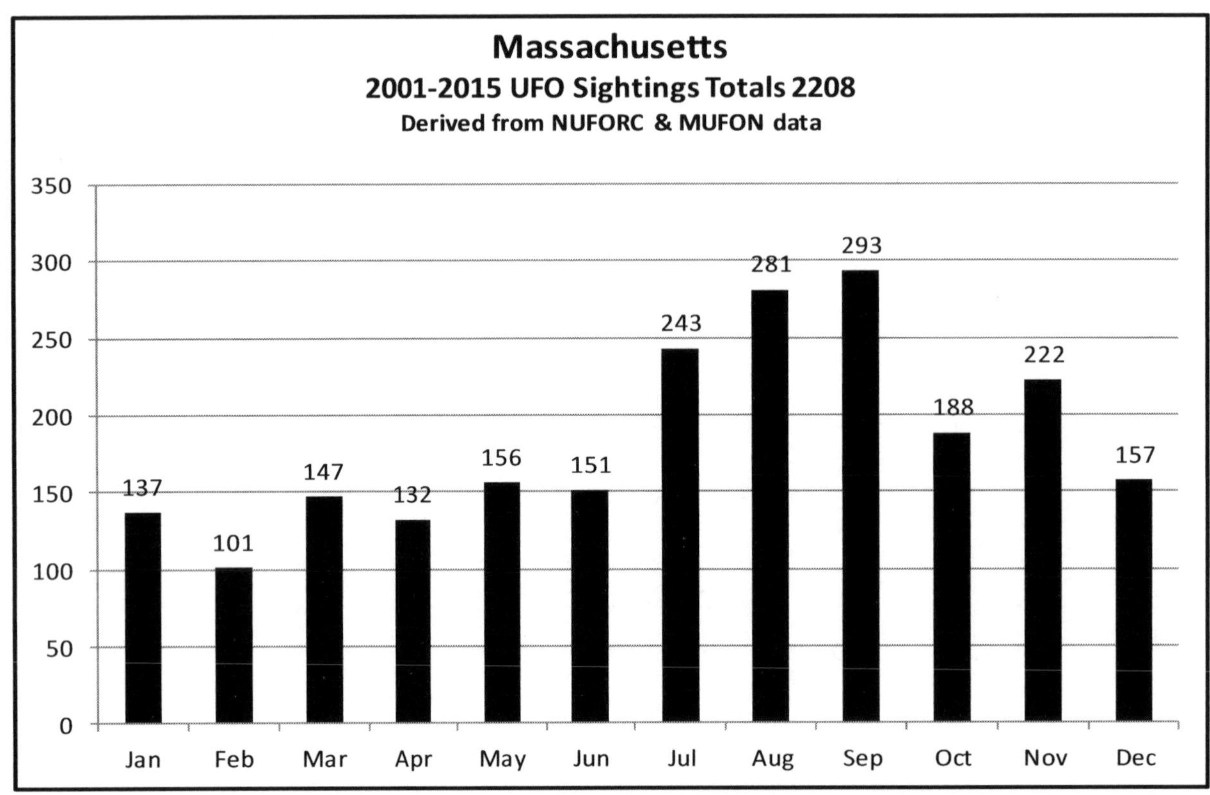

Year	Jan	Feb	Mar	Apr	May	Jun	Jul	Aug	Sep	Oct	Nov	Dec	Total
2001	4	4	1	4	3	6	9	7	8	5	3		54
2002	3	6	4		3	2	7	9	9	4	7	6	60
2003	3	3	3	5	4	6	8	8	10	5	8	9	72
2004	7	4	6	1	6	10	5	8	8	5	9	4	73
2005	4	8	7	11	6	2	4	3	7	6	9	7	74
2006	4	5	9	6	9	7	8	6	8	7	5	4	78
2007	11	6	5	10	10	5	12	10	7	4	17	6	103
2008	14	9	10	13	8	21	20	15	14	12	12	7	155
2009	10	9	10	8	9	9	17	21	30	12	7	8	150
2010	12	7	4	10	16	12	36	18	11	15	8	14	163
2011	8	4	9	6	11	10	26	26	19	17	18	21	175
2012	13	12	25	12	13	10	17	37	36	22	25	22	244
2013	21	9	24	20	19	15	28	39	39	27	33	22	296
2014	14	10	11	12	22	18	29	44	45	32	27	12	276
2015	9	5	19	14	17	18	17	30	42	15	34	15	235
Total	**137**	**101**	**147**	**132**	**156**	**151**	**243**	**281**	**293**	**188**	**222**	**157**	**2208**

BONUS—UFOs by County & Month: Massachusetts

Counties	Jan	Feb	Mar	Apr	May	Jun	Jul	Aug	Sep	Oct	Nov	Dec	Total
Barnstable	4	4	6	4	5	8	19	11	17	11	5	4	98
Berkshire	1	3	5	4	5	1	7	11	7	4	6		54
Bristol	13	7	9	8	7	9	16	16	15	7	16	11	134
Dukes			1				2	1	2			1	7
Essex	50	31	64	59	71	63	118	137	127	88	92	84	984
Franklin	2	1	2	1	2	4	2	5	3	1	3		26
Hampden	10	4	18	9	7	5	13	8	20	7	14	4	119
Hampshire	4	5	3		4		1	4	5	8	3	3	40
Middlesex	10	7	14	13	13	21	20	23	22	14	29	12	198
Norfolk	5	6	6	2	2	8	6	10	10	3	11	9	78
Plymouth	6	3	1	4	14	3	12	7	9	11	6	7	83
Suffolk	8	14	6	11	12	12	11	22	20	11	18	9	154
Unknown	3	3	3	1	5	4	3	4	7	2	3	2	40
Worcester	21	13	9	16	9	13	12	22	29	20	16	11	191
York							1			1			2
Total	**137**	**101**	**147**	**132**	**156**	**151**	**243**	**281**	**293**	**188**	**222**	**157**	**2208**

Distribution of Sightings between Databases: Massachusetts

Database	Count	Percentage
MUFON	750	33.97%
NUFORC	1458	66.03%
Total	2208	100.00%

State Demographic Information: Massachusetts

2010 US Census Statistics	
Population	6,547,629.00
Area in Square Miles	10,554.39
Land Area Sq. Miles	7,800.06
Population/Square mile	89.40

MICHIGAN UFO RANK 9/51

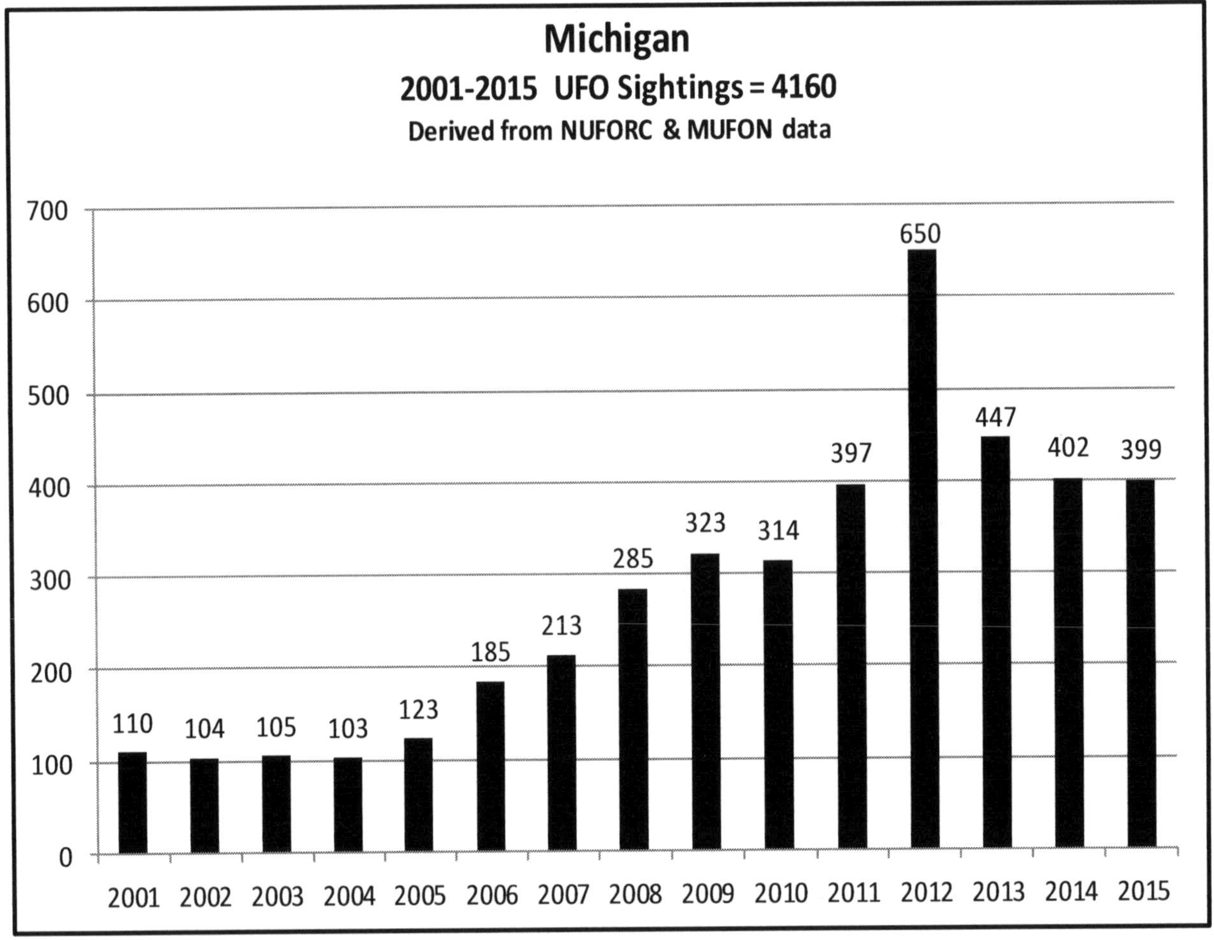

TOP TEN COUNTIES		RANK	TOP TEN SHAPES		
Wayne	501	1	Light	542	11.58%
Oakland	435	2	Circle	537	11.47%
Macomb	333	3	Triangle	494	10.55%
Kent	233	4	Sphere	485	10.36%
Genesee	205	5	Unknown	415	8.86%
Ingham	162	6	Fireball	383	8.18%
Washtenaw	162	7	Other	298	6.36%
Unknown	158	8	Star-like	210	4.49%
Ottawa	108	9	Oval	196	4.19%
Livingston	100	10	Disk	179	3.82%

UFO SHAPES: MICHIGAN

UFO Shapes	2001	2002	2003	2004	2005	2006	2007	2008	2009	2010	2011	2012	2013	2014	2015	Total
Blimp	1				1	1	2	3	3	2	4	8	4	2	2	33
Boomerang	1			1			1	5	3	8	2	13	4	5	3	46
Bullet/Missile				1		1	2	2	2	6	6	3	3	1	3	30
Changing	1	2	3	2	1	2	1	6	2	4	5	5	4		8	46
Chevron	1	1	1		1	1	1	2	3	3	1	4	2	1		22
Cigar	2	1	4		5	7	9	7	8	13	12	11	8	9	5	101
Circle	7	8	10	6	13	17	16	37	50	48	47	101	64	43	37	504
Cone		1	1	2	1	3	1		1		2	7	1	3	2	25
Cross				1				3	4		2	3		1		14
Cylinder	2	1	2	2	4	3	2	3	5		11	16	8	5	9	73
Diamond	6		2	1	4	2	3	4	5	8	5	12	8	8	8	76
Disc	2	1	1	2	2	4	3	7	12	8	8	26	7	16	14	113
Disk	6	7	7	8	6	8	6	5	5	4	1	11	8	6	5	93
Egg	2		2		1	1	3	3	3	3	6	5	3	7	1	40
Fireball	5	11	3	3	3	6	12	21	22	34	46	67	50	32	24	339
Flash			1	1	1	4	4	6	10	10	11	10	9	5	8	80
Formation	4	1	1	3	3	3	9	3	2	3	6	4	6	6	8	62
Light	18	20	19	14	20	22	31	32	30	27	31	63	32	34	56	449
N/A							1					1	2	7	4	15
Other	8	13	5	12	7	23	14	16	22	15	14	36	25	20	25	255
Oval	4	1	9	2	6	6	4	11	10	10	17	21	18	18	22	159
Rectangle	1	3	3	1	2	4	2	2	3	1	3	3	3	2	2	35
Saturn-like								1	2	1	1			2		7
Sphere	5	2	4	11	8	12	12	25	27	31	47	74	71	69	56	454
Sq/Rect				1											3	4
Star-like	2	1	1	2	2	6	11	18	28	15	23	32	23	18	28	210
Teardrop	2		1	1	2	2	3		1	4	1	2	5	4		28
Triangle	18	17	12	11	13	22	31	30	26	34	37	62	38	39	39	429
Unknown	12	13	13	15	17	25	29	33	34	22	48	50	41	39	27	418
Total	**110**	**104**	**105**	**103**	**123**	**185**	**213**	**285**	**323**	**314**	**397**	**650**	**447**	**402**	**399**	**4160**

UFOS BY COUNTY: MICHIGAN

Counties	2001	2002	2003	2004	2005	2006	2007	2008	2009	2010	2011	2012	2013	2014	2015	Total
Alcona		2						1	3	1	1			2	2	12
Alger	1		1				1		1	1		1	1		1	8
Allegan		2		2	1		3	4	5	6	5	10	2	4	7	51
Alpena									2			3			1	6
Antrim	3				1				2	1	2	5	1	4	1	20
Arenac				1		1				2		4			1	9
Baraga									1		2					3
Barry			1	1		1	2	2		2	3	4	2		2	20
Bay		3	1		2	2	1	5	2		7	5	4		7	39
Benzie	1					1	3					2	2			9
Berrien	1	3	1	2		2	2	6	4	2	5	5	12	10	7	62
Branch			2			1	3	3	1		2	1	1	3	1	18
Calhoun	3	1	1	1		1	3		6	10	8	6	1	3	6	50
Cass	1	1	1		1	1		5	2		2	3	1	1	1	20
Charlevoix	2	1				2	1	2	4	3	4	1		1	1	22
Cheboygan			3		1	2	2		3	2	5	3	1		2	24
Chippewa	4	1	1	4	2	6	1		4	2	2	3	2		2	34
Clare	2		1		1	2			1	1	1			1	2	12
Clinton	2		1			1	4	1	1		1	3	8	2	3	27
Crawford												4				4
Delta	5		1	2	1	2		1	5		2	2	2	2	5	30
Dickinson	2	1	1			1		3	1		2	3	1		1	16
Eaton		1	2	1		5	2	2	1	4	3	9	4	2	10	46
Emmet			1	2	3	1	1	1	2	1	2	4	1	3	3	25
Genesee	6	4	5	5	7	10	8	14	19	11	20	42	26	14	14	205
Gladwin								1	1	1	2	1			1	7
Gogebic		1	3	1	1		1			1		2				10
Grand Traverse	4	3	1	1	1	2		1	3	1	6	11	6	5	6	51
Gratiot	1								1		5	1	1	1		10
Hillsdale				1		1				5	2	5	3	1	4	22
Houghton		2	1			2			1	1			2	1	2	12
Huron	1	2		1		1	1	2	2	2		2		2		16
Ingham	5	5	4	2	2	17	8	11	11	15	17	27	14	7	17	162
Ionia	1	1	1	2	1		1	2			1	5	2		2	19
Iosco					2	1	1	2	1	1	3	5	3	3	2	24
Iron						1	1		1						1	4
Isabella		1		1		1	3	3	7	3	3	5	1	3	4	35

Counties	2001	2002	2003	2004	2005	2006	2007	2008	2009	2010	2011	2012	2013	2014	2015	Total
Jackson	3	1	2	2	1	6	6	8	4	1	3	9	6	5	4	61
Kalamazoo		3	3	2	1		4	6	4	10	8	8	7	15	15	86
Kalkaska											1	2	2	1		6
Kent	3	7	2	2	11	7	11	10	21	16	18	47	23	36	19	233
Keweenaw						1										1
Lake	1	1				1	1		1	2				1		8
Lapeer	1		2		3	4	2	6	1	1	4	10	2	4	1	41
Leelanau			1		1		1			1	1	6	5		1	17
Lenawee	1	1	2	3	1	5	3	5	2	3	2	5	7	7	4	51
Livingston	3	5	4	4	6	2	4	5	7	11	11	9	10	12	7	100
Luce	1		1						1							3
Mackinac			1			2		1			1				1	6
Macomb	5	9	10	10	7	10	19	24	21	31	21	58	54	29	25	333
Manistee					2	1		1	1	2	1	2	4	1		15
Marquette	1	1			1	2	3	3	2	8	5	1	5	4	6	42
Mason	1			1			1		2		2	5	3	1	2	18
Mecosta	1	1			1			3	1	1	1	2	2	2	2	17
Menomine e					2							2			2	6
Midland			2			5	3	2	2	3	5	1	2		3	28
Missaukee		1			1				1	1						4
Monroe		2	3	2	3		4	6	3	5	10	18	12	7	5	80
Montcalm		1	1	1	1		3	3				1	2	1	1	15
Montmor-ency	1				1		2		2	1						7
Muskegon	1	3	1	2		1	5	2	1	6	4	9	10	5	11	61
Newaygo			1	1		1		1		1	3	1	1	3	2	15
Oakland	7	4	11	13	14	10	16	38	29	30	38	77	49	54	45	435
Oceana				1	1	1		2		1	1	1	1	2		11
Ogemaw		2	1		1	1	2		4	2	1	1	2		2	19
Ontonagon			3					2	3		2		1		1	12
Osceola	1			2		2	2		1			2			2	12
Oscoda								3	1			1			1	6
Otsego	1	2			3	2		1	1	4	1	1	2		2	20
Ottawa	4	1	1	4	6	7	5	12	12	9	7	10	4	15	11	108
Presque Isle	1		1		1		1		5	1	1	1	2	3	1	18
Roscom-mon	1		1		1		2		1		1	2		2	4	15
Saginaw	2	2		1	1	5	2	4	2	7	4	8	5	4	5	52

Counties	**2001**	**2002**	**2003**	**2004**	**2005**	**2006**	**2007**	**2008**	**2009**	**2010**	**2011**	**2012**	**2013**	**2014**	**2015**	**Total**
Saint Clair	1		3	1		3		1	5	11	6	10	9	6	5	61
Saint Joseph	4			2	3	3	4	4	4		2	5	4	1		36
Sanilac	1	1	1	2	1	1			4	1	12	3	3	2	2	34
Schoolcraft			1									1		2		4
Shiawassee				1			1	1		2		3	1	7	1	17
Tuscola	1	1	2		1		2	2	5	2	1	4	2	3		26
Unknown		2	1	1	3	14	13	17	12	6	23	31	14	10	11	158
Van Buren	1			2		1	3	1	2	3	7	6	3	1	8	38
Washtenaw	2	2	2	5	7	9	9	11	20	7	18	22	21	16	11	162
Wayne	15	15	7	8	10	10	24	28	35	42	51	76	61	64	55	501
Wexford		1					2		2	3	2	2	2	1	2	17
Total	**110**	**104**	**105**	**103**	**123**	**185**	**213**	**285**	**323**	**314**	**397**	**650**	**447**	**402**	**399**	**4160**

If a county is missing from the list, it's because no UFO sightings were logged in either the NUFORC or MUFON databases for the 2001-2015 sample period.

UFOS BY MONTH: MICHIGAN

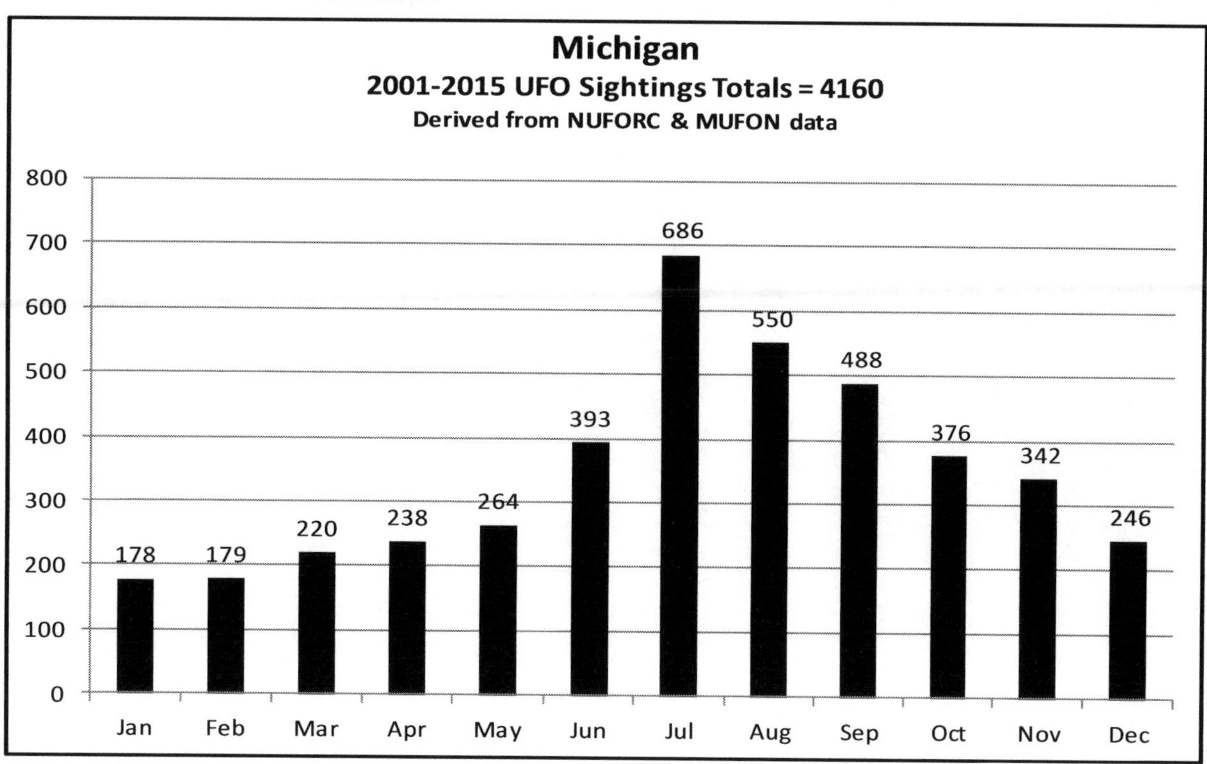

Year	Jan	Feb	Mar	Apr	May	Jun	Jul	Aug	Sep	Oct	Nov	Dec	Total
2001	6	4	5	11	6	11	16	9	20	9	10	3	110
2002	2	9	3	5	6	12	13	23	10	3	13	5	104
2003	5	3	8	8	2	3	16	13	13	11	16	7	105
2004	5	9	2	7	11	16	10	9	8	9	10	7	103
2005	4	3	7	7	11	14	20	9	11	12	16	9	123
2006	8	10	12	7	7	14	20	28	19	14	20	26	185
2007	17	5	10	10	9	32	36	34	24	17	11	8	213
2008	8	13	8	18	16	31	68	37	31	21	18	16	285
2009	9	13	21	15	22	19	68	39	63	25	21	8	323
2010	9	11	26	24	16	30	73	28	20	32	31	14	314
2011	14	16	21	19	16	25	70	59	56	50	28	23	397
2012	17	41	39	32	35	82	101	79	66	47	57	54	650
2013	31	11	16	22	35	39	58	84	52	43	29	27	447
2014	22	17	17	23	42	42	66	58	36	34	27	18	402
2015	21	14	25	30	30	23	51	41	59	49	35	21	399
Total	**178**	**179**	**220**	**238**	**264**	**393**	**686**	**550**	**488**	**376**	**342**	**246**	**4160**

Distribution of Sightings between Databases: Michigan

Database	Count	Percentage
MUFON	2168	52.12%
NUFORC	1992	47.88%
Total	4160	100.00%

State Demographic Information: Michigan

2010 US Census Statistics	
Population	9,883,640.00
Area in Square Miles	96,713.51
Land Area Sq. Miles	56,538.90
Population/Square mile	174.80

MINNESOTA UFO RANK 23/51

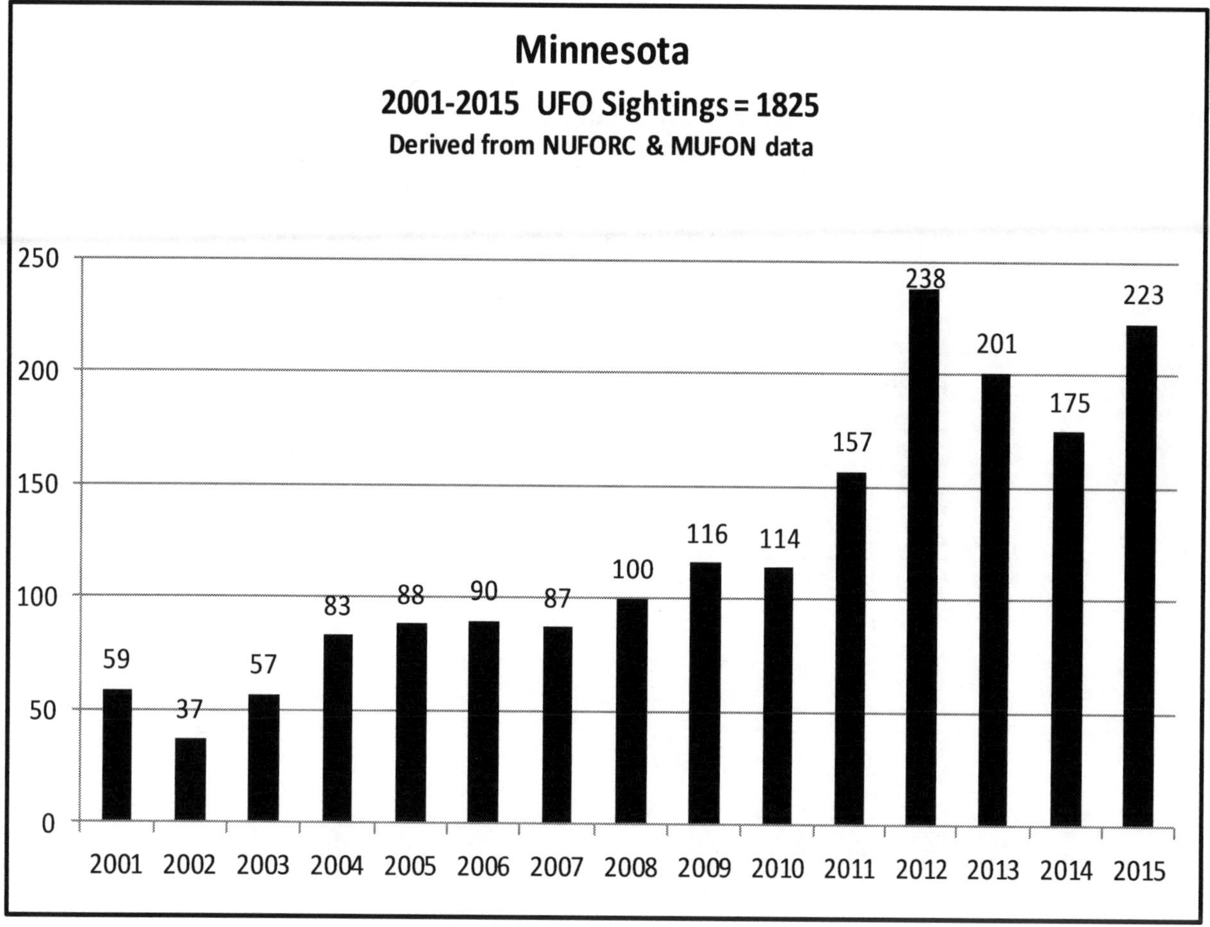

TOP TEN COUNTIES		RANK	TOP TEN SHAPES		
Hennepin	341	1	Light	256	14.03%
Ramsey	156	2	Circle	225	12.33%
Dakota	147	3	Triangle	191	10.47%
Saint Louis	104	4	Unknown	190	10.41%
Anoka	79	5	Sphere	169	9.26%
Washington	77	6	Other	113	6.19%
Unknown	57	7	Fireball	87	4.77%
Wright	54	8	Star-like	83	4.55%
Scott	47	9	Oval	73	4.00%
Olmsted	44	10	Formation	50	2.74%

UFO SHAPES: MINNESOTA

UFO Shapes	2001	2002	2003	2004	2005	2006	2007	2008	2009	2010	2011	2012	2013	2014	2015	Total
Blimp			1	1				1				2			1	6
Boomerang			1	1	1	4		6	3		4	1	4	2	4	31
Changing	1		1		1		3	1	1		2	3	2	1	2	18
Chevron	2	1	2	2	2	2	1	2	1		2	2	2		2	23
Cigar	2	5	1		2	3	3	1	3	2	5	2	6	7	5	47
Circle	2	1	3	13	7	11	4	10	13	18	21	40	26	23	33	225
Cone		1				1	1	1					2	1	2	9
Cross		1						1		1		1	1			5
Cylinder			1	2	2		1	2			1	2	7	4	1	23
Diamond		1		3			2	3	1	3	1	4	4	1	1	24
Disc	1		1		3	2	3	2	2	5		3	7	9	5	43
Disk	1	1	2	3	7	4	4	1	1	2	1	6	5	5	5	48
Egg				1			2	2	2		7	7	3			24
Fireball		1	3	4		4	3	7	4	3	9	15	10	9	15	87
Flash			1	2	1	8	1	1	4		3	4	1	1	7	34
Formation	1	3	3	4	1	2	2	5	4	3	3	9	5	2	3	50
Light	15	6	13	9	16	12	16	17	23	12	17	29	26	25	20	256
Other	5	3	8	5	6	5	9	2	7	7	10	12	14	9	11	113
Oval	3		5	2	5	3	4	4	5	4	6	10	6	4	12	73
Rectangle	1	1		2		2	1	2	1	2	1	5	1		3	22
Saturn-like					1			1		1	1	1				5
Sphere	3	1		8	5	4	2	7	8	15	16	22	25	20	33	169
Star-like			1		1	6	4	5	7	14	10	12	4	10	9	83
Teardrop	1			1		4	1		2	1	2	1	1	1	1	16
Triangle	8	4	7	8	12	5	11	11	11	12	14	27	23	15	23	191
Unknown	13	7	3	12	14	8	8	4	12	8	21	17	16	25	22	190
Bullet					1		1	1	1	1				1	1	7
Square												1			2	3
Total	**59**	**37**	**57**	**83**	**88**	**90**	**87**	**100**	**116**	**114**	**157**	**238**	**201**	**175**	**223**	**1825**

UFOS BY COUNTY: MINNESOTA

Counties	2001	2002	2003	2004	2005	2006	2007	2008	2009	2010	2011	2012	2013	2014	2015	Total
Aitkin	1	1	4			2		1		2	1	2	5	1		20
Anoka		2	3	2	6	6	1	2	4	9	7	10	13	3	11	79
Becker			2	1	1	1	2	2	1			1		1	2	14
Beltrami	1				1		1	4	1	1	3	3	4	8	2	29
Benton															2	2
Blue Earth		1		1			1	1	2	6	14	2		4	4	36
Brown	2															2
Carlton	2		1					1			1	1		4	4	14
Carver		1	1	3	3	1		2		3	2	9	6	4	3	38
Cass			2	1	2	2		1				3	2	3	1	17
Chippewa														1		1
Chisago				1	1	1	2	3	4			2		1	5	20
Clay	2							1		1	1		1	1	1	8
Cook		1		1	3		1	2		1		2	1	1	3	16
Crow Wing			3	1	1		6	1	4	4	3	7	1		1	32
Dakota	1	1	4	8	9	11	3	1	10	7	12	24	19	17	20	147
Dodge						1						1	1	3	2	8
Douglas				1				2			1	3	2		1	10
Faribault			1													1
Fillmore		1					1	1								3
Freeborn	2					1	1			1				3	1	9
Goodhue	1		1			1			2		3	3	3	1	1	16
Grant								1				1			1	3
Hennepin	10	8	5	25	20	21	10	23	29	21	25	36	39	33	36	341
Houston				1				2		1	1	1		1		7
Hubbard			1	2	1	1		1						1	1	8
Isanti	1					1	1	1	1	1		2	2	1		11
Itasca	1			1	2		8	1	2		3	3		3	1	25
Kanabec					1		1						7	2	1	12
Kandiyohi	1		1		1	1		2			1	1	1			9
Kittson			1													1
Koochiching						2				2	4			2		10
Lac qui Parle							1				1		3		6	11
Lake	1	1				3	1	2	1			2			3	14
Lake of the Woods											1				1	2
Le Sueur						1					1		1		2	5

Counties	2001	2002	2003	2004	2005	2006	2007	2008	2009	2010	2011	2012	2013	2014	2015	Total
Lincoln	1										1					2
Lyon									1	4	3	1				9
Mahnomen	1															1
Marshall															1	1
Martin				1						2	2					5
McLeod			1			2	1				1	3	1	1		10
Meeker					1	1				1			1		1	5
Mille Lacs	1						3		1	1	2	2	2	1	1	14
Morrison					2		1							2	3	8
Mower			2						1		1		1			5
Murray		3														3
Nicollet	1			1						1	1		1			5
Nobles											1					1
Norman							1		1							2
Olmsted		1		1	2	1	3			4	8	9	4	3	8	44
Otter Tail	2		1		4	2		1	2	2	2		2	3	4	25
Pennington									1							1
Pine	1	1	2	1		1		4			1	2	4			17
Pipestone				1		1		1	1		3	3	6	2	4	22
Polk	1				2				3			2				8
Pope			2	1				1				2		1		7
Ramsey	6	3	2	15	4	5	9	9	11	10	11	21	15	17	18	156
Red Lake										2						2
Redwood										1	1		1	2	1	6
Renville											1		2		1	4
Rice		1	1	1	3				8		5	1	1		3	24
Rock										1						1
Roseau	1							1								2
Saint Louis	7	5	2	4		1	11	7	8	8	6	21	9	7	8	104
Scott		1		1	2	4	1	2	1	1	1	9	10	4	10	47
Sherburne	1			2	2	1	6	1	2	2	1	3	2	2	2	27
Sibley						1									2	3
Stearns		2		3	2	1		2	3	2	2	11	4	3	6	41
Steele	2	1			1		1	2					1		2	10
Stevens		1													1	2
Swift										1						1
Todd						1		1								2
Traverse										1						1

Counties	**2001**	**2002**	**2003**	**2004**	**2005**	**2006**	**2007**	**2008**	**2009**	**2010**	**2011**	**2012**	**2013**	**2014**	**2015**	**Total**
Unknown			3		1	4	6	4	3	1	5	12	6	4	8	57
Wabasha			1		1			1			1				1	5
Wadena			1													1
Wadena			1													1
Waseca														1		1
Washington	6	1	7	1	2	2		3	4	7	4	8	9	13	10	77
Watonwan			1					1							1	3
Wilkin			1										1			2
Winona	1				2	1					1		1	2	3	11
Wright	1			1	4	4	3	1	3	2	6	9	6	8	6	54
Yellow Medicine					1				1		1				2	5
Total	**59**	**37**	**57**	**83**	**88**	**90**	**87**	**100**	**116**	**114**	**157**	**238**	**201**	**175**	**223**	**1825**

If a county is missing from the list, it's because no UFO sightings were logged in either the NUFORC or MUFON databases for the 2001-2015 sample period.

UFOS BY MONTH: MINNESOTA

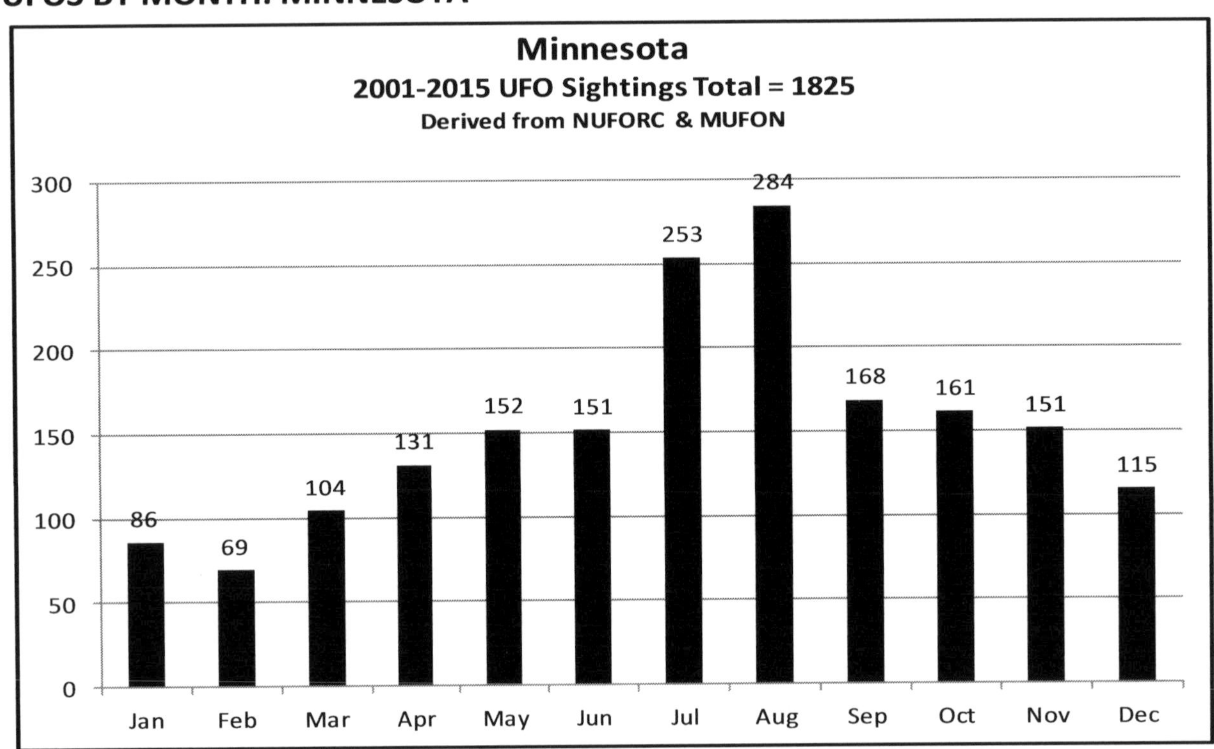

Year	Jan	Feb	Mar	Apr	May	Jun	Jul	Aug	Sep	Oct	Nov	Dec	Total
2001	3	2	5	7	5	3	6	12	3	4	6	3	59
2002	3	3	1	2	2	3	4	4	4	4	4	3	37
2003	2	3	1	4	3	2	7	13	7	7	7	1	57
2004	1	2	7	3	8	5	10	26	10	4	6	1	83
2005	3	4	6	5	7	8	11	12	9	11	12		88
2006	4	4	8	8	8	9	10	11	6	5	9	8	90
2007	8	1	3	6	6	12	11	14	6	9	7	4	87
2008	7	6	3	7	9	8	16	16	4	10	5	9	100
2009	8	4	5	9	12	6	21	14	12	12	7	6	116
2010	4	5	8	10	12	5	24	7	6	17	12	4	114
2011	5	6	12	8	14	10	23	22	23	9	9	16	157
2012	11	12	14	16	20	32	28	36	22	14	18	15	238
2013	8	4	8	19	15	16	24	26	16	19	20	26	201
2014	5	11	10	16	13	10	31	17	18	17	14	13	175
2015	14	2	13	11	18	22	27	54	22	19	15	6	223
Total	**86**	**69**	**104**	**131**	**152**	**151**	**253**	**284**	**168**	**161**	**151**	**115**	**1825**

Distribution of Sightings between Databases: Minnesota

Database	Count	Percentage
MUFON	678	37.15%
NUFORC	1147	62.85%
Total	1825	100.00%

State Demographic Information: Minnesota

2010 US Census Statistics	
Population	
Area in Square Miles	
Land Area Sq. Miles	
Population/Square mile	

MISSISSIPPI

UFO RANK 41/51

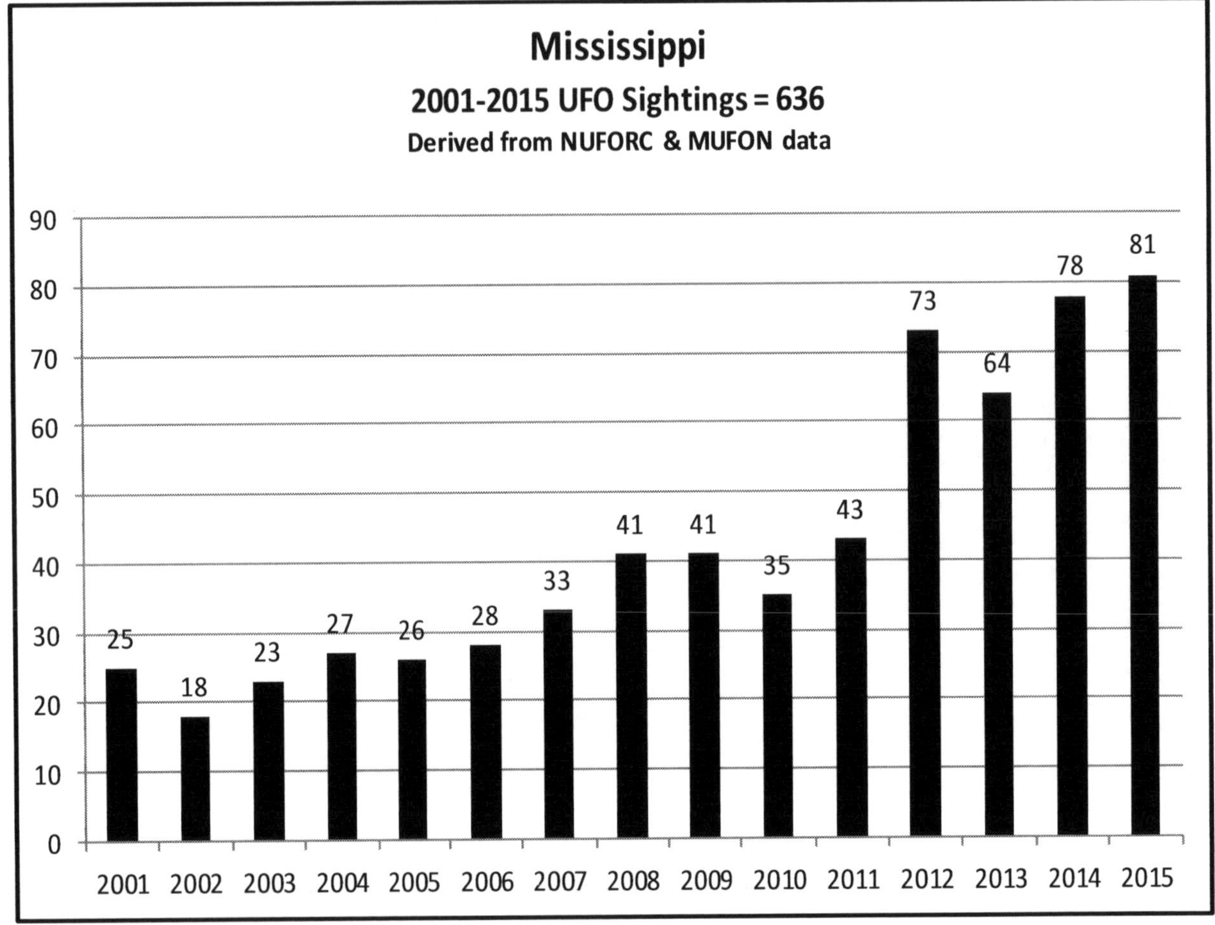

TOP TEN COUNTIES		RANK	TOP TEN SHAPES		
Harrison	76	1	Light	81	12.74%
Desoto	47	2	Circle	77	12.11%
Hinds	41	3	Triangle	66	10.38%
Jackson	37	4	Sphere	64	10.06%
Forrest	30	5	Unknown	57	8.96%
Rankin	29	6	Other	51	8.02%
Lee	22	7	Fireball	40	6.29%
Pearl River	21	8	Disk	23	3.62%
Unknown	21	9	Disc	22	3.46%
Madison	18	10	Star-like	22	3.46%

UFO SHAPES: MISSISSIPPI

UFO Shapes	2001	2002	2003	2004	2005	2006	2007	2008	2009	2010	2011	2012	2013	2014	2015	Total
Blimp													2	1		3
Boomerang		1											1		6	8
Bullet/Missile				2				1		1		1				5
Changing		1	1	1				1				1	1	2	1	9
Chevron				1				1			1				1	4
Cigar					1			1		1		3	1	2		9
Circle	5			1		4	2	4	3	6	10	9	12	13	8	77
Cone												1	1	1		3
Cross							1					1				2
Cylinder		1		1	1	1	2			2		2	5	1	3	19
Diamond						1	1		2			2	1		1	8
Disc	1		1			1	1	3	1	1		4	1	4	4	22
Disk	4	1	3	4		1	2	1	1	2		1	1	1	1	23
Egg			1								1	1	1	2	1	7
Fireball	1		1		3	2	2	3	1	1	2		5	9	10	40
Flash					2		1	4	1		1	1	1	2	1	14
Formation				1					1	1		1	1	1	2	8
Light	5	2	7	6	2	6	3	4	6	7	4	11	8	7	3	81
N/A															1	1
Other		2	2	1	7	6	2	5	3	3	5	4	2	5	4	51
Oval	2							1	3		2	2	2	1	5	18
Rectangle					4				2		1		1			8
Sphere	2	2	3		1	3	3	3	4	4	4	8	7	6	14	64
Star-like					1			4	3		3	1	1	6	3	22
Teardrop	2	1			1					1		1		1		7
Triangle	2	5	1	3	1	1	6	2	7	5	4	6	5	10	8	66
Unknown	1	2	3	6	2	2	7	3	3		5	12	4	3	4	57
Total	**25**	**18**	**23**	**27**	**26**	**28**	**33**	**41**	**41**	**35**	**43**	**73**	**64**	**78**	**81**	**636**

UFOS BY COUNTY: MISSISSIPPI

Counties	2001	2002	2003	2004	2005	2006	2007	2008	2009	2010	2011	2012	2013	2014	2015	Total
Adams				1	1							1	2			5
Alcorn						1		1		1		3				6
Amite								1								1
Attala									2							2
Bolivar				1	1								1	2		5
Calhoun					1											1
Chickasaw													2			2
Choctaw										1				1		2
Claiborne		1													1	2
Clay														1	1	2
Coahoma										1		1	1		1	4
Copiah			1													1
Covington						1		1			2		1			5
Desoto		1	2		3	2	1	1	6	2	2	3	3	9	12	47
Forrest	1		1			2		3	1	2	2	2	5	6	5	30
Franklin					1	1						1	4	1		8
George	1				1	1										3
Greene			1												2	3
Grenada									1			1	2		1	5
Hancock			1					2				3	1	3	2	12
Harrison	3	4	3	4	3	2	3	5	7	3	5	13	4	9	8	76
Hinds	6	3	1	4	1			3	2		6	10	1	1	3	41
Holmes	1															1
Humphreys			1		1											2
Itawamba				1								3		2		6
Jackson	2		3	2	1	2	3		3	3	3	3	5	4	3	37
Jasper									3			2		1		6
Jefferson		1												1		2
Jefferson Davis									1							1
Jones	1			1		1		2			1	1	1	3	1	12
Lafayette							1			1	1	1	1			5
Lamar				2			1	1	1		1			2	3	11
Lauderdale				1	2	1	1	1	1	2	2				2	13
Lawrence														2		2
Leake			1													1
Lee	1	1	2				1	2	1		4	1	3	3	3	22
Leflore							3					1	1			5

Costas' UFO Sightings Desk Reference: USA 2001-2015

Counties	2001	2002	2003	2004	2005	2006	2007	2008	2009	2010	2011	2012	2013	2014	2015	Total
Lincoln			1			1		1			1	1	1			6
Lowndes				5		1	1			1		1	1	3		13
Madison				2	1					2	1	1	2	3	6	18
Marion	1				3		3					1		1	1	10
Marshall	1	1					1		1					2		6
Monroe			1					1					2	1	1	6
Neshoba	1	1							1				1		1	5
Newton					1										1	2
Noxubee						1										1
Oktibbeha			1		2	1					2			2		8
Panola	1							1		1		2	1	2	4	12
Pearl River				1		4	3	5	1	1		1	2		3	21
Perry							1	1								2
Pike							2			2	1	3		1		9
Pontotoc	2	3		1			1					1			2	10
Prentiss							1				1	1				3
Quitman						1	1									2
Rankin		1		1	2	1		3	3	3	2	3	4	2	4	29
Scott			1												1	2
Simpson						1			1					1		3
Smith							1									1
Stone									1	1			2		1	5
Sunflower	1							1						2		4
Tate										1	1		1	2		5
Tippah														1	2	3
Tishomingo								1	1	1				2		5
Tunica										1		2	2			5
Union															1	1
Unknown		1	2		1	1	2	2			3	3	3	1	2	21
Walthall												1				1
Warren	2							1		2	2		1	1		9
Washington							1						3			4
Wayne															1	1
Webster						1									2	3
Wilkinson									2							2
Winston									1			1				2
Yalobusha						1										1
Yazoo							1	1		3		1				6

Counties	2001	2002	2003	2004	2005	2006	2007	2008	2009	2010	2011	2012	2013	2014	2015	Total
Total	25	18	23	27	26	28	33	41	41	35	43	73	64	78	81	636

If a county is missing from the list, it's because no UFO sightings were logged in either the NUFORC or MUFON databases for the 2001-2015 sample period.

UFOS BY MONTH: MISSISSIPPI

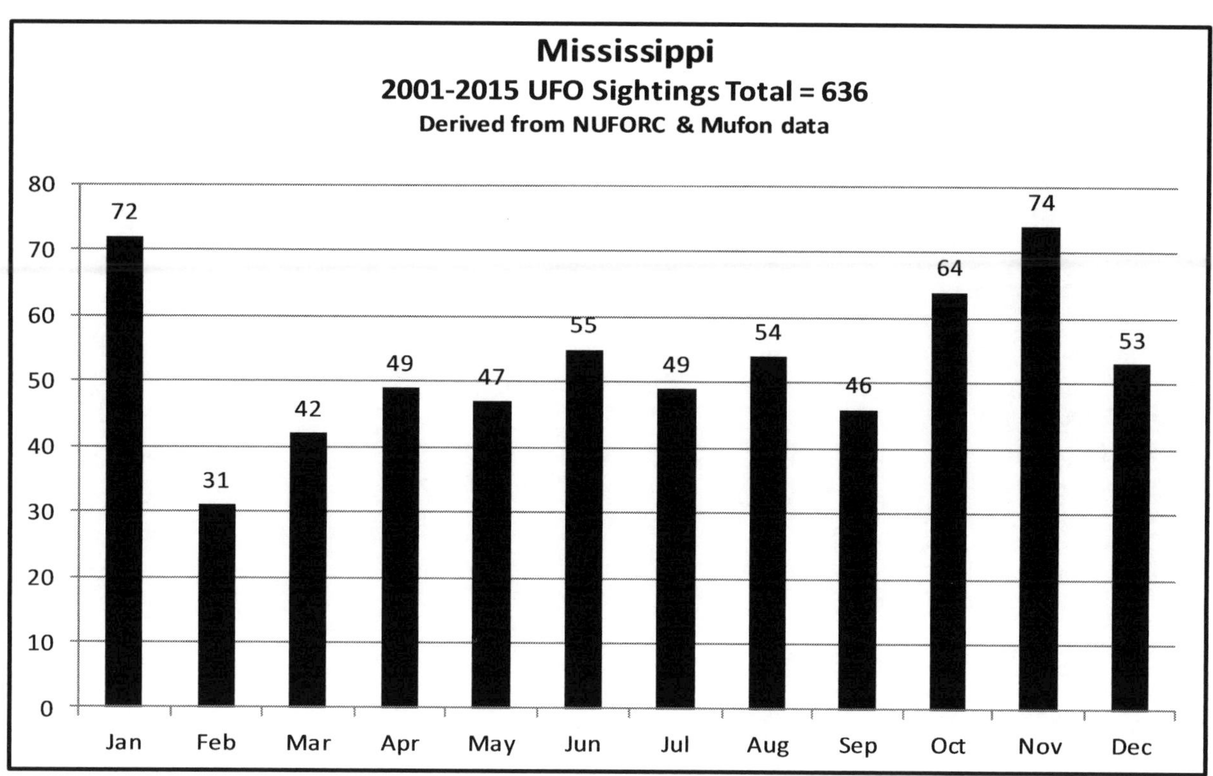

Year	Jan	Feb	Mar	Apr	May	Jun	Jul	Aug	Sep	Oct	Nov	Dec	Total
2001	2	1	4		3	4	3		1	2	3	2	25
2002	5	1	1			1	4	2	2	2			18
2003	2		1	1		2		1	1	1	8	6	23
2004	3	1	1	2	4	3		5	1	3	1	3	27
2005	1	3	4	1	1	1	2	6	3	2	1	1	26
2006	3	3	4		1	1		2	1	5	5	3	28
2007	6	1	4	3	2	1		1	3	3	7	2	33
2008	4	3	4	4	2	5	4	2	3	2	6	2	41
2009	7	1	1	6	7	1	4	1	2	2	6	3	41
2010	4	1	4	3	2	4		3	2	5	6	1	35
2011	6			1	2	3	1	6	6	12	2	4	43
2012	6	4	3	10	3	10	9	5	3	2	11	7	73
2013	5	2	4	4	4	5	6	8	6	7	8	5	64
2014	12	3	3	9	10	4	6	7	3	8	5	8	78
2015	6	7	4	5	6	10	10	5	9	8	5	6	81
Total	**72**	**31**	**42**	**49**	**47**	**55**	**49**	**54**	**46**	**64**	**74**	**53**	**636**

Distribution of Sightings between Databases: Mississippi

Database	Count	Percentage
MUFON	238	37.42%
NUFORC	398	62.58%
Total	636	100.00%

State Demographic Information: Mississippi

2010 US Census Statistics	
Population	2,967,297.00
Area in Square Miles	48,431.78
Land Area Sq. Miles	46,923.27
Population/Square mile	63.20

MISSOURI

UFO RANK 14/51

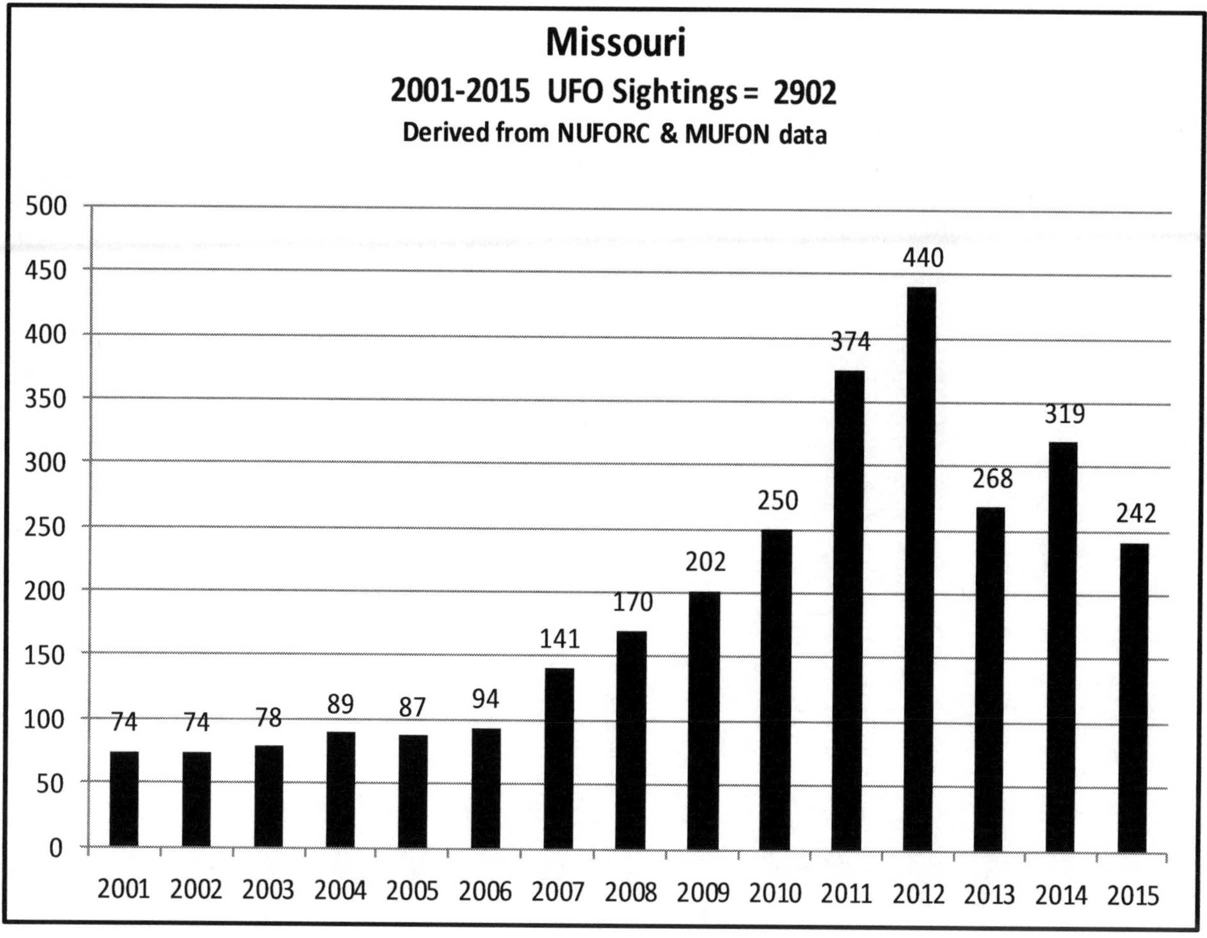

TOP TEN COUNTIES		RANK	TOP TEN SHAPES		
Jackson	584	1	Sphere	329	11.34%
Saint Louis	413	2	Triangle	320	11.03%
Saint Charles	189	3	Circle	315	10.85%
Greene	129	4	Light	296	10.20%
Boone	117	5	Unknown	267	9.20%
Unknown	102	6	Fireball	218	7.51%
Jefferson	91	7	Other	201	6.93%
Clay	65	8	Star-like	130	4.48%
Jasper	50	9	Oval	103	3.55%
Cass	49	10	Disk	95	3.27%

UFO SHAPES: MISSOURI

UFO Shapes	2001	2002	2003	2004	2005	2006	2007	2008	2009	2010	2011	2012	2013	2014	2015	Total
Blimp		1				1		3			8	2	5	1		21
Boomerang	1						2	4	2	4	15	6	6	6	1	47
Bullet/ Missile					1		1	1	1	1	6	2	3	1		17
Changing	2	1	1	2	4	1		2	2	5	2	6	4	4	1	37
Chevron	1	1	1		2	1		2	4	9	5	12	3	3	3	47
Cigar	3	4	3	2	3	1	5	15	4	9	8	11	5	6	6	85
Circle	5	3	4	5	6	10	5	11	24	33	54	64	31	34	26	315
Cone							1	1	2	2	1	1	1			9
Cross	1				1					1	4	1	2	1		11
Cylinder	2	2		3	3	6	3	5	5	4	4	7	6	4	10	64
Diamond	3	1		2		3		4	3	1	6	8	6	6	4	47
Disc		2	2			3	4	5	5	6	21	16	10	9	8	91
Disk	2	11	4	6	4	2	7	9	5	3	14	10	5	9	4	95
Egg					1	1	2	1		1	2	4			3	15
Fireball	4	3	1	5	6	5	6	8	21	21	30	42	27	27	12	218
Flash	1	1	2			2	4		3	3	4	3	5	2	4	34
Formation	3				1	2	2	1	4	4		3	5	1	4	30
Light	15	5	15	17	14	16	24	24	17	29	22	34	25	28	11	296
N/A										1				3	2	6
Other	5	7	11	6	6	5	12	8	11	18	23	27	12	24	26	201
Oval	3	3	4	3	1	2	6	5	9	7	17	13	6	17	7	103
Rectangle		1		1		1	1	1	3	3		3	1	3	6	24
Saturn-like		2							1			1	1			5
Sphere	4	8	7	9	6	8	4	16	20	22	40	69	38	48	30	329
Sq/Rect										1				1	6	8
Star-like					1		2	10	12	13	13	26	19	16	18	130
Teardrop		3	2	2	2	1			4	4		3	1	7	1	30
Triangle	15	7	9	12	10	14	32	16	13	19	40	32	25	45	31	320
Unknown	4	8	12	14	15	9	18	18	27	26	35	34	16	13	18	267
Total	**74**	**74**	**78**	**89**	**87**	**94**	**141**	**170**	**202**	**250**	**374**	**440**	**268**	**319**	**242**	**2902**

UFOS BY COUNTY: MISSOURI

Counties	2001	2002	2003	2004	2005	2006	2007	2008	2009	2010	2011	2012	2013	2014	2015	Total
Adair										2		3	1	1	1	8
Andrew				1	1			1				1	1	1	1	7
Atchison							1	1				2		1		5
Audrain						2	1	1	1			2		1	1	9
Barry			1					1				4	13	3	8	30
Barton		1	1									1				3
Bates	1				1	1	1	3	6	3	1	3	1		3	24
Benton	1		1		2	2	1		1	1	2					11
Bollinger									1		1	1			1	4
Boone	7	5	3	3	7	7	14	9	12	1	5	15	10	7	12	117
Buchanan			2		1	2		1	1	2	8	11	1	1	3	33
Butler		1						1			2		1		2	7
Caldwell				1											1	2
Callaway	2						2	5	1		7	3	8	7	1	36
Camden	1	2	2					1	5	6	7		1	4	3	32
Cape Girardeau		1		2	2			1	1	2	1	6	3	3	6	28
Carroll				1	1	1					1		1			5
Carter			3		2		1				2					8
Cass			4	2	1		3	1	2	2	8	9	6	7	4	49
Cedar							1					1		2		4
Christian	2				2	2	1		1	3	2	5	3	2	1	24
Clay	1	1		1	2	2	4	3	2	7	4	16	6	9	7	65
Clinton							1	1	1			2		2		7
Cole	1			1	1	2	2	2	1	2		3		4	4	23
Cooper	1											1	1			3
Crawford			2					1		2		2	1	2		10
Dade		1							2	1	1					5
Dallas				1						1	3	1		4		10
Daviess												1				1
Dent			1	1		1	5	7	4	1	3	3	2	1		29
Douglas										1						1
Dunklin	1							3	2		1				2	9
Franklin	2	4	1	2	1	1	2		3	1	7	5	2	5	6	42
Gasconade		1		2				2	2	1	1	1		3		13
Gentry				1												1
Greene	6	7	2	4	6	8	12	6	4	10	9	27	11	14	3	129
Grundy			3							1						4

Counties	2001	2002	2003	2004	2005	2006	2007	2008	2009	2010	2011	2012	2013	2014	2015	Total
Hancock	1											1				2
Harrison										2	1				1	4
Henry			5	3		2	2	1	1	4	3	1	2		4	28
Hickory		2		1	1	1	1	1	2		2	1				12
Howard		1		1												2
Howell		1	1	1	2	1	2	1		1	3	5	1	1	1	21
Iron			1	2		1	2			1	4				1	12
Jackson	19	9	12	16	14	11	18	19	38	51	140	103	38	55	41	584
Jasper			1	2		3	3	3	2	2	6	10	2	11	5	50
Jefferson				1	2	1	3	2	3	8	10	22	14	18	7	91
Johnson	2				1	2		5	1	4	3	6	4	1		29
Laclede		1						1	1	1	3	4		1		12
Lafayette	1	2		1			2	1			2	1	1		1	12
Lawrence	1	2		2			1	1								7
Lewis					1								1	1		3
Lincoln			4				1	1	1	3	2	1		3	1	17
Linn						2				1	2				1	6
Livingston										1			1		1	3
Macon						1						1				2
Madison							1					2		2	1	6
Maries				3	1								1			5
Marion			1	1						1	1		2		1	7
Mcdonald					1			3	1	4	1	1		1	1	13
Miller				1		1		1	1		1			2		7
Mississippi				1								1				2
Moniteau			1	1			2				3		1	1	1	10
Monroe		1									1		1		3	6
Montgomery						1	2							1	1	5
Morgan		1		1	2	2	1	1	1	3	2		2	1		17
New Madrid			1							1			1	1		4
Newton				3	2			2	1	1		1	1	4		15
Nodaway			1			1		2			1			2		7
Oregon						2		2			3	1				8
Osage											1	5		1		7
Ozark			1					1		1				2	12	17
Pemiscot		2	1									1				4
Perry							1				2	1			1	5

Counties	2001	2002	2003	2004	2005	2006	2007	2008	2009	2010	2011	2012	2013	2014	2015	Total
Pettis	2						1		3	1			1	1	1	10
Phelps	3		3	2		4	5	3	1	2	4	2	8	1	3	41
Pike									1			1				2
Platte		2	1					2		5		8	2		1	21
Polk		1		5					2	5	1	4		1	1	20
Pulaski							1	1	4	6	1	3		1	2	19
Ralls												1	1			2
Randolph					1	2				1					1	5
Ray		1	1		1							4		3	1	11
Reynolds						1				1			1	1		4
Ripley	1	1		1												3
Saint Charles	2	4	3	1	8	3	5	12	10	19	19	27	34	26	16	189
Saint Clair			1		1		2				3	1			1	9
Saint Francois			1	1	1	2	1	1	6		3	5	3		5	29
Saint Louis	8	13	9	8	13	6	15	29	48	49	41	51	35	49	39	413
Sainte Genevieve													1			1
Saline	1					1	3	1			1	1	1	2	1	12
Scotland											1					1
Scott			1					2		2	1		1	1		8
Shannon												1	1		1	3
Shelby												1				1
Ste. Genevieve											1					1
Stoddard				3					1	2	1	2	1			10
Stone	2	1		1	1				1				2	2		10
Sullivan												1				1
Taney	1	2				1	1	4	3	8	6	5	8	4	1	44
Texas		3		1	1	1	3							2		11
Unknown			1		1	3	5	13	8	6	14	15	10	19	7	102
Vernon	1					1	3	1		1		1	5	3	3	19
Warren	1							1	1	1		1	2	2	1	10
Washington	2			1	1				3		2		2	2	2	15
Wayne			1			3				1	1	4	1	5		16
Webster						1	2	1	1		1	2	2			10
Worth									1							1
Wright				1	1	2			2			1		1		8

Counties	2001	2002	2003	2004	2005	2006	2007	2008	2009	2010	2011	2012	2013	2014	2015	Total
Total	74	74	78	89	87	94	141	170	202	250	374	440	268	319	242	2902

If a county is missing from the list, it's because no UFO sightings were logged in either the NUFORC or MUFON databases for the 2001-2015 sample period.

UFOS BY MONTH: MISSOURI

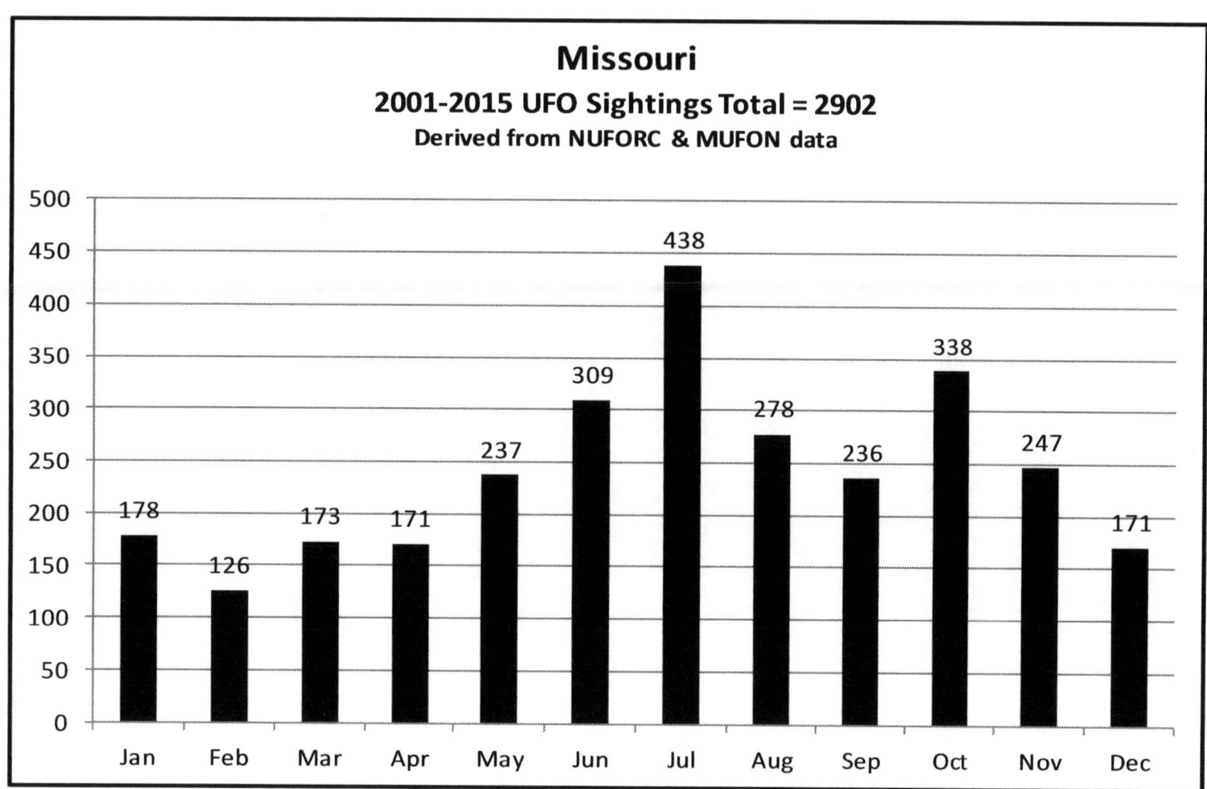

Year	Jan	Feb	Mar	Apr	May	Jun	Jul	Aug	Sep	Oct	Nov	Dec	Total
2001	2	5	4	2	7	5	8	6	11	9	6	9	74
2002	6	4	2	9	6	10	8	5	9	4	6	5	74
2003	3	1	5	2	5	5	10	3	11	13	13	7	78
2004	7	8	5	6	8	7	5	12	10	4	7	10	89
2005		1	8	9	6	17	12	6	6	13	7	2	87
2006	5	3	11	4	9	10	13	7	2	10	10	10	94
2007	16	10	17	11	11	17	12	12	8	9	10	8	141
2008	12	11	9	10	15	16	25	12	16	16	14	14	170
2009	18	9	16	8	17	21	28	14	26	17	19	9	202
2010	11	1	6	18	26	28	54	24	16	38	18	10	250
2011	10	10	10	11	19	26	48	46	25	113	32	24	374
2012	29	27	31	21	45	52	86	40	22	14	47	26	440
2013	9	7	16	12	26	22	47	33	23	27	27	19	268
2014	19	19	9	29	22	49	52	40	32	25	15	8	319
2015	31	10	24	19	15	24	30	18	19	26	16	10	242
Total	**178**	**126**	**173**	**171**	**237**	**309**	**438**	**278**	**236**	**338**	**247**	**171**	**2902**

Distribution of Sightings between Databases: Missouri

Database	Count	Percentage
MUFON	1405	48.41%
NUFORC	1497	51.59%
Total	2902	100.00%

State Demographic Information: Missouri

2010 US Census Statistics	
Population	5,988,927.00
Area in Square Miles	69,706.99
Land Area Sq. Miles	68,741.52
Population/Square mile	87.10

MONTANA

UFO RANK 42/51

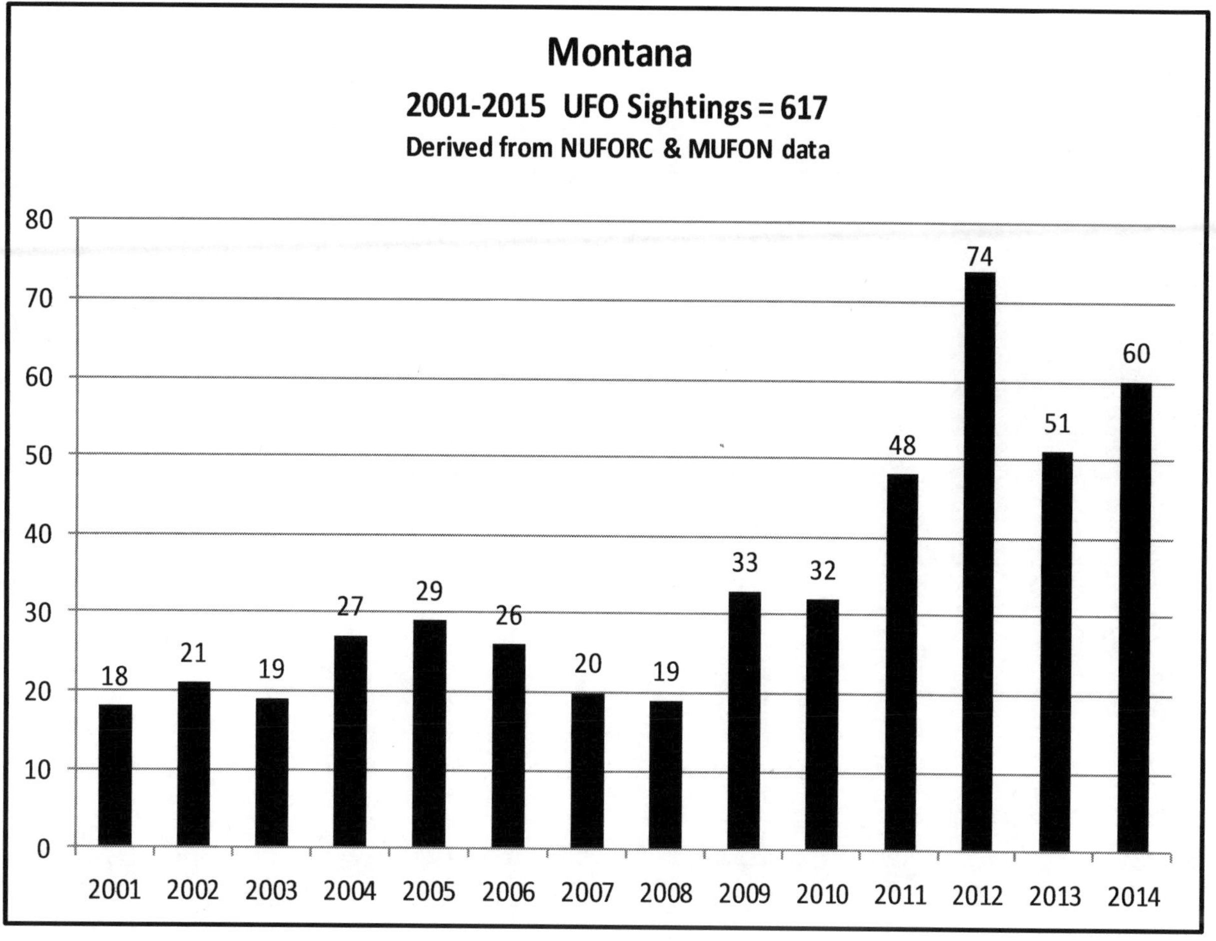

TOP TEN COUNTIES		RANK	TOP TEN SHAPES		
Gallatin	76	1	Light	123	19.94%
Missoula	67	2	Unknown	73	11.83%
Yellowstone	63	3	Fireball	71	11.51%
Flathead	61	4	Triangle	60	9.72%
Cascade	42	5	Circle	52	8.43%
Lewis And Clark	40	6	Sphere	45	7.29%
Silver Bow	37	7	Other	30	4.86%
Ravalli	20	8	Oval	22	3.57%
Lincoln	18	9	Disk	21	3.40%
Glacier	16	10	Formation	17	2.76%

UFO SHAPES: MONTANA

UFO Shapes	2001	2002	2003	2004	2005	2006	2007	2008	2009	2010	2011	2012	2013	2014	2015	Total
Blimp															1	1
Changing	1		1			1			1			2	2	2	1	11
Chevron		1	1			2					1	2		2	3	12
Cigar		2	1		1					1		1	1		2	9
Circle	2		2	2	1	1	1	1	2	1	1	6	6	6	20	52
Cone							1								1	2
Cross			2					1								3
cylinder							1			2				1	2	6
Diamond						1			2			3	2	1		9
Disc														1	6	7
Disk	2	2	1	2	2	1			2	3	1		2	1	2	21
Egg	1				1					1			1			4
Fireball	1	4	2	4	4	5	4		2	2	6	8	6	6	17	71
Flash		1			1				1		1	4	3	3	2	16
Formation		2	1	3	1	1				1	1	2	1	1	3	17
Light	6	2	2	8	6	5	3	6	10	8	12	15	12	11	17	123
N/A		1							1							2
Other			2	2	2	1		1	2	1	5	2	3	1	8	30
Oval	1	1	1		1	1	1	1	1	1	4	2	3	3	1	22
Rectangle	1	1									1	1				4
Sphere			1		1	1	2	1	3	3	5	5	2	6	15	45
Starlike															4	4
Star-like															4	4
Teardrop						1	2	1			1			1	2	8
Triangle	2			4	3	2	1	4		4	5	10	2	4	19	60
Unknown	1	4	2	2	5	3	4	3	6	4	4	11	5	10	9	73
Unspecified															1	1
Total	**18**	**21**	**19**	**27**	**29**	**26**	**20**	**19**	**33**	**32**	**48**	**74**	**51**	**60**	**140**	**617**

UFOS BY COUNTY: MONTANA

Counties	2001	2002	2003	2004	2005	2006	2007	2008	2009	2010	2011	2012	2013	2014	2015	Total
Beaverhead				1						1		1				3
Big Horn		1		1		2		1	1		2	2		1		11
Blaine					1		1				1					3
Broadwater													1			1
Butte												1		1		2
Carbon	1				1				1	1				1	3	8
Cascade	3	1	1	3	4	1	1	1	1	4	1	3	2	4	12	42
Chouteau									1							1
Custer						1					1	1		1	2	6
Daniels		1			1											2
Dawson			1										1			2
Deer Lodge									2			1			2	5
Fergus	1			1								2	1			5
Flathead	2	1	5	4	4	3	2	2	3	1	5	7	7	8	7	61
Gallatin	1	1	2	1	2	2	3	1	2	2	6	19	10	7	17	76
Garfield												1				1
Glacier		1		1	2		1		1	2	1	4			3	16
Golden Valley				1												1
Hill			2		3			1	1	4		1		1		13
Jefferson		3		1						1				1	1	7
Judith Basin												1				1
Lake				1	2				1	2		3	2	1	2	14
Lewis & Clark	2		1	2	2		1		1	3	4	4	3	6	11	40
Liberty														1		1
Lincoln		1				2		1	2		1	1	2		8	18
Madison													3			3
Meagher			1							1		1				3
Mineral				1					1			1				3
Missoula	2	2	2	1	1	4	3	2	7	6	4	7	7	4	15	67
Park	1		1					1	1		1				2	7
Petroleum								1			1				2	4
Phillips	1	1									1					3
Pondera				1		2				1						4
Powell		2														2
Prairie											1				1	2
Ravalli				1		3	3	1	2		1	3	1	2	3	20
Richland													1	1	3	5

Counties	**2001**	**2002**	**2003**	**2004**	**2005**	**2006**	**2007**	**2008**	**2009**	**2010**	**2011**	**2012**	**2013**	**2014**	**2015**	**Total**
Roosevelt					2	1	1	1	2		3			3	3	16
Rosebud	1								1		1			1		4
Sanders		1		1								4	2	2	6	16
Silver Bow		4		2	2	1	2	4	1	1	3	3	3	2	9	37
Stillwater					1	1	1							1		4
Sweet Grass					1											1
Toole				1												1
Unknown	1		1											1	6	9
Valley									1		1					2
Wheatland	1															1
Yellowstone	1	1	2	2		3	1	2		2	9	3	5	10	22	63
Total	**18**	**21**	**19**	**27**	**29**	**26**	**20**	**19**	**33**	**32**	**48**	**74**	**51**	**60**	**140**	**617**

If a county is missing from the list, it's because no UFO sightings were logged in either the NUFORC or MUFON databases for the 2001-2015 sample period.

UFOS BY MONTH: MONTANA

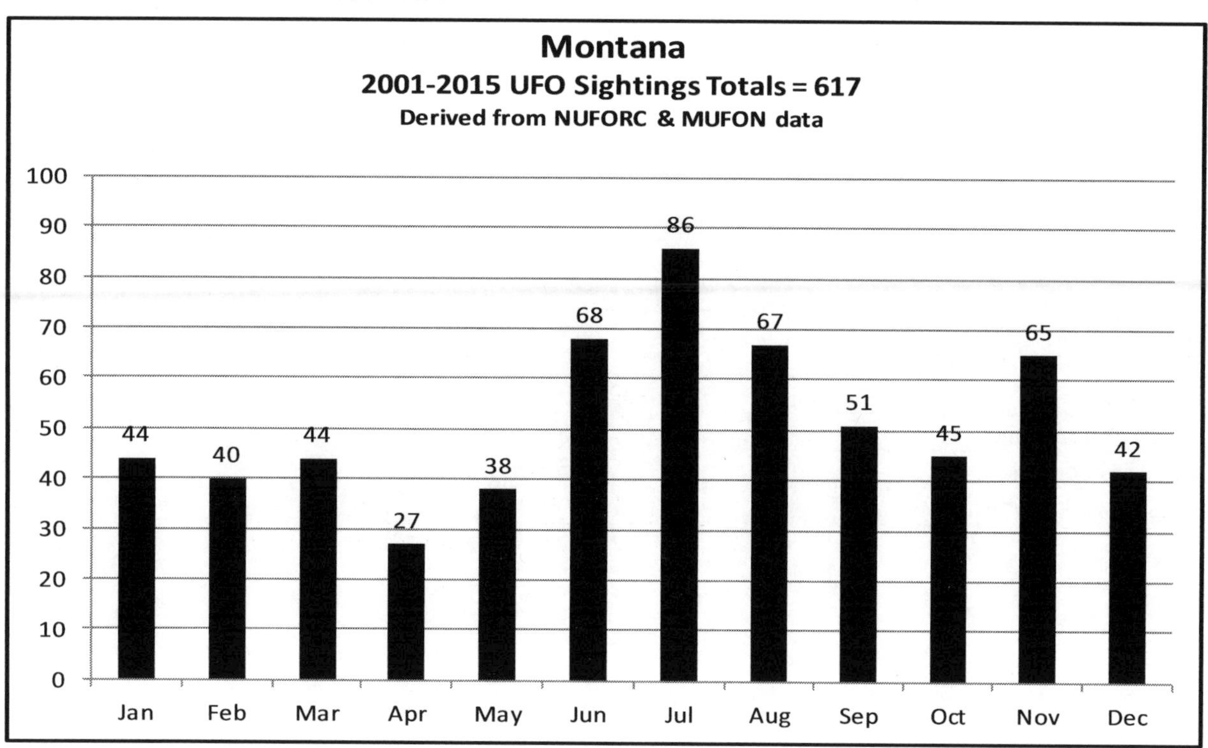

Year	Jan	Feb	Mar	Apr	May	Jun	Jul	Aug	Sep	Oct	Nov	Dec	Total
2001	1		1	2	2	3	4	1				4	18
2002	2	1	1		2	5	5	1	1	2	1		21
2003	1	2	1		1		3	4	1	1	3	2	19
2004	2	1	5	1	3	1		5	2	3	3	1	27
2005	2	2	2	1	1	3	3	2	5	3	3	2	29
2006	2	3	1	1		2	2	4	1	4	4	2	26
2007	1	1	3	1	1	4	3	1	2	2	1		20
2008	1	4	2	2		3	2	1	1	2	1		19
2009	2	2			2	6	6	7	3	1	4		33
2010	3		6	1	3	1	7	4		2	3	2	32
2011	1	1	4	1	1	1	13	10	2	3	4	7	48
2012	4	1	8		10	7	9	8	7	4	10	6	74
2013	4	2	1	1	2	8	11	5	3	2	5	7	51
2014	7	10	1	3	2	9	9	5	4	4	2	4	60
2015	11	10	8	13	8	15	9	9	19	12	21	5	140
Total	**44**	**40**	**44**	**27**	**38**	**68**	**86**	**67**	**51**	**45**	**65**	**42**	**617**

Distribution of Sightings between Databases: Montana

Database	Count	Percentage
MUFON	90	14.59%
NUFORC	527	85.41%
Total	617	100.00%

State Demographic Information: Montana

2010 US Census Statistics	
Population	989,415.00
Area in Square Miles	147,039.71
Land Area Sq. Miles	145,545.80
Population/Square mile	6.80

NEBRASKA

UFO RANK 40/51

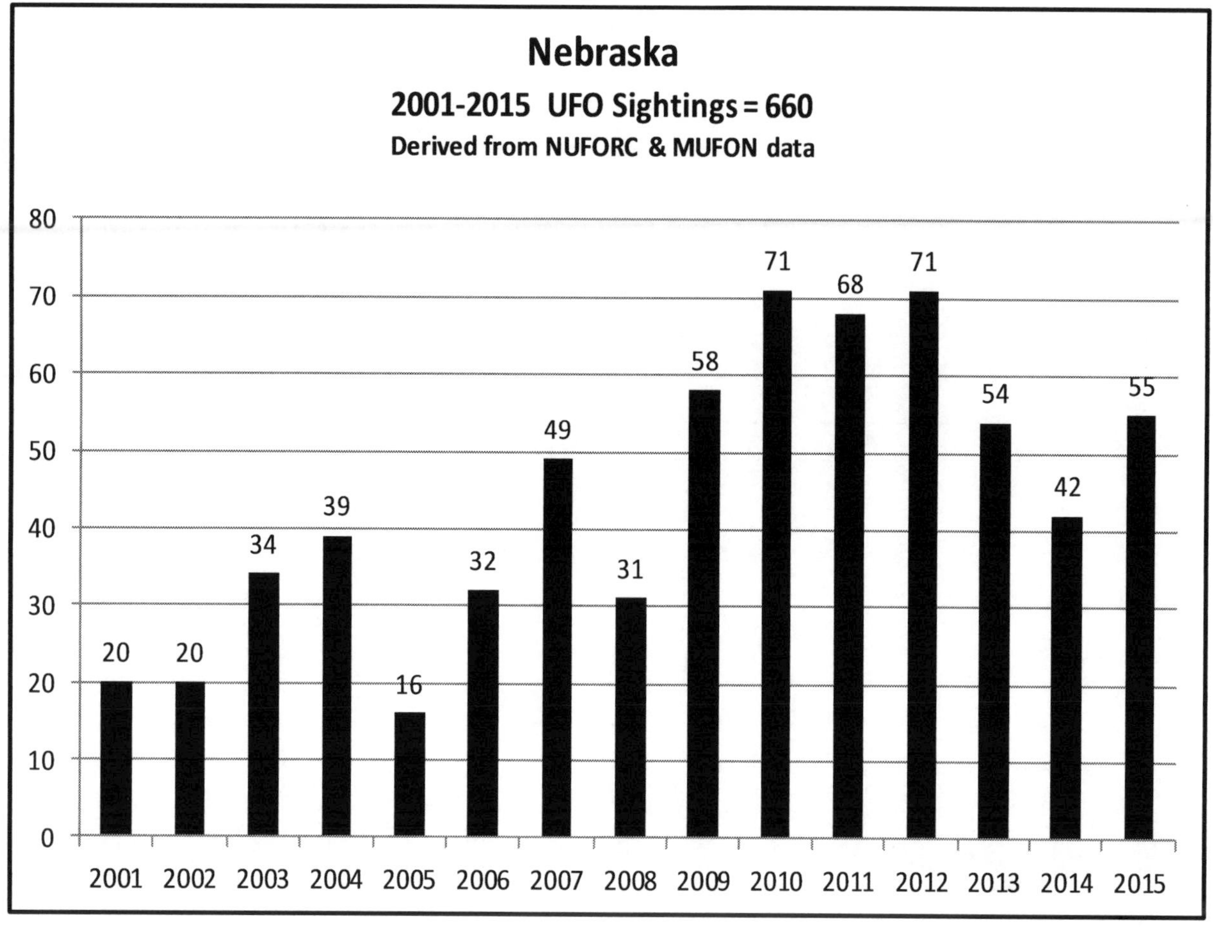

TOP TEN COUNTIES		RANK	TOP TEN SHAPES		
Douglas	230	1	Light	105	13.82%
Lancaster	121	2	Circle	86	11.32%
Sarpy	40	3	Unknown	77	10.13%
Lincoln	25	4	Sphere	73	9.61%
Hall	14	5	Triangle	72	9.47%
Unknown	14	6	Other	60	7.89%
Scotts Bluff	12	7	Fireball	48	6.32%
Dodge	11	8	Cigar	29	3.82%
Keith	11	9	Star-like	27	3.55%
Adams	10	10	Disk	26	3.42%

UFO SHAPES: NEBRASKA

UFO Shapes	2001	2002	2003	2004	2005	2006	2007	2008	2009	2010	2011	2012	2013	2014	2015	Total
Blimp						1										1
Boomerang	1		1				1			1	6	1	2		2	15
Bullet/Missile											1					1
Changing		1	1		2	1	1		2	1					1	10
Chevron											1	1	1			3
Cigar	2	2	1				3	5	3	1	1	1		1	2	22
Circle	1		1	2	2	1	5	3	10	10	10	12	10	7	5	79
Cone				2											1	3
Cross										1			1			2
Cylinder									1		1	3	2		1	8
Diamond					1		1		1	2		1	2	1	1	10
Disc		1	1	1	1	2		1	3	1	4	1	1	2	2	21
Disk			3	1	1		1		1	1	3	2			2	15
Egg								1			1					2
Fireball	4	2		1	2	1	4		3	9	2	6	2	4	3	43
Flash	1		1		1	1	1		1		1			1	1	9
Formation			2	2	1		2	1						2	1	11
Light	3	4	6	6	2	10	7	4	7	10	7	11	6	8	4	95
N/A															1	1
Other	1	3	7	8	1	1	3	1	2	5	5	5	5		4	51
Oval	1		1	3	1	3	1	1	2	2	1	1	1	1		19
Rectangle		1		3	1		2			1		2	1		1	12
Saturn-like							1									1
Sphere	1	2	1	2		3	1	3	10	8	8	7	7	4	9	66
Star-like	1					2	3	1	3	5	5	3	2	2		27
Teardrop		2						1		1	2	1		1	1	9
Triangle	2		3	3		5	9	4	3	4	4	5	5	2	10	59
Unknown	2	2	5	5		1	3	5	6	8	5	8	6	6	3	65
Total	**20**	**20**	**34**	**39**	**16**	**32**	**49**	**31**	**58**	**71**	**68**	**71**	**54**	**42**	**55**	**660**

UFOS BY COUNTY: NEBRASKA

Counties	2001	2002	2003	2004	2005	2006	2007	2008	2009	2010	2011	2012	2013	2014	2015	Total
Adams		1		1				2			3	1	1	1		10
Antelope										1			1	2		4
Arthur			1													1
Boone					1											1
Box Butte									1							1
Boyd	1															1
Brown				1			2	2				1				6
Buffalo			1						1	3		2	1		1	9
Burt				1						1	2					4
Butler												2				2
Cass						1	1		1	2	1	1				7
Cedar							1							1		2
Chase														1		1
Cherry	1						3	1								5
Cheyenne			1													1
Clay				2					1						1	4
Colfax															1	1
Crowley															1	1
Cuming			1				1									2
Custer		1														1
Dakota			1							1			3			5
Dawes			1	1												2
Dawson													3		1	4
Dixon		1										1			1	3
Dodge	1									4	2		1	2	1	11
Douglas	6	5	11	10	5	15	19	8	22	31	22	35	9	19	13	230
Fillmore						1				1		1	1			4
Franklin			1													1
Frontier							1									1
Gage				1			1		2		1	1				6
Garfield											1				1	2
Greeley								1								1
Hall	1			2	2		1	2	3		1		1		1	14
Hamilton												2				2
Harlan															1	1
Hitchcock										1						1
Holt				1								3				4

Counties	**2001**	**2002**	**2003**	**2004**	**2005**	**2006**	**2007**	**2008**	**2009**	**2010**	**2011**	**2012**	**2013**	**2014**	**2015**	**Total**
Hooker		1														1
Jefferson					1				1							2
Johnson												1				1
Keith			1	1	1						2		1	2	3	11
Keya Paha	1			1												2
Knox	1													1		2
Lancaster	3	4	2	8	4	9	10	8	11	9	10	6	18	7	12	121
Lincoln		1	1	2			2	2	4	1	2	4	5		1	25
Madison										2	4				1	7
Merrick		1								1				1		3
Nemaha															1	1
Otoe	1	1						1	1			1	1			6
Pierce						1										1
Platte			1				1	1		2	1		1		2	9
Polk								1								1
Red Willow					1				1			1				3
Richardson				1							1					2
Saline			1							1	1				1	4
Sarpy	2	2	3	3	1	2	2	2	4	2	5	3	4	2	3	40
Saunders			2							2	1				1	6
Scotts Bluff			1			1			3	1	1	3	1	1		12
Seward			1				1			2	1					5
Sheridan														1		1
Stanton										1						1
Thayer				1												1
Thurston				1						1	1					3
Unknown			2			1	1		1		4	1			4	14
Valey															1	1
Valley											1					1
Washington							2		1	1						4
Wayne		2														2
Webster	2												1			3
York			1	1		1						1	1	1	2	8
Total	**20**	**20**	**34**	**39**	**16**	**32**	**49**	**31**	**58**	**71**	**68**	**71**	**54**	**42**	**55**	**660**

If a county is missing from the list, it's because no UFO sightings were logged in either the NUFORC or MUFON databases for the 2001-2015 sample period.

UFOS BY MONTH: NEBRASKA

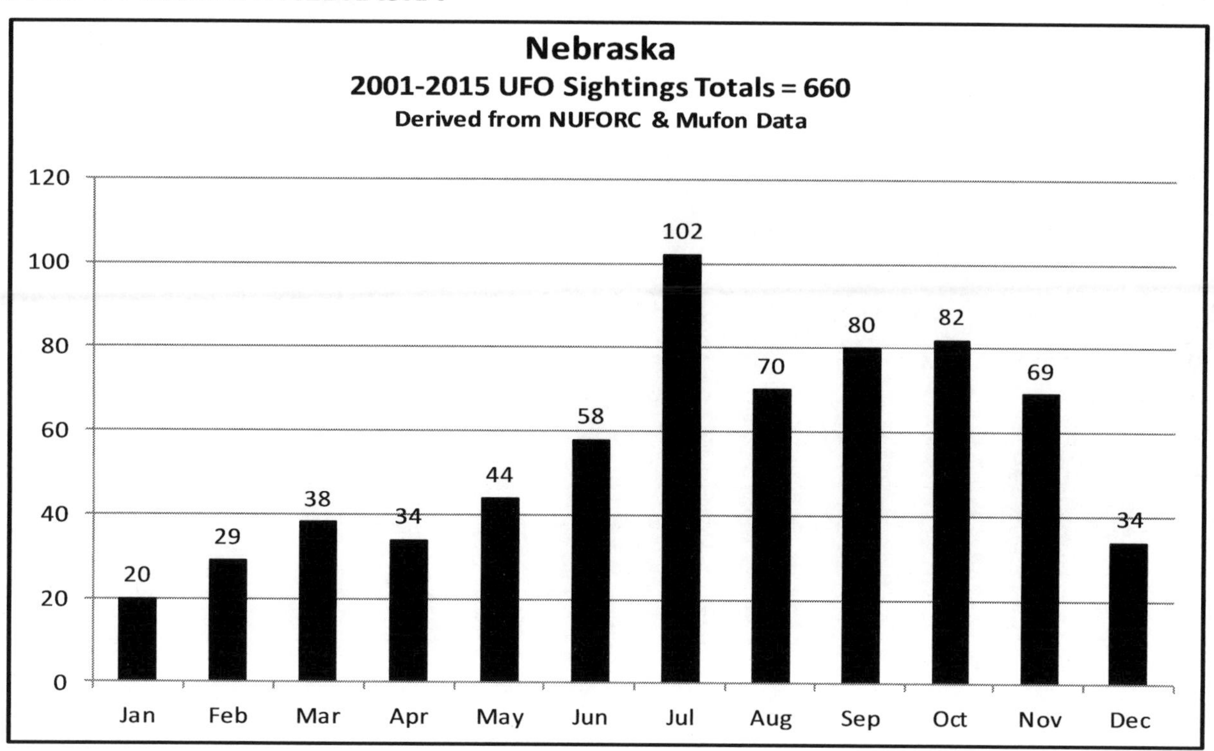

Year	Jan	Feb	Mar	Apr	May	Jun	Jul	Aug	Sep	Oct	Nov	Dec	Total
2001	1		3	3	2			3	2	1	2	3	20
2002		3	1			3		2	3	3	4	1	20
2003	1	3		4	1	4	3	3	5	5	3	2	34
2004	2		4	4	5	2	7	4	2	5		4	39
2005	2	1	3	1	1			3	3	1	1		16
2006			5	2	6		6	5	1	5	1	1	32
2007	3		2	3	4	1	3	4	6	15	6	2	49
2008		2	1			4	4	3	4	2	8	3	31
2009	4	5		2	3	8	14	9	9	3	1		58
2010	1	3	3	3	3	5	21	11	3	6	11	1	71
2011	2	3	3	2	6	5	14	3	10	14	2	4	68
2012	2	2	2	2	9	7	4	6	10	5	15	7	71
2013		2		2		10	12	3	13	4	6	2	54
2014	1		2	3	4	3	4	8	5	6	4	2	42
2015	1	5	9	3		6	10	3	4	7	5	2	55
Total	**20**	**29**	**38**	**34**	**44**	**58**	**102**	**70**	**80**	**82**	**69**	**34**	**660**

Distribution of Sightings between Databases: Nebraska

Database	Count	Percentage
MUFON	267	40.45%
NUFORC	393	59.55%
Total	660	100.00%

State Demographic Information: Nebraska

2010 US Census Statistics	
Population	1,826,341.00
Area in Square Miles	77,347.81
Land Area Sq. Miles	76,824.17
Population/Square mile	23.80

NEVADA

UFO RANK 26/51

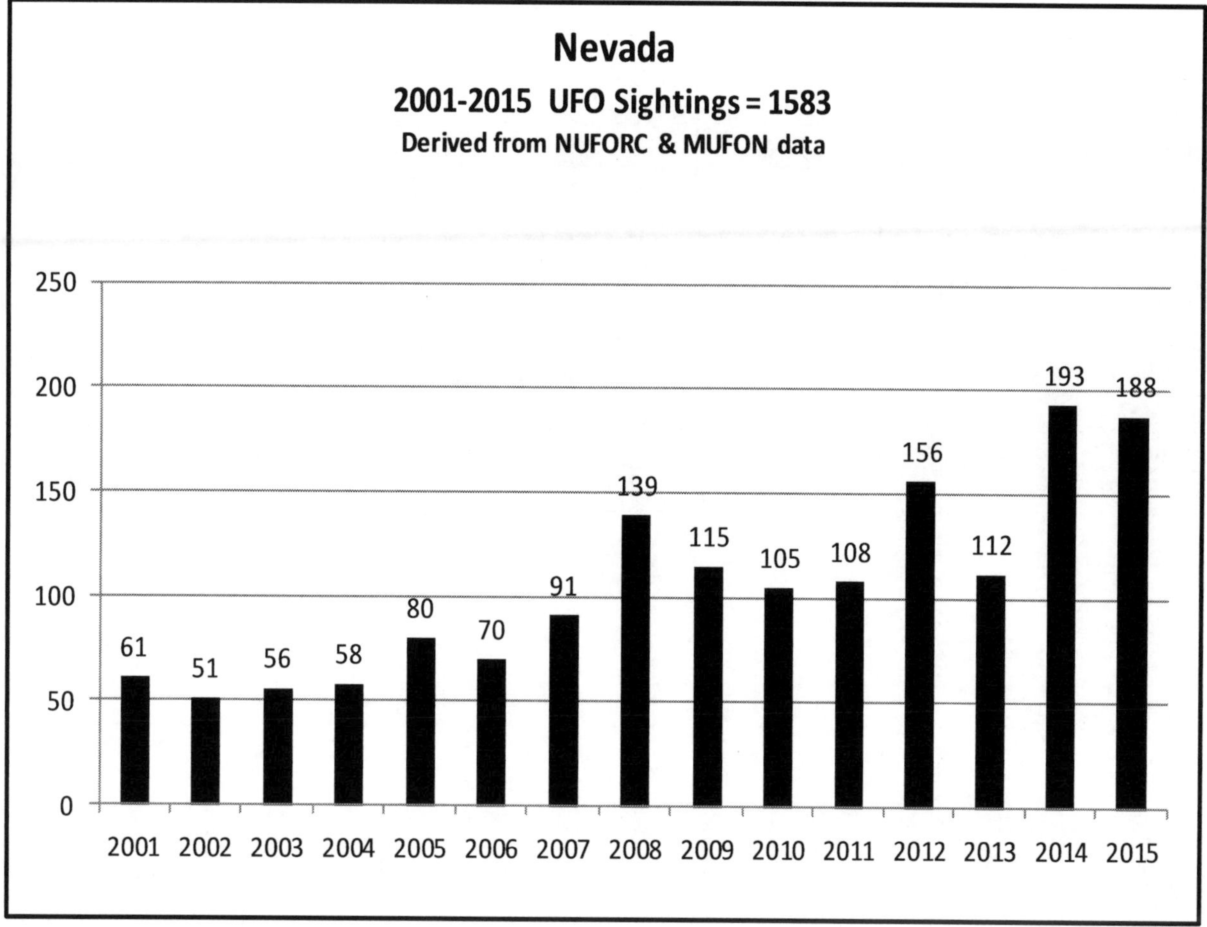

TOP TEN COUNTIES		RANK	TOP TEN SHAPES		
Clark	940	1	Circle	187	11.81%
Washoe	279	2	Light	174	10.99%
Unknown	69	3	Unknown	165	10.42%
Nye	54	4	Sphere	159	10.04%
Elko	46	5	Other	129	8.15%
Lincoln	37	6	Triangle	112	7.08%
Lyon	28	7	Fireball	82	5.18%
Douglas	27	8	Oval	73	4.61%
Carson City	26	9	Star-like	73	4.61%
White Pine	20	10	Disc	53	3.35%

UFO SHAPES: NEVADA

UFO Shapes	2001	2002	2003	2004	2005	2006	2007	2008	2009	2010	2011	2012	2013	2014	2015	Total
Blimp	1				1	2	2			2	1			1	2	12
Boomerang	2	1	1	1		1		1	3	3	4	5	3	3	1	29
Bullet/Missile							1	1		1		1	2		2	8
Changing	1	3		1	2		2	9		2	1	2	1	3	3	30
Chevron	3	1			1	3		2	1	2		1		1		15
Cigar	2					1	5	2	1	3	2	4	1	5	2	28
Circle	4	4	3	6	5	9	7	15	18	10	13	22	15	31	25	187
Cone					4			1			1	2	2		2	12
Cross										1						1
Cylinder	1		2	2	3	1	2	2	3	2	2	4	5	5	3	37
Diamond	1		1			3		4	5	2	2	1	1	1	3	24
Disc	1	1	2	1	3	4	5	7	4	7	1	4	5	3	5	53
Disk	1	1	2	3	3	2	3	9	3	3	3	5		2	5	45
Egg		1	1	1	3			3	1			1		1	1	13
Fireball	3	2	5	2	5	3	1	4	3	4	9	9	11	14	7	82
Flash		1		1			1	2	4	5	4	5	2	6	4	35
Formation	7		1	2	1	2	1	1	3	1	2	5	1	2	6	35
Light	9	6	8	12	12	6	14	14	10	8	7	18	8	19	23	174
N/A														3	4	7
Other	6	7	5	8	9	6	8	14	7	10	7	8	6	15	13	129
Oval	3	3	4	2	3	2	5	2	6	6	8	6	6	15	2	74
Rectangle	1				1	1	1	1	1	4		2	1		5	18
Saturn-like						1				1						2
Sphere	3	3	4	5	4	9	13	10	14	5	10	20	10	22	27	159
Sq/Rect								2							5	7
Star-like	1	1			3	2	2	12	8	8	6	8	5	10	7	73
Teardrop	1	1	2	2				1	1	2	2		1	1	3	17
Triangle	1	6	6	4	7	4	7	7	9	5	7	9	12	15	13	112
Unknown	9	9	9	5	10	7	11	13	10	8	16	14	14	15	15	165
Total	**61**	**51**	**56**	**58**	**80**	**70**	**91**	**139**	**115**	**105**	**108**	**156**	**112**	**193**	**188**	**1583**

UFOS BY COUNTY: NEVADA

Counties	**2001**	**2002**	**2003**	**2004**	**2005**	**2006**	**2007**	**2008**	**2009**	**2010**	**2011**	**2012**	**2013**	**2014**	**2015**	**Total**
Carson City			1				1	3	5	1	1	4	2	6	2	26
Churchill		1	1	1		1	2		2	1					3	12
Clark	46	34	28	28	46	37	49	71	56	66	67	103	72	131	106	940
Douglas	1	1			1	3	1	3	4	2	1	4	1	1	4	27
Elko	2	3	2	1	4	2	5	6	6		1	4	2	2	6	46
Esmeralda	1													1	2	4
Eureka						1		1		2	2					6
Humboldt	1		2	1	2		1			1	2	1	1	3	1	16
Lander									1	1	1			1	1	5
Lincoln	2		3	2	3	2	2	5		4	2	4	3	2	3	37
Lyon	1		1		1	2	1	1	5	1	1	3	3	5	3	28
Mineral	1												1			2
Mohave								1		1						2
Nevada		1											1			2
Nye	1	2		5	2	3	2	2	7	2	6	7	3	7	5	54
Pershing				1		1	1	1				1				5
Placer						1									1	2
Storey								1								1
Unknown		1		2	9	2	4	13	1	4	5	6	1	5	16	69
Washoe	5	7	17	17	11	13	22	31	20	19	17	18	20	29	33	279
White Pine		1	1		1	2			8		2	1	2		2	20
Total	**61**	**51**	**56**	**58**	**80**	**70**	**91**	**139**	**115**	**105**	**108**	**156**	**112**	**193**	**188**	**1583**

If a county is missing from the list, it's because no UFO sightings were logged in either the NUFORC or MUFON databases for the 2001-2015 sample period.

UFOS BY MONTH: NEVADA

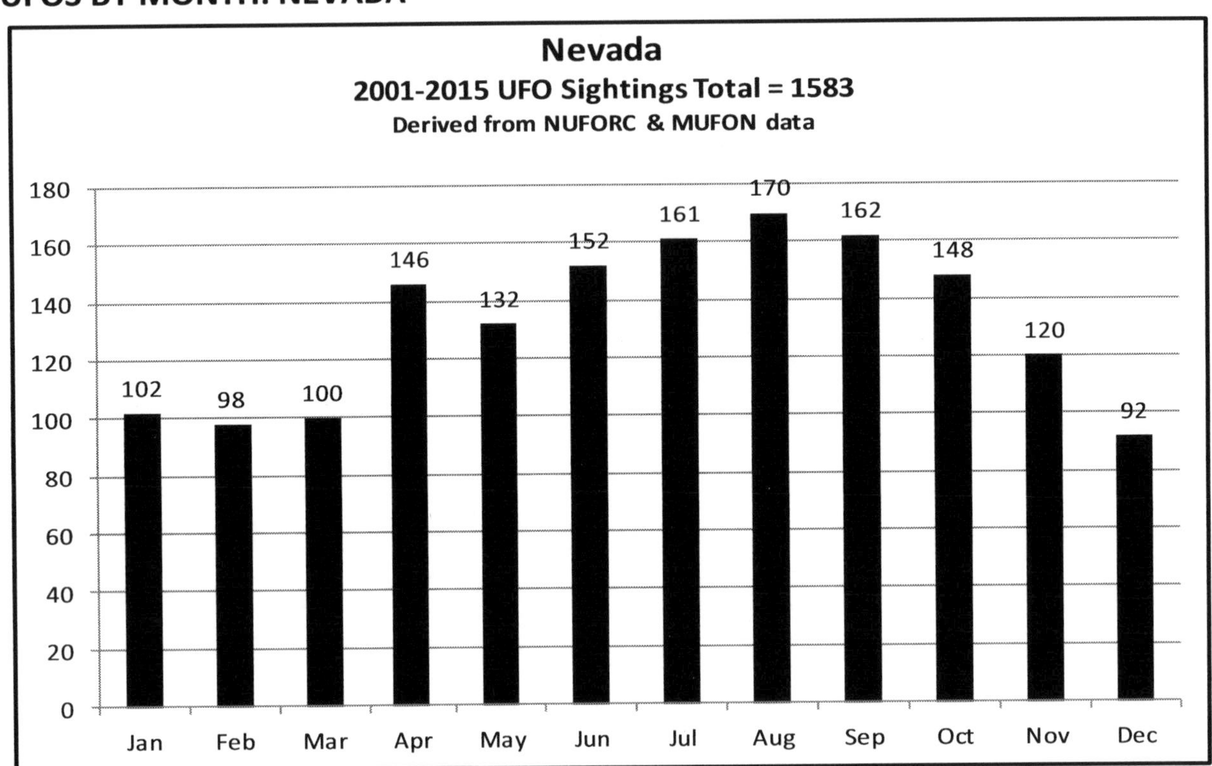

Year	Jan	Feb	Mar	Apr	May	Jun	Jul	Aug	Sep	Oct	Nov	Dec	Total
2001	5	3	11	8	5	6	5	4	6	3	4	1	61
2002	3	2	4	2	3	8	2	5	7	6	4	5	51
2003	5	2	2	1	2	8	6	11	6	8	3	2	56
2004	6	1	2	7	7	8	9	6	2	4	5	1	58
2005	4	6	11	6	9	8	5	10	8	5	4	4	80
2006		6	6	4	7	5	8	3	10	8	7	6	70
2007	3	1	4	5	8	7	4	13	10	13	12	11	91
2008	10	10	7	21	6	14	13	18	14	13	5	8	139
2009	8	1	3	6	14	11	20	15	11	13	7	6	115
2010	10	5	6	13	11	7	14	7	9	9	6	8	105
2011	5	7	8	17	9	6	6	14	19	9	6	2	108
2012	11	7	10	13	14	19	16	17	11	11	16	11	156
2013	8	10	8	5	7	14	8	13	9	13	4	13	112
2014	15	16	9	23	19	17	21	16	23	16	11	7	193
2015	9	21	9	15	11	14	24	18	17	17	26	7	188
Total	**102**	**98**	**100**	**146**	**132**	**152**	**161**	**170**	**162**	**148**	**120**	**92**	**1583**

Distribution of Sightings between Databases: Nevada

Database	Count	Percentage
MUFON	705	44.54%
NUFORC	878	55.46%
Total	1583	100.00%

State Demographic Information: Nevada

2010 US Census Statistics	
Population	2,700,551.00
Area in Square Miles	110,571.82
Land Area Sq. Miles	109,781.18
Population/Square mile	24.60

NEW HAMPSHIRE UFO RANK 38/51

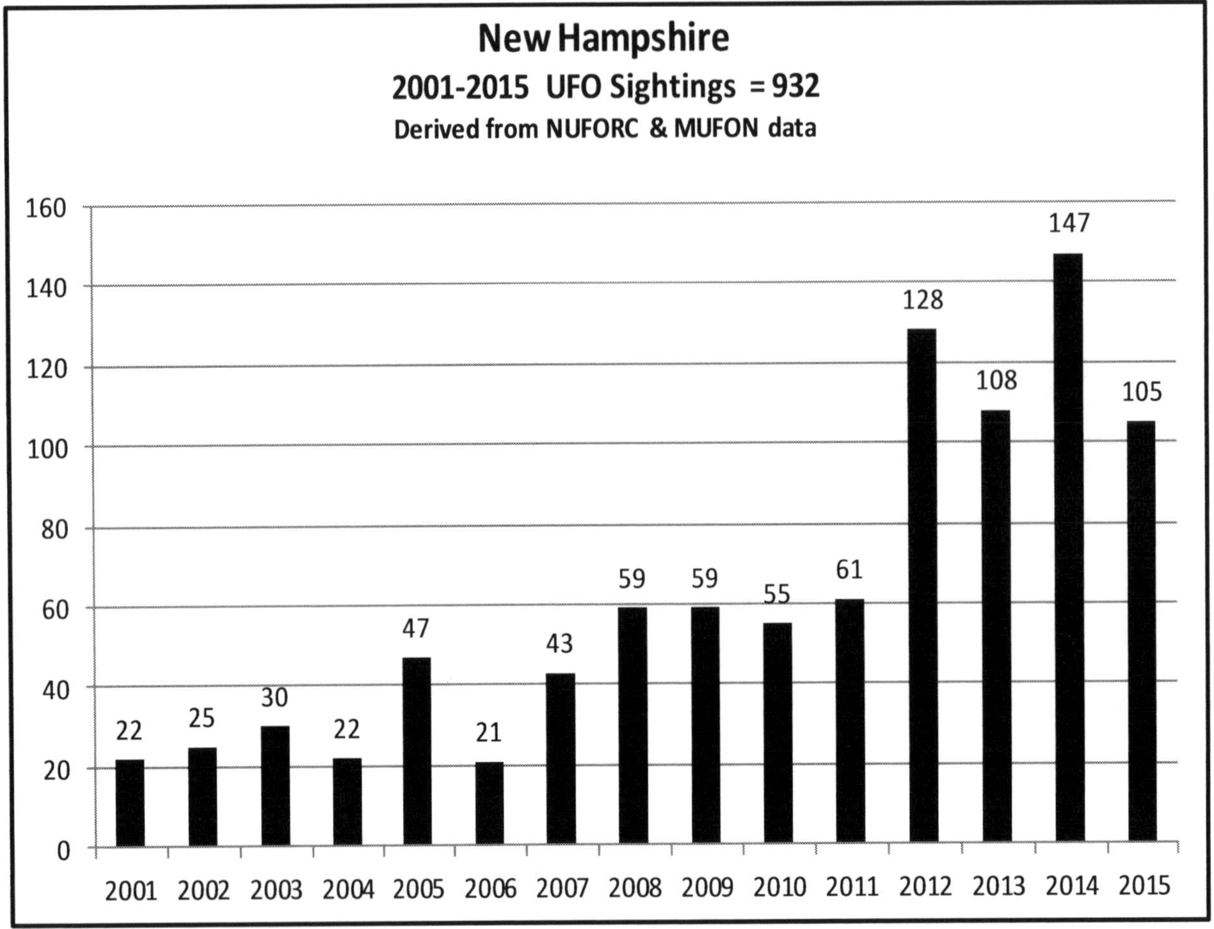

TOP TEN COUNTIES		RANK	TOP TEN SHAPES		
Rockingham	197	1	Light	134	14.38%
Hillsborough	159	2	Circle	109	11.70%
Merrimack	109	3	Unknown	107	11.48%
Grafton	104	4	Sphere	98	10.52%
Strafford	80	5	Triangle	91	9.76%
Belknap	76	6	Fireball	64	6.87%
Carroll	64	7	Other	45	4.83%
Coos	60	8	Star-like	43	4.61%
Cheshire	41	9	Oval	34	3.65%
Sullivan	22	10	Disk	33	3.54%

UFO SHAPES: NEW HAMPSHIRE

UFO Shapes	2001	2002	2003	2004	2005	2006	2007	2008	2009	2010	2011	2012	2013	2014	2015	Total
Blimp										1	1	1				3
Boomerang										1	2	1	1	3		8
Bullet/Missile										1		2				3
Changing	1	1	1	2		1	3	1	1	2	1			3	1	18
Chevron							1	1		2	1	2		3	1	11
Cigar	2				3	1	3	1	2	1	3	2	2	4	5	29
Circle	4		2	2	1	3	2	4	9	5	5	23	19	20	10	109
Cone									3			2				5
Cross							1	1					1	1		4
Cylinder						1		1				9	1	1	1	14
Diamond			2				2	1	2		1		3	4	1	16
Disc					2		1	1		1		1	3	1	1	11
Disk	2	5	5	1	6	1	4		1		1	3	1	1	2	33
Egg				1				1			1	1				4
Fireball		2	3			1	1	3	2	4	6	12	12	12	6	64
Flash				2					2			2	1	1		8
Formation					1			4	1			2	4	6	2	20
Light	3	5	5	5	12	3	8	11	7	7	7	16	17	13	15	134
N/A														1	2	3
Other	2	1	2	4	5	1	2	2	3	2	2	9		3	7	45
Oval			2		2	1	2	3		2	2	6	4	8	2	34
Rectangle	1		1				1	1	1			4	1		1	11
Sphere	3	4	2	1	3	2	2	1	6	7	9	9	13	20	16	98
Star-like						1	4	3	5	6	4	4	6	5	5	43
Teardrop	1				1							3	1			6
Triangle	1	2	1	3	2	3	1	7	8	7	7	7	9	18	15	91
Unknown	2	5	4	1	9	2	5	12	6	6	8	7	9	19	12	107
Total	**22**	**25**	**30**	**22**	**47**	**21**	**43**	**59**	**59**	**55**	**61**	**128**	**108**	**147**	**105**	**932**

UFOS BY COUNTY: NEW HAMPSHIRE

Counties	2001	2002	2003	2004	2005	2006	2007	2008	2009	2010	2011	2012	2013	2014	2015	Total
Belknap	1	2	2		14	3	5	3	1	7	4	7	6	14	7	76
Carroll	2	4	3	3	1	1	1	4	2	5	7	8	11	9	3	64
Cheshire				1	1	3	2	6	1	3	2	3	6	9	4	41
Coos	1	1		1	5		4	7	3	5	3	8	5	11	6	60
Grafton	8	3	4	3	3		12	7	13	6	3	11	8	14	9	104
Hillsborough	2	7	5	6	5	3	4	9	7	6	6	14	28	32	25	159
Merrimack	5	2		3	7	3	4	11	5	6	3	18	16	16	10	109
Rockingham	1	5	11	1	7	5	8	10	15	9	22	35	20	23	25	197
Strafford	2	1	2	2	2	2	2	2	6	4	8	17	4	13	13	80
Sullivan			3		2				3	1	1	4	3	3	2	22
Unknown				2		1	1		3	3	2	3	1	3	1	20
Total	**22**	**25**	**30**	**22**	**47**	**21**	**43**	**59**	**59**	**55**	**61**	**128**	**108**	**147**	**105**	**932**

If a county is missing from the list, it's because no UFO sightings were logged in either the NUFORC or MUFON databases for the 2001-2015 sample period.

UFOS BY MONTH: NEW HAMPSHIRE

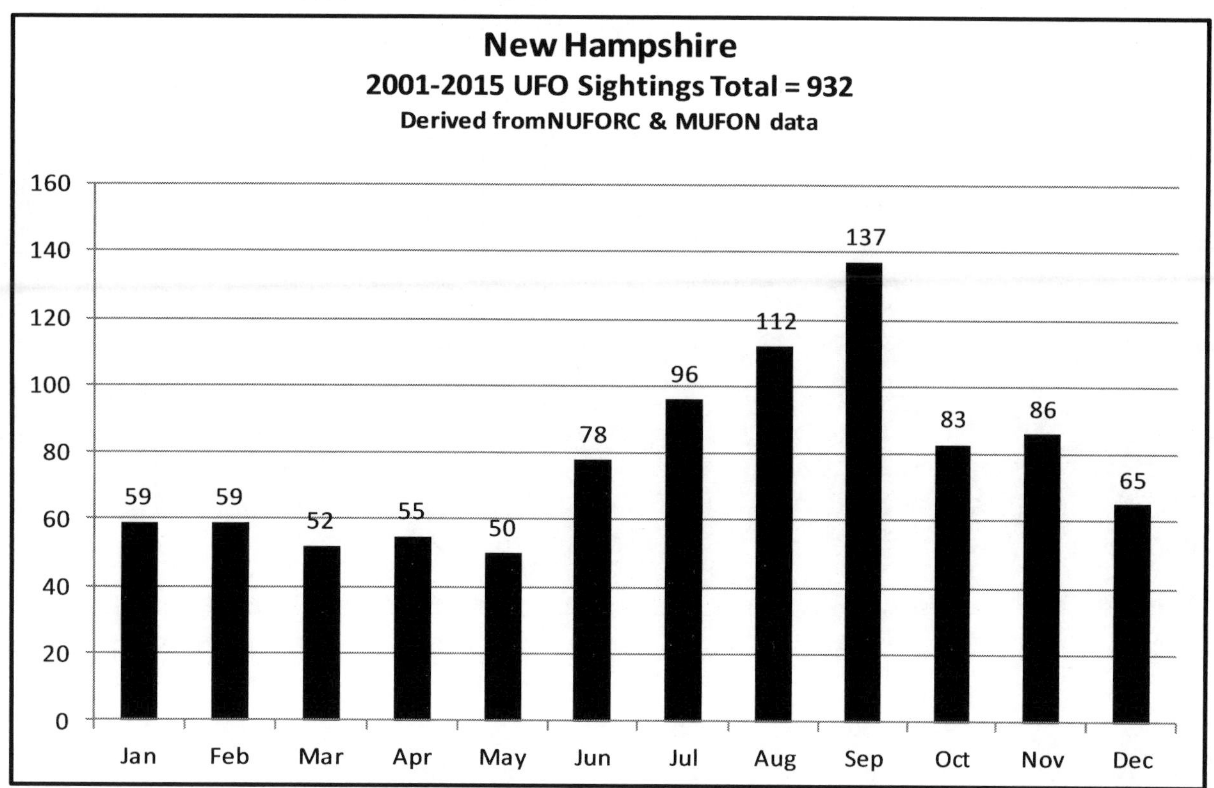

Year	Jan	Feb	Mar	Apr	May	Jun	Jul	Aug	Sep	Oct	Nov	Dec	Total
2001	3	1	1		2	1	1	2	3	3	2	3	22
2002	2	2	1	2		10	3	2	2		1		25
2003	4	2	4	1	2	2	3	2	3	2	4	1	30
2004	2	1	3	1		2	3	7	1	1		1	22
2005	2	2	4	5	2	4	4	5	15	2	1	1	47
2006	2		4	1		3	1	3	4	1		2	21
2007	3	3		4	1	2	4	8	12	2		4	43
2008	4	7	3	5	5	2	4	4	14	5	3	3	59
2009	5	2	6	2	4	1	4	3	13	6	8	5	59
2010	2	3	6	2	4	8	4	8	2	8	3	5	55
2011	3	7	2	2	1	1	6	5	8	10	10	6	61
2012	7	10	7	7	2	11	15	19	16	4	9	21	128
2013	4	2	1	7	4	15	10	16	15	12	18	4	108
2014	9	12	4	10	9	13	23	17	13	17	12	8	147
2015	7	5	6	6	14	3	11	11	16	10	15	1	105
Total	**59**	**59**	**52**	**55**	**50**	**78**	**96**	**112**	**137**	**83**	**86**	**65**	**932**

BONUS - UFOs by County & Month: New Hampshire

Counties	Jan	Feb	Mar	Apr	May	Jun	Jul	Aug	Sep	Oct	Nov	Dec	Total
Belknap	4	6	5	4	4	4	9	10	13	8	4	5	76
Carroll	6	3	2	4	4	11	4	6	6	10	4	4	64
Cheshire	2		1	6	3	4	7	7	2	5	2	2	41
Coos	3	4	1	5	3	8	3	6	17	4	3	3	60
Grafton	7	4	6	4	8	9	8	15	20	6	12	5	104
Hillsborough	11	8	9	7	8	10	17	14	32	20	10	13	159
Merrimack	4	6	9	9	7	11	10	13	10	6	11	13	109
Rockingham	15	13	10	10	10	14	26	30	22	15	19	13	197
Strafford	3	10	6	3	3	6	7	8	10	6	13	5	80
Sullivan	2	3	1	3			2	3	2		5	1	22
Unknown	2	2	2			1	3		3	3	3	1	20
Total	**59**	**59**	**52**	**55**	**50**	**78**	**96**	**112**	**137**	**83**	**86**	**65**	**932**

Distribution of Sightings between Databases: New Hampshire

Database	Count	Percentage
MUFON	328	35.19%
NUFORC	604	64.81%
Total	932	100.00%

State Demographic Information: New Hampshire

2010 US Census Statistics	
Population	1,316,470.00
Area in Square Miles	9,349.16
Land Area Sq. Miles	8,952.65
Population/Square mile	147.00

NEW JERSEY

UFO RANK 16/51

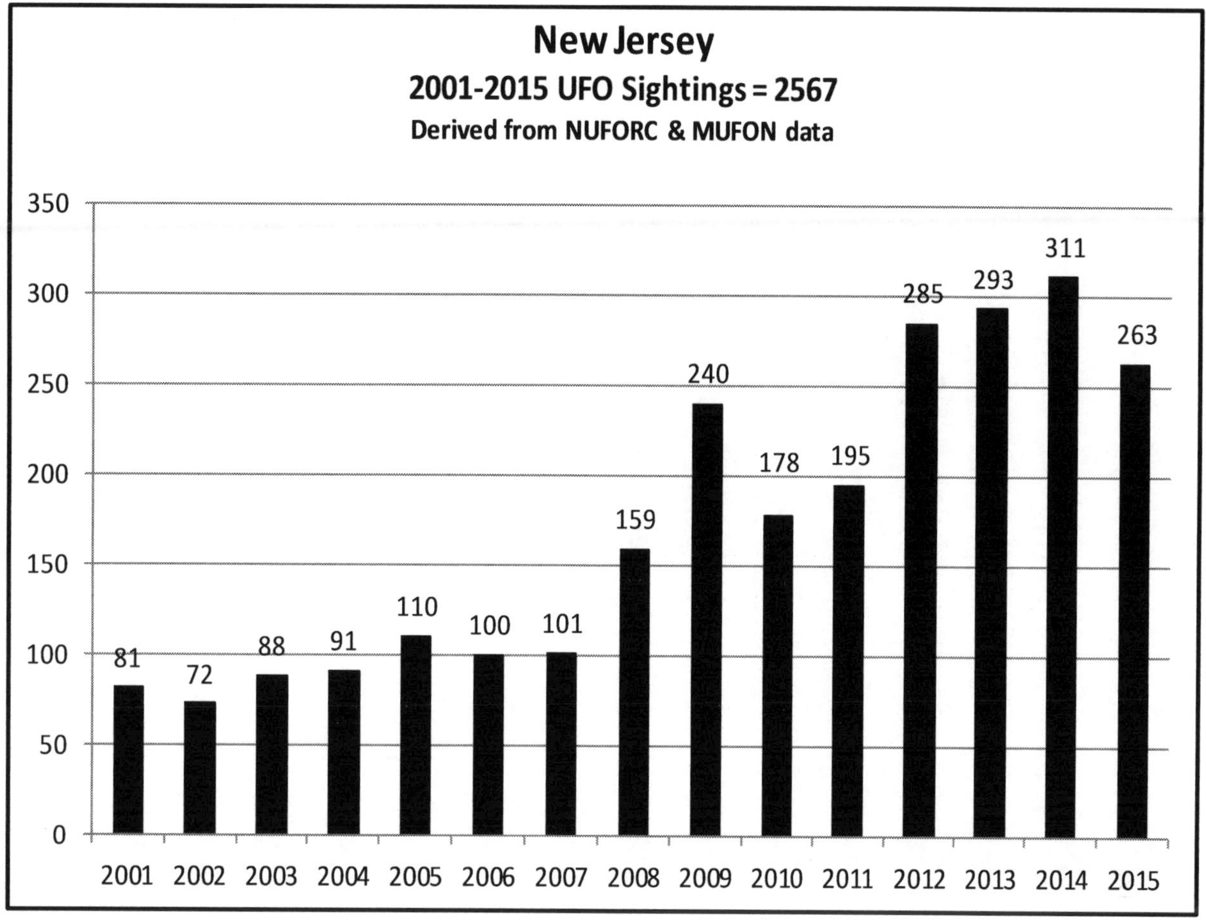

TOP TEN COUNTIES		RANK	TOP TEN SHAPES		
Burlington	139	1	Circle	331	12.89%
Atlantic	136	2	Light	303	11.80%
Cape May	120	3	Triangle	251	9.78%
Morris	120	4	Unknown	225	8.77%
Somerset	117	5	Fireball	215	8.38%
Ocean	249	6	Sphere	203	7.91%
Monmouth	248	7	Other	195	7.60%
Middlesex	207	8	Oval	127	4.95%
Bergen	170	9	Star-like	91	3.54%
Camden	144	10	Disk	85	3.31%

UFO SHAPES: NEW JERSEY

UFO Shapes	2001	2002	2003	2004	2005	2006	2007	2008	2009	2010	2011	2012	2013	2014	2015	Total
Blimp				1			2	3	1	2	1	3	1	1	2	17
Boomerang						1		1	4	4	6	4	5	2	3	30
Bullet/Missile						1		2	2		4	4	3	5	1	22
Changing	3		2	3	1		3	3	1	1	1	2	1	1	1	23
Chevron	3	1		1		1		1	1		1	2	4	1	1	17
Cigar	1	2	1		2	9	6	5	4	5	6	1	1	4	5	52
Circle	5	5	9	7	12	11	6	14	41	18	34	42	46	44	37	331
Cone			2	1	1	2			12	3		2	4		1	28
Cross		1	1			1				1			3	1		8
Cylinder	3	2	2		3	1	2	2	2	4	1	4	5	7	4	42
Diamond		1			5	1	2	1	4	2	1	5	5	8	6	41
Disc		3	2	1	1		4	6	15	4	7	7	9	8	8	75
Disk	5	8	7	6	6	12	4	7	5	4	1	7	5	8		85
Egg	1			1	1	3	1	2	1	4	1	2	5	4	1	27
Fireball	2	3	5	1	2	8	1	7	11	10	22	47	34	33	29	215
Flash		3	1	1	1	2	4	8	7	4	4	8		4	6	53
Formation	8	2	3	5	1	1	1	2	4	2	4	2	6		5	46
Light	13	9	19	15	13	13	13	20	34	24	15	25	35	30	25	303
N/A									1					2	1	4
Other	8	7	9	11	15	5	8	10	18	18	17	19	15	16	19	195
Oval	4		7	7	8	3	9	12	6	11	15	4	18	18	5	127
Rectangle	1	2	1	1	1		1	3	3	2	1	2	3	2	2	25
Saturn-like						1	1							3	3	8
Sphere	3	5	2	4	4	7	13	11	11	7	18	26	33	33	26	203
Sq/Rect														2	5	7
Star-like		1			1	2	1	11	11	18	4	15	7	13	7	91
Teardrop	1		1	1	2		2	3		1	1			2	2	16
Triangle	9	6	5	14	9	8	11	13	25	17	15	25	26	33	35	251
Unknown	11	11	9	10	21	7	6	12	16	12	15	27	19	26	23	225
Total	**81**	**72**	**88**	**91**	**110**	**100**	**101**	**159**	**240**	**178**	**195**	**285**	**293**	**311**	**263**	**2567**

UFOS BY COUNTY: NEW JERSEY

Counties	2001	2002	2003	2004	2005	2006	2007	2008	2009	2010	2011	2012	2013	2014	2015	Total
Atlantic	1	3	4	2	4	7	4	15	15	11	14	23	11	11	11	136
Bergen	6	10	7	9	10	8	8	14	11	8	7	16	10	21	25	170
Burlington	6	3		3	8	6	7	4	14	9	8	10	18	21	22	139
Camden	1	2	4	5	5	6	8	6	8	7	6	18	27	21	20	144
Cape May	1		6	4	2	2	7	7	10	7	14	11	21	15	13	120
Cumberland			4	1	4	3	4	4	2	4	1	3	3	3	1	37
Essex	4	3	3	3	3	5	5	7	7	12	9	15	13	15	6	110
Gloucester		4	2	3	1	4	6	7	12	10	7	12	12	14	10	104
Hudson	4	4	7	3	5	5	8	5	11	10	16	10	12	6	5	111
Hunterdon	2	1	3	2	3	4	3	7	6	7	6	7	3	9	6	69
Mercer	2		1	4	2	4	2	5	6	4	6	7	7	13	8	71
Middlesex	22	3	6	9	7	5	12	9	10	12	15	25	23	32	17	207
Monmouth	7	15	6	12	20	13	7	9	25	14	17	23	27	29	24	248
Morris	4	5	3	5	4	3	4	6	32	3	12	7	8	16	8	120
Ocean	5	4	10	9	11	10	6	13	13	19	17	39	35	26	32	249
Passaic	4	5	5	2	3	3	1	6	8	12	4	9	15	21	14	112
Salem		1		1	1			2	7	3	2	5	3	4		29
Somerset	2	4	8	6	10	4	2	9	8	4	11	17	11	8	13	117
Sussex	1	1	1	2	1	1		4	8	4	4	5	4	9	7	52
Union	5	3	6		3	5	3	13	6	8	10	9	9	12	8	100
Unknown	4		1	1	2	2		4	15	3	7	10	12	2	8	71
Warren		1	1	5	1		4	3	6	7	2	4	9	3	5	51
Total	**81**	**72**	**88**	**91**	**110**	**100**	**101**	**159**	**240**	**178**	**195**	**285**	**293**	**311**	**263**	**2567**

If a county is missing from the list, it's because no UFO sightings were logged in either the NUFORC or MUFON databases for the 2001-2015 sample period.

UFOS BY MONTH: NEW JERSEY

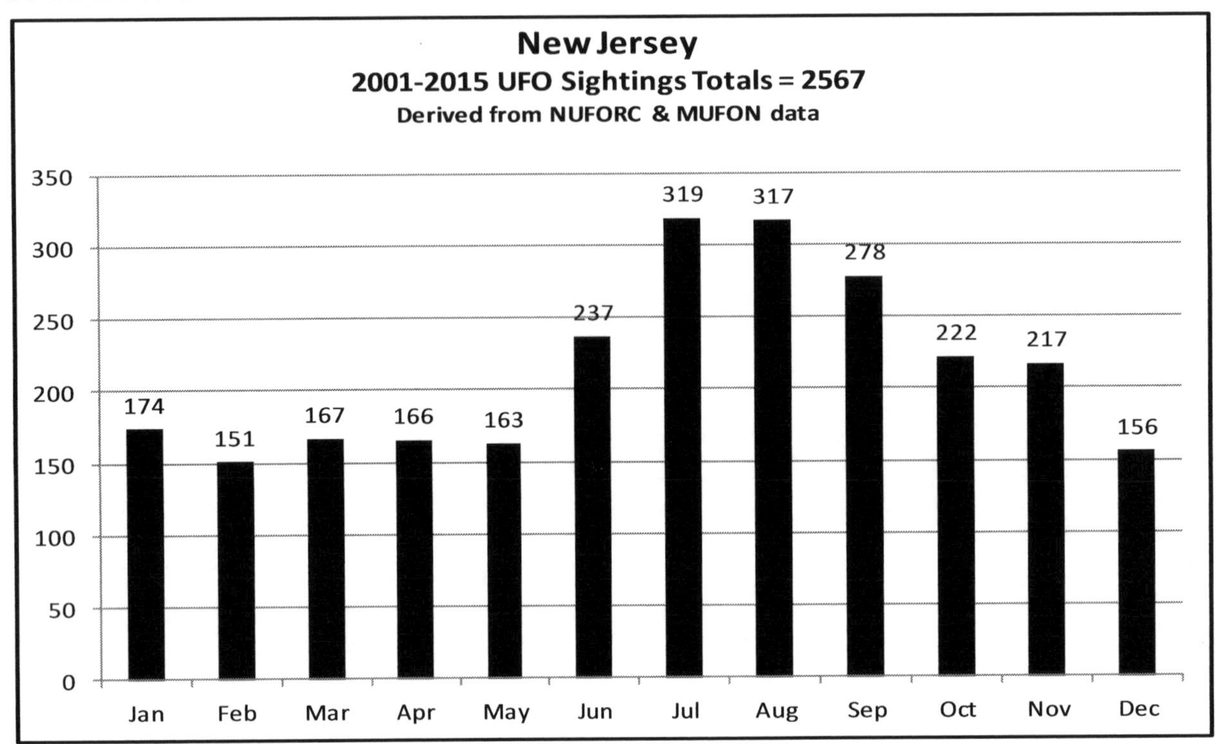

Year	Jan	Feb	Mar	Apr	May	Jun	Jul	Aug	Sep	Oct	Nov	Dec	Total
2001	3	4	3	6	3	4	30	8	13	1	3	3	81
2002	3	7	5	5	2	8	10	13	5	6	4	4	72
2003	6	3	2	1	5	8	8	14	16	2	10	13	88
2004	10	10	10	6	6	4	7	10	8	10	6	4	91
2005	3	6	13	9	5	14	7	12	12	14	9	6	110
2006	7	6	13	9	6	8	13	12	3	7	10	6	100
2007	6	6	7	5	12	14	8	14	7	5	9	8	101
2008	13	13	12	7	14	16	13	29	12	5	16	9	159
2009	35	30	11	9	16	15	21	20	46	11	15	11	240
2010	14	3	9	8	16	14	30	17	12	22	16	17	178
2011	5	4	14	14	13	22	24	23	16	25	19	16	195
2012	11	21	20	19	14	28	29	44	33	25	25	16	285
2013	10	8	9	17	23	17	46	33	42	32	37	19	293
2014	25	17	19	31	13	38	39	34	32	31	14	18	311
2015	23	13	20	20	15	27	34	34	21	26	24	6	263
Total	**174**	**151**	**167**	**166**	**163**	**237**	**319**	**317**	**278**	**222**	**217**	**156**	**2567**

Distribution of Sightings between Databases: New Jersey

Database	Count	Percentage
MUFON	1042	40.59%
NUFORC	1525	59.41%
Total	2567	100.00%

State Demographic Information: New Jersey

2010 US Census Statistics	
Population	8,791,894.00
Area in Square Miles	8,722.58
Land Area Sq. Miles	7,354.22
Population/Square mile	1,195.50

NEW MEXICO UFO RANK 29/51

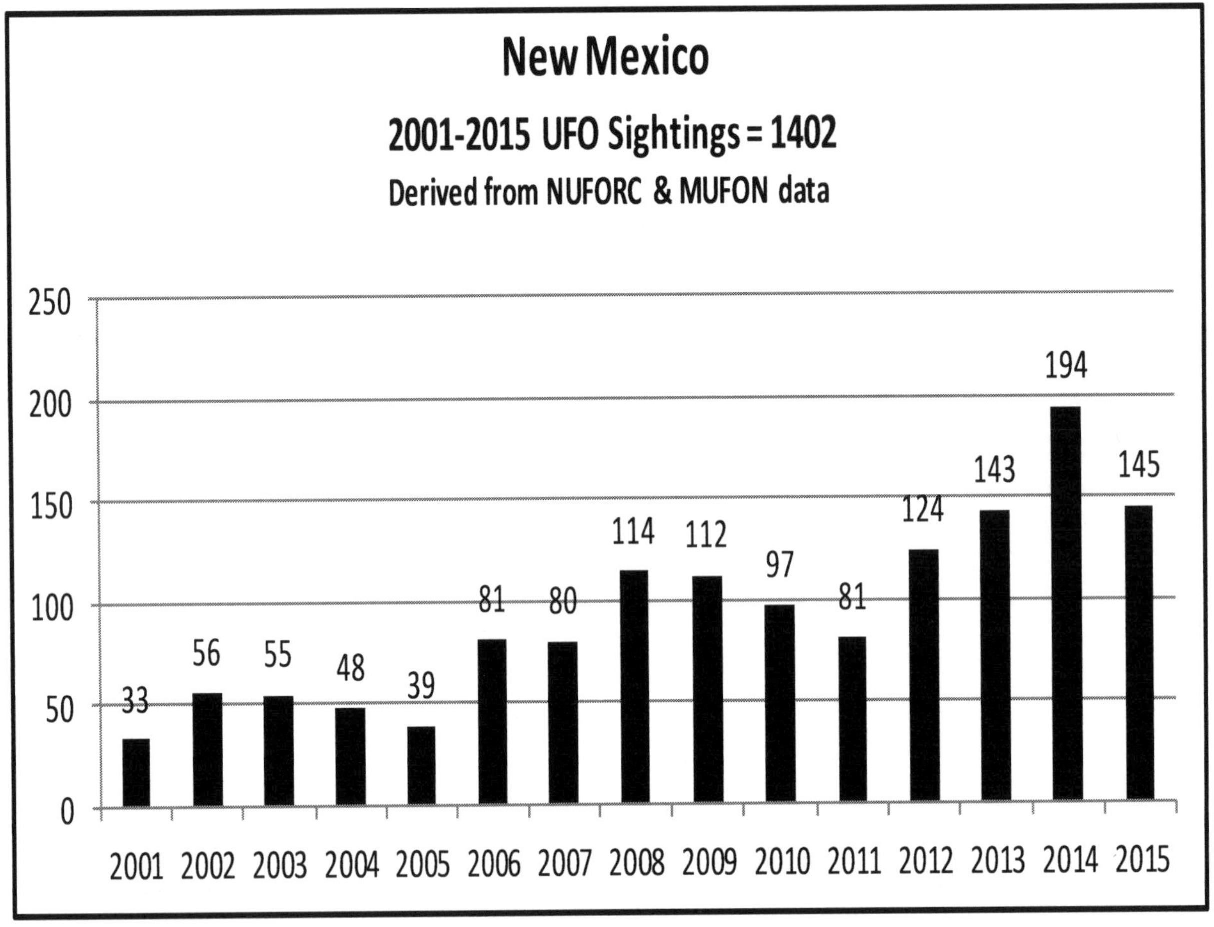

TOP TEN COUNTIES		RANK	TOP TEN SHAPES		
Bernalillo	385	1	Light	173	12.34%
Santa Fe	134	2	Unknown	156	11.13%
Dona Ana	101	3	Circle	153	10.91%
Sandoval	76	4	Sphere	124	8.84%
Chaves	64	5	Other	112	7.99%
San Juan	57	6	Triangle	90	6.42%
Otero	48	7	Fireball	63	4.49%
Grant	44	8	Star-like	60	4.28%
Luna	43	9	Oval	56	3.99%
Rio Arriba	42	10	Disk	52	3.71%

UFO SHAPES: NEW MEXICO

UFO Shapes	2001	2002	2003	2004	2005	2006	2007	2008	2009	2010	2011	2012	2013	2014	2015	Total
Blimp		1				2					1		1	3	4	12
Boomerang						3			2	2	1	3	1	2	3	17
Bullet/Missile		1		1			2	2	1	3	1		1	1		13
Changing		1		1	2	3	3	2	2		1	2	4	5	1	27
Chevron	1	1	1	1		1	1	1	2		1		1	1	2	14
Cigar	1		1		1	2	5	3	3	2	2	1	2	4	2	29
Circle	1	2	3	4	6	5	9	12	10	11	16	16	22	26	10	153
Cone	1	1				3		1	3	3	2	3	2		1	20
Cross										2				1		3
Cylinder		3	1				3	2	4	2	3	3	6	6	3	36
Diamond		1			1	2	1	3	1	2	2	6	2	2	1	24
Disc		2		1		2	3	6	3	4	2	2	2	8	8	43
Disk	4	3	3	5	3	7	4	2	2	3		4	1	4	7	52
Egg		2	1			1	1		1	2	3	2	2	2	1	18
Fireball	3	2	1	1	1	2	3	7	4	3	2	6	7	11	10	63
Flash	2	3	1			3	1	2		3	4	8	3	2	4	36
Formation	1					3	1	1	3	3			2	5	1	20
Light	6	10	9	12	10	14	6	16	13	3	9	10	27	17	11	173
N/A														2	1	3
Other	1	4	6	3	1	5	1	11	10	6	6	10	16	17	15	112
Oval	1	2	4	5		2	6	3	2	5	4	3	3	12	4	56
Rectangle			1			3	2	1	3	2		3	1	1		17
Saturn-like													1	1		2
Sphere	1		3	5	4	1	8	11	10	12	2	10	8	21	28	124
Sq/Rect												1			3	4
Star-like	2	2	1			1	1	3	9	8	4	7	7	9	6	60
Teardrop		1	2				4	2	7		4	2		3		25
Triangle	3	4	7	1	2	6	7	4	9	1	7	9	8	15	7	90
Unknown	5	10	10	8	8	10	8	19	8	15	4	13	13	13	12	156
Total	**33**	**56**	**55**	**48**	**39**	**81**	**80**	**114**	**112**	**97**	**81**	**124**	**143**	**194**	**145**	**1402**

UFOS BY COUNTY: NEW MEXICO

Counties	2001	2002	2003	2004	2005	2006	2007	2008	2009	2010	2011	2012	2013	2014	2015	Total
Bernalillo	8	5	16	12	9	19	25	32	24	31	21	38	57	52	36	385
Catron		3		1		2		2						2	1	11
Chaves	3	4	3	3	1	4	4	7	5	5	6	6	2	7	4	64
Cibola		3	1		2			1	1			1	3	4	1	17
Colfax		1		1		3		7		2	1		1	2	1	19
Curry		1			4	1	2		1	1	2	1	1	7		21
De Baca		2							2							4
Dona Ana		7	2	2		5	7	6	12	8	5	12	11	10	14	101
Eddy				1		5	2	3	6		2	2	5	2	5	33
Grant	2	1	3	3	4	4	3	2	3	1	2	7	1	6	2	44
Guadalupe				1	1		1	2	2					3		10
Harding														2		2
Hidalgo									1		1			3	1	6
Lea	1	1	2	1		1	1	2	1	5	1	2	1	5	3	27
Lincoln	1	1			2	2		3	1		4	1	1	3	5	24
Los Alamos	1						3	3	1			1		1		10
Los Lunas						1										1
Luna		3	3	1	2	2	2	2	4	2	3	2	3	9	5	43
McKinley	1	2	3	3	2	1	2	3	3			1	1	2	4	28
Mora															1	1
Otero	3	1	2	1	2	1		2	4	13	1	4		5	9	48
Quay						1		2	1	1	3	1	1			10
Rio Arriba	1	2	1	3	2	1	2	3	7	2		4	4	5	5	42
Roosevelt				1			1		3			1	1	1		8
San Juan	1	4	2	1	2	6	3	3	4	3	8	4	6	5	5	57
San Miguel	3	1	1			1		1		1		1		3	1	13
Sandoval	2	2	4	2	1	2		1	7	4	7	12	11	14	7	76
Santa Ana		1	2	1		1	3	1	1		1		1			12
Santa Fe	4	4	5	5	3	9	15	9	8	4	3	7	20	17	21	134
Sierra		1		1		1	2	3	2	1	1	1	1	2		16
Socorro	1	2	1	3		1			2	4	2	1		2		19
Santa Fe						1										1
Taos		2	1	1	1	4	1	2		3	2	7	3	6	6	39
Torrance		1				1		4	1		1	2	1	1	3	15
Union								1	1				2	2		6
Unknown	1	1				1	1	5	2	5		4	4	5	5	34
Valencia			3		1			2	2	1	4	1	1	6		21

Counties	2001	2002	2003	2004	2005	2006	2007	2008	2009	2010	2011	2012	2013	2014	2015	Total
Total	33	56	55	48	39	81	80	114	112	97	81	124	143	194	145	1402

If a county is missing from the list, it's because no UFO sightings were logged in either the NUFORC or MUFON databases for the 2001-2015 sample period.

UFOS BY MONTH: NEW MEXICO

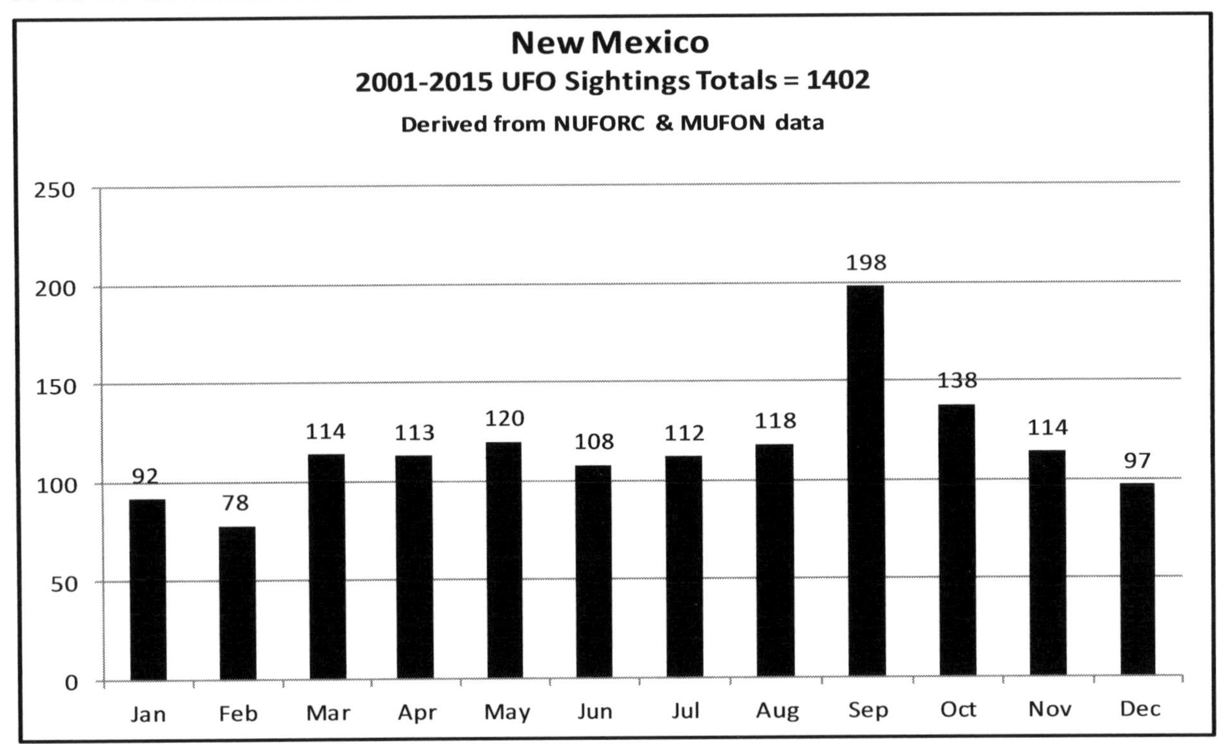

Year	Jan	Feb	Mar	Apr	May	Jun	Jul	Aug	Sep	Oct	Nov	Dec	Total
2001	3	1	5	1	3	3	2	4	3	1	2	5	33
2002	5	3	4	4	2	5	10	7	6	8	2		56
2003	2		2	4	1	5	7	8	11	6	5	4	55
2004	5	1	5	5	7	4	5	8	4	1	2	1	48
2005			2	1	7	4	2	5	11	5	1	1	39
2006	3	9	1	5	6	4	9	4	7	15	6	12	81
2007	4	1	13	4	8	8	7	2	15	7	5	6	80
2008	4	11	23	6	8	10	10	11	10	12	7	2	114
2009	6	2	4	10	17	13	15	10	12	8	11	4	112
2010	17	7	8	4	11	7	5	13	5	9	5	6	97
2011	3	6	6	6	8	4	5	4	14	9	8	8	81
2012	11	7	10	11	9	10	5	6	20	15	12	8	124
2013	6	4	8	15	9	5	8	13	26	16	19	14	143
2014	11	12	14	27	7	13	10	11	40	17	14	18	194
2015	12	14	9	10	17	13	12	12	14	9	15	8	145
Total	**92**	**78**	**114**	**113**	**120**	**108**	**112**	**118**	**198**	**138**	**114**	**97**	**1402**

Distribution of Sightings between Databases: New Mexico

Database	Count	Percentage
MUFON	597	42.58%
NUFORC	805	57.42%
Total	1402	100.00%

State Demographic Information: New Mexico

2010 US Census Statistics	
Population	2,059,179.00
Area in Square Miles	121,590.30
Land Area Sq. Miles	121,298.15
Population/Square mile	17 .0

NEW YORK

UFO RANK 6/51

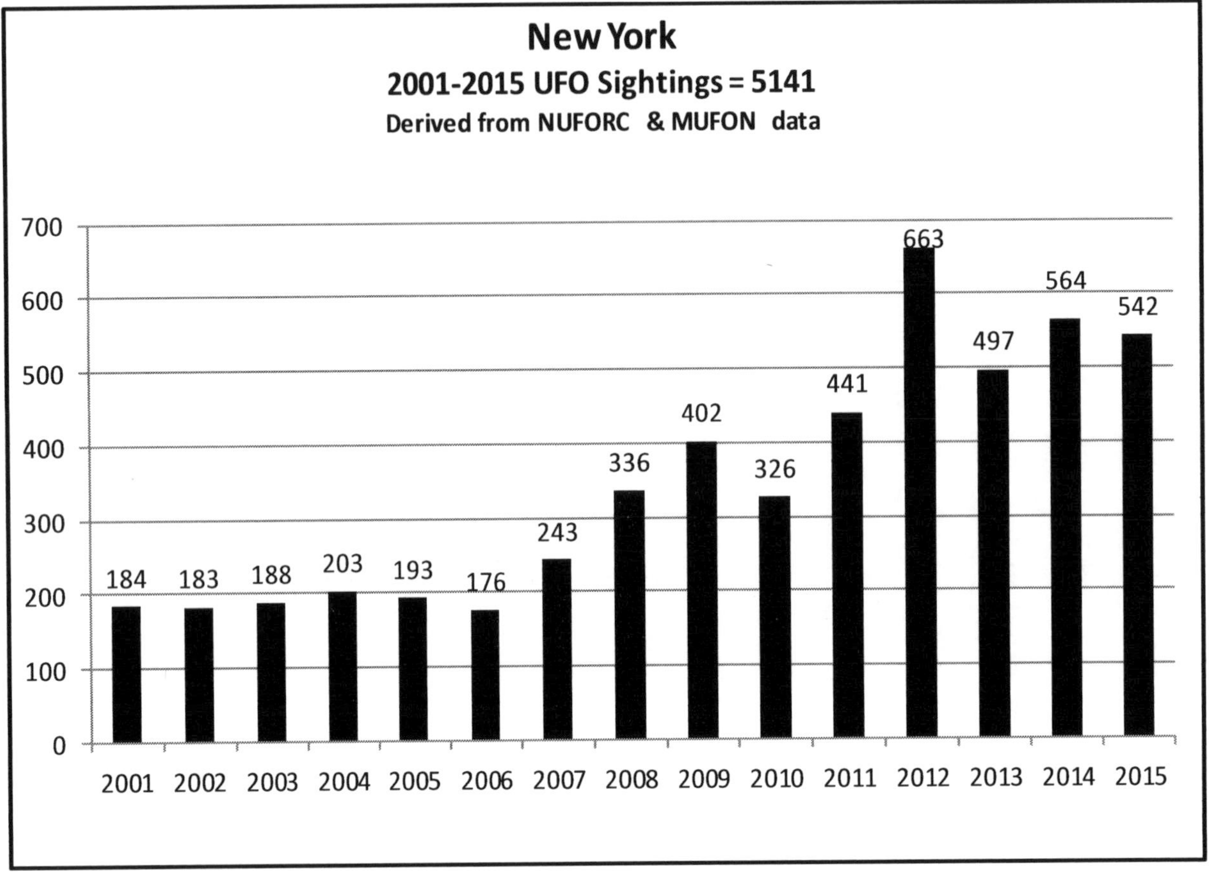

TOP TEN COUNTIES		RANK	TOP TEN SHAPES		
Suffolk	554	1	Triangle	414	8.05%
New York	426	2	Other	316	6.15%
Erie	352	3	Oval	241	4.69%
Nassau	276	4	Star-like	207	4.03%
Monroe	236	5	Disk	165	3.21%
Kings	225	6	Circle	657	12.78%
Queens	210	7	Light	643	12.51%
Unknown	203	8	Unknown	473	9.20%
Onondaga	161	9	Sphere	457	8.89%
Westchester	153	10	Fireball	430	8.36%

UFO SHAPES: NEW YORK

UFO shapes	2001	2002	2003	2004	2005	2006	2007	2008	2009	2010	2011	2012	2013	2014	2015	Total
Blimp	2	1	1	1		1	3	3	2	3	3	3	1			24
Boomerang				2		2	1	3	1	7	3	5	6	5	7	42
Bullet/Missile	1	1	1		1		1	2	1	4	1	8	5		4	30
Changing	6	6	6	2	5	2	3	4	5	6	4	6	5	8	6	74
Chevron	3	1	3	4	2	3	1	7	7	9	11	10	7	8	4	80
Cigar	3	7	5	4	6	6	7	11	12	9	8	18	4	9	13	122
Circle	13	13	14	19	15	17	34	42	61	39	66	90	87	71	76	657
Cone	2	2	1	1			1	1	11	3	1	1	5	2	3	34
Cross		2				2	2	2	7		1	2	4		3	25
Cylinder	3	5	4		4	5	5	4	10	7	9	10	8	16	11	101
Diamond	9	6	2		3	3	2	4	12	3	12	9	13	10	10	98
Disc	6	5	3	2	3	2	6	12	16	14	15	22	8	18	19	151
Disk	10	9	16	18	13	3	11	14	12	11	4	13	9	10	12	165
Egg	2	6	4	2	6		2	5	3	2	2	5	3	1	5	48
Fireball	5	8	6	10	10	3	7	12	21	18	51	91	64	83	41	430
Flash	4	4	3		4	10	6	8	5	9	10	11	11	9	4	98
Formation	6	6	8	5	5	4	2	5	5	5	5	10	6	8	14	94
Light	23	31	27	34	31	19	35	45	49	41	45	82	54	67	60	643
N/A								2	1				2	3	5	13
Other	10	7	15	17	14	17	14	22	28	27	20	29	31	30	35	316
Oval	16	9	10	14	10	5	21	13	18	12	22	29	16	21	25	241
Rectangle		1		4	3	4	5	5	2	1	3	3	2	6	6	45
Saturn-like						1		1	2	1		1	1	1	1	9
Sphere	11	5	15	11	10	19	13	29	22	23	36	77	55	65	66	457
Sq/Rect															7	7
Star-like			3	3	5	3	11	17	20	17	28	27	18	30	25	207
Teardrop	4	2	1	4	4	4	6	1	2	1	2	4	1	5	2	43
Triangle	23	18	23	27	12	14	21	31	29	27	33	41	35	42	38	414
Unknown	22	28	17	19	27	27	23	31	38	27	46	56	36	36	40	473
Total	**184**	**183**	**188**	**203**	**193**	**176**	**243**	**336**	**402**	**326**	**441**	**663**	**497**	**564**	**542**	**5141**

UFOS BY COUNTY: NEW YORK

Counties	2001	2002	2003	2004	2005	2006	2007	2008	2009	2010	2011	2012	2013	2014	2015	Total
Albany	3	14	5	1	2	8	5	10	5	11	14	7	19	9	10	123
Allegany	1	1	3	4		1	1		3	1	2	4	2	3	6	32
Bronx	3	3	4	3	4	4	6	2	3	4	1	9	13	10	8	77
Broome	5	2	10	4	2	4	3	6	8	4	14	15	13	8	5	103
Cattaraugus		1		2	4	3	1		5	3	2	4	5	6	3	39
Cayuga	1		1	1				4	3	5	3	3	3	3	4	31
Chautauqua	1	1		4	1	1	5	1	1	2	5	7	10	9	7	55
Chemung	2	1	1		2	1		1	11	1	2	4	2	2	1	31
Chenango				1			2		3		1		2	2	2	13
Chester											1				1	2
Clinton	1	2	2	3	1		2			3		6	6	1	5	32
Columbia	2	2		2	1		1			4	3	3	4	1		23
Cortland		1		2	1				2	1	3	4	4	3	2	23
Delaware					2	1	2	1	3		2	1	2	4	2	20
Dutchess	7	1	2	4	7	3	10	10	9	9	13	17	16	17	19	144
Erie	5	10	8	13	10	13	17	28	17	20	35	63	27	36	50	352
Essex	3	1			1	3	3				2	1	1	1	3	19
Franklin	2	1	1		1		1		1	1	2	6	2	1	1	20
Fulton	1				1		2	2		2	1		3		3	15
Genesee				3	3		2	4	7	2	3	4	5	3	9	45
Greene	1		1	2	2	4		6	2	3	4	3	1	2		31
Hamilton								1			1		1			3
Herkimer	1			1	2				4	3	3	3	3	1	2	23
Jefferson		2	1		2	3		2	3	6	8	8	2	5	2	44
Kings	9	7	14	15	11	12	13	8	12	8	14	31	21	35	15	225
Lewis	1	1	1		3			1				1	1		3	12
Livingston	3	1	1	3	3	1		1		1		5	4	1	3	27
Madison	1	4			1		2		2		2	6	6	2	5	31
Monroe	9	12	4	8	13	4	8	7	21	21	24	31	20	28	26	236
Montgomery	1	2	1	3	1		1	3		3		3	2	1	2	23
Nassau	14	11	11	11	11	6	11	19	24	14	22	31	26	30	35	276
New York	33	22	22	18	12	22	31	27	54	36	35	30	19	32	33	426
Niagara	1	2	2	1	2	1	3	6	7	2	9	16	9	17	17	95
Oneida	5	4	5	7	6	6	3	3	2	6	10	10	14	10	14	105
Onondaga	3	3	7	6	5	4	2	11	9	7	14	18	22	21	29	161
Ontario	1	1	2	4	1		1	3	3	2	6	3		6	4	37
Orange	3	4	1	3	3	8	3	17	13	14	12	21	7	21	21	151

Counties	2001	2002	2003	2004	2005	2006	2007	2008	2009	2010	2011	2012	2013	2014	2015	Total
Orleans	2				1			1		1	2	2	1	2	2	14
Oswego	1	1	2	1	3	1	2	3	7	2	7	10	2	7	6	55
Otsego		1		3	1	1	1	2	4	3	1	2	1		3	23
Putnam	2	3	1	2		2	3	2	5			6	5	3	4	38
Queens	10	7	10	7	11	6	23	15	21	11	12	24	16	24	13	210
Rensselaer		1	2	1	1	3	1	3	4	3	3	7	2	4	6	41
Richmond	6	5	6	3	3	2	4	7	9	9	12	8	7	11	13	105
Rockland	1		3	4	2	2	1	3	7	5	1	8	5	6	2	50
Saratoga	3	3	5	2	1	2	5	6	5	4	2	10	5	13	9	75
Schenectady	1	1	2	1			1	5		2	2	7	6	9	3	40
Schoharie					1						2		4	1		8
Schuyler	2		1			1	1	1	1	4	3	3	1	1	1	20
Seneca				1	1	2		2	1		2	1		1	1	12
St. Lawrence	2	2	8		2	2	4	9	5	3	2	14	7	13	5	78
Steuben		1	2			1	1	1	2	2	4	1	3	5	4	27
Suffolk	14	20	18	17	20	14	24	43	34	37	58	88	51	64	52	554
Sullivan		2			1	2	1	7	5	6	3	3	2	5	4	41
Tioga						1	1	5		1	4	4	2	4		22
Tompkins	1	2	1	5	2	2	1	1	2	2	5	8	5	1	1	39
Ulster	1	3		4	2	5	2	7	7	8	3	13	12	8	6	81
Unknown	4	5	3	6	4	4	6	9	14	8	13	33	36	24	34	203
Warren	2		2	4	6	1	3	3	11	1	3	5	8	5	6	60
Washington		2	4			4	3	2	3	2	5	5	3	2	1	36
Wayne		2	3	1	2	1			2		4	7	4	4	1	31
Westchester	9	4	3	12	8	4	12	13	15	12	14	13	9	14	11	153
Wyoming		1					1			1		1			2	6
Yates			2				1	2	1		1	2	3	2		14
Total	**184**	**183**	**188**	**203**	**193**	**176**	**243**	**336**	**402**	**326**	**441**	**663**	**497**	**564**	**542**	**5141**

If a county is missing from the list, it's because no UFO sightings were logged in either the NUFORC or MUFON databases for the 2001-2015 sample period.

UFOS BY MONTH: NEW YORK

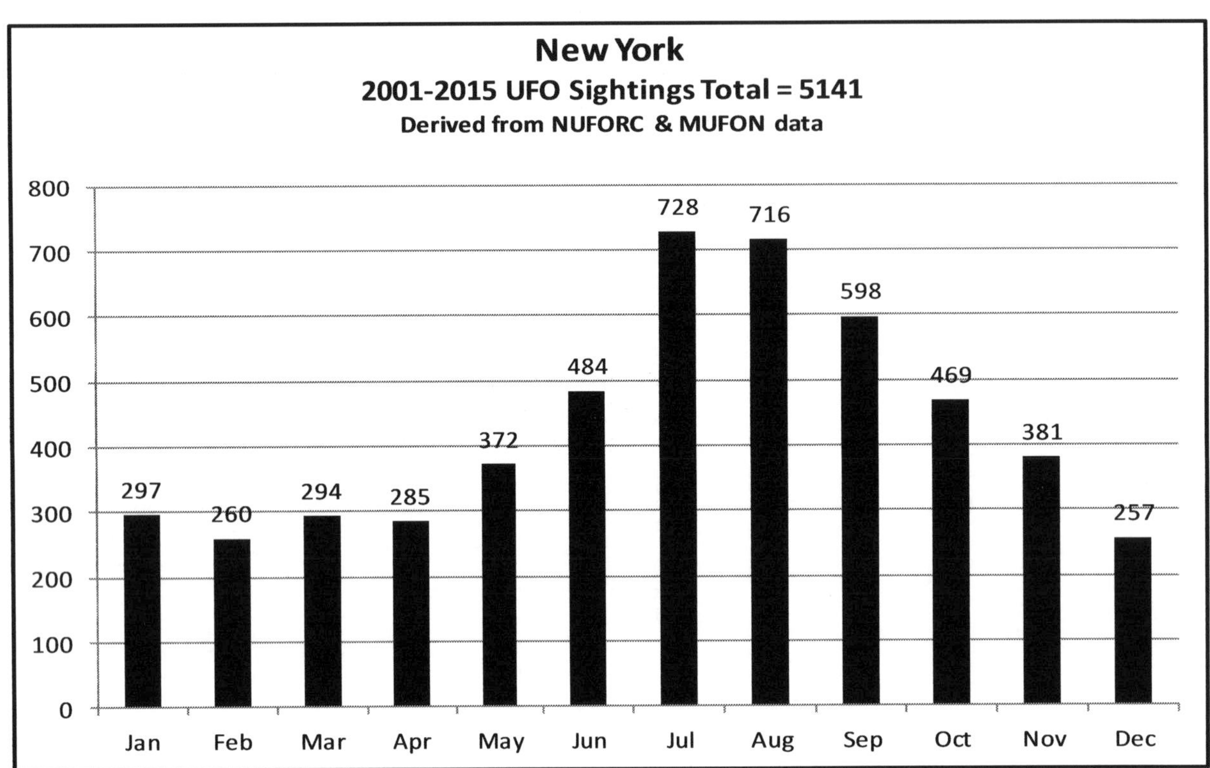

Year	Jan	Feb	Mar	Apr	May	Jun	Jul	Aug	Sep	Oct	Nov	Dec	Total
2001	13	11	11	13	14	9	23	16	42	10	14	8	184
2002	15	7	10	12	12	16	28	24	26	24	5	4	183
2003	10	7	8	6	3	12	26	22	32	21	28	13	188
2004	11	20	11	10	15	15	11	33	19	34	15	9	203
2005	6	16	15	9	10	28	17	23	25	11	21	12	193
2006	12	11	13	15	8	13	16	26	18	24	11	9	176
2007	21	8	18	11	28	20	21	34	27	27	18	10	243
2008	31	14	20	21	25	33	42	50	27	30	24	19	336
2009	27	24	25	22	24	26	57	31	69	32	38	27	402
2010	16	11	19	24	12	33	66	36	23	48	23	15	326
2011	13	19	14	19	26	42	62	81	52	34	37	42	441
2012	51	41	59	35	46	80	95	79	61	45	43	28	663
2013	25	19	25	26	51	43	89	90	54	33	30	12	497
2014	20	39	25	30	51	61	72	90	64	48	27	37	564
2015	26	13	21	32	47	53	103	81	59	48	47	12	542
Total	**297**	**260**	**294**	**285**	**372**	**484**	**728**	**716**	**598**	**469**	**381**	**257**	**5141**

Distribution of Sightings between Databases: New York

Database	Count	Percentage
MUFON	1978	38.48%
NUFORC	3162	61.52%
Total	5141	100.00%

State Demographic Information: New York

2010 US Census Statistics	
Population	19,378,102.00
Area in Square Miles	54,554.98
Land Area Sq. Miles	47,126.40
Population/Square mile	411.20

NORTH CAROLINA UFO RANK 11/51

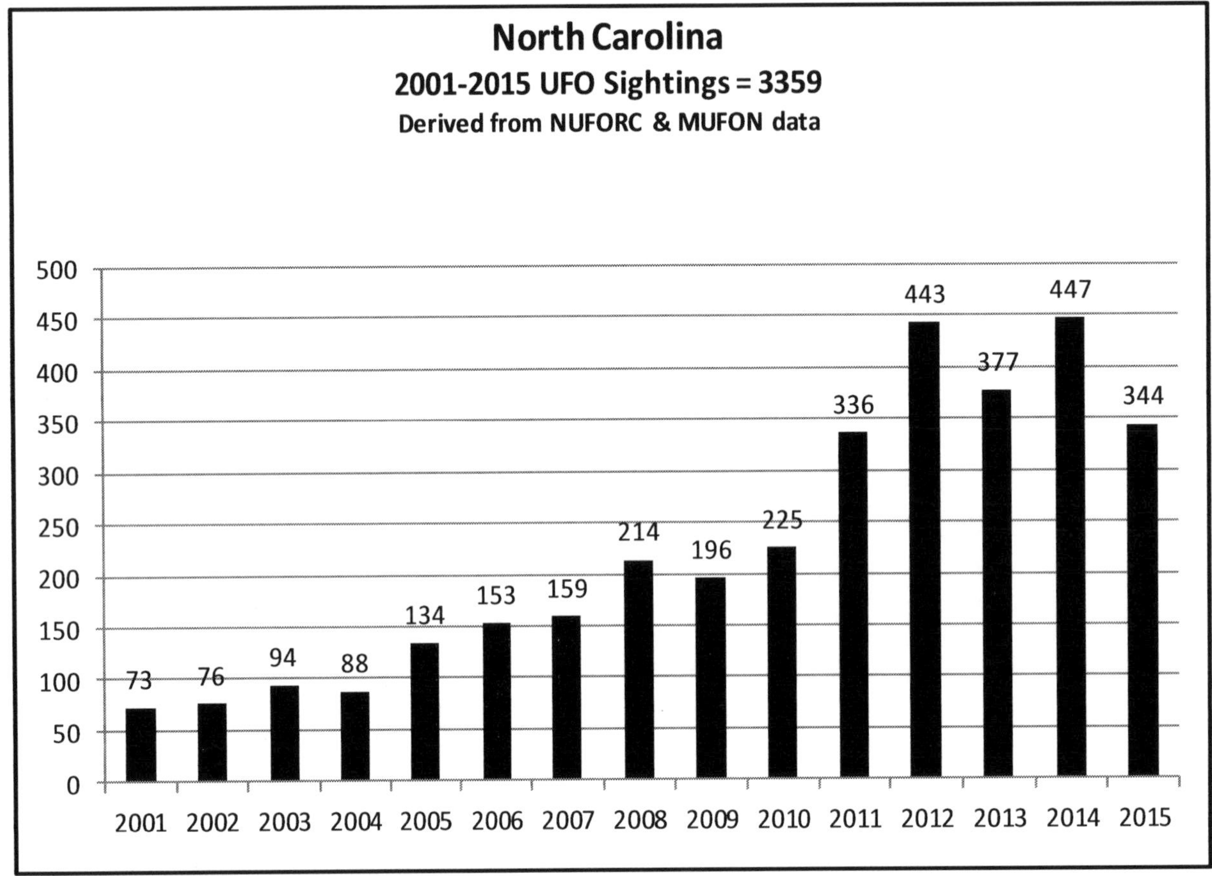

TOP TEN COUNTIES		RANK	TOP TEN SHAPES		
Wake	276	1	Light	458	13.64%
Mecklenburg	272	2	Circle	430	12.80%
New Hanover	224	3	Sphere	360	10.72%
Brunswick	164	4	Unknown	312	9.29%
Buncombe	116	5	Triangle	308	9.17%
Dare	109	6	Other	227	6.76%
Forsyth	102	7	Fireball	214	6.37%
Caswell	91	8	Oval	133	3.96%
Catawba	89	9	Star-like	118	3.51%
Unknown	89	10	Disc	97	2.89%

UFO SHAPES: NORTH CAROLINA

UFO Shapes	2001	2002	2003	2004	2005	2006	2007	2008	2009	2010	2011	2012	2013	2014	2015	Total
Blimp					1	1		1		1	1	1		1	1	8
Boomerang					2		2	2		3	5	4	9	3	6	36
Bullet/Missile					1	1				3	4	2	4	1	1	17
Changing			3	3	6	3	2	2	3	5	3	4	4	8	5	51
Chevron	1	2		3	4	4	2	5	4	1	4	2	1	4	4	41
Cigar	4	3	2	3	5	4	7	6	4	9	8	12	6	10	8	91
Circle	8	6	5	5	4	21	21	30	15	28	44	71	58	65	49	430
Cone		1					1		4	4		2	1	1		14
Cross								2			2	4	2	2	2	14
Cylinder			1		1	3	3	10	5	4	7	3	9	4	6	56
Diamond		1			2	3	5	4	2	4	5	1	10	6	5	48
Disc	3	1		1		15	1	6	9	7	9	16	8	14	7	97
Disk	9	4	3	7	6	4	9	6	8	6	4	7	5	11	4	93
Egg	2	1	3		2	1		1	2		3	2	1	6		24
Fireball	2	5	8	6	11	8	8	7	12	13	20	35	29	28	22	214
Flash	1	2	2	5	4	3	1	8	3	5	2	5	7	5	5	58
Formation		5	2	3	4	3		3	4	4	10	13	5	11	6	73
Light	11	17	19	15	17	13	20	30	29	30	51	52	52	66	36	458
N/A											1			5	3	9
Other	2	3	6	3	9	24	20	17	8	20	17	24	31	22	21	227
Oval	3	4	4	5	3	12	11	6	8	10	16	19	8	11	13	133
Rectangle		3	3	2		1	6	1	2	2	3	3	3	6	5	40
Saturn-like							2			1			1			4
Sphere	6	4	6	8	8	8	7	16	19	17	38	59	55	62	47	360
Sq/Rect														1	1	2
Star-like			2	1		3	7	10	13	9	13	16	11	16	17	118
Teardrop		1	1	1	2		2		3		2	4		5	2	23
Triangle	10	6	7	9	13	9	11	19	18	18	29	46	30	43	40	308
Unknown	11	7	17	8	29	9	11	22	21	21	35	36	27	30	28	312
Total	**73**	**76**	**94**	**88**	**134**	**153**	**159**	**214**	**196**	**225**	**336**	**443**	**377**	**447**	**344**	**3359**

UFOS BY COUNTY: NORTH CAROLINA

Counties	2001	2002	2003	2004	2005	2006	2007	2008	2009	2010	2011	2012	2013	2014	2015	Total
Alamance	3	1	2		2		1	3	1	2	3	7	8	5	13	51
Alexander			1						1			1	2	1		6
Anson								1		2						3
Ashe	1				1		1	1	1	2		1	2		2	12
Avery	1	1	1	2	1			1		1	1		2	2		13
Beaufort	2		1	1	1				1			4	5	4		19
Bertie											2					2
Bladen		1					1		1		1					4
Brunswick	1	4		3	1	6	2	5	8	8	28	33	25	36	5	165
Buncombe	1		6	5	5	1	10	8	11	5	15	15	12	11	11	116
Burke	2	1			2	2			3	1	4	3	1	5	4	28
Cabarrus	1	2	3		2		7		2	2	3	6	6	6	11	51
Caldwell		1					1		4	2	3	7	2	3	3	26
Camden	1			1												2
Carroll														1		1
Carteret	1	3	2		2	1	3	2	4	13	6	8	6	9	4	64
Caswell	2	1	3	3	5	2		6	6	11	9	10	7	14	12	91
Catawba	2		1	2	3			5	8	5	8	19	15	13	8	89
Chatham		2					2	4		1	1			3	1	14
Cherokee	1				1	2				1				1		6
Clay			1				1						1			3
Cleveland		1	1		1		3	3	1	1	1	5	8	2	5	32
Columbus	1		2		2				2	1		3	1		4	16
Craven	1		2	2	1		1	4		2	1	8	1	2	3	28
Cumberland			1	4	5	4	4	9	3	2	10	11	14	15	5	87
Currituck		1	1	1		2		1			5	3		4		18
Dare	1	2	2	3	5	1	3	5	3	4	10	26	10	21	13	109
Davidson		1	2	3	3	1		2	4	1	2	5	4	5	4	37
Davie			1	2		1		1	1				3	1	2	12
Duplin			1			1	1	2	1		1	2		2	1	12
Durham	2	1		2	2	1	1	8	10	9	7	5	9	8	8	73
Edgecombe		2	1		1		2	3	1	1	4		3	1	1	20
Forsyth	1	3	1		3	4	4	8	5	6	12	12	21	8	14	102
Franklin					1		2	2	1		4	3	4	5	3	25
Gaston	3		3	1	2		2	4	3	5	11	8	12	9	6	69
Gates				2						1	2					5
Granville		1						1				2		2		6

Counties	2001	2002	2003	2004	2005	2006	2007	2008	2009	2010	2011	2012	2013	2014	2015	Total
Greene													1	1	1	3
Guilford		1	4	1	3	2	5		4	8	2	5	10	6	10	61
Halifax			1		1	2			3		1		2		1	11
Hanover														1		1
Harnett		1	1		1	1	6	1	3	2	3	4	4	3	5	35
Haywood					1	1	2		1		1	1		2	2	11
Henderson	1				4	6	5	5	4	3	4	4	6	5	5	52
Hoke				2		1		2		2			1	1	1	10
Horry						1			1					1		3
Hyde	1			1		1				1	2		1	1	2	10
Iredell	1	2	1	2	3		3	2	4	2	1	7	7	3	6	44
Jackson			4				1		1	2	1		1	4	4	18
Johnston	1	1	3	1	1	1	6	5	3	2	5	3	6	6	6	50
Jones			1			1			2							4
Lee			1			2	1	1	1		3	1			3	13
Lenoir					1			1	1	2			1	1		7
Lincoln		2	1	1			3	2	1	1			1	2	1	15
Macon		1				2	1	1	1		2	2	1	2	3	16
Madison		1			1	2	1		1	1		3		4		14
Martin							1			1	1	2	2	2	1	10
McDowell	1		1		1	1	1	1		4		3	2	7	1	23
Mecklenburg	11	9	13	8	10	13	16	19	14	16	32	31	19	34	27	272
Mitchell		1		1	1	1	1		1	2	1			1		10
Montgomery			1		1			1		1	3			1		8
Moore	2		1	2				1	1	1	3	2	3	4	1	21
Nash				1				1	2	2	2	2		1		11
New Hanover	3	8	3	4	8	59	11	12	9	15	12	26	19	23	12	224
Newberry								1								1
Northampton				1							1					2
Onslow	1	2		1	5	2	4	3	5	2	5	8	5	8	9	60
Orange	2				3		2	3	1	2	1	5	4	1	6	30
Pamlico	1			1	1							1	1			5
Pasquotank					3	1		1	1		3	4	2	2	2	19
Pender			2	1	1	2	1		2	2	6	7	11	11	7	53
Perquimans			1				1								2	4
Person				1		1		1					1			4
Pitt		3			1			3	1	3	4	2	3	4	5	29
Polk				1			1					1				3

Counties	**2001**	**2002**	**2003**	**2004**	**2005**	**2006**	**2007**	**2008**	**2009**	**2010**	**2011**	**2012**	**2013**	**2014**	**2015**	**Total**
Randolph		1	2	1	1	1	3	3	3		6	4	1	7	3	36
Richmond							1		3	2	3	2	2	1	1	15
Robeson		1		1		2	1	1	2	1	2	3		1	2	17
Rockingham	1						1	1		2		4	2	1	2	14
Rowan	4	2		2	2	1	2	3		1	3	4	1	3	3	31
Rutherford	1		1				2	1		1	4	3	3	2		18
Sampson								2							1	3
Scotland						1		2		3	1	1	1	1	1	11
Stanly					1		1	2				2	2	2	3	13
Stokes				1			2	2		1	3	1	2			12
Surry	1		1		1		1		1	1	1	2	7	2	1	19
Swain		1									1	2	5	2	1	12
Sylva										1						1
Transylvania	1						2		2	1		2		1		9
Tuxedo									2							2
Tyrrell														4		4
Union		1	1		3	1	3	3	1	2	5	11	7	13	7	58
Unknown				1	1	2	4	9	7	7	8	17	15	11	7	89
Vance			2										1			3
Wake	7	5	6	8	10	7	9	18	15	24	28	36	26	46	31	276
Warren				1				1			1	1		1		5
Washington			1					1			1					3
Watauga	3	1		3	1	2		2	2	4	3	2	1		4	28
Wayne				1	1	1					2	2		1	3	11
Wilkes	1		2		3	2	1	4	1	2	3	4		3	3	29
Wilson		3			1	1	1	3			3	4	1	1	4	22
Yadkin				1	1				2	3	1	4	1	3		16
Yancey	1			1	5				1	3	4	1	1		1	18
Total	**73**	**76**	**94**	**88**	**134**	**153**	**159**	**214**	**196**	**225**	**336**	**443**	**377**	**447**	**344**	**3359**

If a county is missing from the list, it's because no UFO sightings were logged in either the NUFORC or MUFON databases for the 2001-2015 sample period.

UFOS BY MONTH: NORTH CAROLINA

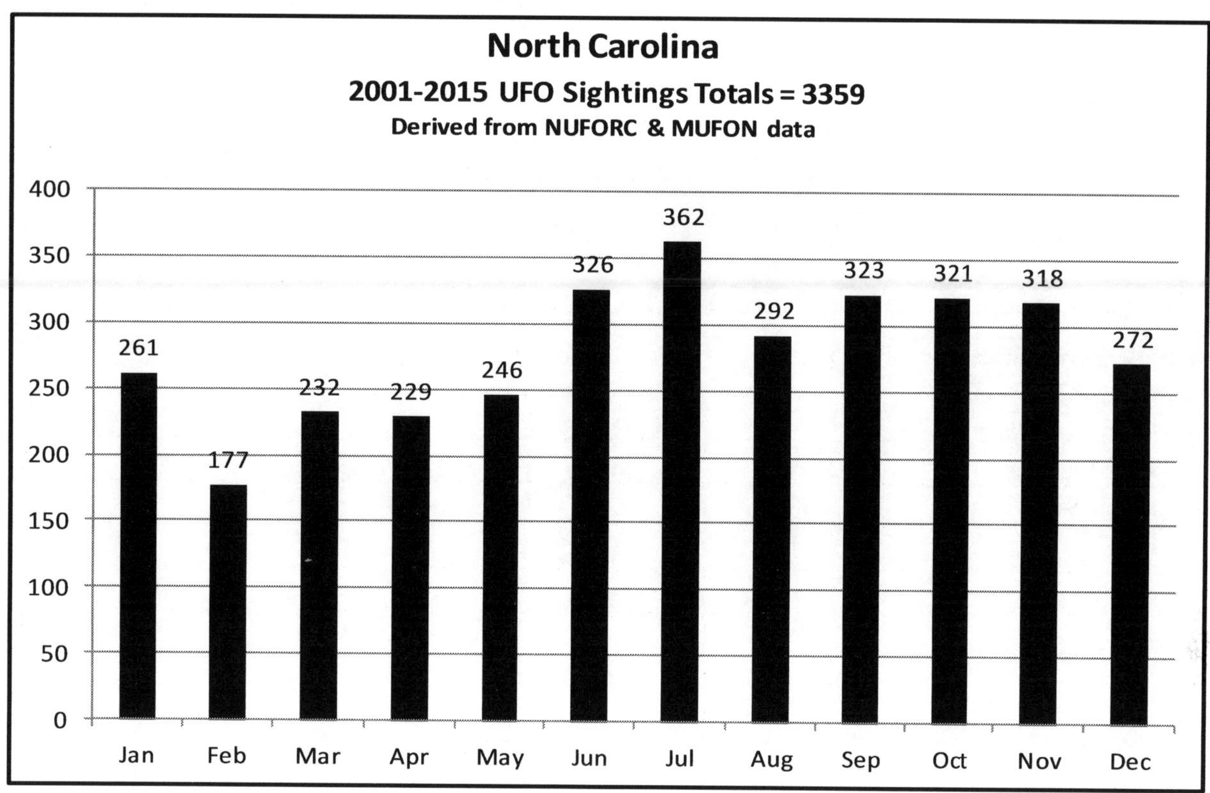

Year	Jan	Feb	Mar	Apr	May	Jun	Jul	Aug	Sep	Oct	Nov	Dec	Total
2001	6	4	6	3	4	11	7	6	6	6	8	6	73
2002	6	3	3	6	3	7	8	9	9	5	8	9	76
2003	7	4	3	4	4	10	9	6	16	11	12	8	94
2004	6	11	11	10	4	7	6	5	13	8	5	2	88
2005	8	8	6	11	9	19	10	6	19	14	15	9	134
2006	6	10	11	9	10	14	22	9	13	12	24	13	153
2007	25	15	10	11	7	8	10	16	14	17	9	17	159
2008	19	12	21	19	14	18	20	8	15	32	18	18	214
2009	17	14	15	21	15	7	22	7	21	20	24	13	196
2010	25	7	19	16	12	13	39	11	19	30	20	14	225
2011	19	16	16	15	14	37	27	29	29	44	35	55	336
2012	26	11	32	37	41	38	63	48	46	31	38	32	443
2013	27	22	17	25	25	39	24	52	43	28	43	32	377
2014	42	25	31	25	50	63	45	50	30	38	25	23	447
2015	22	15	31	17	34	35	50	30	30	25	34	21	344
Total	**261**	**177**	**232**	**229**	**246**	**326**	**362**	**292**	**323**	**321**	**318**	**272**	**3359**

Distribution of Sightings between Databases: North Carolina

Database	Count	Percentage
MUFON	1300	38.70%
NUFORC	2059	61.30%
Total	3359	100.00%

State Demographic Information: North Carolina

2010 US Census Statistics	
Population	9,535,483.00
Area in Square Miles	53,819.16
Land Area Sq. Miles	48,617.91
Population/Square mile	196. 1

NORTH DAKOTA UFO RANK 50/51

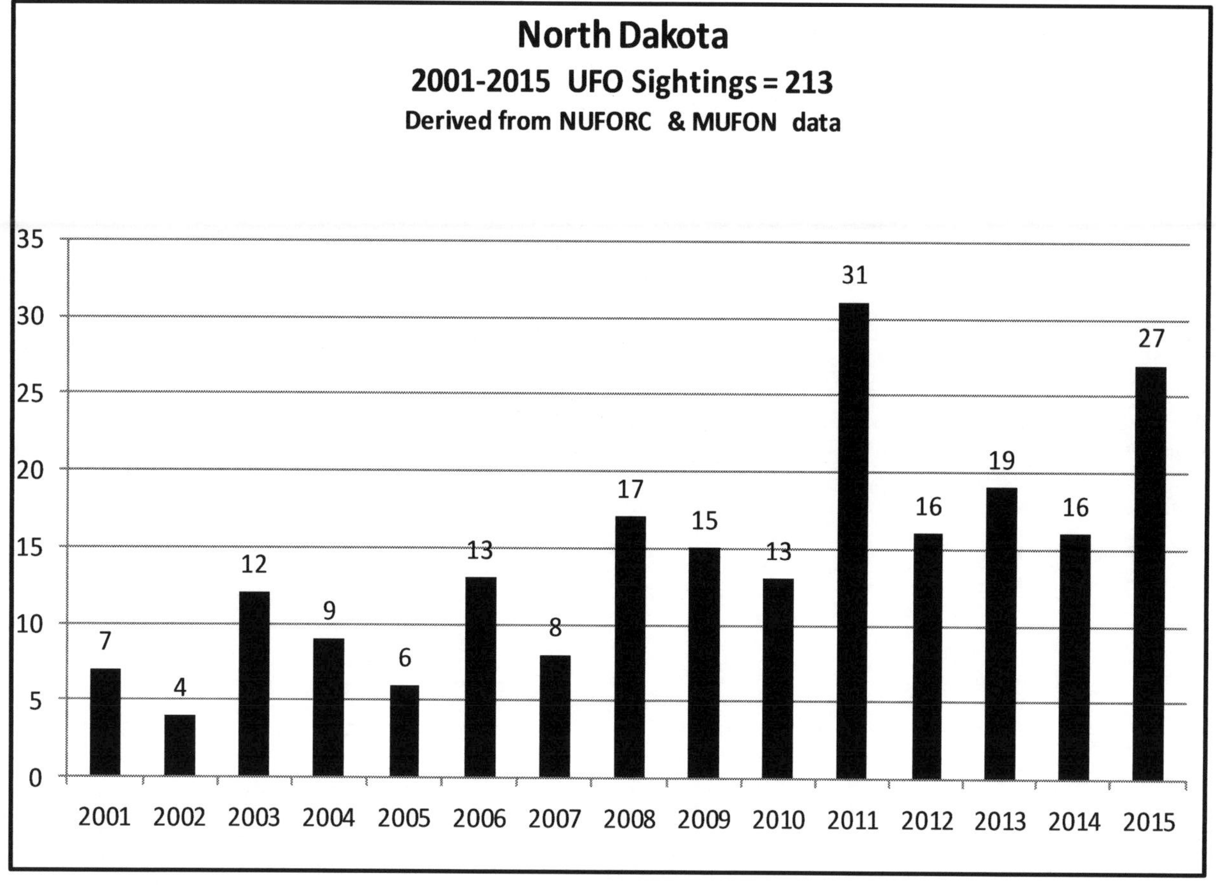

TOP TEN COUNTIES		RANK	TOP TEN SHAPES		
Cass	35	**1**	Triangle	33	15.49%
Ward	25	**2**	Unknown	26	12.21%
Burleigh	24	**3**	Sphere	21	9.86%
Grand Forks	22	**4**	Light	20	9.39%
Williams	13	**5**	Circle	18	8.45%
Mclean	7	**6**	Other	15	7.04%
Stutsman	7	**7**	Star-like	10	4.69%
Rolette	6	**8**	Oval	9	4.23%
Stark	6	**9**	Cigar	7	3.29%
Mercer	5	**10**	Disc	6	2.82%

UFO SHAPES: NORTH DAKOTA

UFO Shapes	2001	2002	2003	2004	2005	2006	2007	2008	2009	2010	2011	2012	2013	2014	2015	Total
Blimp											1					1
Changing							1	1			1	1				4
Chevron					1				1							2
Cigar				1				1			2		1	1	1	7
Circle	2			1		3	1	1	1		1	2	4		2	18
Cylinder								1		3			1			5
Diamond		1	2								1		1			5
Disc							1	2			1			1	1	6
Disk		1	1		1			1	1						1	6
Egg	1				1		1									3
Fireball				1		1					1				1	4
Flash				1		2		2						1		6
Formation										1		1		2	1	5
Light	2	1	1		1	2	2		1	1	4		1	2	2	20
N/A														1		1
Other	1		1	2		1			2	1	2	3	1		1	15
Oval	1		2						1	1	2		1	1		9
Rectangle								1								1
Sphere			1			1	1	1	1	1	5	1	4	2	3	21
Star-like								1			1		2	3	3	10
Teardrop						1				1	2					4
Triangle		1	2	2	1	1	1	2	5	2	4	7	1	1	3	33
Unknown			2	1	1	1		3	2	1	3	1	2	1	8	26
Boomerang										1						1
Total	**7**	**4**	**12**	**9**	**6**	**13**	**8**	**17**	**15**	**13**	**31**	**16**	**19**	**16**	**27**	**213**

UFOS BY COUNTY: NORTH DAKOTA

Counties	**2001**	**2002**	**2003**	**2004**	**2005**	**2006**	**2007**	**2008**	**2009**	**2010**	**2011**	**2012**	**2013**	**2014**	**2015**	**Total**
Barnes								1							1	2
Burleigh			1	1				2	2	3	6	1	1	1	6	24
Cass	1	1	1	2	1	3	3	1	2	1	2	4	5	3	5	35
Cavalier								1					1			2
Dunn											1					1
Eddy								1								1
Emmons			1			1	1									3
Foster											1					1
Grand Forks				1		3	2	2	3	1	1	5	1	3		22
Griggs											1					1
Hettinger						1					1					2
Kidder					1	1										2
Logan	2															2
McHenry															1	1
Mclean		1		1	1	1			1					1	1	7
Mercer					1			1			1		2			5
Morton		1			1	1			1					1		5
Mountrail								1				1			1	3
Nelson	1															1
Oliver													1			1
Pembina										1			1			2
Pierce															1	1
Ramsey						1				1		1		1		4
Renville											1					1
Richland	1		1					2							1	5
Rolette	1											2	1	2		6
Sheridan			2							1	2					5
Sioux				1							1					2
Slope	1															1
Stark		1	1							1	2		1			6
Steele								1								1
Stutsman				1					2		2		1		1	7
Traill											2			1		3
Unknown										1	1				3	5
Walsh						1									1	2
Ward			2	2			1	1	4	1	6	1	3	2	2	25
Wells								2							1	3

Counties	**2001**	**2002**	**2003**	**2004**	**2005**	**2006**	**2007**	**2008**	**2009**	**2010**	**2011**	**2012**	**2013**	**2014**	**2015**	**Total**
Williams			3		1		1	1		2		1	1	1	2	13
Total	**7**	**4**	**12**	**9**	**6**	**13**	**8**	**17**	**15**	**13**	**31**	**16**	**19**	**16**	**27**	**213**

If a county is missing from the list, it's because no UFO sightings were logged in either the NUFORC or MUFON databases for the 2001-2015 sample period.

UFOS BY MONTH: NORTH DAKOTA

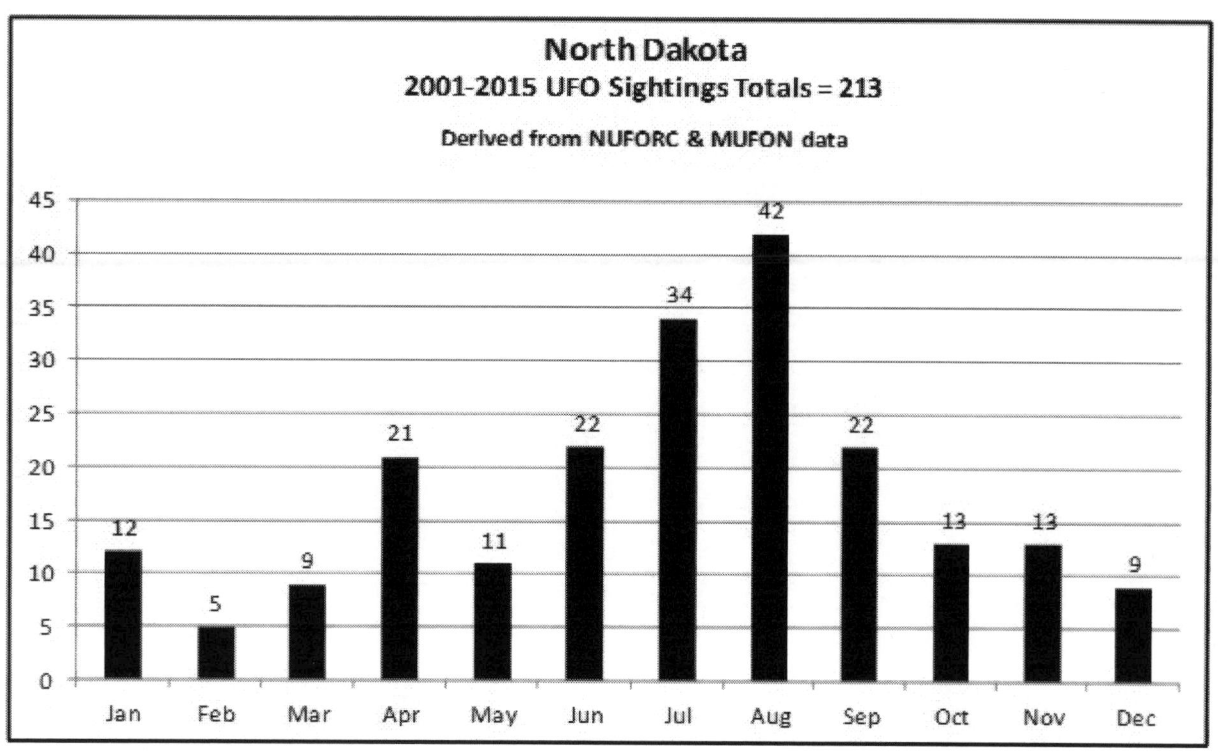

Year	Jan	Feb	Mar	Apr	May	Jun	Jul	Aug	Sep	Oct	Nov	Dec	Total
2001							2	1		3		1	7
2002		1						1			1	1	4
2003	1					1	3	5			1	1	12
2004	1					1		3	2		2		9
2005		1	1		1		3						6
2006	1			3		1	3	2		2	1		13
2007	1			1	1	2	1	1	1				8
2008	4					2	3	4	2	1	1		17
2009				2	5		1	5		1	1		15
2010	1			1		2	5	1		1	1	1	13
2011	1	1	3	5		1	5	6	5		1	3	31
2012			2	5	1	3		2	2			1	16
2013				1	2	5	2	5	2	1		1	19
2014	2		2	1	1	1	4		2	1	2		16
2015		2	1	2		3	2	6	6	3	2		27
Total	**12**	**5**	**9**	**21**	**11**	**22**	**34**	**42**	**22**	**13**	**13**	**9**	**213**

Distribution of Sightings between Databases: North Dakota

Database	Count	Percentage
MUFON	94	44.13%
NUFORC	119	55.87%
Total	213	100.00%

State Demographic Information: North Dakota

2010 US Census Statistics	
Population	672,591.00
Area in Square Miles	70,698.32
Land Area Sq. Miles	69,000.80
Population/Square mile	9.70

OHIO

UFO RANK 10/51

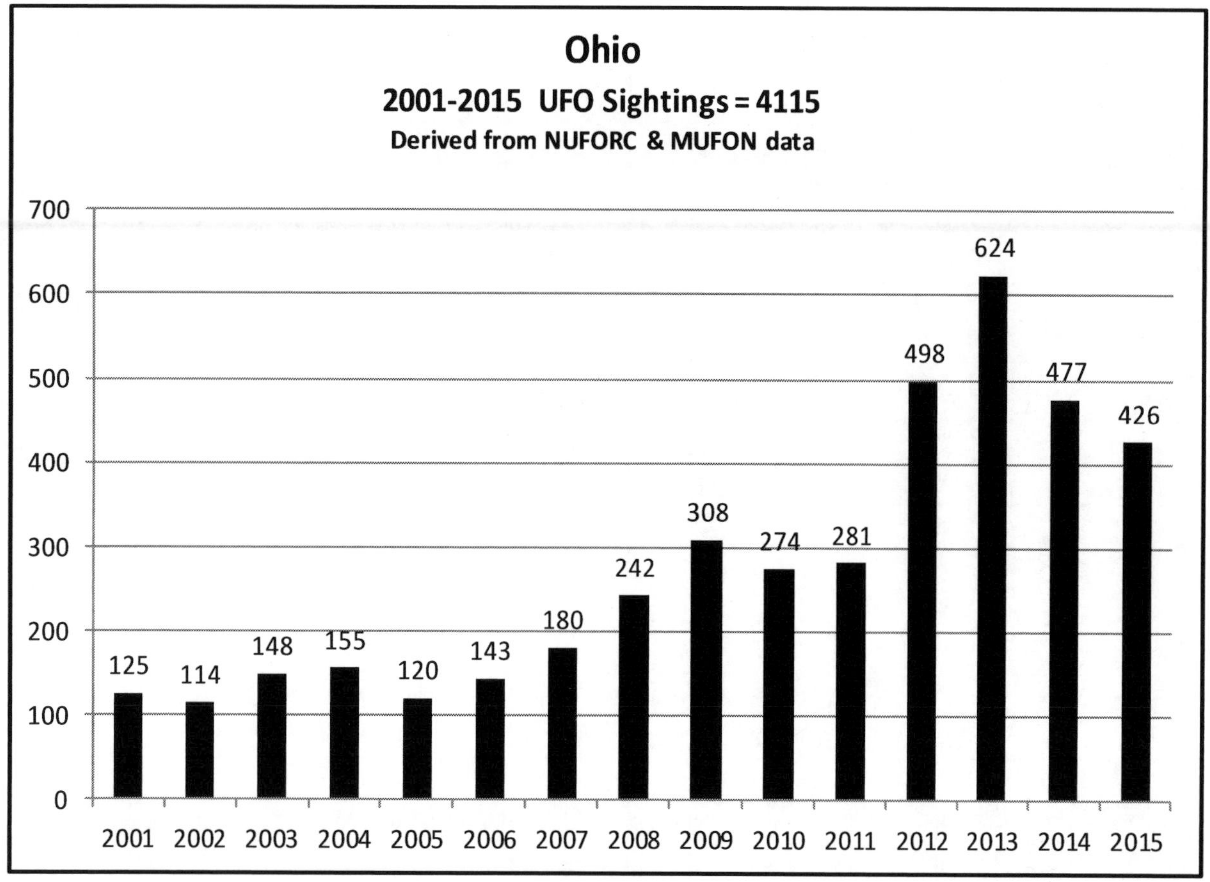

TOP TEN COUNTIES		RANK	TOP TEN SHAPES		
Franklin	392	1	Circle	515	12.52%
Cuyahoga	354	2	Light	473	11.49%
Hamilton	212	3	Sphere	464	11.28%
Montgomery	203	4	Triangle	435	10.57%
Butler	164	5	Fireball	375	9.11%
Summit	157	6	Unknown	347	8.43%
Lucas	136	7	Other	230	5.59%
Stark	134	8	Oval	175	4.25%
Unknown	117	9	Star-like	140	3.40%
Clermont	94	10	Disc	103	2.50%

UFO SHAPES: OHIO

UFO Shapes	2001	2002	2003	2004	2005	2006	2007	2008	2009	2010	2011	2012	2013	2014	2015	Total
Blimp						2		3	3	1	5	3	3			20
Boomerang	1	1	1	1			6	2	10	5	5	4	4	6	5	51
Bullet/Missile	2				1	1		2	5	2	1	6	2	1	2	25
Changing	4	3	4	5	2	5	3	4	5	5		1	10	10	6	67
Chevron	1	1	3			2	3	5	1	2	4	1	3	2	2	30
Cigar	5	7	4	5	3	5	3	18	6	8	6	6	9	3	6	94
Circle	6	11	6	10	7	11	22	27	40	44	38	81	97	66	49	515
Cone	2		1		2	3	1		1	1	3	7	3	1	4	29
Cross		2						3	1	2		3	3	5	2	21
Cylinder	6	3	5	3	3	2	4	6	4	2	4	7	17	10	8	84
Diamond	2	2	1	2		2	5	6	9	4	3	8	8	6	11	69
Disc	3	2	1	2	3	3	6	11	12	6	8	23	5	8	10	103
Disk	4	10	7	9	4	9	4	7	3	11	3	6	4	6	8	95
Egg	2	1		1		2	2	2	3	5	1	5	3	3	3	33
Fireball	4	1	2	7	3	11	7	6	24	24	37	73	107	40	29	375
Flash	1	1	3	4	5	5	1	4	10	7	4	5	9	4	3	66
Formation	2	2	3	1	5	3	7	5	5	3	4	11	16	13	6	86
Light	26	10	29	39	20	10	30	26	30	19	34	51	58	53	38	473
N/A					1					1			1	4	4	11
Other	3	7	15	14	9	10	11	11	22	20	13	15	24	33	23	230
Oval	3	8	12	8	7	6	6	14	13	8	9	20	24	23	14	175
Rectangle	1		2	1	1	2	2	3	1	1	1	7	7		7	36
Saturn-like							1			2	1				1	5
Sphere	10	9	10	6	7	9	12	28	20	21	34	65	82	80	71	464
Sq/Rect									1						9	10
Star-like	1		1		1	5	4	6	17	9	9	24	25	17	21	140
Teardrop	2		1		1	1		2	2	1	6	3	6	1		26
Triangle	19	20	16	14	15	15	22	21	34	33	31	34	55	51	55	435
Unknown	15	13	21	23	20	19	18	20	26	27	17	29	39	31	29	347
Total	**125**	**114**	**148**	**155**	**120**	**143**	**180**	**242**	**308**	**274**	**281**	**498**	**624**	**477**	**426**	**4115**

UFOS BY COUNTY: OHIO

Counties	2001	2002	2003	2004	2005	2006	2007	2008	2009	2010	2011	2012	2013	2014	2015	Total
Adams				2	1	1		3	3	2	1		1	2	2	18
Allen	4		3	1	1		4	2	1	2	3	7	10	6	7	51
Ashland					1	1			1		2	1			2	8
Ashtabula	3	2	3	2	4	1	1	6	5	3	2	13	4	6	5	60
Athens				1	3	3		2	2		2	4	10	6	7	40
Auglaize			3			1		3		1	1	1	2		1	13
Belmont	1	1	1	1	1	2		1	2	3	3	4	2		2	24
Brook Park				1	1											2
Brown	1					1	1	1			1	1	3		1	10
Butler	8	7	11	2	1	3	3	6	22	16	13	14	30	14	14	164
Carroll			1	1	2						1			1	1	7
Champaign					2					1		1	1	1	2	8
Clark	3	1	2		1		4	1		4	1	7	7	5	7	43
Clermont	3	3	2	2	2	6	3	11	7	6	9	12	7	13	8	94
Clinton	3	1				2		2	2	2	3	6	3	3	5	32
Columbiana	3	2	3		3	2	1	1	6		4	9	2	10	4	50
Coshocton			2			1		1					2	1	2	9
Crawford	2	2				1	2		1			3	6	4	2	23
Cuyahoga	9	17	9	23	15	13	17	24	17	37	23	49	41	40	20	354
Darke								1	1	1		2	2	1	1	9
Defiance	1				1		2	1	1		1	3	2		1	13
Delaware	1		8		1	3	6	3	6	1	5	4	6	1	10	55
Erie		1	1	1		3	4	2	3		1	5	5	3	4	33
Fairfield	5			2	1	1	2	3	5	3	3	5	6	6	7	49
Fayette			2			2	1		1			1		2	1	10
Franklin	8	9	14	13	8	8	11	15	23	30	27	55	78	46	47	392
Fulton						1		1	1	1	1	2	2		1	10
Gallia			1	1								4	2	1	5	14
Geauga	2	2	2	1	1			1		2	1		5		4	21
Greene	1	4	3		3	7	2	2	5	6	1	10	11	11	8	74
Guernsey				1		1	1	1		1	1	1		2		9
Hamilton	2	9	1	6	7	10	9	12	28	18	16	27	36	15	16	212
Hancock	2		1	1	3	1	2	2	1	1	3	1	8	3	4	33
Hardin		1	1							1		1			1	5
Harrison	2					2				1	1		1			7
Henry												2	1	1		4
Highland		1	4	2		1	2	2	3	2			2	3	6	28

Counties	2001	2002	2003	2004	2005	2006	2007	2008	2009	2010	2011	2012	2013	2014	2015	Total
Hocking					2	2	1	1			1	1	2	2	1	13
Holmes	2					1									1	4
Huron			2	1			1	1	1	2	1	4	7	6	2	28
Jackson		1	1					3	3		1		3	3		15
Jefferson	1				1			1	1	1		1	2	1	3	12
Knox	1				1		1	1	1	2	3	2	5	2	4	23
Lake	2	1	3	4	3	2	3	7	5	3	2	12	6	11	8	72
Lawrence	1	1	1	1	1		3		2	1	4	4	2	7	3	31
Licking	2	4	5	3		1	5	6	12	1	5	16	5	9	7	81
Logan		1		2	1		3	1			1	2	2	1		14
Lorain		3	2	5		3	6	9	2	6	9	14	10	9	16	94
Lucas	4	1	4	9	2	3	10	6	13	13	10	15	23	10	13	136
Madison				1				1	1		1	1	1	1	2	9
Mahoning	2	2	1	1		4	4	5	11	9	7	7	15	5	11	84
Marion		2				1		1				2	1	3	2	12
Marshall											1					1
Medina	3	1	2	3	2	1		2	3	1	2	5	11	8	9	53
Meigs				1			1	1	1	2		1		1		8
Mercer					1		1	1		1			1			5
Miami	1	2	1	1			1	2	4	1	5	6	2	11	1	38
Monroe														1	1	2
Montgomery	9	1	7	6	2	9	8	6	10	12	13	21	35	34	30	203
Morgan	1															1
Morrow	1		1		1	2							1	2	2	10
Muskingum	2		1	1	4		3		1	2	3	3	2	7	3	32
Noble				1				1	4	1	1	6	7	3		24
Ottawa			1			1	1	3	4	2	6	2	5	4	3	32
Paulding						1	1		2			1		1	1	7
Perry				1	2		1		1	1		3	2		2	13
Pickaway		1	2	3	3	3	2	4	2	4		1	3	5	1	34
Pike	1					1	1	2	1		1		1	1		9
Portage		3	1	2	1	3	1	6	3	5	5	1	9	11	7	58
Preble			1	1				1	3	1	2	2	2		1	14
Putnam		1				1			1	1	1		1	2		8
Reynoldsburg			1	2						1	1	2	3	2	2	14
Richland		1	1	7	2	1	2	1	1	2	5	4	8	3	1	39
Ross		2	4	2	3	2	5	1	1	2	3	4	4	7	8	48
Sandusky		1						1	2	1	3	1	1	2	3	15
Scioto	2	2	3	6	1	1	4	2	3	4	2	1	3	2	3	39

Counties	**2001**	**2002**	**2003**	**2004**	**2005**	**2006**	**2007**	**2008**	**2009**	**2010**	**2011**	**2012**	**2013**	**2014**	**2015**	**Total**
Seneca	1	1		1	1			1	1	2		2			1	11
Shelby	2			2			1	1	1	3	2	4	5	7	5	33
Stark	5	3		4	1	4	6	12	10	5	4	12	35	24	9	134
Summit	5	2	11	5	2	5	7	16	9	10	13	15	20	20	17	157
Sylvania															1	1
Trumbull	2	2	4	6	5	1	2		2	3	8	13	8	9	4	69
Tuscarawas	3			2	2	3	1	2	4	1		2	4	2	6	32
Union		1							2	1		1	2	2		9
Unknown	3	1	1		5	3	5	8	9	8	10	20	19	14	11	117
Van Wert				2			2				2	1	2		2	11
Vinton			1						2			2				5
Warren		2	2	2	3	2	1	3	15	7	7	13	25	6	3	91
Washington	2	1	1		1	1	3	4	3	1	1	2	3	2	1	26
Wayne	2	4	1	3	2		1	1	1	3	1	3	6	2	3	33
Westerville		1	1		1			1				1	3		2	10
Williams			3			1	2	1					5		1	13
Wood	1	2			1	2	2	5	3	3	4	5	4	5	1	38
Wyandot												2				2
Total	**125**	**114**	**148**	**155**	**120**	**143**	**180**	**242**	**308**	**274**	**281**	**498**	**624**	**477**	**426**	**4115**

If a county is missing from the list, it's because no UFO sightings were logged in either the NUFORC or MUFON databases for the 2001-2015 sample period.

UFOS BY MONTH: OHIO

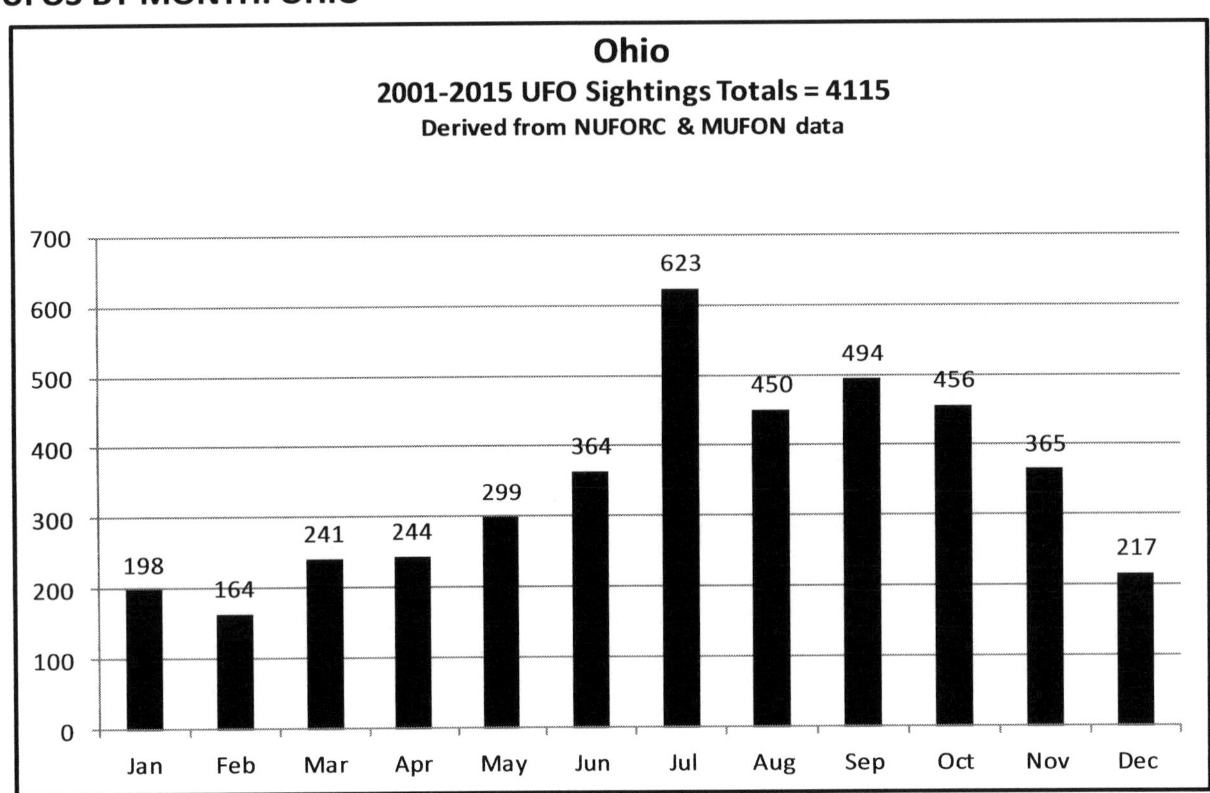

Year	Jan	Feb	Mar	Apr	May	Jun	Jul	Aug	Sep	Oct	Nov	Dec	Total
2001	6	7	7	6	9	7	19	11	26	9	9	9	125
2002	8	9	4	3	7	7	20	19	18	11	5	3	114
2003	14	7	11	5	10	8	9	17	13	24	12	18	148
2004	4	7	12	6	11	25	14	14	19	13	18	12	155
2005	6	9	17	5	4	5	25	4	14	18	10	3	120
2006	5	5	11	12	9	12	13	11	14	13	14	24	143
2007	8	13	12	17	17	13	22	13	30	14	14	7	180
2008	12	10	14	30	22	21	23	27	18	32	23	10	242
2009	13	21	17	20	22	23	47	29	50	26	29	11	308
2010	11	3	20	15	18	24	72	16	26	36	26	7	274
2011	15	8	12	5	11	24	54	35	25	35	43	14	281
2012	22	14	30	22	42	52	68	72	61	34	46	35	498
2013	25	12	29	28	39	66	102	86	73	87	45	32	624
2014	21	20	23	42	38	49	81	49	59	49	25	21	477
2015	28	19	22	28	40	28	54	47	48	55	46	11	426
Total	**198**	**164**	**241**	**244**	**299**	**364**	**623**	**450**	**494**	**456**	**365**	**217**	**4115**

Distribution of Sightings between Databases: Ohio

Database	Count	Percentage
MUFON	1713	41.63%
NUFORC	2402	58.37%
Total	4115	100.00%

State Demographic Information: Ohio

2010 US Census Statistics	
Population	11,536,504.00
Area in Square Miles	44,825.58
Land Area Sq. Miles	40,860.69
Population/Square mile	282.30

OKLAHOMA UFO RANK 28/51

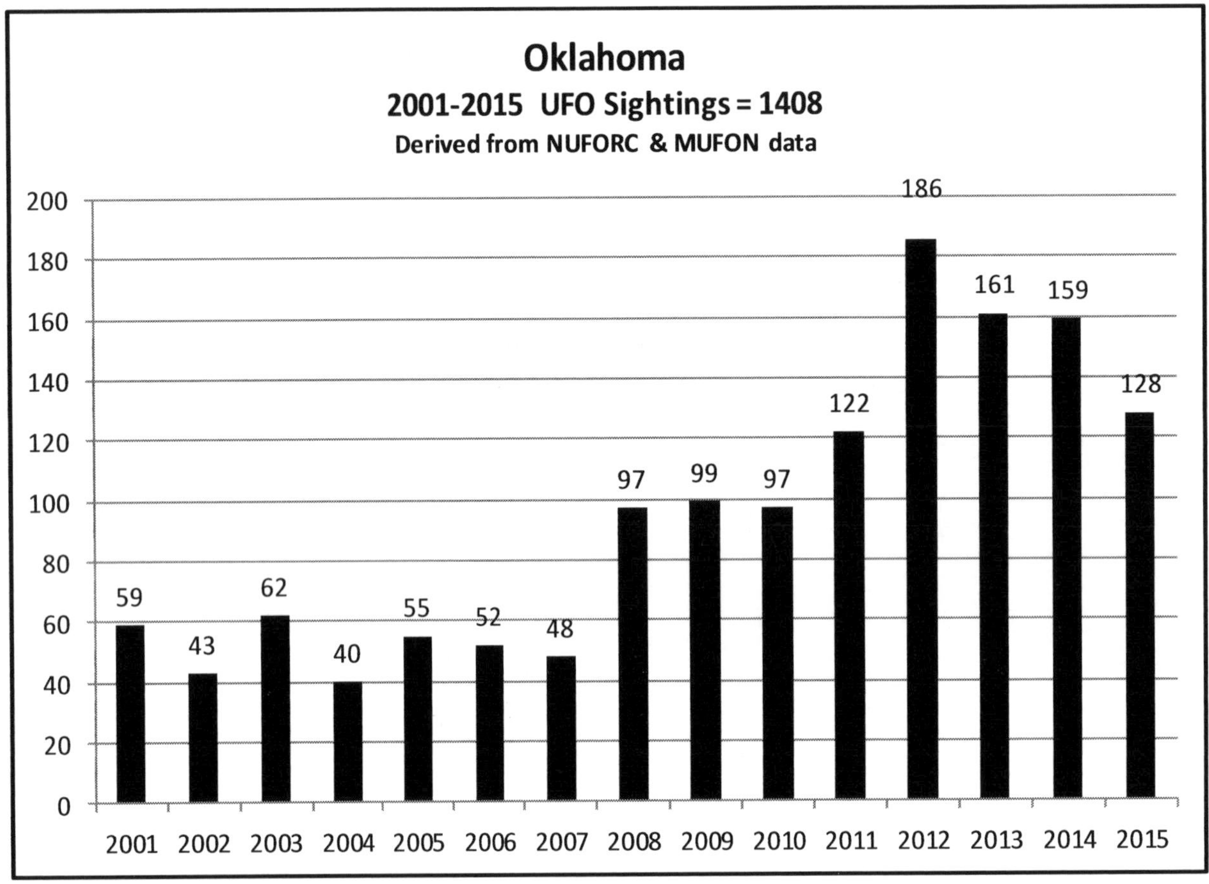

TOP TEN COUNTIES		RANK
Tulsa	271	1
Oklahoma	260	2
Cleveland	103	3
Unknown	44	4
Canadian	40	5
Comanche	40	6
Creek	29	7
Muskogee	29	8
Le Flore	27	9
Rogers	27	10

TOP TEN SHAPES		
Light	166	11.79%
Unknown	158	11.22%
Circle	149	10.58%
Triangle	134	9.52%
Sphere	115	8.17%
Other	104	7.39%
Fireball	86	6.11%
Oval	56	3.98%
Star-like	53	3.76%
Disk	43	3.05%

UFO SHAPES: OKLAHOMA

UFO Shapes	**2001**	**2002**	**2003**	**2004**	**2005**	**2006**	**2007**	**2008**	**2009**	**2010**	**2011**	**2012**	**2013**	**2014**	**2015**	**Total**
Blimp		1				1					2		1	1	1	7
Boomerang					1	1			2	6	5	3	3	4	2	27
Bullet/Missile	1					1	1		1	2	1	1				8
Changing	3	2	1	2	1	2	2	2		2	1	1		6	1	26
Chevron			1	2			2		2	3	1	1	2	1	1	16
Cigar	1	2	1		3	4		3	5	2	2	4	8	3	4	42
Circle	3		1	3	1	3	6	12	11	9	20	34	21	16	9	149
Cone		1					1	3					2	2		9
Cross	2	1						1			1	1				6
Cylinder	1	1	5	1	3		2	1	4	2	6	6	2	1	6	41
Diamond	1	3	1	2			2	2		1	2	2	1	2	3	22
Disc		4	4	1		7	1	4	2	4	3	4	4	1	3	42
Disk	4		7	4	2	1	3	2			4	2	7	4	3	43
Egg										2	1	1	1	4		9
Fireball	2	1	2	3	2	3	2	6	6	8	6	23	10	7	5	86
Flash		1	1			2	1	3	2	2	3	4	1	2	3	25
Formation	6	1	2	1	1		1	3			1	5	5	2	1	29
Light	9	6	14	3	8	9	9	12	13	10	17	14	19	14	9	166
N/A														3		3
Other	3	4	4	2	5	1	4	3	11	6	4	13	12	18	14	104
Oval	2	3	2	2	3	3		4	4	4	7	6	6	8	2	56
Rectangle	3	1	1				2	1		2		1	1	2	3	17
Saturn-like									1			1	1			3
Sphere		1	1	1	2	4	2	3	10	8	7	19	24	15	18	115
Sq/Rect									1			1			1	3
Star-like					1	2		5	5	3	7	6	7	8	9	53
Teardrop			1				1	1		1		3	1	1		9
Triangle	11	3	5	4	5	5	2	15	6	6	16	13	11	18	14	134
Unknown	7	7	8	9	17	3	4	11	13	14	5	17	11	16	16	158
Total	**59**	**43**	**62**	**40**	**55**	**52**	**48**	**97**	**99**	**97**	**122**	**186**	**161**	**159**	**128**	**1408**

UFOS BY COUNTY: OKLAHOMA

Counties	2001	2002	2003	2004	2005	2006	2007	2008	2009	2010	2011	2012	2013	2014	2015	Total
Adair											1			1		2
Alfalfa										1						1
Athens			1													1
Atoka												2	1			3
Beaver	1				1											2
Beckham	1	3	2		1				1		2				1	11
Blaine			2		2									1	1	6
Bryan		1			1	1		3		3	2	3		1		15
Caddo	1	1	1		1	1						3	1	2		11
Calera									1							1
Canadian	2	1	5	1	2		1	3	3	2	3	3	9	2	3	40
Carson								1								1
Carter							1	3	3		3	5	2	1	3	21
Cherokee			1	1	1	1	1		1			1		2	2	11
Choctaw			1		1				2	3	2	3				12
Cimarron	1															1
Cleveland	1	3	1	2	3	1	5	6	4	3	18	20	22	7	7	103
Coal					1				1						1	3
Comanche	2	3	1	2	3	1	2	2	1		4	6	6	4	3	40
Cotton								1		1			1			3
Craig		1									1					2
Creek	4	1					1	2	3	3	3	2	3	3	4	29
Custer	1		1	1				1	1	1	1					7
Delaware	1		1	1	1		2	1		2		4			2	15
El Flore										1						1
Ellis			1		1		1				1					4
Garfield	1		1			5		1	2		2	2			4	18
Garvin	1	2				2	2		2			1	1			11
Grady		1	1			1				4	1		4	3	1	16
Grant									1			1				2
Greer				2												2
Harmon						1						1		3		5
Haskell									1	2	1			1	2	7
Hughes							1		1			1				3
Jackson	2	1										1	1		1	6
Jefferson								1								1
Johnston											1			2		3

Counties	2001	2002	2003	2004	2005	2006	2007	2008	2009	2010	2011	2012	2013	2014	2015	Total
Kay	1	1	3				1	1	1		2	1	1	3	2	17
Kingfisher				2				1				2				5
Kiowa									1							1
Latimer		1							2	1	1	6				11
Le Flore	1	1	2	2	1	3		1	2	4		5	3		2	27
Lincoln	1					1		1	2			2	1	2	1	11
Logan							1	1			1		2	1	1	7
Love						1		1							1	3
Marshall			1		1		1	1	2				1	2	1	10
Mayes									1					1	1	3
McClain		1			2				2	1			4	1		11
McCurtain	1		1						1		1				1	5
McIntosh								3			2	5		1		11
Murray	1				1		1			2	2	1		1	1	10
Muskogee		1	3					1	1	2	2	5	6	3	5	29
Nowata							1					2			1	4
Oklahoma	11	6	9	8	13	8	13	17	21	22	14	33	31	33	21	260
Okmulgee	1	3			1		1	2		2	1	1	3	2		17
Osage							1					1		1	4	7
Ottawa		1	1		2	2	1			1	2	2	3	6	1	22
Pawnee			1		2				1		2		1	1	1	9
Payne	1		1	2			2	1	1	1	3	2	6	1	2	23
Pittsburg		2		2		1		1	2	1			5	2	3	19
Pontotoc	2		1	1	1				2		1	3	1	5	1	18
Pottawatomie			2			2	1	1	2	4	4	1	5	1	1	24
Pushmataha													1			1
Roger Mills								1				1				2
Rogers	3		2			4		3		1	2	2	4	5	1	27
Seminole								4		2	2	5			2	15
Sequoyah			1	1		2				1	1		2		1	9
Stephens			1			1	3	2			1	1	1			10
Texas								1			2			2		5
Tillman					1											1
Tulsa	12	4	8	8	8	9	3	21	23	21	28	36	19	41	30	271
Unknown		2	1	1		2		5	3	1	2	6	7	8	6	44
Wagoner					1					2		1	2			6
Washington	1	1	3	1	1	2						1		1	2	13
Washita			1									1	1	1		4
Washita									1							1

Counties	2001	2002	2003	2004	2005	2006	2007	2008	2009	2010	2011	2012	2013	2014	2015	Total
Woods		1						1		1		1				4
Woodward	4			2	1		1	1		1				1		11
Total	**59**	**43**	**62**	**40**	**55**	**52**	**48**	**97**	**99**	**97**	**122**	**186**	**161**	**159**	**128**	**1408**

If a county is missing from the list, it's because no UFO sightings were logged in either the NUFORC or MUFON databases for the 2001-2015 sample period.

UFOS BY MONTH: OKLAHOMA

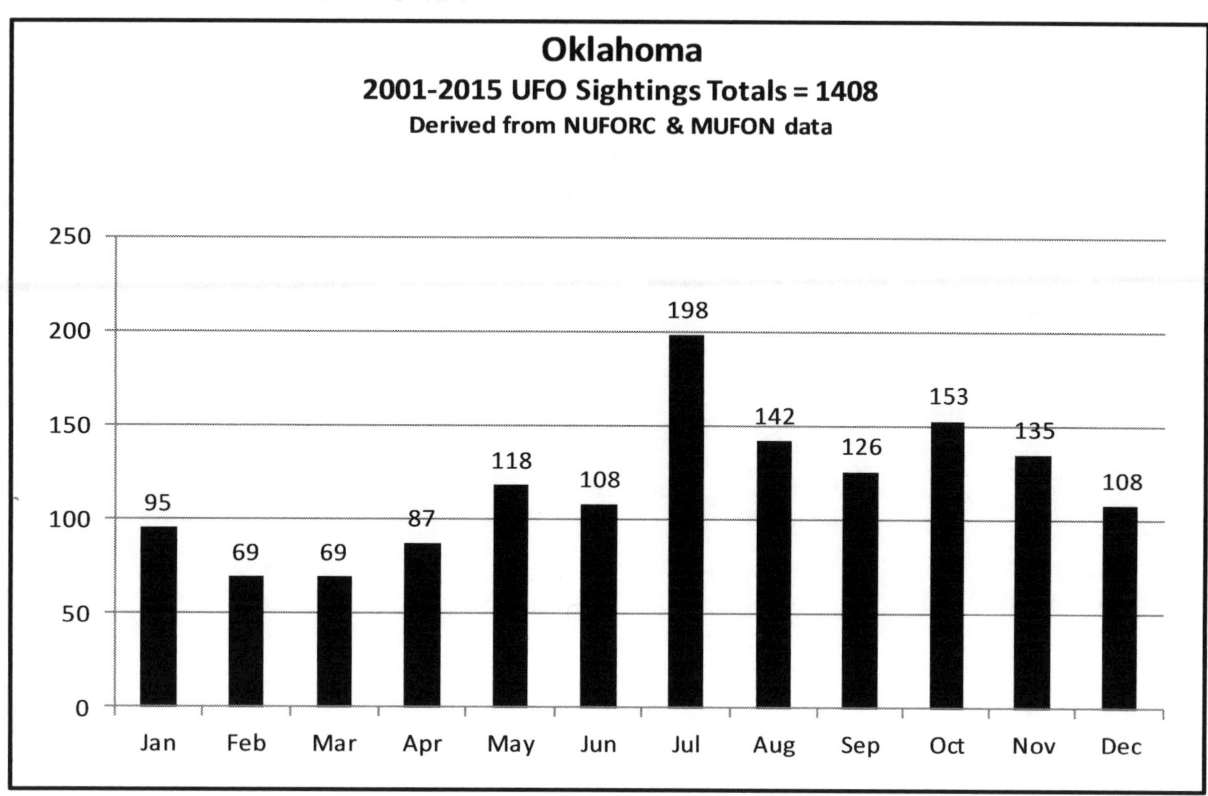

Year	Jan	Feb	Mar	Apr	May	Jun	Jul	Aug	Sep	Oct	Nov	Dec	Total
2001	4	3	2	2	6	4	7	6	7	3	3	12	59
2002	4	2	3	2	2	2	6	6	5	3	5	3	43
2003	7		5		4	6	8	4	9	6	6	7	62
2004		3	8	3	5	1	5	6	1	3	2	3	40
2005	1	4	1	1	7	7	9	1	3	10	6	5	55
2006	4	1	5	7	4	5	4	3	7	8	1	3	52
2007	5	3		5	1		5	8	3	4	8	6	48
2008	12	10	3	4	7	7	8	4	14	11	9	8	97
2009	3	6	6	8	12	5	19	5	5	9	12	9	99
2010	5		5	7	9	6	14	9	8	19	11	4	97
2011	12	4	4	4	6	12	23	14	10	9	16	8	122
2012	17	9	12	14	10	20	33	15	15	11	15	15	186
2013	3	7	5	10	14	12	28	21	14	15	15	17	161
2014	10	9	4	9	15	12	17	23	14	27	16	3	159
2015	8	8	6	11	16	9	12	17	11	15	10	5	128
Total	**95**	**69**	**69**	**87**	**118**	**108**	**198**	**142**	**126**	**153**	**135**	**108**	**1408**

Distribution of Sightings between Databases: Oklahoma

Database	Count	Percentage
MUFON	623	44.25%
NUFORC	785	55.75%
Total	1408	100.00%

State Demographic Information: Oklahoma

2010 US Census Statistics	
Population	3,751,351.00
Area in Square Miles	69,898 .87
Land Area Sq. Miles	68,594 .92
Population/Square mile	54 .7

OREGON

UFO RANK 13/51

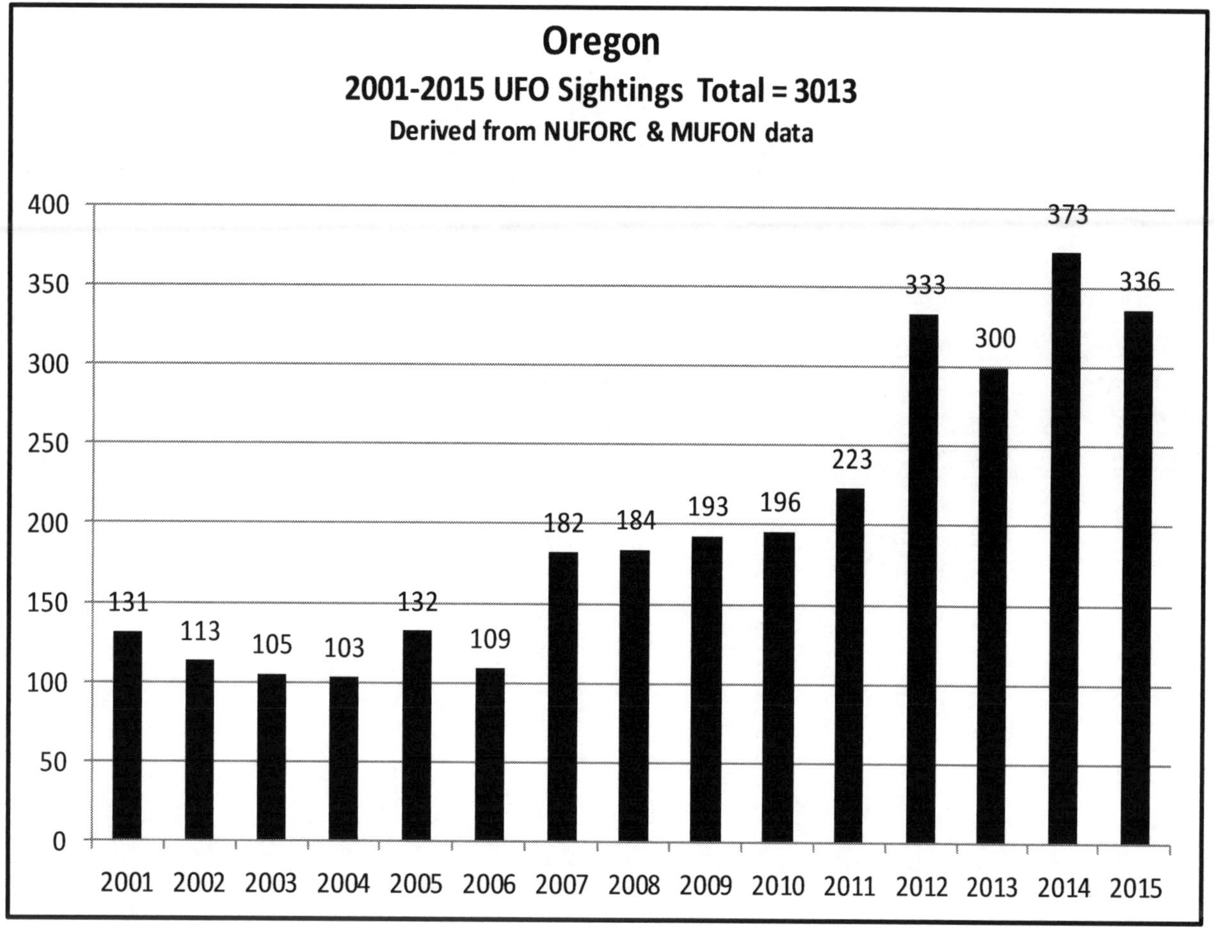

TOP TEN COUNTIES		RANK	TOP TEN SHAPES		
Multnomah	621	1	Light	430	14.27%
Lane	323	2	Circle	369	12.25%
Washington	249	3	Sphere	330	10.95%
Marion	214	4	Unknown	306	10.16%
Clackamas	195	5	Other	232	7.70%
Jackson	186	6	Triangle	230	7.63%
Deschutes	123	7	Fireball	185	6.14%
Josephine	93	8	Star-like	128	4.25%
Lincoln	90	9	Oval	118	3.92%
Linn	90	10	Flash	93	3.09%

UFO SHAPES: OREGON

UFO Shapes	2001	2002	2003	2004	2005	2006	2007	2008	2009	2010	2011	2012	2013	2014	2015	Total
Blimp		1					3	1		1		1		3	2	12
Boomerang				1			1	1	3	4	3	2	1	3	2	21
Bullet/Missile		1			2	1	1	1	1	1	3	1	1			13
Changing	3	2	3	5	4	4	5		5	3	2	5	2	7	6	56
Chevron	3	3		2	2	1	4	1	3	2	3		2	1		27
Cigar	2	2	3	3	6	4	8	8	6	5	6	6	6	1	7	73
Circle	7	11	8	15	12	11	15	21	21	21	33	57	49	48	40	369
Cone					1		2	1		1		1	2	2		10
Cross							1			3	1	4	2	1	1	13
Cylinder			2	3	3		5	5	1	3	3	8	6	5	5	49
Diamond	4			2	2	3	4	3	1	2	3	4	2	3	5	38
Disc				1	2	4	4	2	8	10	8	6	8	10	10	73
Disk	5	8	4	7	4	6	3	3	5	2		5	3	6	8	69
Egg	1			1		2	1	2	4	2	2	3	2	2		22
Fireball	9	3	4	4	6	4	1	11	8	8	19	32	21	27	28	185
Flash	3	1	3	2	6	4	2	6	8	4	9	9	8	17	11	93
Formation	2	2	1	1	2	4	2	2	3		3	8	7	10	7	54
Light	27	23	20	12	24	15	29	24	20	22	34	40	48	47	45	430
N/A													1	2	3	6
Other	8	6	10	5	8	9	15	22	16	14	17	22	20	29	31	232
Oval	4	7	10	2	3	8	8	8	5	2	5	18	7	15	16	118
Rectangle	2	1	2	2	2	2	1	1		1	2	1	2	1	5	25
Saturn-like								1				1			1	3
Sphere	10	10	14	9	14	8	18	17	20	25	20	42	32	42	49	330
Sq/Rect														1	3	4
Star-like					3	3	11	11	13	17	15	10	7	17	21	128
Teardrop	1	1		1	2			1		1	3	3	5	2	4	24
Triangle	20	15	9	11	9	7	13	14	21	23	12	12	23	29	12	230
Unknown	20	16	12	14	15	9	25	17	21	19	17	32	33	42	14	306
Total	**131**	**113**	**105**	**103**	**132**	**109**	**182**	**184**	**193**	**196**	**223**	**333**	**300**	**373**	**336**	**3013**

UFOS BY COUNTY: OREGON

Counties	2001	2002	2003	2004	2005	2006	2007	2008	2009	2010	2011	2012	2013	2014	2015	Total
Baker		1	2	1	4	1					3		2	2	2	18
Benton	4	2	2	1	1		2	8	1	3	4	4	5	8	5	50
Canyon					1											1
Clackamas	10	8	3	3	8	7	9	11	14	20	19	16	18	30	19	195
Clackamas										1				1		2
Clatsop	2		1		1	1	2	1	3	4	4	8	10	7	14	58
Columbia	3	3	3	1	2	2		2	3	1	3	3	6	2	8	42
Coos	1	1	2	3	2	1	3	6	3	6	2	3	12	16	7	68
Crook						1	3	2	1	1	1	3	1	2	2	17
Curry	1	2	1	1	1	3	3	5	6	3	1	1	3	1	1	33
Deschutes	5	4	3	7	3	2	5	8	5	10	11	17	7	17	19	123
Douglas	2	1	1	3	4	1	6	3	4	3	6	8	8	13	8	71
Gilliam															1	1
Grant						1					1		1	1	1	5
Harney	1	1		1		1	3	1	3	3		3		2	3	22
Hood River					1			1	1	1	1	2	6			13
Jackson	10	5	4	4	9	12	32	16	7	15	14	18	7	12	21	186
Jefferson		1	2	2				4	1	2	4	2	3		1	22
Josephine	4	8	2	3	1	3	5	12	7	9	6	10	9	11	3	93
Klamath	4	4	2	3	5	2	5	6	4	4	2	6	5	4	6	62
Lake		1		1	1		1	2	2	3	4	2	2	2	1	22
Lane	12	7	14	14	17	9	8	18	29	16	28	44	33	35	39	323
Lincoln	2	2	2	4	6	3	6	4	3	9	8	14	14	7	6	90
Linn	1	1	3	2	2		7	4	4	1	7	9	19	9	21	90
Malheur	1	1	1	1	2		1		2		1	1			1	12
Marion	10	6	12	6	9	7	16	3	12	15	14	26	20	32	26	214
Morrow	1							1								2
Multnomah	27	33	30	24	28	31	25	30	40	42	43	73	49	85	61	621
Polk	2	1	3	4	2	2		2	4	4	1	5		6	2	38
Sherman					1											1
Tillamook	2	2	1	3	4	1	1		2	1	4	4	5	4	3	37
Umatilla				1	2	1	3	2	3	1	3	7	9	5	6	43
Union		1	1	1	2	1		3	2	1		1	4	3	3	23
Unknown	1	2	1		2	2	8	1	9	2	7	14	8	12	10	79
Wallowa		1						1				1			1	4
Wasco	1		1	1	2	3	1	4			1	4	1	2		21
Washington	21	9	8	7	8	9	22	19	15	8	17	18	27	34	27	249

Counties	**2001**	**2002**	**2003**	**2004**	**2005**	**2006**	**2007**	**2008**	**2009**	**2010**	**2011**	**2012**	**2013**	**2014**	**2015**	**Total**
Yamhill	3	5		1	1	2	5	4	3	7	3	6	6	8	8	62
Total	**131**	**113**	**105**	**103**	**132**	**109**	**182**	**184**	**193**	**196**	**223**	**333**	**300**	**373**	**336**	**3013**

If a county is missing from the list, it's because no UFO sightings were logged in either the NUFORC or MUFON databases for the 2001-2015 sample period.

UFOS BY MONTH: OREGON

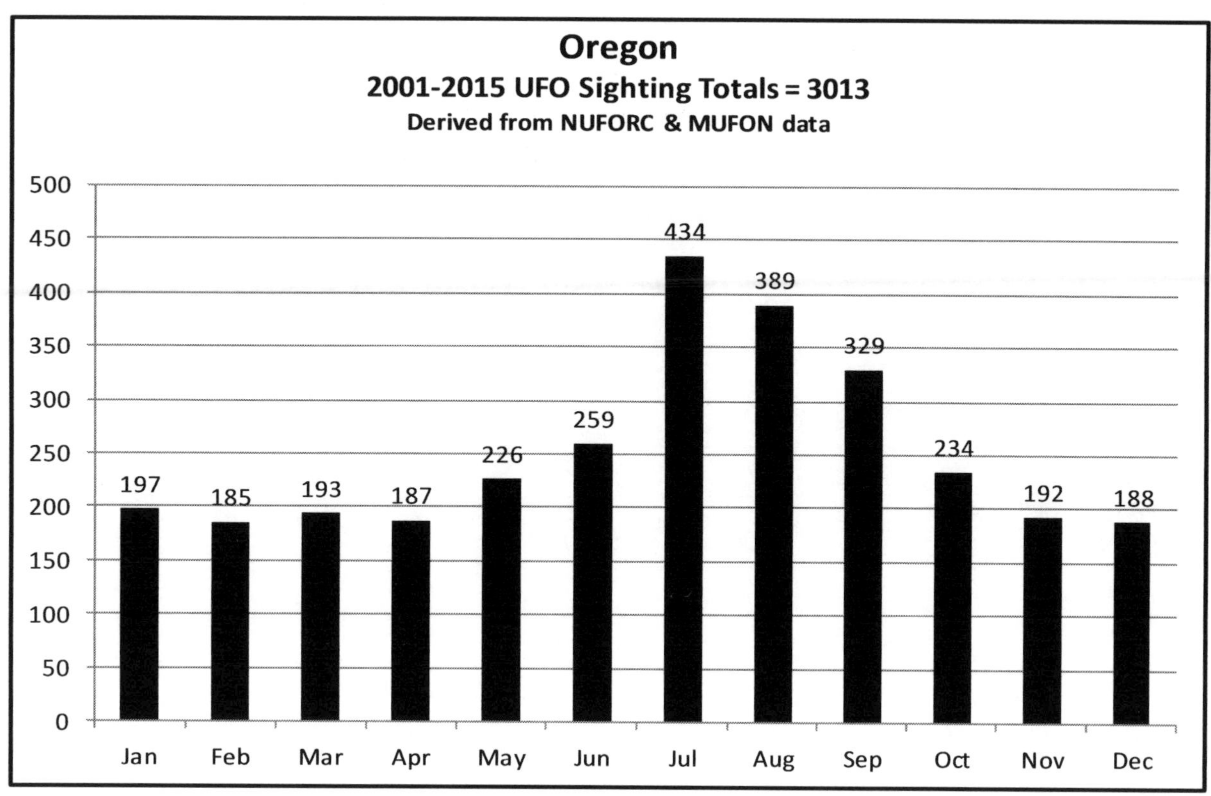

Year	Jan	Feb	Mar	Apr	May	Jun	Jul	Aug	Sep	Oct	Nov	Dec	Total
2001	7	18	16	4	5	3	24	24	10	3	14	3	131
2002	5	9	4	6	7	17	20	17	8	11	4	5	113
2003	7	10	1	4	3	6	14	16	19	6	13	6	105
2004	6	8	8	7	7	12	13	17	6	10	5	4	103
2005	7	10	15	7	9	17	26	12	15	5	4	5	132
2006	3	3	7	19	5	7	18	18	8	15	4	2	109
2007	15	8	20	10	18	20	15	18	21	20	7	10	182
2008	9	12	16	6	10	10	23	23	16	12	26	21	184
2009	10	10	11	8	22	13	37	25	27	10	11	9	193
2010	7	10	10	13	24	19	30	19	24	20	11	9	196
2011	14	7	8	12	12	15	35	36	34	18	15	17	223
2012	20	20	7	10	35	32	52	61	36	14	16	30	333
2013	12	16	22	22	25	32	40	24	21	25	27	34	300
2014	42	21	19	23	29	30	49	46	38	34	18	24	373
2015	33	23	29	36	15	26	38	33	46	31	17	9	336
Total	**197**	**185**	**193**	**187**	**226**	**259**	**434**	**389**	**329**	**234**	**192**	**188**	**3013**

Distribution of Sightings between Databases: Oregon

Database	Count	Percentage
MUFON	1155	38.33%
NUFORC	1858	61.67%
Total	3013	100.00%

State Demographic Information: Oregon

2010 US Census Statistics	
Population	3,831,074.00
Area in Square Miles	98,378 .54
Land Area Sq. Miles	95,988 .01
Population/Square mile	39 .9

PENNSYLVANIA

UFO RANK /51

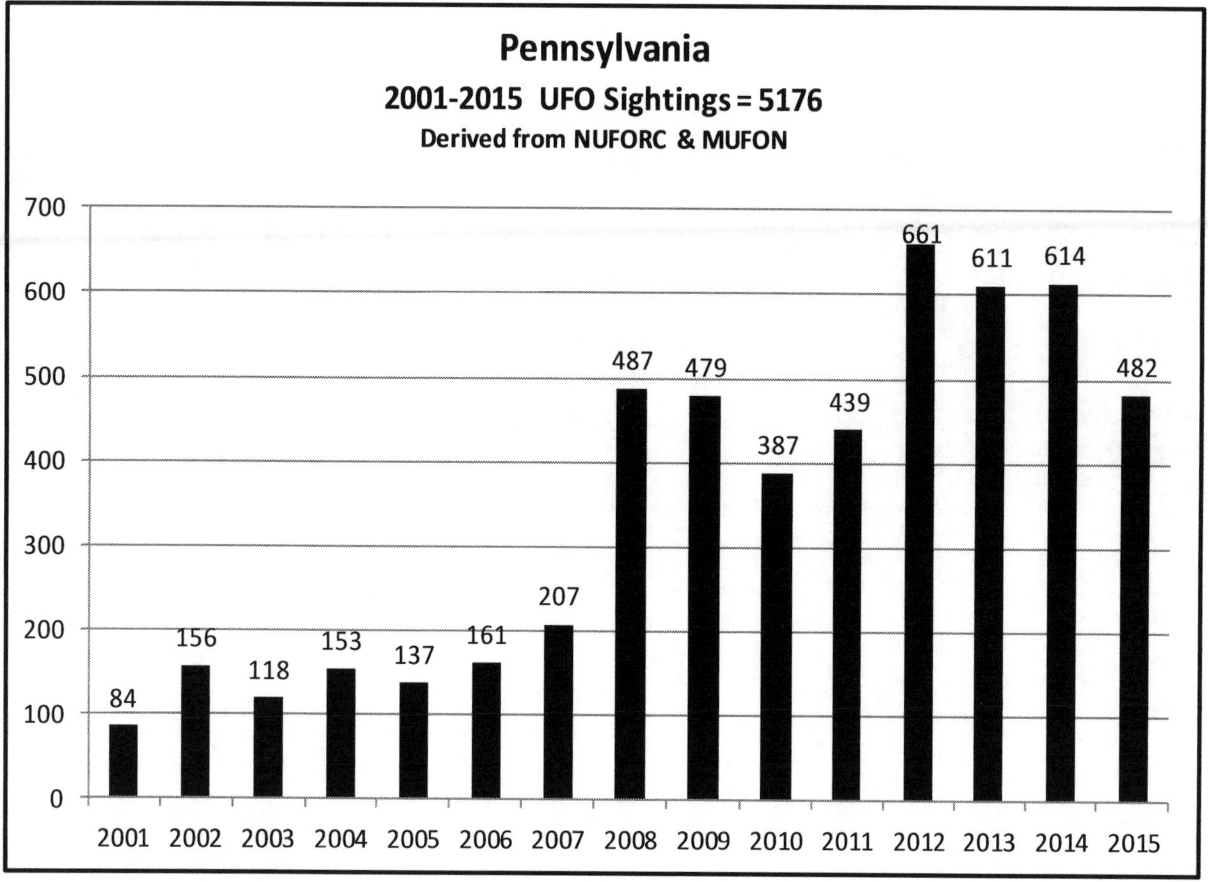

TOP TEN COUNTIES		RANK	TOP TEN SHAPES		
Allegheny	477	1	Circle	664	12.83%
Bucks	397	2	Light	592	11.44%
Philadelphia	336	3	Unknown	510	9.85%
Montgomery	282	4	Sphere	497	9.60%
Westmoreland	212	5	Fireball	456	8.81%
Unknown	201	6	Triangle	436	8.42%
Chester	197	7	Other	349	6.74%
Lancaster	194	8	Star-like	236	4.56%
Berks	181	9	Oval	213	4.12%
York	165	10	Cigar	128	2.47%

UFO SHAPES: PENNSYLVANIA

UFO Shapes	2001	2002	2003	2004	2005	2006	2007	2008	2009	2010	2011	2012	2013	2014	2015	Total
Blimp		1				1	1	4	2	1	2	5	3			20
Boomerang		1	1		2	2		16	11	5	8	9	3	2	6	66
Bullet/Missile		1					3	5	2	4	4	9	3	3	1	35
Changing	2	5	2	4	2		3	1	3	6	6	5	4	3	11	57
Chevron		2		2	2	1	4	6	3	2	7	2	2	3	1	37
Cigar	4	5	1	4	3	5	9	20	14	5	16	11	8	17	6	128
Circle	7	12	13	12	7	14	17	56	63	57	68	103	89	87	59	664
Cone	1	1		1	1	2		3	12		4	3	4	2	5	39
Cross				2		1		1	2	8	1		1	1		17
Cylinder	1	5	4		2	3	5	8	8	7	3	10	15	13	14	98
Diamond	2	2	3	3	2	2	2	10	9	9	8	11	10	6	7	86
Disc		1	4	5	3	4	8	15	14	12	11	12	9	9	13	120
Disk	9	11	6	14	5	7	12	10	3	7	8	4	5	17	4	122
Egg	3	4	1	2	2	2		7	5	1	4	6	5	6	1	49
Fireball	7	8	2	7	9	4	12	35	17	40	36	80	90	73	36	456
Flash		1	2	2	5	2	2	16	15	14	14	8	11	12	7	111
Formation	1	2	5	5	1	9	5	3	7	3	6	7	22	12	5	93
Light	18	30	10	30	24	30	33	34	34	42	28	66	65	84	64	592
N/A		1								1	1	2	2	7	9	23
Other	4	15	13	13	13	11	13	48	38	18	31	32	32	32	36	349
Oval	2	6	5	4	9	9	9	23	23	12	9	38	21	21	22	213
Rectangle	1	3		1	2	4	1	2	3		5	6	5	5	3	41
Saturn-like	1				1		1	5	2	2	3	2		1	1	19
Sphere	3	9	10	6	8	6	16	19	34	36	46	79	90	81	54	497
Sq/Rect														3	11	14
Star-like		2		1		5	6	35	48	20	23	29	14	19	34	236
Teardrop	1		2			3		7	3	7	7	8	3	3	4	48
Triangle	7	10	14	11	14	16	26	45	56	30	34	49	47	44	33	436
Unknown	10	18	20	24	20	18	19	53	48	38	46	65	48	48	35	510
Total	**84**	**156**	**118**	**153**	**137**	**161**	**207**	**487**	**479**	**387**	**439**	**661**	**611**	**614**	**482**	**5176**

UFOS BY COUNTY: PENNSYLVANIA

Counties	2001	2002	2003	2004	2005	2006	2007	2008	2009	2010	2011	2012	2013	2014	2015	Total
Adams		1	1	2	1		4	7	4	3	5	3	4	2	2	39
Allegheny	7	5	11	16	6	8	11	38	48	39	34	75	70	67	42	477
Armstrong		2	1	2	1				2	1	6	2	1		2	20
Beaver		4	1		1	2	3	5	4	3	5	15	9	5	5	62
Bedford			3		3		1	3	4					4	2	20
Berks	3	6	2	3	2	13	8	19	15	17	11	22	23	23	14	181
Blair	1	2	1	6	1	5	2	9	12	2	8	3	2	11	3	68
Bradford	1	2	1	1	1	2	3	3	2	1			4	1	1	23
Bucks	4	11	7	10	7	7	7	64	40	29	29	48	43	49	42	397
Butler		1	4	3	3	2	1	3	3	3	2	12	11	7	6	61
Cambria	1	1		1	5		4	2	3	2	4	8	4	3	2	40
Cameron														1		1
Carbon		3	1			2	2	4	3		2	2	6	3	1	29
Centre	1	4	2	5	3	1	2	9	4	7	7	11	4	8	4	72
Chester	2	2	3	10	7	8	9	7	18	13	18	24	32	23	21	197
Clarion	2		1	2	2		1	2	4	2		1		1	1	19
Clearfield			2		2	1		5	3	1	2	9	3	6	2	36
Clinton									2	1	2		4	2	3	14
Columbia			2			1		5	3	6	1	5	4		3	30
Crawford		2	3	3	1	3	1		3	6	4	3	5		2	36
Cumberland	3	3	4	1	4	3	6	7	5	8	6	9	8	6	15	88
Dauphin	2	6	1	1	10	8	12	7	3	6	9	14	10	18	7	114
Delaware	2	2	3	4	5	6	2	8	12	8	13	18	14	13	17	127
Elk							1		2	2				3	4	12
Erie	1	3	1	4	4	3	11	6	8	11	11	26	19	15	15	138
Fayette		1		2	2	2	3	6	8	5	2	4	5	7	7	54
Forest	1			1						1						3
Franklin		2	1	1	3	2	3	4	2	4	4	12	4	7	6	55
Fulton															3	3
Greene				2	1		1				2	5	3	4	1	19
Huntingdon			2	2			1		1	3	1			2		12
Indiana		2		1	1	4		1	1	2	3	4	3	1	2	25
Jefferson					1	1		2	3	2		2		3		14
Juniata					1				1	1	3	1		1		8
Lackawanna	1	3		2	4	4	3	10	13	7	13	8	8	7	6	89
Lancaster	3	5	5	10	4	9	10	13	12	14	24	16	30	23	16	194
Lawrence		1	1		2		1	4	4	5	6	5	6	3	6	44

Lebanon				1	2	1	3	3	4	1	2	9	7	11	7	51
Lehigh	1	4		3	1	6	6	13	17	8	7	28	20	28	22	164
Luzerne	4	6	4	2	2	8	9	6	15	13	10	22	22	12	9	144
Lycoming	2	5	3	1	1	1	3	4	2	4	6	5	7	9	8	61
McKean		1		4		1	1	1	3	1	2	1	2	1	2	20
Mercer	2	10			1	1	3	4	10	2	5	13	4	5	7	67
Mifflin		1	1			1	1	1	1		2	1	1	2		12
Monroe	1	1	5	4	2	2	2	5	4	5	8	11	11	6	5	72
Montgomery	5	7	10	10	8	7	12	25	20	26	34	43	30	42	19	298
Montour			1										1			2
Northamp-ton	4	1	1	2	2		2	6	12	22	12	10	25	19	19	137
Northumberland	1	10		5	1			15	9	4	8	5		4	2	64
Perry		1				1			1	1	1	1	2	3	1	12
Philadelphia	8	5	8	7	7	13	11	75	42	24	20	33	25	38	20	336
Pike	1		1	1		1	3	2	1	2	1	3	5	2	1	24
Potter				1		2	1		1	1	2	1	3	1	1	14
Schuylkill	1	1	4	4	2	1	4	2	9	4	11	7	1	5	3	59
Shickshinny										1			2			3
Snyder	1				1	1			1	1			1	2		8
Somerset		2					1	2	5	2	2	2	2	1	2	21
South Greensburg														1		1
Sullivan						1									1	2
Susquehanna					1			4		3			2	2	2	14
Tioga			1	1				2	1	2			2	2	1	12
Union	1					1	2	3	2	3			2	1	1	16
Unknown	1	1	5	4	3	5	6	9	8	9	26	32	42	23	27	201
Venango	3	1		1						2	2	1	1	2	3	16
Warren		1	1		1	1	2	3	1		2	2		2		16
Washington	2	2	2		1	1	2	12	5	4	7	13	6	13	8	78
Wayne		2		1	2	2		1	2	2	4	12	3	5	4	40
Westmoreland	10	9	1	1	8	3	10	20	34	12	16	27	23	18	20	212
Wyoming		2	1			1		1		2	1		1	2	2	13
York	1	9	5	4	3	2	10	16	17	11	11	12	19	23	22	165
Total	**84**	**156**	**118**	**152**	**137**	**161**	**207**	**488**	**479**	**387**	**439**	**661**	**611**	**614**	**482**	**5176**

If a county is missing from the list, it's because no UFO sightings were logged in either the NUFORC or MUFON databases for the 2001-2015 sample period.

UFOS BY MONTH: PENNSYLVANIA

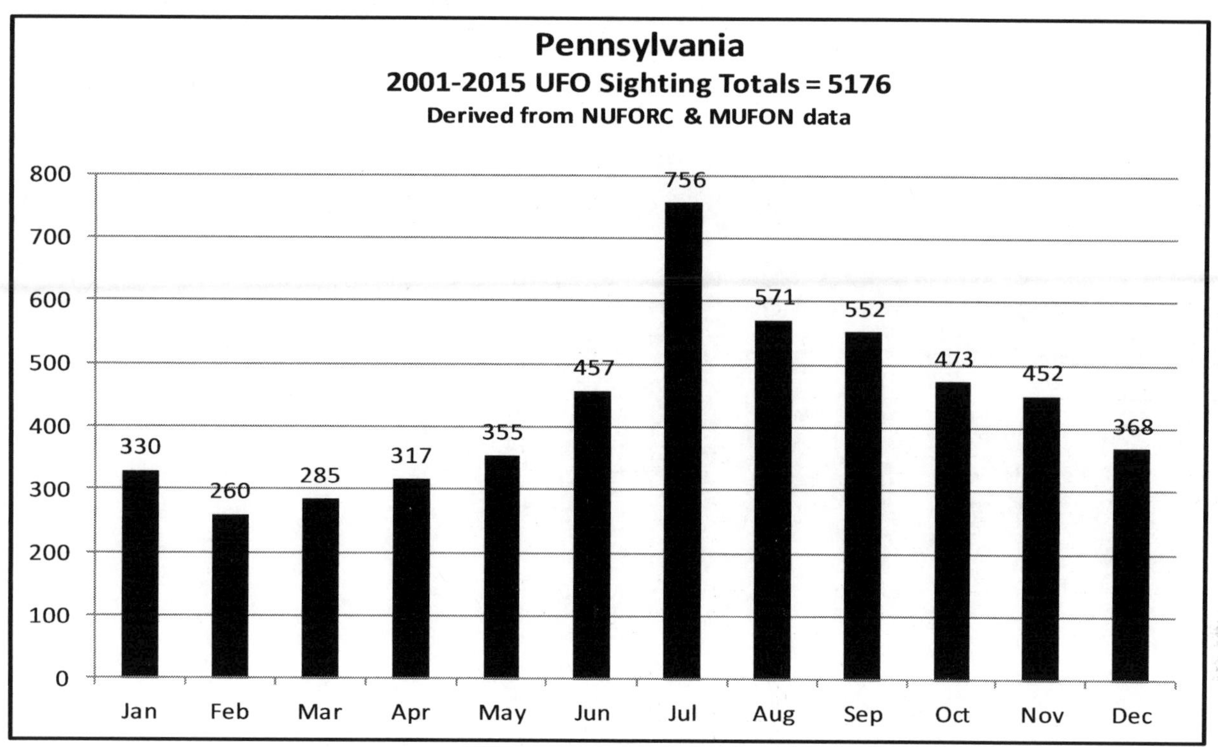

Year	Jan	Feb	Mar	Apr	May	Jun	Jul	Aug	Sep	Oct	Nov	Dec	Total
2001	3	9	12	6	5	5	14	8	6	5	7	4	84
2002	8	13	5	13	10	10	19	21	16	11	15	15	156
2003	14	3	9	7	3	10	18	6	7	18	16	7	118
2004	6	8	11	12	10	21	13	22	12	11	15	11	152
2005	3	7	10	9	10	14	9	13	13	21	17	11	137
2006	9	9	3	16	8	8	14	21	13	13	20	27	161
2007	21	7	11	13	9	20	19	15	29	20	13	30	207
2008	30	16	23	21	31	51	73	59	41	53	49	41	488
2009	42	33	23	27	39	26	77	35	90	16	38	33	479
2010	24	16	31	20	32	37	78	28	30	43	20	28	387
2011	28	22	28	17	14	32	68	52	40	50	43	45	439
2012	49	37	44	53	45	58	95	77	55	58	60	30	661
2013	23	16	21	40	52	76	91	71	63	66	58	34	611
2014	42	35	23	33	51	52	102	75	76	49	41	35	614
2015	28	29	31	30	36	37	66	68	61	39	40	17	482
Total	**330**	**260**	**285**	**317**	**355**	**457**	**756**	**571**	**552**	**473**	**452**	**368**	**5176**

Distribution of Sightings between Databases: Pennsylvania

Database	Count	Percentage
MUFON	2446	47.26%
NUFORC	2730	52.74%
Total	5176	100.00%

State Demographic Information: Pennsylvania

2010 US Census Statistics	
Population	12,702,379.00
Area in Square Miles	46,054 .34
Land Area Sq. Miles	44,742 .70
Population/Square mile	283 .9

RHODE ISLAND

UFO RANK 44/51

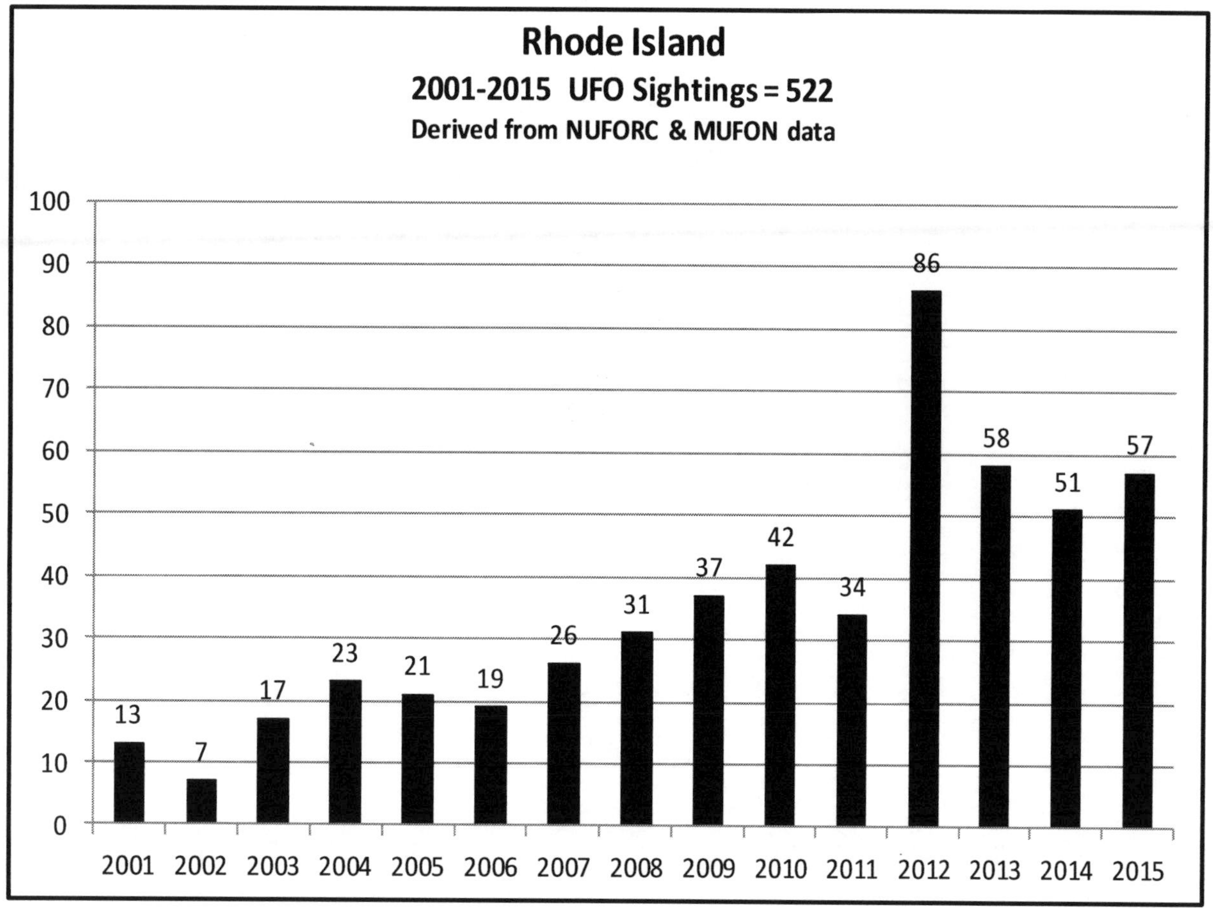

TOP TEN COUNTIES		RANK
Providence	254	1
Washington	108	2
Kent	77	3
Newport	51	4
Unknown	22	5
Bristol	9	6
South	1	7
NA		8
NA		9
NA		10

TOP TEN SHAPES		
Circle	71	13.60%
Light	64	12.26%
Unknown	54	10.34%
Sphere	46	8.81%
Triangle	43	8.24%
Fireball	40	7.66%
Other	40	7.66%
Star-like	22	4.21%
Disk	18	3.45%
Oval	16	3.07%

UFO SHAPES: RHODE ISLAND

UFO Shapes	2001	2002	2003	2004	2005	2006	2007	2008	2009	2010	2011	2012	2013	2014	2015	Total
Blimp										2	1	1				4
Boomerang					1		2									3
Bullet/Missile								1								1
Changing			1		2										1	4
Chevron	1					1	1		1	3	1	2				10
Cigar				1			2		2	1	1	1	1	1		10
Circle	1			2	2	4	2	5	4	5	5	17	8	9	7	71
Cone								2	1							3
Cylinder								1	1	5		1	1	1	1	11
Diamond			1							1	1		3	1	3	10
Disc	1		1				1		1	2		4	1	1	1	13
Disk	1	1	1	1		1	1	2	2	4	1		2		1	18
Egg				2		1						1		1		5
Fireball		1	1	1			1		2		4	9	10	7	4	40
Flash								2		1	1			1		5
Formation		1	2	2				1	1	1	1		1		5	15
Light	2	2		6	3	5	5	1	2	1	4	9	7	8	9	64
Other	1		1	3	2	2	1	6	3	6	1	5	2		7	40
Oval			3					1	4	2	2	1		3		16
Rectangle	1												1		2	4
Saturn-like					1											1
Sphere	1	1			1	2		1	4		2	15	10	3	6	46
Star-like							2	2		3	3	4		3	5	22
Teardrop				1		1			1			3	2		1	9
Triangle	3		2	3	5	2	4	4	5	1	2	1	3	7	1	43
Unknown	1	1	4	1	4		4	2	3	4	4	12	6	5	3	54
Total	**13**	**7**	**17**	**23**	**21**	**19**	**26**	**31**	**37**	**42**	**34**	**86**	**58**	**51**	**57**	**522**

UFOS BY COUNTY: RHODE ISLAND

Counties	2001	2002	2003	2004	2005	2006	2007	2008	2009	2010	2011	2012	2013	2014	2015	Total
Bristol	1	1					2					1	1	2	1	9
Kent	1	2	4	2	3	2	2	4	4	9	8	15	8	8	5	77
Newport	2		1	1	1	2	8	6	3	5	1	6	2	4	9	51
Providence	6	2	4	12	13	8	5	12	22	16	17	43	40	27	27	254
South				1												1
Unknown	1		3		2		2	3			1	5	1	1	3	22
Washington	2	2	5	7	2	7	7	6	8	12	7	16	6	9	12	108
Total	**13**	**7**	**17**	**23**	**21**	**19**	**26**	**31**	**37**	**42**	**34**	**86**	**58**	**51**	**57**	**522**

If a county is missing from the list, it's because no UFO sightings were logged in either the NUFORC or MUFON databases for the 2001-2015 sample period.

Bonus Chart- UFOs by Cities: Rhode Island

Cities	Jan	Feb	Mar	Apr	May	Jun	Jul	Aug	Sep	Oct	Nov	Dec	Total
Ashaway		1						1					2
Barrington		1											1
Block Island								1	1				2
Bristol							2	2					4
Burrillville										1			1
Charlestown					1			3		1			5
Chepachet								1	1				2
Coventry		2		1		1	3	1	1	1	6	1	17
Cranston	2		3	1	2	2	2	4	1	4	2		23
Cumberland	1			1			2	1	1	1	3		10
East Greenwich		1		1		2	1		1				6
East Providence	2	1	1		3	1	1	4	2	2		1	18
Exeter				1	1						1	1	4
exit 8 off interstate 9			1										1
Fall River								1					1
Fall river Mass						1							1
Glocester	1												1
Greenville				1		1							2
Harmony		1											1
Harrisville			2										2
Hope										1			1
Hope Valley					1		1				1		3
Hopkinton									1				1
Interstate 95		1					1						2
Jamestown					1		1	1	1		2		6

Cities	Jan	Feb	Mar	Apr	May	Jun	Jul	Aug	Sep	Oct	Nov	Dec	Total
Johnston	2		1		1	1	4	3	2				14
Kingston					2				1	2	1	1	7
Lincoln		1				1	2		1	1			6
Little Compton								2					2
Mapillville							1						1
Matunuck								1					1
Middletown		1		1	1		2	2	1				8
Narragansett					3	2	2	2	3				12
Newport	1		1			3	5	4		3	2	4	23
North Kingstown	1	3	1	1			1	1	4	2	1		15
North Providence		1		1			2	1	2		3	1	11
North Scituate												1	1
North Smithfield	1					1			1	2	3		8
Pascoag	1								1				2
Pawtucket	3		1	1	3	3	5	1	8	3		1	29
Perryville				1									1
Portsmouth		1	3		1		1	1	1		1		9
Providence	4	2	2	3	2	7	5	6	10	9	7	6	63
Richmond			1						1	1	2		5
Riverside					2	1	1					1	5
Rumford										1		1	2
Scituate		1					1	1					3
Smithfield	1	1			2		2		2				8
South Kingstown	5	6			3	1	3	2		2	1		23
Tiverton					1	2	1		2		2	1	9
Unspecified		1	1		3	2	4	3	3	1	2	2	22
Wakefield	3		1	1	1		1	1	2	4	1		15
Warren				1			1						2
Warwick	2	3	2	5			3	5	7	5	1	2	35
Watch Hill							1						1
West Greenwich	2		1				1		2	2		1	9
West Warwick	2		2			1	2		2			1	10
Westerly	1		1			1	1	2	2			1	9
Woonsocket	1	4	1	1	5	3	3	6		5	3	1	33
Wyoming											1		1
Total	**36**	**33**	**26**	**22**	**39**	**37**	**69**	**64**	**68**	**54**	**46**	**28**	**522**

UFOS BY MONTH: RHODE ISLAND

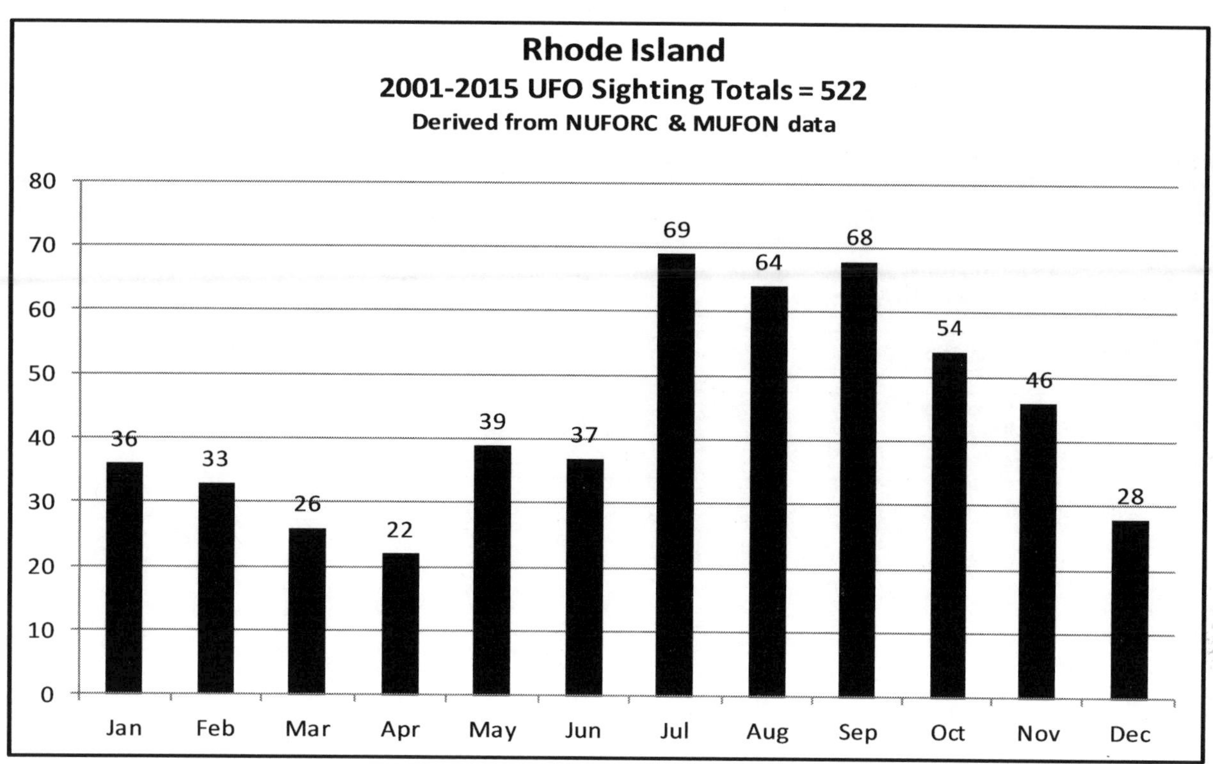

Year	Jan	Feb	Mar	Apr	May	Jun	Jul	Aug	Sep	Oct	Nov	Dec	Total
2001	2		2				5	1	2		1		13
2002		1	1	1		1				1	1	1	7
2003	2	1	2	1	1		3	2	1	3	1		17
2004	2	2	2		1	1	2	7	3		1	2	23
2005	2	3	1	2	1	2	1		1	2	4	2	21
2006	3	4				1	2		2	6		1	19
2007		1	1	2	1	2	2	5	5	3	2	2	26
2008	2	1	1	2	1	1	4	3	4	8	1	3	31
2009	4	2		2	4	2		6	10	6	1		37
2010	4	2	2	6	8	3	8	3	2		1	3	42
2011	5	1	2	1	2	3	4	3	6	2	2	3	34
2012	2	7	5		12	7	14	9	6	6	13	5	86
2013	1	3	4	2	1	3	6	13	9	4	8	4	58
2014	4	2	2	2	3	6	9	7	3	8	3	2	51
2015	3	3	1	1	4	5	9	5	14	5	7		57
Grand Total	**36**	**33**	**26**	**22**	**39**	**37**	**69**	**64**	**68**	**54**	**46**	**28**	**522**

Distribution of Sightings between Databases: Rhode Island

Database	Count	Percentage
MUFON	197	37.74%
NUFORC	325	62.26%
Total	522	100.00%

State Demographic Information: Rhode Island

2010 US Census Statistics	
Population	1,052,567.00
Area in Square Miles	1,544 .89
Land Area Sq. Miles	1,033 .81
Population/Square mile	1,018 .1

SOUTH CAROLINA UFO RANK 22/51

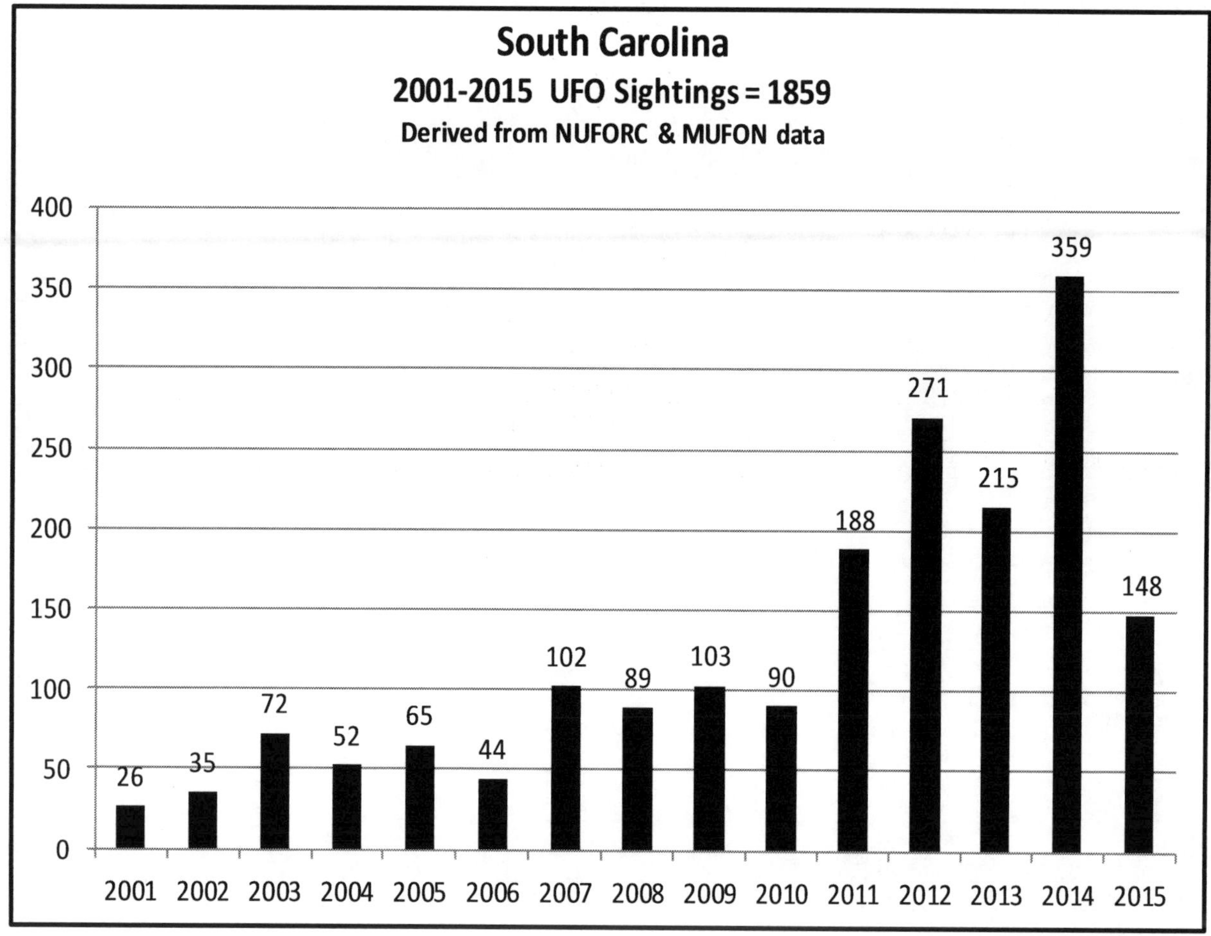

TOP TEN COUNTIES		RANK	TOP TEN SHAPES		
Horry	627	1	Light	331	17.81%
Charleston	186	2	Circle	228	12.26%
Greenville	126	3	Sphere	187	10.06%
York	86	4	Fireball	160	8.61%
Richland	85	5	Triangle	154	8.28%
Berkeley	66	6	Unknown	152	8.18%
Georgetown	66	7	Other	113	6.08%
Lexington	59	8	Oval	66	3.55%
Anderson	51	9	Star-like	57	3.07%
Florence	46	10	Formation	55	2.96%

UFO SHAPES: SOUTH CAROLINA

UFO Shapes	2001	2002	2003	2004	2005	2006	2007	2008	2009	2010	2011	2012	2013	2014	2015	Total
Blimp						1	1	2	1		1		1		1	8
Boomerang						1		1			2	2		2	1	9
Bullet/Missile		1					1	4					1	1		8
Changing		1	2		5	1				4	3	10	5	7	2	40
Chevron			2	3			1	2	1		1			2		12
Cigar	1		1	1		1	7	7	2	5	1	9	3	4	2	44
Circle	3	2	13	4	8	5	9	5	15	11	16	36	29	50	22	228
Cone		1			3		1					1	2	2		10
Cross							1			1		1	2	1		6
Cylinder	1			2	1	1	3		1		3	8	4	5	6	35
Diamond	1		1				2		2	2	3	1	4	6	1	23
Disc		2		1			1	4	2		6	1	5	3	3	28
Disk	1		7		4	2	1		3	2	2	5	4	7	6	44
Egg				1			1	1				1	1			5
Fireball	2	1		1		1	6	2	5	6	21	42	21	43	9	160
Flash		2	1	1		2		2	6	4	4	7	2	8	3	42
Formation			4	1	1	1	1	2	2	5	8	6	9	14	1	55
Light	7	7	13	15	11	13	28	13	20	18	32	40	39	53	22	331
N/A							2							4	2	8
Other		4	6	3	8	5	5	9	4	5	12	9	15	24	4	113
Oval	2	2	4	2	2	2	9	2	7	3	10	8	4	8	1	66
Rectangle				2	1	2		1	1			2	1	7	2	19
Saturn-like															1	1
Sphere	4	2	9	2	1	1	6	11	11	4	18	27	23	52	16	187
Sq/Rect														1		1
Star-like	1	2	1		2	1	2	2	1	3	6	15	5	11	5	57
Teardrop	1	1		1			1	1	1	1		1		1	4	13
Triangle	1	2	2	6	10	2	5	9	4	12	17	18	19	27	20	154
Unknown	1	5	6	6	8	2	8	9	14	4	22	21	16	16	14	152
Total	**26**	**35**	**72**	**52**	**65**	**44**	**102**	**89**	**103**	**90**	**188**	**271**	**215**	**359**	**148**	**1859**

UFOS BY COUNTY: SOUTH CAROLINA

Counties	2001	2002	2003	2004	2005	2006	2007	2008	2009	2010	2011	2012	2013	2014	2015	Total
Abbeville		1					1						1	1		4
Aiken			3	2	1		1	3	2	5	8	4	4	4	4	41
Anderson	3		2	2	1		4	3	4	5	3	3	7	7	7	51
Barnwell							1	1	1	1						4
Beaufort	1	2			2	2	5	2	2	4	4		3	7	1	35
Berkeley			1	1			1	6		6	10	11	8	12	10	66
Calhoun										1				2		3
Charleston	3	5	15	5	21	5	4	11	8	9	9	19	16	40	16	186
Cherokee				3		2		1		1			1			8
Chester				1	2				1		1	1	2		1	9
Chesterfield			1													1
Clarendon									2					1		3
Colleton		2	1		1		1			3	2	2	1		2	15
Columbia	1															1
Darlington		1					3	1	3	2		1	2	3	1	17
Dillon						1	2				1	1				5
Dorchester	1		2		2	1	3	1	1	2	4	8	4	4	4	37
Fairfield			1						1				2	1		5
Florence	3		3	1		2	1	3	4	1	6	6	8	5	3	46
Georgetown		1	1		1	3	4	1	3	2	9	13	4	22	2	66
Greenville	1	3	2	2	4	3	7	5	8	5	14	25	13	19	15	126
Greenwood	1				2				2		1	3	2	2	1	14
Hampton				1							1					2
Horry	2	9	27	20	13	17	32	26	30	16	53	115	88	152	27	627
Jasper											2	3			1	6
Kershaw		1	1		1			1	1		1	1	3	4	1	15
Lancaster				1	1				1		1			2	4	10
Laurens	1	2					1		2		3	2	2	3		16
Lee				1	1				1		1	1	1			6
Lexington	1	1	2		1	4	1	1	5	7	4	11	10	7	4	59
Marion							1							1	1	3
Marlboro	1															1
McCormick		1							1			1		2	3	8
Newberry				1							2			1		4
Oconee			1		1		3	1			4			4	2	16
Orangeburg				1	1		2	3			1	1		2	1	12
Pickens		1	1	1	2		5	2	3	4	2	1	2	12	5	41

Counties	**2001**	**2002**	**2003**	**2004**	**2005**	**2006**	**2007**	**2008**	**2009**	**2010**	**2011**	**2012**	**2013**	**2014**	**2015**	**Total**
Richland	3	1	4	2	4		3	4	7	4	10	11	9	12	11	85
Saluda	1			1						1						3
Spartanburg	1	1	2				2	4	3	2	9	4	5	5	4	42
Sumter		1		1		2	2		1	2	3	5	2	3	4	26
Union								1							1	2
Unknown		1				1	2	2	2		6	9	8		1	32
Williamsburg		1		3	2		1	1			4			1	1	14
York	2		2	2	1	1	9	5	4	7	9	9	7	18	10	86
Total	**26**	**35**	**72**	**52**	**65**	**44**	**102**	**89**	**103**	**90**	**188**	**271**	**215**	**359**	**148**	**1859**

If a county is missing from the list, it's because no UFO sightings were logged in either the NUFORC or MUFON databases for the 2001-2015 sample period.

UFOS BY MONTH: SOUTH CAROLINA

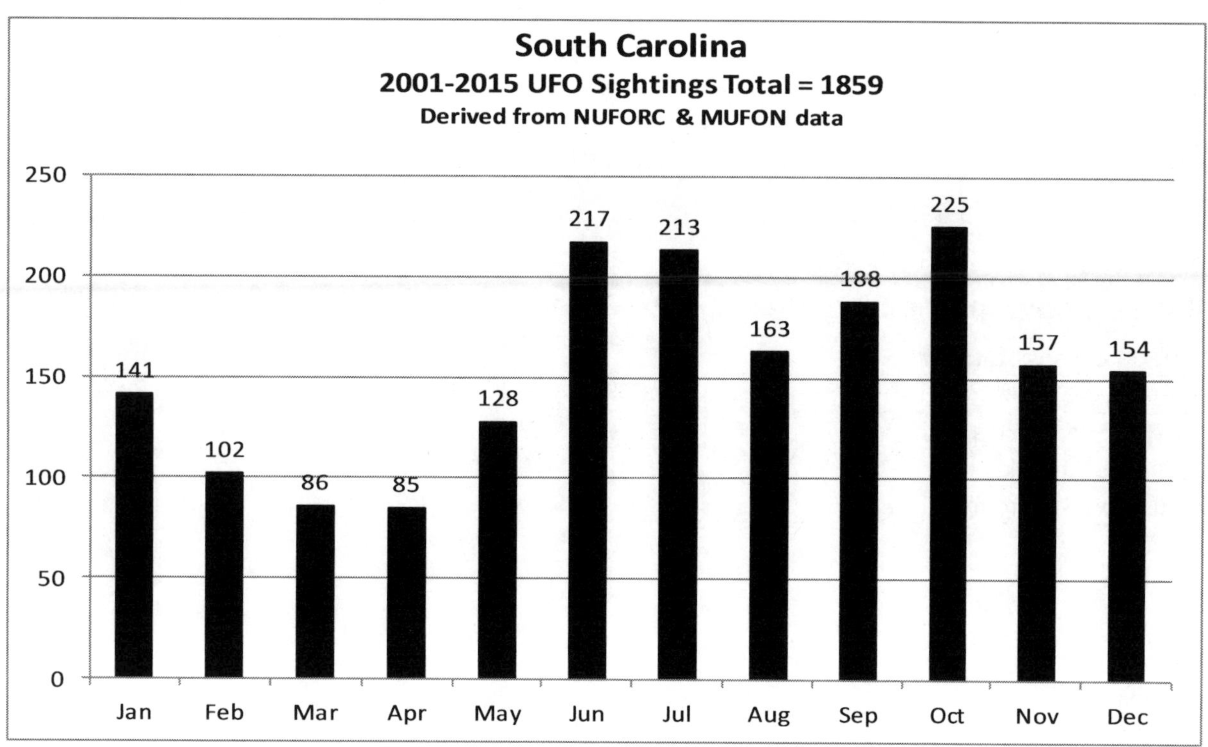

Year	Jan	Feb	Mar	Apr	May	Jun	Jul	Aug	Sep	Oct	Nov	Dec	Total
2001	2	4	1	1	1	6	2		1	2	1	5	26
2002	1	2		2	2	5	4	5	6		5	3	35
2003	5	4	2	3	2	4	7	6	16	9	7	7	72
2004	4	5	1	3	1	2	4	5	4	8	4	11	52
2005	3	6		3	4	12	5		3	9	13	7	65
2006	3	3	2	1	3	5	11	3	3	2	4	4	44
2007	10	8	3	3	8	10	9	12	12	12	6	9	102
2008	10	11		6	8	8	6	7	6	11	11	5	89
2009	12	5	6	3	13	9	9	10	11	8	11	6	103
2010	2	5	3	4	6	4	12	10	17	15	11	1	90
2011	6	5	11	6	16	20	18	10	21	22	19	34	188
2012	22	7	16	11	9	16	33	35	33	50	25	14	271
2013	19	16	12	13	11	22	31	14	30	11	18	18	215
2014	30	14	18	16	26	77	43	34	17	49	14	21	359
2015	12	7	11	10	18	17	19	12	8	17	8	9	148
Total	**141**	**102**	**86**	**85**	**128**	**217**	**213**	**163**	**188**	**225**	**157**	**154**	**1859**

Distribution of Sightings between Databases: South Carolina

Database	Count	Percentage
MUFON	543	29.21%
NUFORC	1316	70.79%
Total	1859	100.00%

State Demographic Information: South Carolina

2010 US Census Statistics	
Population	4,625,364.00
Area in Square Miles	32,020 .49
Land Area Sq. Miles	30,060 .70
Population/Square mile	153 9

SOUTH DAKOTA UFO RANK 49/51

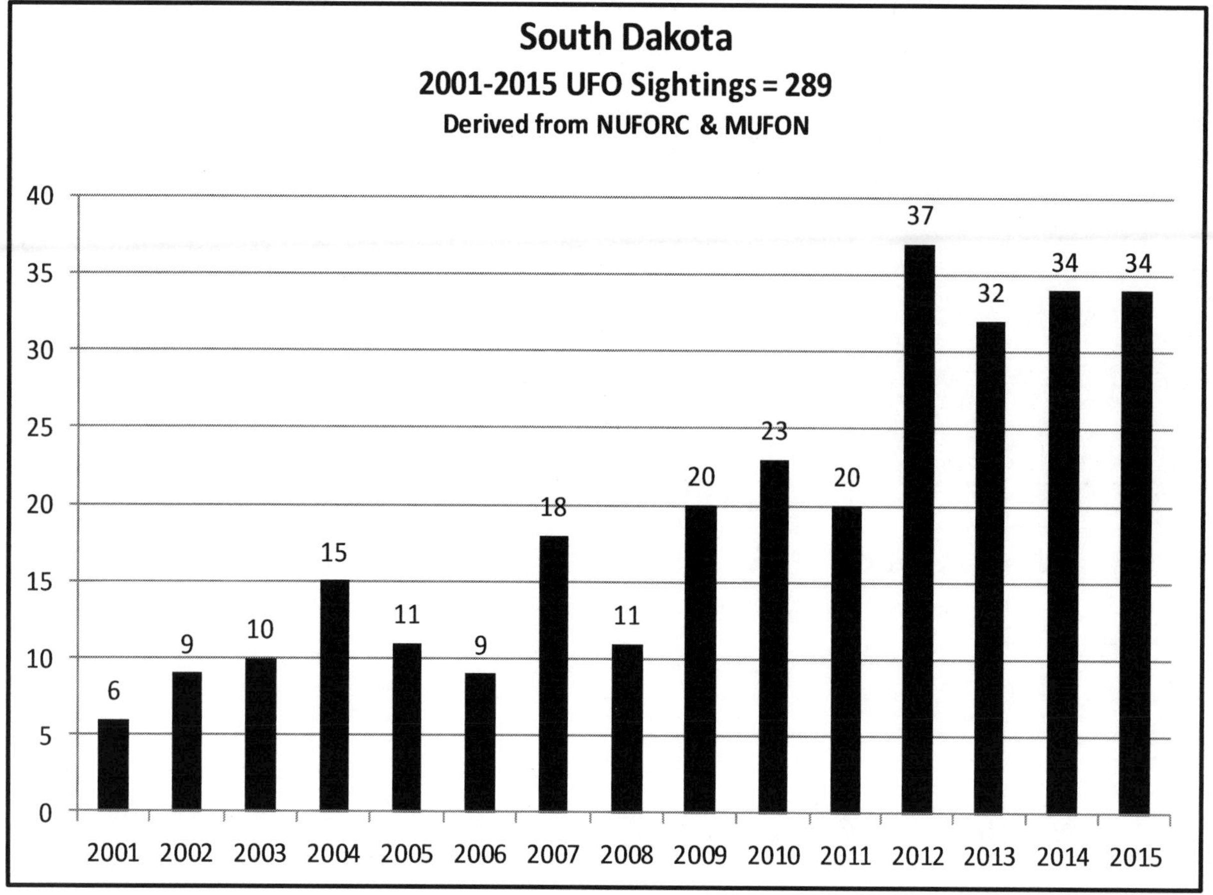

TOP TEN COUNTIES		RANK	TOP TEN SHAPES		
Minnehaha	58	1	Light	54	18.69%
Pennington	51	2	Unknown	34	11.76%
Unknown	15	3	Triangle	33	11.42%
Yankton	13	4	Circle	26	9.00%
Beadle	12	5	Other	22	7.61%
Lawrence	12	6	Sphere	19	6.57%
Roberts	12	7	Fireball	16	5.54%
Codington	10	8	Oval	14	4.84%
Todd	8	9	Star-like	13	4.50%
Davison	7	10	Cylinder	6	2.08%

UFO SHAPES: SOUTH DAKOTA

UFO Shapes	2001	2002	2003	2004	2005	2006	2007	2008	2009	2010	2011	2012	2013	2014	2015	Total
Blimp												1				1
Boomerang												1	1		1	3
Changing					1		1					1				3
Chevron						1					1				2	4
Cigar		1					1	1	1						1	5
Circle			1	1	1		1		3	1	3	6	3	3	3	26
Cone													1			1
Cylinder							1						1		4	6
Diamond									1				1		2	4
Disc										1		1	1			3
Disk						1		2					1		1	5
Egg			1					1								2
Fireball				1		1				2	1	4	1	5	1	16
Flash				1	1			1			2					5
Formation			1						1			1	2	1		6
Light	2	4	2	4	3		4		4	5	4	6	7	5	4	54
N/A														1		1
Other					1	1	2	1	1	2	1	5	3	1	4	22
Oval	1		2				1	2	1	1		2	1	2	1	14
Rectangle			1				1		1	1						4
Saturn-like														1		1
Sphere				1	1	2	1	1			2	3	1	4	3	19
Sq/Rect															1	1
Star-like				1			1		2	3			2	2	2	13
Teardrop		2												1		3
Triangle	1	1	2	2	1	2	1	1	2	5	3	1	2	7	2	33
Unknown	2	1		4	2	1	3	1	3	2	3	5	4	1	2	34
Total	**6**	**9**	**10**	**15**	**11**	**9**	**18**	**11**	**20**	**23**	**20**	**37**	**32**	**34**	**34**	**289**

UFOS BY COUNTY: SOUTH DAKOTA

Counties	2001	2002	2003	2004	2005	2006	2007	2008	2009	2010	2011	2012	2013	2014	2015	Total
Beadle			1		1	1			1	1	1		2	3	1	12
Bon Homme	1								1		1					3
Brookings									1		1			1		3
Brown									3						1	4
Brule											1	1				2
Buffalo			1				1					1				3
Charles Mix				1								2		1		4
Clay			1				2					1				4
Codington				1	1	1			1			4		2		10
Corson															1	1
Custer								1		2	1			1		5
Davison					1					1	1	1	3			7
Day			1													1
Dewey		1	1		3				1		1					7
Douglas												1				1
Edmunds										2						2
Fall River			1						1							2
Gregory					1			1				1				3
Hughes										2			1	2		5
Harding																0
Hutchinson												1				1
Hyde							1									1
Kingsbury	1											2				3
Lake												1	1			2
Lawrence	1	1		2		2					1	2		2	1	12
Lincoln				1						2	1	1				5
Lyman							1									1
Marshall												1				1
McCook				1												1
Meade				1	1	1							3		1	7
Minnehaha		3		1		2	2	4	1	5	3	6	5	10	16	58
Moody									2			1			1	4
Oglala											1					1
Pennington	2	3	1	2	3	1	5	1	6	2	3	5	6	7	4	51
Perkins				1												1
Potter													1			1
Roberts		1	1	2				2	1	1			1	2	1	12

Counties	**2001**	**2002**	**2003**	**2004**	**2005**	**2006**	**2007**	**2008**	**2009**	**2010**	**2011**	**2012**	**2013**	**2014**	**2015**	**Total**
Shannon			1	1			1			1						4
Todd	1						2	1		2	1		1			8
Tripp														1		1
Turner							2									2
Union												1			2	3
Unknown						1	1	1	1	2		2	4		3	15
Walworth			1													1
Yankton											3	2	4	2	2	13
Ziebach				1												1
Total	**6**	**9**	**10**	**15**	**11**	**9**	**18**	**11**	**20**	**23**	**20**	**37**	**32**	**34**	**34**	**289**

If a county is missing from the list, it's because no UFO sightings were logged in either the NUFORC or MUFON databases for the 2001-2015 sample period.

UFOS BY MONTH: SOUTH DAKOTA

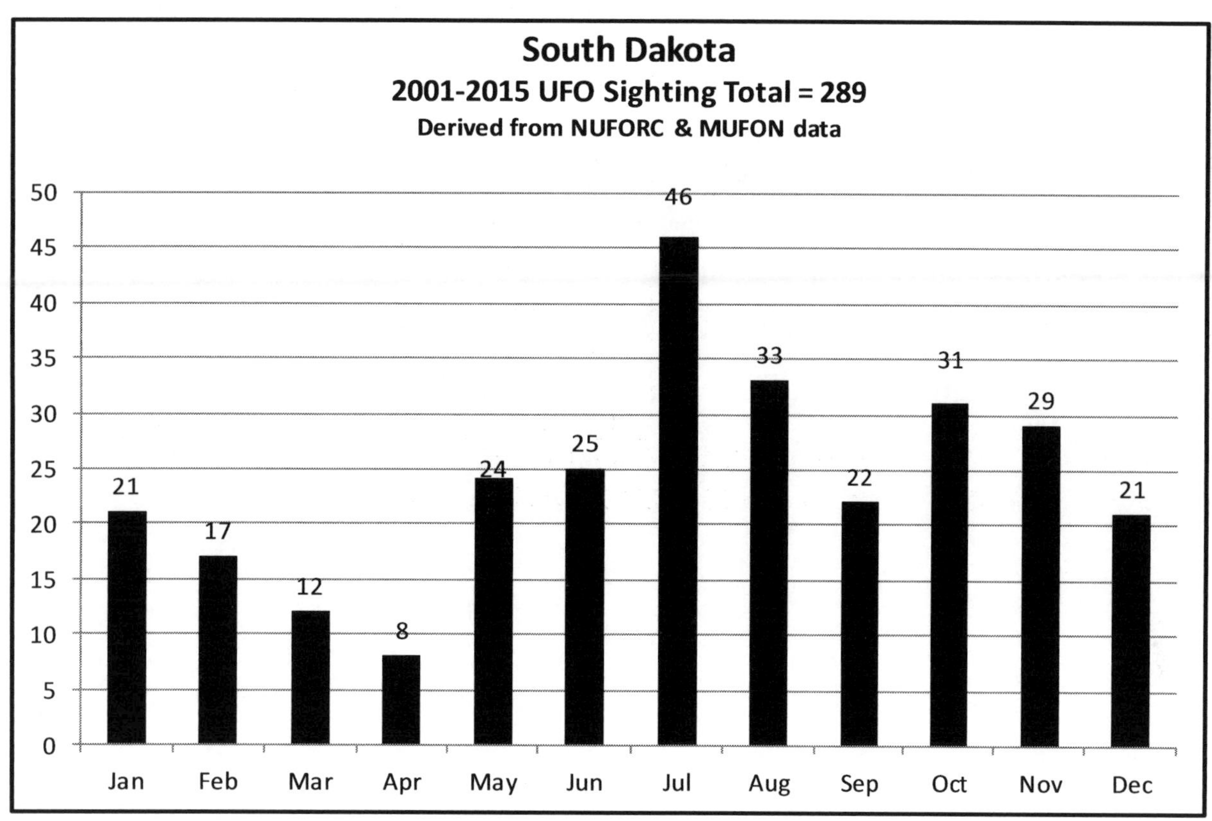

Year	Jan	Feb	Mar	Apr	May	Jun	Jul	Aug	Sep	Oct	Nov	Dec	Total
2001						2		2		1		1	6
2002		1					3	1	1		1	2	9
2003	1	1		1	1		1	2	1		1	1	10
2004	2	2	1			2	2		2		4		15
2005		1		1	1		2	4	1		1		11
2006		1		1	1		1		1	3	1		9
2007	1		2				2	1	1	10	1		18
2008	1	1	1			2	3			2	1		11
2009		2	1		6	2	4	2			2	1	20
2010	2	2			1	2	5	4	3	3	1		23
2011			2		2		3	2	2	4	1	4	20
2012	1	2	2	2	9	3	4	2	1	1	5	5	37
2013	9			1	1	1	8	1	3	3	2	3	32
2014	3	2		2	1	6	3	8	3	1	3	2	34
2015	1	2	3		1	5	5	4	3	3	5	2	34
Total	**21**	**17**	**12**	**8**	**24**	**25**	**46**	**33**	**22**	**31**	**29**	**21**	**289**

Distribution of Sightings between Databases: South Dakota

Database	Count	Percentage
MUFON	90	31.14%
NUFORC	199	68.86%
Total	289	100.00%

State Demographic Information: South Dakota

2010 US Census Statistics	
Population	814,180.00
Area in Square Miles	77,115.68
Land Area Sq. Miles	75,811.00
Population/Square mile	10.7

TENNESSEE UFO RANK 20/51

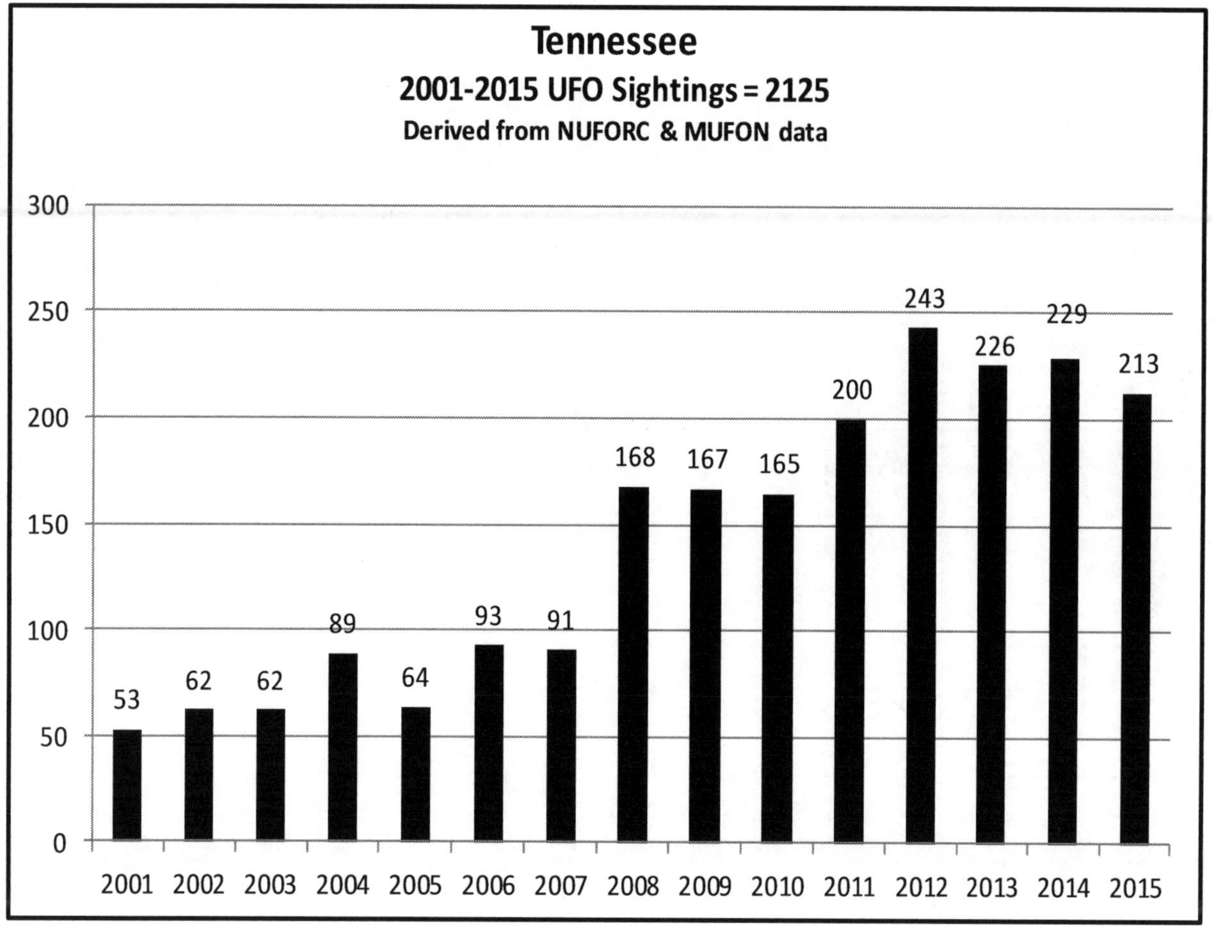

TOP TEN COUNTIES		RANK	TOP TEN SHAPES		
Davidson	244	1	Circle	249	11.83%
Shelby	173	2	Light	233	11.07%
Knox	163	3	Triangle	216	10.26%
Hamilton	113	4	Unknown	201	9.55%
Rutherford	105	5	Sphere	190	9.03%
Sullivan	99	6	Fireball	130	6.18%
Unknown	85	7	Other	129	6.13%
Williamson	70	8	Oval	88	4.18%
Washington	65	9	Disc	87	4.13%
Sumner	57	10	Star-like	85	4.04%

UFO SHAPES: TENNESSEE

UFO Shapes	2001	2002	2003	2004	2005	2006	2007	2008	2009	2010	2011	2012	2013	2014	2015	Total
Blimp		1						1	2	2	1	2	1			10
Boomerang							3	5	1	5	5	1			1	21
Bullet/Missile						3	1		3	1	2	2	4	2		18
Changing	1	1	3	4	1	2	1	3	3	1		1	3	1	3	28
Chevron	2	2	1	1	1	1	1	1		2	1			3	2	18
Cigar				2	4	6	4	6	7	5	12	9	11	6	4	76
Circle	5	7	7	2	2	10	10	16	16	19	21	41	40	34	19	249
Cone	1					1		1		1	1	2	2		3	12
Cross	1					1		1	1							4
Cylinder	1	1		4	1	2	2	3	8	1	8	15	7	5	12	70
Diamond		1		3	1	1	3	6	5	7	3	2	5	4	1	42
Disc			4	1	2	1	1	6	18	12	9	10	9	7	7	87
Disk	2	6	4	8	6	3	3	7	6	4	8	5	4	4	3	73
Egg			1	3			1	2	1	1	3	1	4	3		20
Fireball	4	1		4	3	7	2	6	4	12	22	18	16	21	10	130
Flash	1	1		2	1	2	1	3	1		2	6	2	1	4	27
Formation	1	1	2	2	1		1	3			2	1	6	6	5	31
Light	12	8	9	9	9	19	14	18	20	10	15	22	17	30	21	233
N/A														1	2	3
Other	4	7	5	15	4	6	5	15	7	7	11	10	10	14	9	129
Oval	5	1	4	4	2	5	4	8	2	7	8	9	12	11	6	88
Rectangle	2		1		1			2		3	1	3	2	1	1	17
Saturn-like									1			1			2	4
Sphere	2	8	3	5	3	8	2	6	12	11	19	32	24	27	28	190
Sq/Rect														3	4	7
Star-like			1		1	5	4	4	10	11	15	5	5	9	15	85
Teardrop		1		1			1	1	1			3	3	1	4	16
Triangle	5	4	9	12	8	4	14	19	13	16	17	18	24	23	30	216
Unknown	3	11	7	6	13	5	11	22	23	24	13	23	14	10	16	201
Total	**52**	**62**	**61**	**88**	**64**	**92**	**89**	**165**	**165**	**162**	**199**	**242**	**225**	**227**	**212**	**2105**

UFOS BY COUNTY: TENNESSEE

Counties	2001	2002	2003	2004	2005	2006	2007	2008	2009	2010	2011	2012	2013	2014	2015	Total
Anderson		2	1	1		2	2	3	1			1	1	6		20
Bedford		1		1			2	2	1	5	3	4	2	3	2	26
Benton							1				1			2		4
Bledsoe									1							1
Blount				2	3	4	2	1	2		1	3	4	6	5	33
Bradley	1			1				1		5		3	5	4	1	21
Campbell	1									1	1	2	1			6
Cannon					1					1				1		3
Carroll					1								1		2	4
Carter	1	1		5			1	2	2	2	4	2	4		2	26
Cheatham	1	1		2	1			2			1	1	2	1		12
Chester															2	2
Claiborne							1	1		2	2		2		1	9
Clay	1			1			2							1	1	6
Cocke	1			1							1			1	3	7
Coffee	2		3	1				3	5		6	6	2	1	2	31
Crockett									5	1	2	1				9
Cumberland		1			1	1	1		1	1	2	1	3	4	2	18
Davidson	9	9	7	7	11	6	8	14	30	26	20	16	37	21	23	244
Decatur											1					1
DeKalb		1								1			2		1	5
Dickson	1						1		1	2	1	1	2		1	10
Dyer		1	1					2		1		2	2	2		11
Fayette								2			1	3	2			8
Fentress													1		2	3
Franklin	1						1	3	2	1		2	1	1	2	14
Gibson		1		1	1			2	2	2		2	2		1	14
Giles		1	1							1		1			2	6
Grainger						1			1	2		2		1		7
Greene				2			2	3	7	4	6	4	1	3	2	34
Grundy				1												1
Hamblen	1		1		2		1	1	2	1	2	3	4	6		24
Hamilton	1	1	3	2	4	7	7	12	8	11	9	5	13	12	18	113
Hancock													1			1
Hardeman				1									1		1	3
Hardin	1		1	2		1	2		1	4	6		2	1		21
Hawkins	1		1		4						1	1		2	2	12

Counties	**2001**	**2002**	**2003**	**2004**	**2005**	**2006**	**2007**	**2008**	**2009**	**2010**	**2011**	**2012**	**2013**	**2014**	**2015**	**Total**
Haywood					1							1				2
Henderson								1						1		2
Henry	1		1	1				1			1		2	2		9
Houston							1	1		2						4
Humphreys			1				1	1		2	1	2	1	3		12
Jackson												2				2
Jefferson		1	1		1	1		2	2	1	1	7	2	5	2	26
Johnson							1	1						2	2	6
Knox		4	4	11	1	6	5	14	19	12	21	24	13	16	13	163
Lake	1															1
Lauderdale								1				1	1	2		5
Lawrence						1		1	1		2	2	1	1		9
Lewis											1	1	1		1	4
Lincoln					1							1		3	1	6
Loudon					2	8		2	5	5	1		1	1	4	29
Macon			1						1				1		1	4
Madison	2		1	2	1	3		6	2		3	1	1	3	1	26
Marion					1		1			1						3
Marshall		2			1	1		1		1		1	2	2	2	13
Maury			3	1		3		4	7	1	2	3	6	5	4	39
McMinn				1	1			1		3		3		1	1	11
McNairy													1		2	3
Meigs											1		1	1	2	5
Monroe	2		1					2	2	1		2		1	2	13
Montgomery			1	1	4	4	1	1	4	7	3	4	6	13	5	54
Moore												2		1		3
Morgan				1								1			1	3
Obion		1										2	1		1	5
Overton						1		1		1					2	5
Perry			1			1		1		1		3			1	8
Pickett		1							1							2
Polk	1		1					1		1		1				5
Putnam		1	1	1		3	2		3	3	1	2			1	18
Rhea										1	1		1		1	4
Roane		2	1			2		1	2	1	1	1	1	1	4	17
Robertson	1		1	1	2		1		1		4	5		3		19
Rutherford	5	3	2	4	4	3	5	6	1	9	13	16	10	16	8	105
Scott											1	1				2
Sequatchie									1		1	1		1		4

Counties	**2001**	**2002**	**2003**	**2004**	**2005**	**2006**	**2007**	**2008**	**2009**	**2010**	**2011**	**2012**	**2013**	**2014**	**2015**	**Total**
Sevier	1	3	1	1	1	3	2	1		3		5	8	6	5	40
Shelby	5	10	6	8	4	6	10	21	12	11	21	14	14	20	11	173
Smith								3	2	1	3					9
Stewart		2								1	1	2				6
Sullivan	4	2	11	14	3	3	4	5	3	2	10	16	6	7	9	99
Sumner	1	3	1	1	1	1	5	2	5	6	6	5	11	3	6	57
Swain	1															1
Tipton				1	1	1	1	3			4	2	4	6	3	26
Trousdale	1														2	3
Unicoi									2			1	1	1	1	6
Union						1				1	2					4
Unknown				1	1	6	5	7	9	5	13	13	10	4	11	85
Warren						2						2	1	1	1	7
Washington		1		4	2	3	5	10	5	2	2	13	5	6	7	65
Wayne			1				2	1								4
Weakley	1	1						2					1	1		6
White		1	1			1						3				6
Williamson	2	2	1	3	1	5	3	8	2	6	8	6	9	5	9	70
Wilson	1	2		1	1	2	2	1	3			5	5	6	8	37
Total	**53**	**62**	**62**	**89**	**64**	**93**	**91**	**168**	**167**	**165**	**200**	**243**	**226**	**229**	**213**	**2125**

If a county is missing from the list, it's because no UFO sightings were logged in either the NUFORC or MUFON databases for the 2001-2015 sample period.

UFOS BY MONTH: TENNESSEE

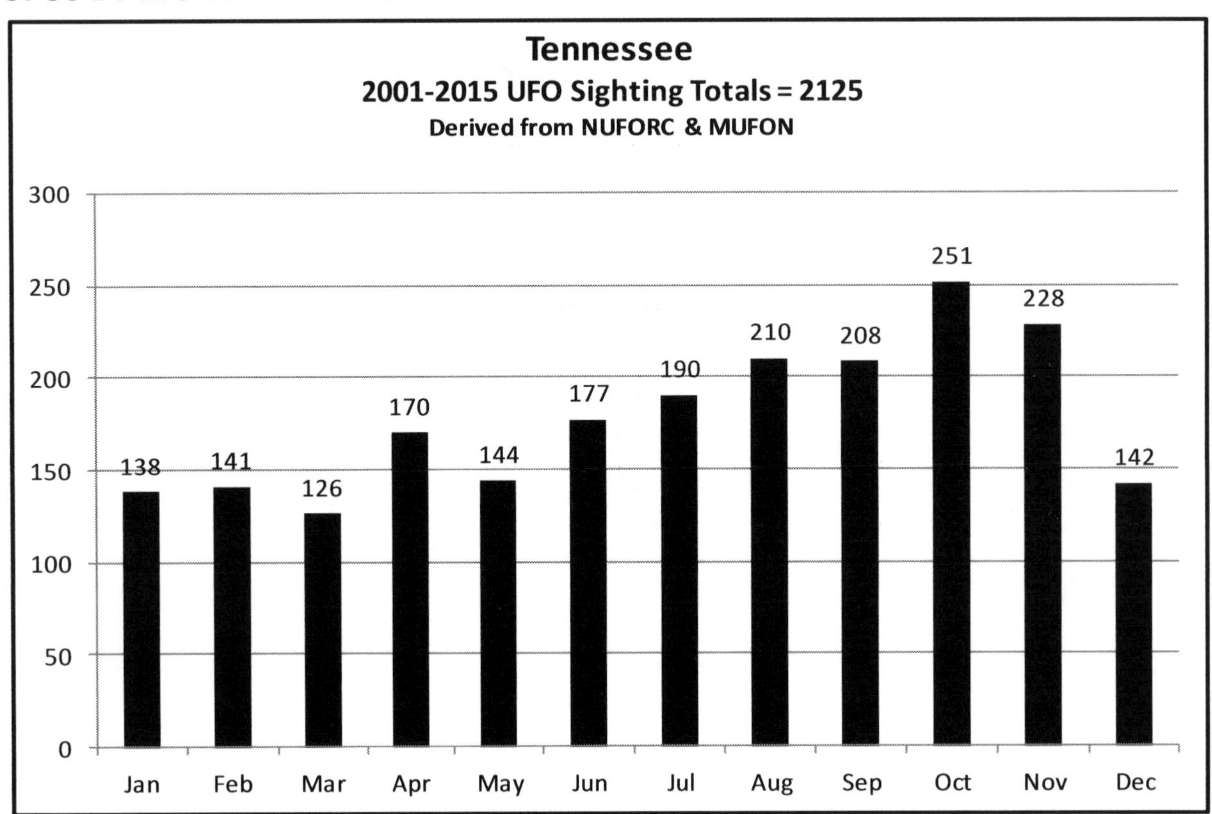

Year	Jan	Feb	Mar	Apr	May	Jun	Jul	Aug	Sep	Oct	Nov	Dec	Total
2001	1	7	2	7	4	6	1	3	3	8	9	2	53
2002	4	5	5	4	2	6	6	9	8	4	7	2	62
2003			3	4	5	12	8	9	8	7	4	2	62
2004	5	4	8	10	7	9	9	9	8	5	6	9	89
2005	4	7	5	4	2	6	5	13	6	5	6	1	64
2006	5	5	7	5	4	8	4	7	14	9	16	9	93
2007	10	4	8	7	8	4	8	6	11	10	5	10	91
2008	15	11	6	22	16	14	7	3	13	31	19	11	168
2009	12	20	12	19	11	8	14	11	8	20	18	14	167
2010	9	7	11	10	13	7	26	15	21	20	17	9	165
2011	13	8	7	18	11	21	24	26	20	27	13	12	200
2012	22	14	16	18	11	26	13	23	20	35	27	18	243
2013	12	18	5	13	11	20	24	22	28	31	31	11	226
2014	13	17	14	20	21	15	22	23	22	26	24	12	229
2015	13	14	17	9	18	15	19	31	18	13	26	20	213
Total	**138**	**141**	**126**	**170**	**144**	**177**	**190**	**210**	**208**	**251**	**228**	**142**	**2125**

Distribution of Sightings between Databases: Tennessee

Database	Count	Percentage
MUFON	886	41.69%
NUFORC	1239	58.31%
Total	2125	100.00%

State Demographic Information: Tennessee

2010 US Census Statistics	
Population	6,346,105.00
Area in Square Miles	42,144 .25
Land Area Sq. Miles	41,234 .90
Population/Square mile	153 .9

TEXAS

UFO RANK 3/51

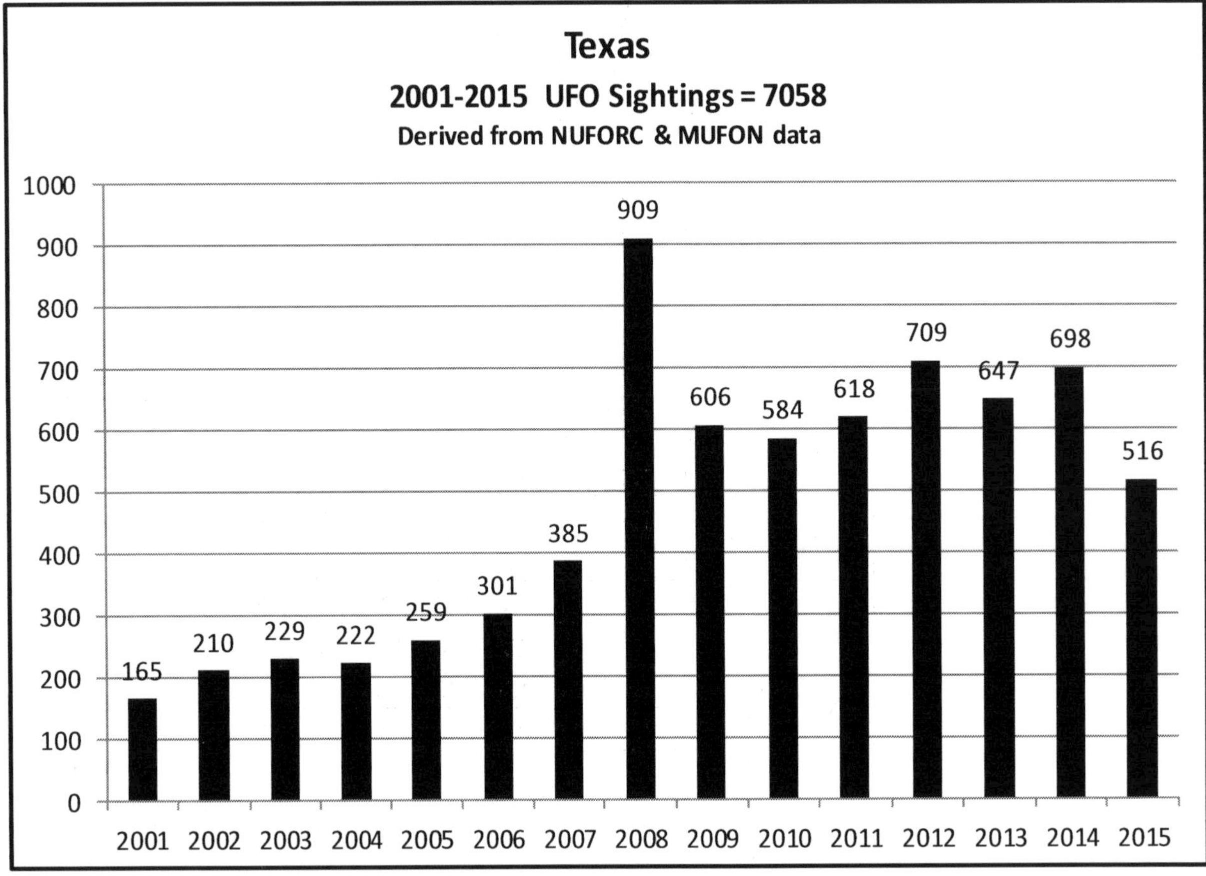

TOP TEN COUNTIES		RANK
Harris	792	1
Tarrant	537	2
Dallas	477	3
Travis	465	4
Bexar	379	5
Collin	253	6
Denton	201	7
Unknown	154	8
Williamson	138	9
El Paso	137	10

TOP TEN SHAPES		
Circle	813	11.52%
Light	711	10.07%
Unknown	682	9.66%
Triangle	680	9.63%
Sphere	665	9.42%
Other	550	7.79%
Star-like	373	5.28%
Fireball	357	5.06%
Oval	323	4.58%
Cigar	224	3.17%

UFO SHAPES: TEXAS

UFO Shapes	2001	2002	2003	2004	2005	2006	2007	2008	2009	2010	2011	2012	2013	2014	2015	Total
Blimp		1	1	1	1	2	3	16	3	5	5	6	6		1	51
Boomerang	1	3	2		1	3	10	15	13	14	15	23	19	4	10	133
Bullet/Missile		1	1		1		6	12	6	7	7	7	8	6	2	64
Changing	6	4	3	10	8	8	4	9	8	11	7	8	6	7	3	102
Chevron		4	3		1	3	8	11	5	10	3	9	3	5	8	73
Cigar	7	3	9	5	8	11	21	46	15	15	19	15	19	13	18	224
Circle	6	17	21	16	22	26	34	111	70	76	86	112	90	74	52	813
Cone	3			2		3		5	5	2	3	4	2	4	1	34
Cross						1		5	2	5	3	3	2			21
Cylinder	9	8	7	5	6	5	10	20	10	5	9	17	19	28	17	175
Diamond	4	5	1	5	3	3	8	8	10	11	11	14	10	8	8	109
Disc	2	1	5	3	3	10	16	33	17	19	23	27	17	23	12	211
Disk	6	11	9	12	12	17	7	28	9	13	13	8	9	9	6	169
Egg	1	4		7	3	3	2	6	5	2	9	6	5	3	2	58
Fireball	11	9	5	12	8	14	21	25	21	28	34	59	46	33	31	357
Flash	3	3	4	1	7	4	8	29	28	18	15	21	12	14	5	172
Formation	5	9	5	6	4	4	5	13	6	6	8	8	10	9	6	104
Light	28	29	43	41	63	37	39	83	59	44	52	51	48	66	28	711
N/A									2		1	1	6	9	7	26
Other	12	17	13	19	16	26	37	73	64	58	35	48	32	60	40	550
Oval	18	12	13	10	11	10	23	52	26	19	29	30	16	26	28	323
Rectangle	3	2	3	5	4	4	4	9	5	3	11	5	3	9	2	72
Saturn-like			2		1	1		8	4	5	1		1	3	1	27
Sphere	10	16	16	15	13	20	22	63	49	57	49	58	103	97	77	665
Sq/Rect														7	12	19
Star-like			2	1	3	8	10	70	44	40	37	39	42	36	41	373
Teardrop		2	3	1	2	2	9	9	5	2	6	3	2	6	8	60
Triangle	10	20	21	27	24	45	30	71	57	60	63	64	69	72	47	680
Unknown	20	29	37	18	34	31	48	79	58	49	64	63	42	67	43	682
Total	**165**	**210**	**229**	**222**	**259**	**301**	**385**	**909**	**606**	**584**	**618**	**709**	**647**	**698**	**516**	**7058**

UFOS BY COUNTY: TEXAS

Counties	2001	2002	2003	2004	2005	2006	2007	2008	2009	2010	2011	2012	2013	2014	2015	Total
Anderson	1		1				1	5			1		2	3	2	16
Andrews															1	1
Angelina		1	1	1			1	4	1	1		2		2	1	15
Aransas					1		1				2	1				5
Archer						1			1	1						3
Armstrong														2		2
Atascosa	1						1			2	1	1	3	2		11
Austin						1		2	1			1				5
Bailey						1		1	2							4
Bandera					1			1	2		5	2	3	5	2	21
Bastrop				2	4	3	2	5	1	1	6	2	8	3	1	38
Bee	1	1	1		1							2	2		2	10
Bell	1	3	4	1	7	6	2	9	10	7	3	18	5	10	9	95
Bexar	9	13	14	13	16	21	14	39	24	32	29	43	34	39	39	379
Blanco			1						1		2	2	2	2	2	12
Borden					1						1					2
Bosque		1					1	2	5		2	1		2	1	15
Bowie	1	2	3	1	1	2		6	3	1	3	3	2	4	2	34
Brazoria	3		1	5	2	2	5	9	4	6	6	5	11	10	8	77
Brazos	2		2	8	2	2	1	7	2	5	4	1	5	7	3	51
Brewster	1						2	3		1	3	1	2		2	15
Briscoe												1				1
Brown		1				1	4	7	6	3	6	3			1	32
Bryan								1			1					2
Bucks														1		1
Burleson		2		1	1		1	2	1		1	2	1	2		14
Burnet		1			5	2	3			1	1	1	3	3	1	21
Caldwell		1				1		1		1			3	1	2	10
Callahan	1							4	1	2	3		2	2	1	16
Cameron		1	1	1	3	5	2	11	4	4	8	14	10	6	6	76
Camp											1					1
Carson									2	1	2					5
Cass					5						1				2	8
Chambers			1			1		1	2	4	1					10
Cherokee	1					1		1			1		2	3		9
Childress													1			1
Clay	1															1

Counties	2001	2002	2003	2004	2005	2006	2007	2008	2009	2010	2011	2012	2013	2014	2015	Total
Cochran									1					3		4
Coke	1															1
Gillespie							1	2	2	2	1	1	6	1		16
Glasscock												1				1
Gonzales					1	1		1			1	1				5
Gray						1			2	1			1		1	6
Grayson		1	4	4	1		2	1		3	6	4	3	1		30
Gregg		1	3		2	2	1	2	4	1	3	4	2	3	1	29
Grimes											2					2
Guadalupe			1	1		2	1	5	2	1	2	5	1	5	3	29
Hale						1				1	1				1	4
Hall				1	1											2
Hamilton							3	4		1	2	1	1	1		13
Hansford									1							1
Hardeman		1					1									2
Hardin	2				1	1	1	2	3		2	1	1	2		16
Harris	27	27	36	24	28	32	38	88	66	51	67	75	91	94	48	792
Harrison			1				2	5	3	2	2	1	1	2		19
Haskell							1									1
Hays	2	5		5	4	4	1	4	9	3	3	4	4	13	6	67
Hemphill		1														1
Henderson		1	3	1	1	3	1	4	2	5	2	4	4	5	1	37
Hidalgo	1		3	2	1	3	6	10	14	1	9	10	6	10	4	80
Hill	2			1	1		2	1	2		1	4	3	2	1	20
Hockley										1			1			2
Hood							3	6	1	2	1	2	3	1		19
Hopkins								1	3	1		3	2	5	2	17
Houston	1	1		1	1				4			1	5			14
Howard	1	1	1						1	1	1	1			3	10
Hudspeth						1		1	2		2					6
Hunt				1				7	3	3		3	1	2		20
Hutchinson		1	1							3				4		9
Jack												1	2			3
Jackson								1	1	1		2	1			6
Jasper	1				2			1	3				1		1	9
Jeff Davis				1			2	2				1				6
Jefferson	2	6	1	4	1	2	3	5	5	6	1	7	8	5	3	59
Jim Hogg						1		1	1	1						4
Jim Wells			1		1	1	2				2	2		3	2	14

Counties	2001	2002	2003	2004	2005	2006	2007	2008	2009	2010	2011	2012	2013	2014	2015	Total
Johnson			3	1	1		2	4	5	3	2	10	3	2	1	37
Jones									1	1	1			1		4
Karnes												1			1	2
Kaufman						1	2	4	1	2	2	4	1	7	2	26
Kendall					2	3			1	1	1		4	1	1	14
Kenedy								1								1
Kent											1		1			2
Kerr			1		2	1			1	1	2	3	6	1	1	19
Kimble	1	1	1	2		1				1						7
Kinney				1				1						1		3
Kleberg		2		2	3	1	1		1		1					11
La Salle	1							3	1	1	2	4	3			15
Lamar		3						6	1	1	4	2		2	1	20
Lamb	1					1		2				1				5
Lampasas			1				1	1			1	1	1	1		7
Lavaca		1		1			1		1	1			1	2	1	9
Lee			1				2	1					1		2	7
Leon			1	1				2		2			3	2	1	12
Liberty	1	1	1	2			1	1	1			5	3	1	1	18
Limestone				1		1		2	1		1					6
Lipscomb									1							1
Live Oak						3			1			2				6
Llano		1				1		2			1	1	3	3	1	13
Lubbock				1	2	3	5	5	8	1	6	11	5	11	4	62
Madison						1		1			1			1	1	5
Marion			1													1
Martin													1			1
Mason			1									2				3
Matagorda					2	1	1	3	3	1	4		2	1	2	20
Maverick		1			1		3			1	2		3	1		12
McCulloch							1	1			1				1	4
McLennan		4	1	1	5	5	3	6	5	3	7	3	3	4	7	57
McMullen											1		2			3
Medina		1	2		1		1		2	1	1	1			1	11
Menard						1								1	1	3
Midland	1	2		2		6	3	1		1	4	3	1	5	3	32
Milam							1		1				1	1		4
Mills								1	1		3	1	2	1		9
Mitchell						1						1				2

Counties	2001	2002	2003	2004	2005	2006	2007	2008	2009	2010	2011	2012	2013	2014	2015	Total
Montague			1			1		1				2			1	6
Montgomery	2	2	1	3	1	5	1	7	6	3	10	15	17	11	11	95
Moore													1			1
Morris				1	1	1								1		4
Motley				1												1
Nacogdoches		1	1				2	3	4	1	2	1	2	7	1	25
Navarro			1		2	1	1	2	1	1			1	1	4	15
Newton	1								1		2				1	5
Nolan	1	1						1								3
Nueces	2	3	2	5	2	4	8	6	7	10	11	15	11	9	10	105
Ochiltree											1	1			1	3
Oldham						1										1
Orange						1		2	2	2	3	1	2	2	2	17
Palo Pinto								6	4	1		2				13
Panola					1	2			1		1	1				6
Parker	5	1	3	2			3	14		2	7	3	1	1	8	50
Parmer							1									1
Pecos			1							1		1		2	2	7
Polk					1		1	1	1	1	1	4	1	3		14
Potter	1		2	1	3	4	2	6	6	7	4	4	4	5	6	55
Presidio			2		1		1				4		2		3	13
Rains		1	1	1	1					1						5
Randall	1			1			1	1	1					1		6
Reagan		1			1									1		3
Real					1	1	1	1	1	1		1	1		1	9
Red River			1	1		2		1		1						6
Reeves			1			1		1	1	1		1			1	7
Refugio							1		1	1						3
Roberts			1												1	2
Robertson							1	2				1				4
Rockwall		1		2	1		1	1		2	5	2	2	1		18
Runnels					1		1	1	2	1	3		1	1		11
Rusk	1	1	1			1		2		3		4	1	1	2	17
San Augustine								1								1
San Jacinto		1					1	1	2			1		1		7
San Patricio	1									1		1				3
San Saba			1			1					2	1		1		6
Scurry								1		1	1		2	1	1	7
Shackelford							1	1	1	1			1		1	6

Counties	2001	2002	2003	2004	2005	2006	2007	2008	2009	2010	2011	2012	2013	2014	2015	Total
Shelby		1	1					1	1	1	1					6
Smith		1		2		4	4	11	7	6	3	7	1	5	3	54
Somervell		1	2					4	2	2	1		3	3		18
Starr	1		2	1						1	1	1	1	1	1	10
Stephens			1					3	9	3				1		17
Stonewall									3							3
Sutton												1				1
Tarrant	15	15	23	20	24	15	50	73	39	46	49	44	48	46	30	537
Taylor		3		1	9	6	2	18	21	21	12	11		3	3	110
Terrell	2												1		1	4
Terry											2	2				4
Throckmorton										1						1
Titus	1							1	1		2	1			2	8
Tom Green			1	2	2	1	1			15	3	3	3	7		38
Travis	9	15	15	11	15	19	24	58	40	46	33	39	56	56	29	465
Trinity						2		2		2	1	3				10
Tyler			1			1	2	1		1	1		3	4		14
Unknown	3	4	7	3	3	5	17	40	16	12	8	4	3	8	21	154
Upshur				1			1	2			1	4		1	1	11
Upton	2				2	1				1					1	7
Uvalde				1									2			3
Val Verde	1	1	1	1	1	3	4	1		1	1	3	1	3		22
Van Zandt					1		1	1	4	4	1	1	2		3	18
Victoria		1				1		6	6	2		3			4	23
Walker	2	1				1	1	3	3	2	1	3		5	3	25
Waller					2	1				1						4
Ward								1			1		1	1		4
Washington	1	1				1			1			1	2	2	1	10
Webb		1	2	1		2	2	6	2	3	8	3	2			32
Wharton	1								1	2		1				5
Wheeler						1	2									3
Wichita	2	2	3	1		3	5	7	4	5	2	4	6	4	2	50
Wilbarger							2									2
Willacy			1	1								1				3
Wilbarger								1								1
Williamson	2	4	4	9	4	4	6	10	9	9	21	18	10	15	13	138
Wilson										2		2	1	3		8
Winkler				1	1					1	2			1		6
Wise				1		2		3	2	1	4	2	1	1	2	19

Counties	**2001**	**2002**	**2003**	**2004**	**2005**	**2006**	**2007**	**2008**	**2009**	**2010**	**2011**	**2012**	**2013**	**2014**	**2015**	**Total**
Wood		1		1	1	1		1	1	1	1			1		9
Yoakum											1					1
Young		1		1				2			2		1			7
Zapata								1	1					1		3
Zavala								1						3		4
Total	**165**	**210**	**229**	**222**	**259**	**301**	**385**	**909**	**606**	**584**	**618**	**709**	**647**	**698**	**516**	**7058**

If a county is missing from the list, it's because no UFO sightings were logged in either the NUFORC or MUFON databases for the 2001-2015 sample period.

UFOS BY MONTH: TEXAS

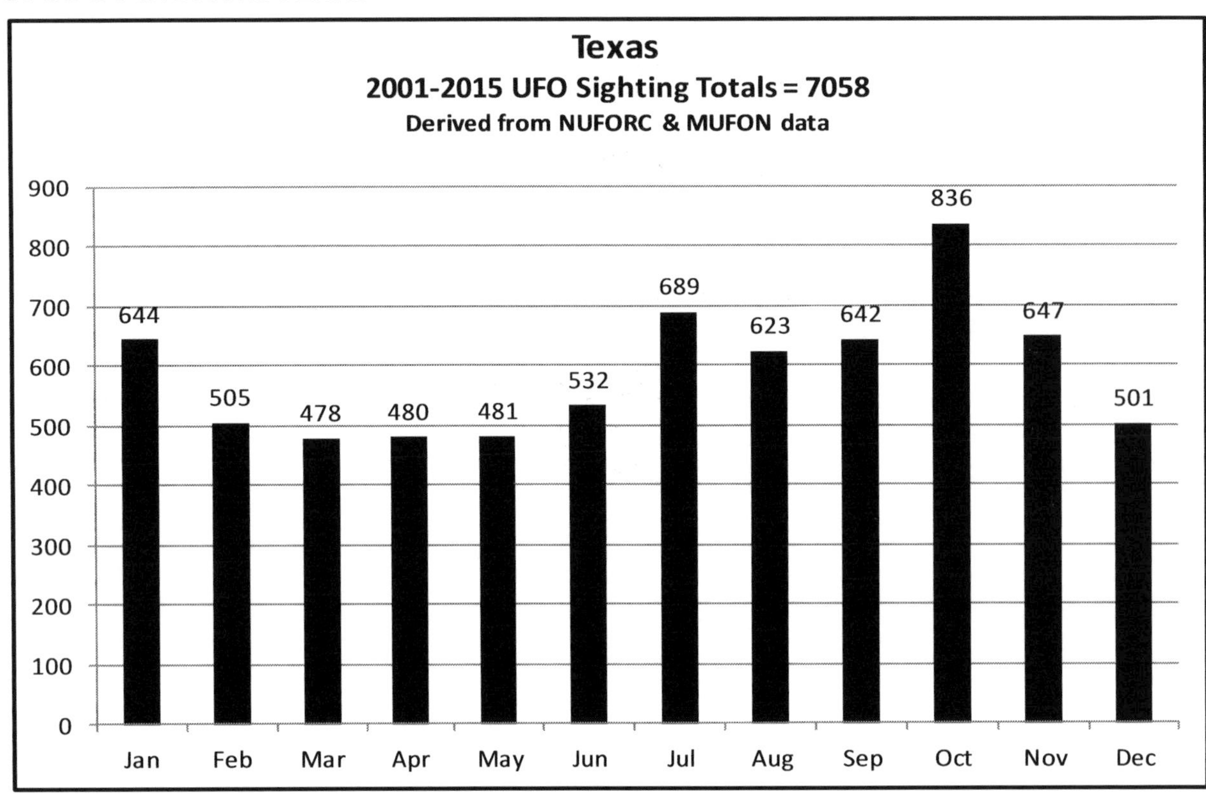

Year	Jan	Feb	Mar	Apr	May	Jun	Jul	Aug	Sep	Oct	Nov	Dec	Total
2001	9	13	14	9	10	13	16	13	19	18	11	20	165
2002	19	12	17	9	18	13	23	25	15	22	21	16	210
2003	19	13	8	11	15	7	25	23	32	31	23	22	229
2004	13	14	11	19	16	22	28	20	21	18	17	23	222
2005	13	11	23	16	22	25	28	19	27	26	33	16	259
2006	25	20	14	27	29	34	22	31	32	26	29	12	301
2007	28	14	37	22	22	25	29	37	25	53	46	47	385
2008	145	74	44	56	40	64	54	75	57	146	105	49	909
2009	67	81	40	31	32	64	54	53	38	54	60	32	606
2010	38	42	52	41	45	34	50	40	60	92	47	43	584
2011	43	46	54	34	40	37	69	64	77	81	43	30	618
2012	55	52	43	63	51	42	65	67	69	58	69	75	709
2013	48	57	37	55	55	40	58	50	63	76	54	54	647
2014	63	23	44	49	46	56	128	66	54	81	47	41	698
2015	59	33	40	38	40	56	40	40	53	54	42	21	516
Total	**644**	**505**	**478**	**480**	**481**	**532**	**689**	**623**	**642**	**836**	**647**	**501**	**7058**

Distribution of Sightings between Databases: Texas

Database	Count	Percentage
MUFON	3656	51.80%
NUFORC	3402	48.20%
Total	7058	100.00%

State Demographic Information: Texas

2010 US Census Statistics	
Population	25,145,561.00
Area in Square Miles	268,596 .46
Land Area Sq. Miles	261,231 .71
Population/Square mile	96 .3

UTAH

UFO RANK 32/51

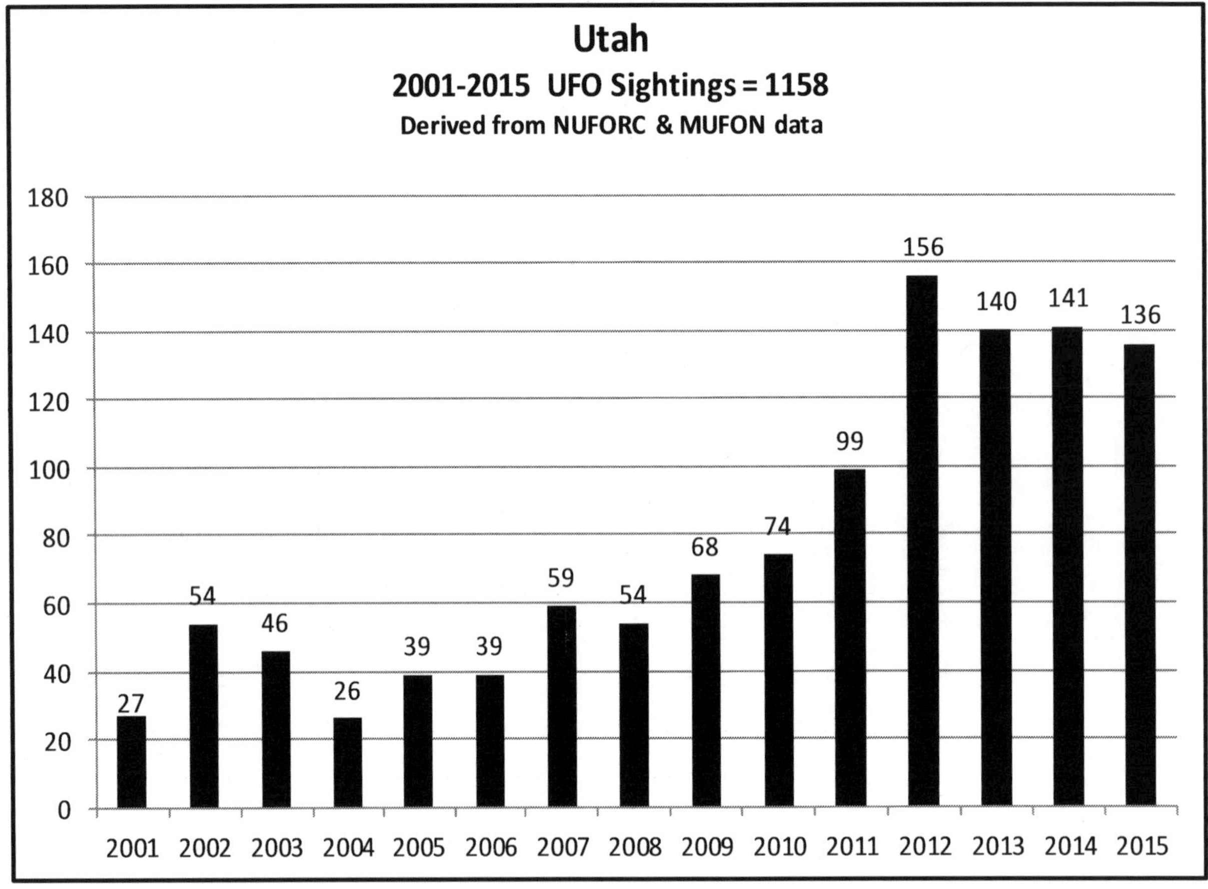

TOP TEN COUNTIES		RANK	TOP TEN SHAPES		
Salt Lake	424	1	Light	165	14.25%
Utah	165	2	Circle	131	11.31%
Davis	106	3	Sphere	119	10.28%
Washington	63	4	Unknown	114	9.84%
Weber	63	5	Triangle	102	8.81%
Tooele	52	6	Other	91	7.86%
Unknown	35	7	Fireball	82	7.08%
Iron	30	8	Disc	68	5.87%
Box Elder	25	9	Star-like	46	3.97%
Summit	21	10	Oval	38	3.28%

UFO SHAPES: UTAH

UFO Shapes	**2001**	**2002**	**2003**	**2004**	**2005**	**2006**	**2007**	**2008**	**2009**	**2010**	**2011**	**2012**	**2013**	**2014**	**2015**	**Total**
Blimp											2					2
Boomerang					1		2	2	1		1	1	2	3	2	15
Bullet/Missile					1	1		1								3
Changing		1	1		1		3	1		2	1	3	3	5	3	24
Chevron		1						1	1	1	1	1	4	1	1	12
Cigar	1	1	1		2	1	1	2	1	2	2	1	1			16
Circle	2	3	1	1	3	2	9	6	9	16	10	26	18	12	13	131
Cone	1		1			1			2			1		2		8
Cross		1			1						1		1			4
Cylinder				1						1	2	3	4	2	2	15
Diamond		1	1		3	2	1	1		1		1		3	1	15
Disc	1	6	3	2	3	3	3	2	7	3	8	10	3	6	8	68
Egg	1			1	1	1			1			2	2	2		11
Fireball		6	7	1	2	4	4	1	2	1	12	16	13	6	7	82
Flash		2	3			2	1		3	4	3	3	3	3	3	30
Formation		2	1		1		1	2	1	1	4	3	2	3	2	23
Light	6	7	8	3	3	2	5	4	9	12	19	26	23	15	23	165
Other	1	5	2	2	5	3	7	4	7	3	6	11	7	16	12	91
Oval	3	1	1	1		1	5	3	1	2	2	4	5	5	4	38
Rectangle					2						1	3	1	3	1	11
Saturn-like						1										1
Sphere	1	4	3	4	1		4	8	5	5	4	8	28	27	17	119
Sq/Rect															1	1
Star-like		1			1	1		3	6	5	5	6	5	6	7	46
Teardrop		1		1		5	2		1			1				11
Triangle	6	5	6	7	3	6	5	8	5	5	7	12	5	7	15	102
Unknown	4	6	7	2	5	3	6	5	6	10	8	14	10	14	14	114
Total	**27**	**54**	**46**	**26**	**39**	**39**	**59**	**54**	**68**	**74**	**99**	**156**	**140**	**141**	**136**	**1158**

UFOS BY COUNTY: UTAH

Counties	2001	2002	2003	2004	2005	2006	2007	2008	2009	2010	2011	2012	2013	2014	2015	Total
Beaver						1		1						1	1	4
Box Elder				1	3				2	3	4		5	2	5	25
Cache		1	1		1						1	5	3	1	1	14
Carbon			3			1				1			1	2	2	10
Davis	2	6	4		2	3	1	9	2	4	11	18	13	16	15	106
Duchesne			1		1		1	1		1	1				3	9
Emery	2	1				2	1			3		1			2	12
Garfield			1				2								2	5
Grand		1	2			2	4	2		3	1	2		1	2	20
Iron	1	1			2		1	2	1	2	8	5	4	1	2	30
Juab					2	1	1			1	1			2	1	9
Kane	1		1		1	2	1		2				1	4	2	15
Millard						2					1			1	1	5
Rich							1							1	4	6
Salt Lake	10	21	11	9	11	9	26	19	38	30	29	66	52	47	46	424
San Juan		1	1	2	2	1	2			1	2	1	1	3		17
Sanpete			1	1	1					1						4
Sevier		1	3				1		2			1		3	2	13
Summit	1			2	1	1	1	1		1		2	5	3	3	21
Tooele		4	4		3	1	1	2	7	1	7	9	6	3	4	52
Uintah			2	1			1		2		3	3	2	2	2	18
Unknown	1	1	1		1	2	4	1	3	1	5	2	2	8	3	35
Utah	7	12	3	7	1	4	6	7	2	11	14	24	25	20	22	165
Wasatch			1	1		1					1	1	2			7
Washington	1	2	3		1	3	1	7	3	2	5	8	8	13	6	63
Wayne	1				1	1	1	1			1					6
Weber		2	3	2	5	2	2	1	4	8	4	8	10	7	5	63
Total	**27**	**54**	**46**	**26**	**39**	**39**	**59**	**54**	**68**	**74**	**99**	**156**	**140**	**141**	**136**	**1158**

If a county is missing from the list, it's because no UFO sightings were logged in either the NUFORC or MUFON databases for the 2001-2015 sample period.

UFOS BY MONTH: UTAH

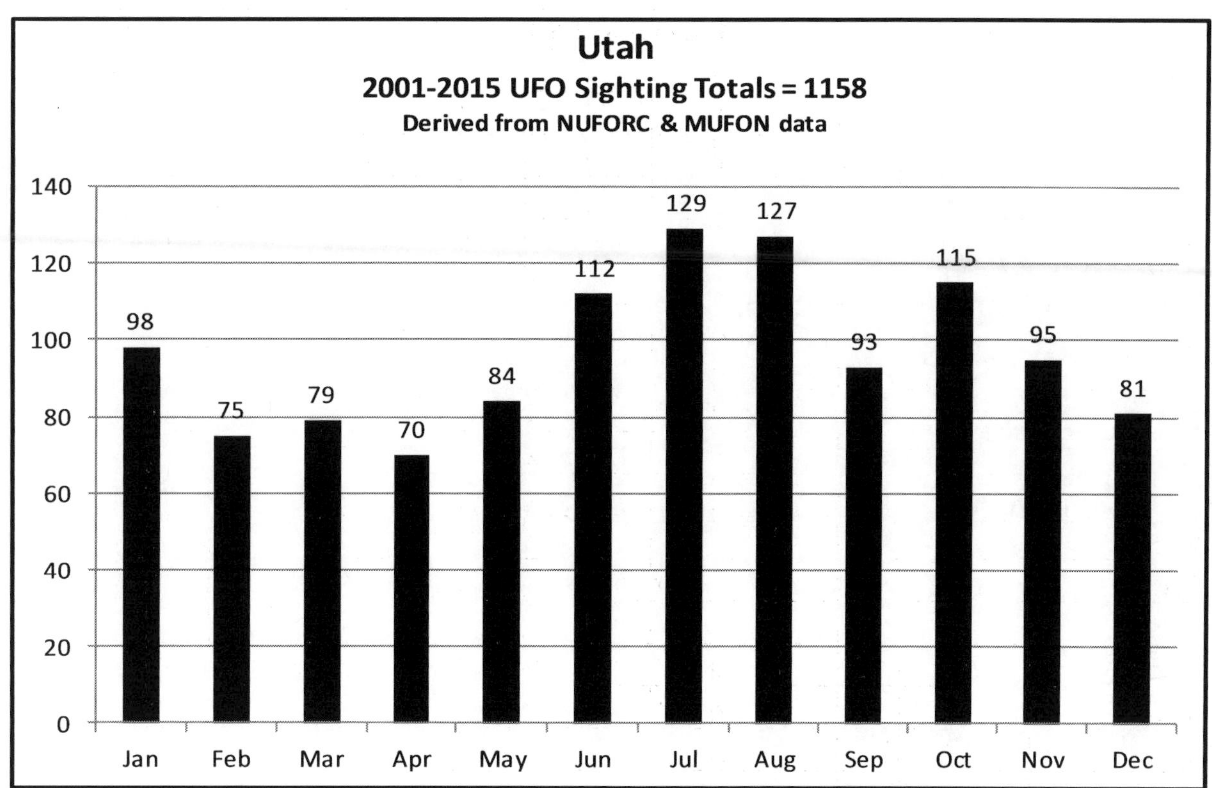

Year	Jan	Feb	Mar	Apr	May	Jun	Jul	Aug	Sep	Oct	Nov	Dec	Total
2001	1	1	3	2	3	1	6	3	4	2		1	27
2002	3	5	1	2	5	7	6	6	3	9	5	2	54
2003	4	3	1	2	3	9	6	3	6	6	1	2	46
2004		1		2	3	5	4	4	5			2	26
2005	1	2		3	1	5	2	2	6	10	7		39
2006	2	1		4	4	7	2	7	3	2	4	3	39
2007	3	1	5	1	3	7	11	11	4	9	2	2	59
2008	3	1	4	5	1	5	1	7	6	8	8	5	54
2009	8	4	15		3	6	12	10	3	1	4	2	68
2010			2	4	9	13	15	8	9	3	5	6	74
2011	9	8	6	3	10	5	10	8	9	10	9	12	99
2012	22	16	12	13	17	6	18	14	6	10	14	8	156
2013	14	3	9	12	10	12	8	13	10	15	17	17	140
2014	16	12	14	8	6	13	15	14	5	19	5	14	141
2015	12	17	7	9	6	11	13	17	14	11	14	5	136
Total	**98**	**75**	**79**	**70**	**84**	**112**	**129**	**127**	**93**	**115**	**95**	**81**	**1158**

Distribution of Sightings between Databases: Utah

Database	Count	Percentage
MUFON	440	38.00%
NUFORC	718	62.00%
Total	1158	100.00%

State Demographic Information: Utah

2010 US Census Statistics	
Population	2,763,885.00
Area in Square Miles	84,896 .88
Land Area Sq. Miles	82,169 .62
Population/Square mile	33 .6

VERMONT

UFO RANK 45/51

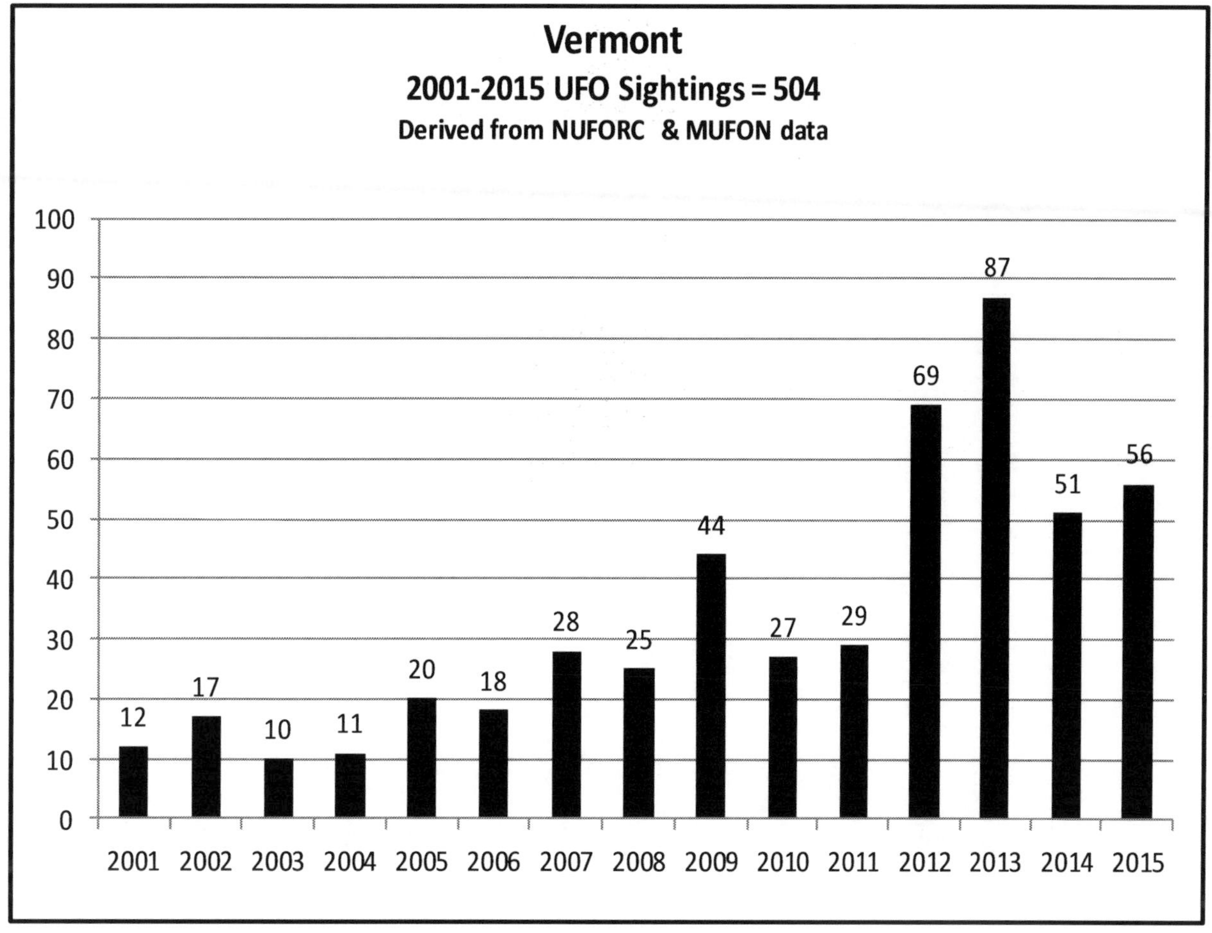

TOP TEN COUNTIES		RANK	TOP TEN SHAPES		
Chittenden	116	1	Light	81	16.07%
Washington	62	2	Circle	61	12.10%
Rutland	48	3	Unknown	57	11.31%
Bennington	43	4	Sphere	54	10.71%
Windham	39	5	Triangle	38	7.54%
Windsor	33	6	Other	34	6.75%
Orange	28	7	Fireball	33	6.55%
Addison	27	8	Oval	16	3.17%
Caledonia	26	9	Formation	15	2.98%
Franklin	26	10	Star-like	14	2.78%

UFO SHAPES: VERMONT

UFO Shapes	2001	2002	2003	2004	2005	2006	2007	2008	2009	2010	2011	2012	2013	2014	2015	Total
Blimp												2	1			3
Boomerang										1			2	1		4
Bullet/Missile						1	1		1						1	4
Changing				1	1				1		1	1	2	3		10
Chevron											1			1		2
Cigar		1					2		2	2	1	1			1	10
Circle		3			1	3	3	2	9	2	2	9	11	7	9	61
Cone		1							4				1	1		7
Cross									1	1		1				3
Cylinder		1			1		1		1			1	2	1	1	9
Diamond								1	1			1	2			5
Disc								1	1		1		3	1	2	9
Disk		1	1		1		4	2				1	1	1	1	13
Egg					1	1										2
Fireball							1			3	4	11	8	5	1	33
Flash	2				2				1		1	1	1		1	9
Formation	2	1					1	1	1			1	5	1	2	15
Light	2	1	5	3	1	4	2	4	7	2	6	8	20	7	9	81
Other	2	3	1	3	2	3	1		1	1	1	5	3	3	5	34
Oval		1					2	1	1	1	1	1	5		3	16
Rectangle		1				1					1		1	3	1	8
Sphere				1	3	2	1	1	3	8	1	9	10	6	9	54
Star-like						1	1	1	2	1	2	1	1	2	2	14
Teardrop							1		1		1					3
Triangle	2	1	2		1		1	4	1	1	4	12	4	3	2	38
Unknown	2	2	1	3	6	2	6	7	5	4	1	3	4	5	6	57
Total	**12**	**17**	**10**	**11**	**20**	**18**	**28**	**25**	**44**	**27**	**29**	**69**	**87**	**51**	**56**	**504**

UFOS BY COUNTY: VERMONT

Counties	**2001**	**2002**	**2003**	**2004**	**2005**	**2006**	**2007**	**2008**	**2009**	**2010**	**2011**	**2012**	**2013**	**2014**	**2015**	**Total**
Addison	2	1	2			1		4	4		1	5	4	1	2	27
Bennington	2	2	1	1	2	5	2	2	3	1	3	11	4	2	2	43
Caledonia	1	1	2				3	1	3		1	3	4	4	3	26
Chittenden		2	2	2	4	2	6	3	16	5	8	13	21	13	19	116
Essex					4		1		1				1	1	1	9
Franklin	1			1			1	2	4	2	1	3	5	4	2	26
Grand Isle	1	2	2								1				1	7
Lamoille	1					1	4			1	3	1	3	3	1	18
Orange		1		1	2	1	5	1	2		1	3	3	4	4	28
Orleans		1		1					1	1	1	3		3		11
Rutland		3		2		2	2		2	6	3	4	9	8	7	48
Unknown	1					1		2	1				4	1	1	11
Washington	2			1	3	3	3	2	4	6	3	10	17	2	6	62
Windham	1	1			3	2	1	7	2	3	1	5	7	3	3	39
Windsor		3	1	2	2			1	1	2	2	8	5	2	4	33
Total	**12**	**17**	**10**	**11**	**20**	**18**	**28**	**25**	**44**	**27**	**29**	**69**	**87**	**51**	**56**	**504**

If a county is missing from the list, it's because no UFO sightings were logged in either the NUFORC or MUFON databases for the 2001-2015 sample period.

UFOS BY MONTH: VERMONT

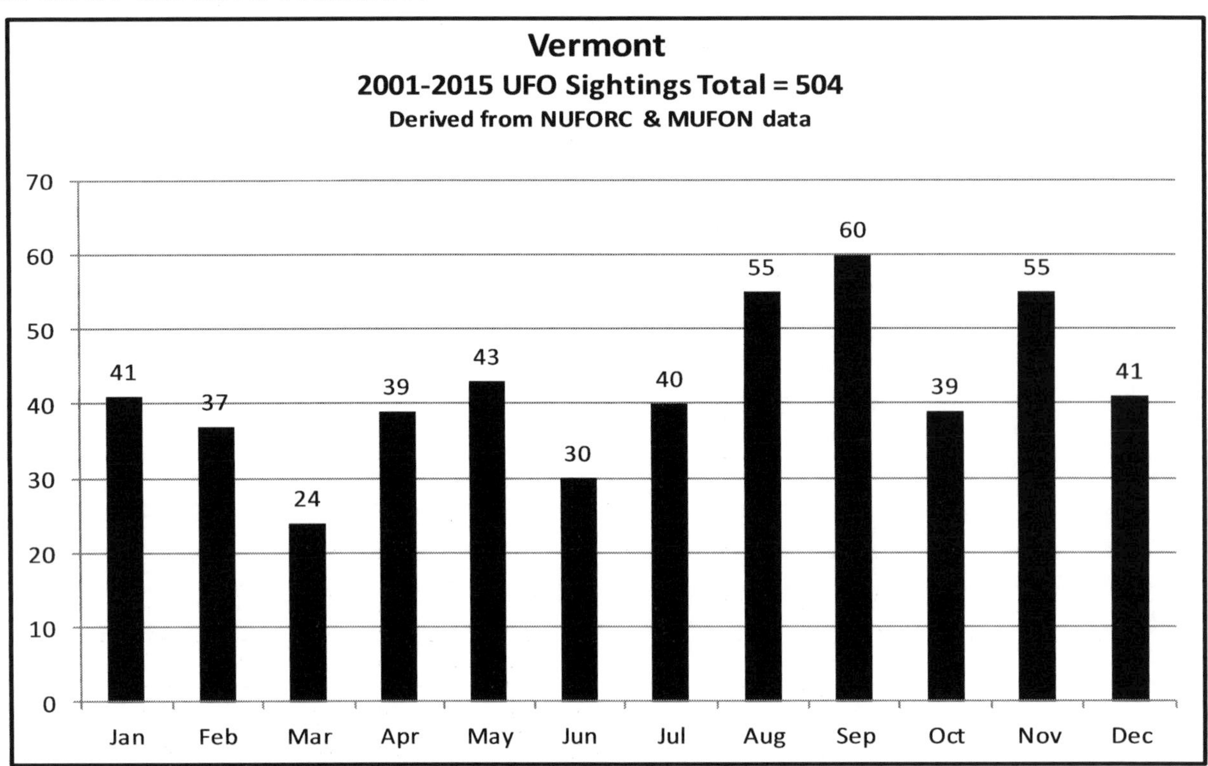

Year	Jan	Feb	Mar	Apr	May	Jun	Jul	Aug	Sep	Oct	Nov	Dec	Total
2001	1	2	4	1				2			1	1	12
2002	3	2			2		2	2	3	2	1		17
2003				1	1	2		1	1	1	2	1	10
2004	1		1			1		3	1	3	1		11
2005	2	2	5	1		2	3	1	1	2		1	20
2006	3	2		1	3		1	3	3		1	1	18
2007	2	4	3	1	2	2		3	3	1	1	6	28
2008	2	1		2	4	3			7	3		3	25
2009	4	1	2	6	4	2	2	1	14	1	6	1	44
2010		2	2	8	1	1	5	2	3		3		27
2011	2	3			1	3	5	4	7			4	29
2012	8	5	2	4	8	4	1	12	3	6	8	8	69
2013	2	7			8	3	6	9	5	13	24	10	87
2014	2	6	2	4	1	5	8	5	5	6	2	5	51
2015	9		3	10	8	2	7	7	4	1	5		56
Total	**41**	**37**	**24**	**39**	**43**	**30**	**40**	**55**	**60**	**39**	**55**	**41**	**504**

BONUS - UFOs by County & Month: Vermont

Counties	Jan	Feb	Mar	Apr	May	Jun	Jul	Aug	Sep	Oct	Nov	Dec	Total
Addison	1	1	1	2	4	2	1	3	6	1	3	2	27
Bennington	3	1		4	3	6	5	5	6	2	6	2	43
Caledonia	1	2	2	2	2		3	1	1	3	4	5	26
Chittenden	7	12	4	17	8	4	10	13	9	16	8	8	116
Essex	1	1	1	1		1	1		2			1	9
Franklin				1	5	1	4	2	5	2	4	2	26
Grand Isle	1		1	1		2		1			1		7
Lamoille		1		1	1		2	5	5		2	1	18
Orange	6	1	2		1	1	2	1	4	1	4	5	28
Orleans		1			3		1	3	1		1	1	11
Rutland	5		5	6	2	3	3	11	5	1	6	1	48
Unknown	2	3		1		1			1		2	1	11
Washington	3	5	2	1	8	5	5	3	8	4	10	8	62
Windham	5	6	3	2	4	2	2	3	5	5		2	39
Windsor	6	3	3		2	2	1	4	2	4	4	2	33
Total	**41**	**37**	**24**	**39**	**43**	**30**	**40**	**55**	**60**	**39**	**55**	**41**	**504**

Distribution of Sightings between Databases: Vermont

Database	Count	Percentage
MUFON	139	27.58%
NUFORC	365	72.42%
Total	504	100.00%

State Demographic Information: Vermont

2010 US Census Statistics	
Population	625,741.00
Area in Square Miles	9,616 .36
Land Area Sq. Miles	9,216 .66
Population/Square mile	67 .9

VIRGINIA UFO RANK 18/51

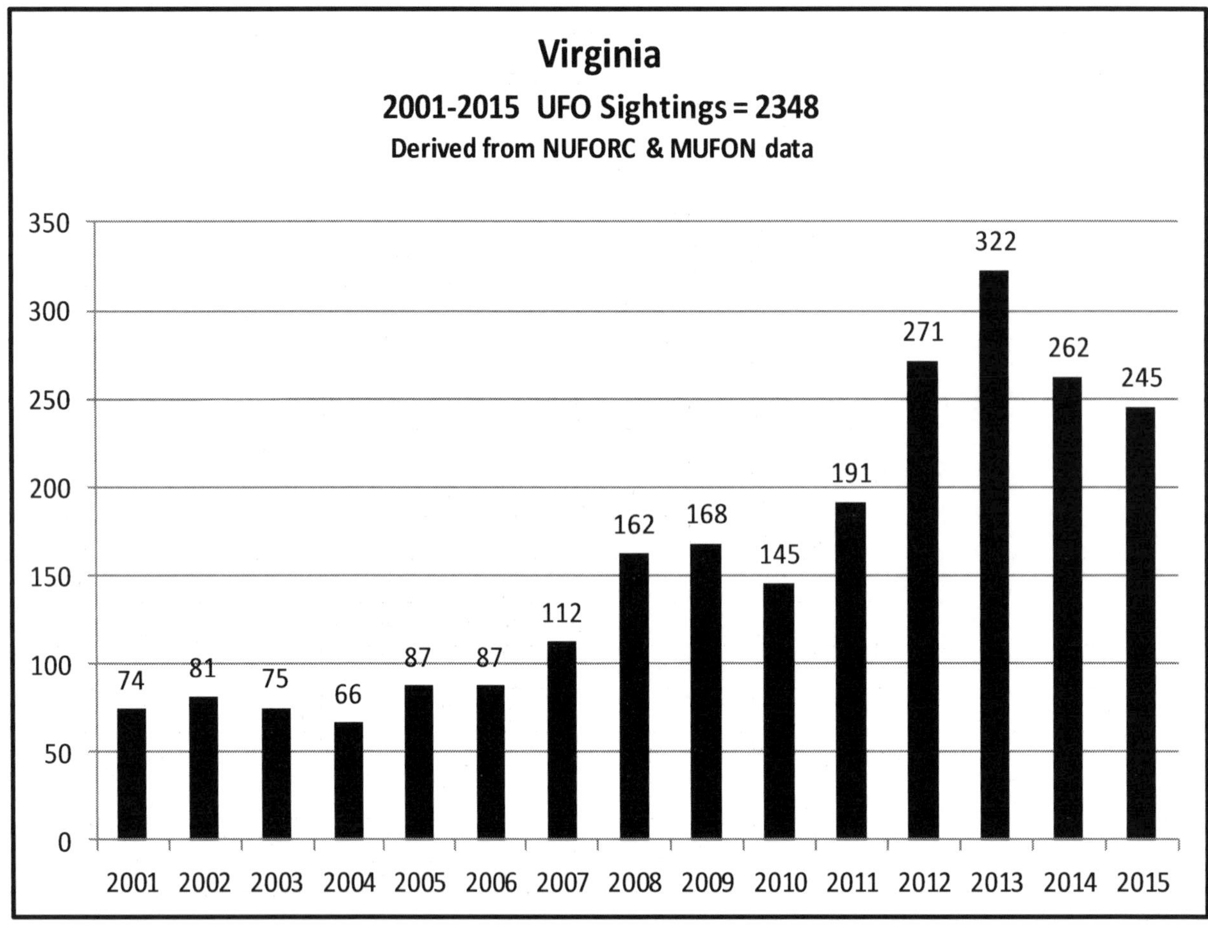

TOP TEN COUNTIES		RANK	TOP TEN SHAPES		
Fairfax	191	1	Light	310	13.20%
Virginia Beach City	161	2	Circle	273	11.63%
Richmond City	148	3	Sphere	256	10.90%
Unknown	112	4	Unknown	240	10.22%
Prince William	106	5	Triangle	221	9.41%
Loudoun	96	6	Fireball	152	6.47%
Alexandria City	63	7	Other	148	6.30%
Fredericksburg City	53	8	Oval	87	3.71%
Roanoke City	52	9	Star-like	80	3.41%
Chesapeake City	51	10	Cigar	71	3.02%

UFO SHAPES: VIRGINA

UFO Shapes	**2001**	**2002**	**2003**	**2004**	**2005**	**2006**	**2007**	**2008**	**2009**	**2010**	**2011**	**2012**	**2013**	**2014**	**2015**	**Total**
Blimp								1	1		1	1	2		2	8
Boomerang			1			1		1			4		3	4	2	16
Bullet/Missile					1	1	2	1		1	1	2	1		1	11
Changing	2	1	2	1	4	3	1	1	3	2	1	7	5	2	5	40
Chevron	1	5	1			1	1	1		1	4	2	4	5	2	28
Cigar	4		6	3	5	1	3	2	7	11	8	5	8	5	3	71
Circle	2	4	10	6	6	10	15	22	21	10	21	44	45	27	30	273
Cone			1		2		1		3	1		3				11
Cross		1					1	1			1	2				6
Cylinder	1	1	1	3	2		2	4	4	3	5	10		4	3	43
Diamond	5			3	2		1	4	5	3	4	3	9	5	4	48
Disc	1	1		4	1	2	10	5	2		2	8	9	5	5	55
Disk	3	5	3	1	5	3	2	6	4	8	4	2	5	9	2	62
Egg		2		1		2		1		1		1	4	2	3	17
Fireball	2	3	7	2	5	5	4	9	10	7	9	21	25	26	17	152
Flash	2		3		1	1	3	4	8	2	7	5	5	7	5	53
Formation	2	2		2		2		3	4		5	5	8	12	3	48
Light	8	17	11	12	6	13	13	14	24	13	20	22	54	34	49	310
N/A														4	3	7
Other	7	14	3	4	11	7	9	6	8	9	7	13	20	17	13	148
Oval	3	2		1	3	2	4	11	6	7	13	9	9	10	7	87
Rectangle	4	1		1			2	4	1		1	3	1	5	4	27
Saturn-like								1			1		2	3		7
Sphere	4	4	6	4	7	7	11	21	14	21	25	28	41	33	30	256
Squ/Rect													1	2	6	9
Star-like					2	2	1	3	11	15	11	14	4	9	8	80
Teardrop		2	2	1			1	2		1		4	1			14
Triangle	10	6	9	6	12	13	9	18	10	10	19	26	35	14	24	221
Unknown	13	10	9	11	12	11	16	16	22	19	17	31	21	18	14	240
Total	**74**	**81**	**75**	**66**	**87**	**87**	**112**	**162**	**168**	**145**	**191**	**271**	**322**	**262**	**245**	**2348**

UFOS BY COUNTY: VIRGINIA

Counties	2001	2002	2003	2004	2005	2006	2007	2008	2009	2010	2011	2012	2013	2014	2015	Total
Accomack			1			1		4	2	1	1		4	2	5	21
Albemarle	3	1	2	3	4	3	1	1	2	2		6	10	6	6	50
Alexandria City	1	1	11	4	1	4	3	3	1	4	5	7	6	3	9	63
Alleghany						1	2	1			2			1	1	8
Amelia					1											1
Amherst	2				1				1	7	4		2		1	18
Appomattox															1	1
Arlington		3	2	2		6	5	3	5	3	1	3	5	5	3	46
Augusta	1	1			1		1			5		6	2	2	1	20
Bath										1		1		1		3
Bedford				1	1		2	2	1			10	1	2	2	22
Botetourt				1	1			2		3	1					8
Bristol									1		3	2	2	1	2	11
Buchanan					1							3	1	1		6
Buckingham		2												1		3
Buena Vista City	1															1
Campbell					1				1	1		2			1	6
Caroline					1				1		1		1	1	1	6
Carroll				1		1	1		1	1	3	6	2	1		17
Charlotte										1	1		1	1	1	5
Chesapeake City	2	1	1		1		2	1	4	4	2	7	11	8	7	51
Chesterfield	1	1	3	1	3	2	1	2	2	5	1	4	9	6	9	50
Clarke		1								1	1	1	1		1	6
Colonial Heights City						1						2	1		2	6
Covington City	1	1			1								1	1		5
Craig						1							2		1	4
Culpeper			1	2	1	1		3		1	1		1	2	2	15
Danville City	1			1			2	1	2	4	2	3	1	4	1	22
Dickenson								1						1	1	3
Dinwiddie														2		2
Essex											1		1	4		6
Fairfax	7	12	7	10	9	8	13	10	15	12	9	15	27	23	14	191
Falls Church City	1	2	1			1		1	1		4	1	3	3	2	20
Fauquier		3	1		1					1	4	1	2	4	1	18
Fayette	1									1			1			3
Floyd									1				1			2
Fluvanna									1		1	2	1			5

Counties	2001	2002	2003	2004	2005	2006	2007	2008	2009	2010	2011	2012	2013	2014	2015	Total
Franklin	1					2	2			1	1	3	1	2	1	14
Franklin City							4	1				1				6
Frederick								1	1	1		3	2	2		10
Fredericksburg City	1		1	3	2	2	1	2	3	2	10	8	9	3	6	53
Giles		1					10	6	2		1					20
Gloucester					1				1		3	2	2		2	11
Goochland										1		2	2	1		6
Grayson	1		1		1				1	1		1	2		2	10
Greene									1	1			1	1		4
Greensville											1					1
Halifax	7		1			1						1			2	12
Hampton														1		1
Hampton City	1	1	1	2		1		1	1	3	6	4	6	3	5	35
Hanover	1				3	2			1		1	2	4	4	5	23
Harrisonburg City	1						1	2	2	2	5	1	2		3	19
Henrico		1			1	1	1	3	2	1	4	3	5	2	2	26
Henry										2	1				1	4
Hopewell City						2	1	1	1		2	2		2		11
Howard															1	1
Isle Of Wight				1		1	1	2			1		1	2	2	11
James City	1	2	1	1	1	1	1	3	1	3		2	4	2		23
Kanawha									1				1			2
King And Queen				1												1
King George						1		1			1	1	1	2	3	10
King William									1	1		1			2	5
Lancaster		1								1		2		3	1	8
Lee					1				1			3	1		1	7
Lexington City								1								1
Loudoun	4	2		1	5	1	4	7	8	4	13	10	12	14	11	96
Louisa	1							1	2	1		2		1	1	9
Lunenburg													1			1
Lynchburg City		1		2	4			2	1	4	2	3	3	5	3	30
Madison							3	1		1						5
Manassas Park City										1				1		2
Martinsville City											1	1		1		3
Mecklenburg						1			2					2	1	6
Middlesex						1		1	1		1			2		6

Counties	2001	2002	2003	2004	2005	2006	2007	2008	2009	2010	2011	2012	2013	2014	2015	Total
Montgomery		2	1			1		1	2		3	4	4	1		19
Nelson			1	1	1	2				1		1				7
New Kent		1				1				1		1	1			5
Newport News City	4	2				1	2	3	2	1	2	2	4	4	4	31
Norfolk	1	3		1	2		3	2	7	4	2	9	6	4	2	46
Northampton													1		1	2
Northumberland								1	3	2	1					7
Norton												1				1
Norton City							1				3					4
Nottoway	1						1							1		3
Orange														1		1
Orange				3							1					4
Page		1	1		4	1			2			1	1	2	1	14
Patrick			1				1		3			1	1			7
Petersburg City									1		1		1	2		5
Pittsylvania	2	1	3			1	3		2			2			2	16
Poquoson City		2						1	1							4
Portsmouth City				1		1	2	1	1	1	1	2	2	4	8	24
Powhatan						1						1	1	1	1	5
Prince Edward	1					1			1			1			1	5
Prince George	1	1	1								1		1			5
Prince William	4	1	4	4	5	3	1	11	10	8	5	3	21	14	12	106
Princess Anne													1			1
Pulaski		2		1	3	1							1	2	1	11
Radford								1	1		1	1				4
Richmond									1		1					2
Richmond City	5	9	5	7	5	9	7	7	8	9	10	10	27	14	16	148
Roanoke							1	1			1	2		2		7
Roanoke City	2	1	2		2	1	1	7	6	1	6	7	9	4	3	52
Rockbridge	1										2			1		4
Rockingham									3	2	2	1	1	2	2	13
Russell			1		2							2	1	2		8
Salem					1		1	1	2	1			1		3	10
Scott			1			1	2					3				7
Shenandoah			1	1			4	1	1	1	3	3	2			17
Smyth	3	1	1		1	1	1	1	2			2	1		2	16
Southampton		1						1			2	1	1		1	7
Spotsylvania		1			1		1	1	1	1	2	3		1	1	13

Counties	2001	2002	2003	2004	2005	2006	2007	2008	2009	2010	2011	2012	2013	2014	2015	Total
Stafford			1			2	2	3			2	7	3		2	22
Staunton City			1				1	1		2	1	1	3	1	4	15
Suffolk City				1	1	1		1	2		1		6	1	1	15
Surry			1					6			1	2	3			13
Tazewell					1	1	1	5				1				9
Unknown	2	4	1	1	1	3	4	8	5	2	17	21	12	16	15	112
Virginia Beach										1						1
Virginia Beach City	4	7	9	3	5	3	6	12	16	8	12	12	28	23	13	161
Warren		1	1	1		1		1	3	3	1	5	3	5	9	34
Washington			2	1	1			4	1	3		5	2	3	3	25
Waynesboro City	1			1	1	1		1			1	1	4	1	1	13
Westmoreland										1					2	3
Wight								1								1
Winchester City			1	1				2	4	1		5	4	4	1	23
Wise		2			1	1	2	2		2	1	2		1	1	15
Wood				1		1										2
Wythe							2		1		1	3	3	1	2	13
York	1				1			3			1	2	2	2		12
Total	**74**	**81**	**75**	**66**	**87**	**87**	**112**	**162**	**168**	**145**	**191**	**271**	**322**	**262**	**245**	**2348**

If a county is missing from the list, it's because no UFO sightings were logged in either the NUFORC or MUFON databases for the 2001-2015 sample period.

UFOS BY MONTH: VIRGINIA

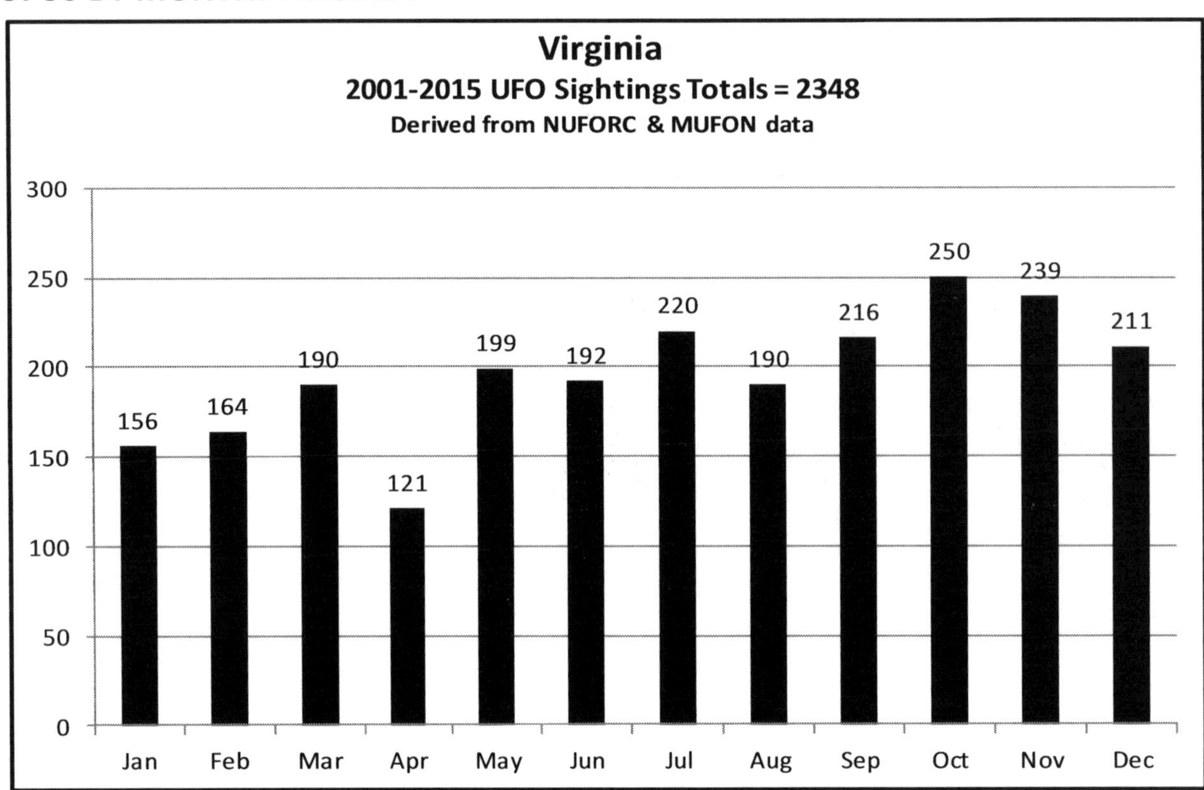

Year	Jan	Feb	Mar	Apr	May	Jun	Jul	Aug	Sep	Oct	Nov	Dec	Total
2001	4	7	6	5	4	4	5	5	11	8	8	7	74
2002	10	6	2	2	7	11	8	8	6	4	8	9	81
2003	2	3	6	1	6	9	4	6	9	8	8	13	75
2004	4	6	11	3	7	2	3	6	5	5	8	6	66
2005	2	4	11	4	9	6	12	1	7	14	7	10	87
2006	6	5	10	5	5	6	5	5	8	10	12	10	87
2007	6	9	7	7	5	14	9	9	8	12	13	13	112
2008	10	15	10	10	19	12	10	11	7	30	13	15	162
2009	11	13	29	9	17	13	10	8	22	8	15	13	168
2010	8	4	9	9	10	13	10	9	13	25	21	14	145
2011	9	7	11	15	11	16	9	29	14	30	14	26	191
2012	29	28	24	9	21	23	23	22	20	25	28	19	271
2013	18	19	19	17	22	35	40	30	35	25	36	26	322
2014	28	23	20	14	21	14	39	19	20	25	20	19	262
2015	9	15	15	11	35	14	33	22	31	21	28	11	245
Total	**156**	**164**	**190**	**121**	**199**	**192**	**220**	**190**	**216**	**250**	**239**	**211**	**2348**

Distribution of Sightings between Databases: Virginia

Database	Count	Percentage
MUFON	857	36.50%
NUFORC	1491	63.50%
Total	2348	100.00%

State Demographic Information: Virginia

2010 US Census Statistics	
Population	8,001,024.00
Area in Square Miles	42,774 .93
Land Area Sq. Miles	39,490 .09
Population/Square mile	202 .6

WASHINGTON

UFO RANK 4/51

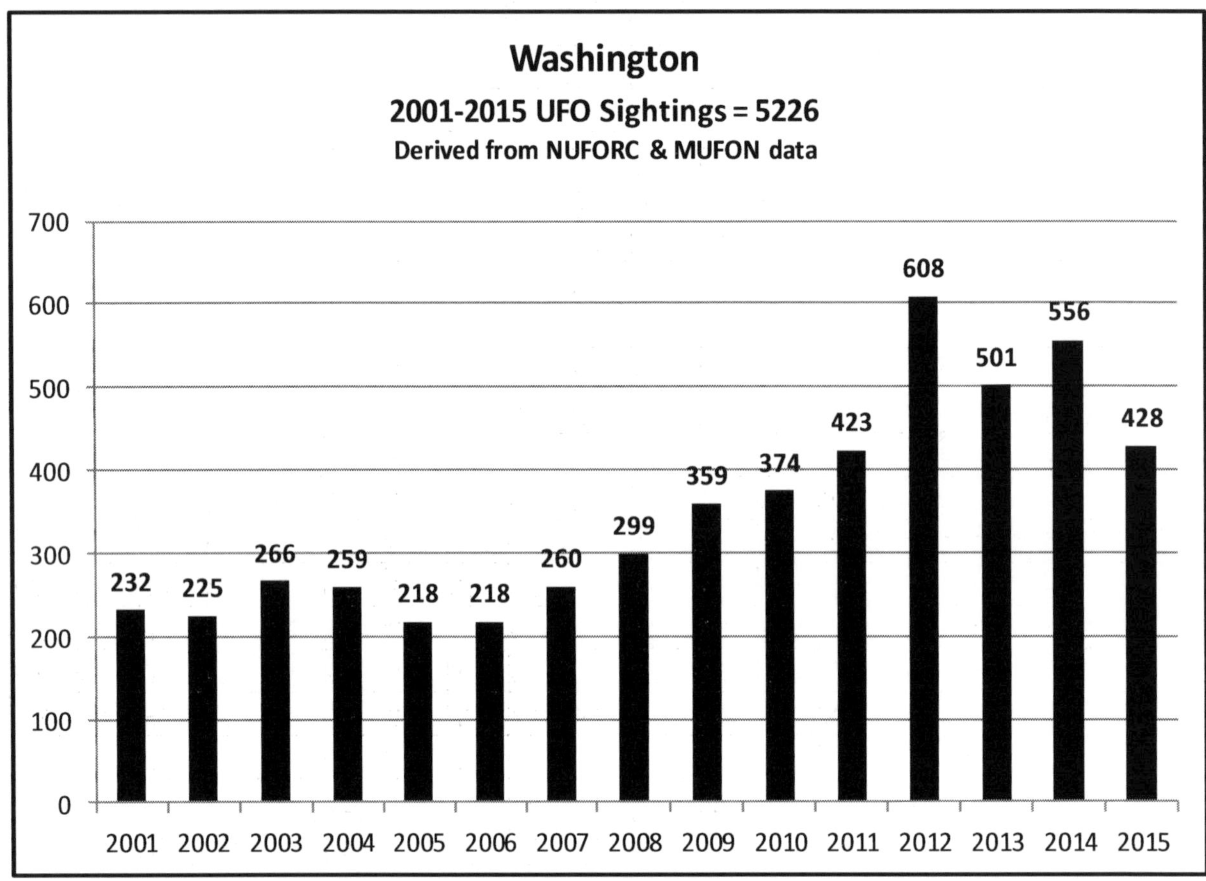

TOP TEN COUNTIES		RANK	TOP TEN SHAPES		
King	1393	1	Light	935	17.89%
Snohomish	555	2	Circle	629	12.04%
Pierce	473	3	Unknown	535	10.24%
Clark	305	4	Sphere	508	9.72%
Spokane	241	5	Fireball	433	8.29%
Kitsap	232	6	Triangle	413	7.90%
Whatcom	211	7	Other	340	6.51%
Thurston	200	8	Oval	226	4.32%
Yakima	182	9	Star-like	173	3.31%
Skagit	126	10	Disk	147	2.81%

UFO SHAPES: WASHINGTON

UFO Shapes	2001	2002	2003	2004	2005	2006	2007	2008	2009	2010	2011	2012	2013	2014	2015	Total
Blimp							2	3			2	4	1			12
Boomerang				2		3		1	4	3	3	6	4	4	2	32
Bullet/Missile	1							1	5	1	3	1	3	2	2	19
Changing	2	4	6	5	3	6	6	8	10	6	5	8	6	11	4	90
Chevron	6	3	3	3	1	4	3	5	3	2	1	8	6	9	4	61
Circle	32	17	34	20	30	21	33	32	42	42	53	87	66	56	64	629
Cone	1		1				3	1	1	2	1	7	1	3	3	24
Cross		1	2						3		2	2		3	1	14
Cylinder	3	4	9	6	4	6	2	5	5	9	5	6	8	6	7	85
Diamond	5	3	4	6	2	1	2	3	5	5	7	11	6	10	5	75
Disc	1			1	1	7	3	13	9	8	11	11	7	9	15	96
Disk	6	14	10	9	9	11	10	9	9	10	13	10	13	8	6	147
Egg	3	1	5	1	4	1	3	3	2	3	2	7	3	4		42
Fireball	24	16	17	20	11	12	8	14	15	37	34	88	64	46	27	433
Flash	4	4	5	6	8	4	9	9	6	7	10	13	12	8	14	119
Formation	7	3	6	8	3	3	7	3	5	11	10	10	7	16	6	105
Light	45	54	47	55	41	35	59	62	62	68	90	84	75	95	63	935
N/A									2				1	2	8	13
Other	17	27	16	11	21	16	16	12	22	27	23	27	25	45	35	340
Oval	10	9	10	10	8	9	11	24	18	17	14	33	27	16	10	226
Rectangle	3	3	3	2	3	4	7	3	3	4	4	5	3	7	4	58
Sphere	15	14	15	22	14	10	25	12	32	30	41	73	76	82	47	508
Sq/Rect													1		3	4
Star-like			2	2	6	7	5	20	22	14	15	17	17	24	22	173
Teardrop	1	1	2	5	2	2	2	2	4	3	1	3	2	5		35
Triangle	23	16	30	29	24	18	20	19	32	31	31	38	27	37	38	413
Unknown	23	31	39	36	23	38	24	35	38	33	41	49	39	48	38	535
Saturn-like										1	1		1			3
Total	**232**	**225**	**266**	**259**	**218**	**218**	**260**	**299**	**359**	**374**	**423**	**608**	**501**	**556**	**428**	**5226**

UFOS BY COUNTY: WASHINGTON

Counties	2001	2002	2003	2004	2005	2006	2007	2008	2009	2010	2011	2012	2013	2014	2015	Total
Adams			1	1	1		1	1				1		4	2	12
Asotin		2			1			2	3	1			4	2		15
Auburn						1			5	3	1	2	1	2	3	18
Benton	6	1	6	5	2	7	4	5	9	12	11	19	14	18	6	125
Chelan	1	5	5	8	2	5	3	6	3	9	13	15	13	9	8	105
Clallam	7	6	5	6	1	5	2	5	5	6	5	8	8	6	8	83
Clark	15	8	8	6	11	10	12	11	22	25	34	50	26	31	36	305
Columbia													1			1
Cowlitz	4	2	2	1	3	3	2	8	5	5	11	14	13	10	14	97
Douglas			2	2	1	1	1	1	1	3	3	2	3	4	1	25
Ferry		3	1	1							3	1	2	2		13
Franklin			1			1	2	1	1	1	5	4	4	5	3	28
Grant	5	2	5	2	6	4	4	4	1	10	5	3	1	2	6	60
Grays Harbor	3	3	1	2	3	4	4	2	5	7	2	8		15	6	65
Island	3	2	1	2	2	3	4		6	5	6	9	10	10	3	66
Jefferson	2	5	2	3	2		1		3	2	2	2	6	3	5	38
King	93	80	77	87	76	62	64	72	91	109	106	145	107	139	85	1393
Kitsap	8	8	12	14	8	8	24	14	11	14	10	27	30	24	20	232
Kittitas	4	2	2	2	1		3	3	2	1	4	3	3	2	3	35
Klickitat		5	1		2	10	4	4	2	1	2	3	4	4	3	45
Kootenai															1	1
Lewis	3	1	2	2	6	4	5	6	7	6	5	10	6	7	5	75
Lincoln	2		1		1			4	4		4	4	3	5	2	30
Mason	1	2	1	6	4	2	2	3	3	1	2	5	4	5	6	47
Okanogan	3		4	7	2	1	1	2	7	2	5	7		3	2	46
Pacific				2		1	1		1		1	4	1	4	3	18
Pend Oreille	1			1	1		1			1	2	3			1	11
Pierce	14	14	31	20	27	11	30	27	31	21	38	56	48	56	49	473
Port Ludlow				1				1					1	1		4
Porter							1									1
San Juan	1	1	2	1	2			1	2		3	4	2	2	2	23
Skagit	2	4	4	13	5		3	8	16	12	10	20	8	9	12	126
Skamania	1			3		1		1	1		1	7				15
Spokane			1						1			1	1			4
Snohomish	22	27	49	25	19	25	28	37	43	50	40	47	51	63	29	555
Spokane	7	13	7	7	9	10	14	14	16	15	18	32	23	32	24	241

Counties	**2001**	**2002**	**2003**	**2004**	**2005**	**2006**	**2007**	**2008**	**2009**	**2010**	**2011**	**2012**	**2013**	**2014**	**2015**	**Total**
Stevens	1	2	1		1	6		3	1	2	4	9	2	3	2	37
Thurston	7	10	9	10	5	7	4	14	12	18	13	23	29	14	25	200
Umatilla											1					1
Unknown			1	1		3	4	12	9	3	9	4	15	12	10	83
Wahkiakum				1							1	1			1	4
Walla Walla		3				3	4	3	2	2	5	11	5	5	4	47
Washington				1			1				1		1			4
Whatcom	9	9	7	5	11	4	10	15	9	9	15	24	32	30	22	211
Whitman	1	1		2	1	2	2		1	1	1	1	5	4	4	26
Yakima	6	4	14	9	2	14	14	9	18	17	21	19	14	9	12	182
Total	**232**	**225**	**266**	**259**	**218**	**218**	**260**	**299**	**359**	**374**	**423**	**608**	**501**	**556**	**428**	**5226**

If a county is missing from the list, it's because no UFO sightings were logged in either the NUFORC or MUFON databases for the 2001-2015 sample period.

UFOS BY MONTH: WASHINGTON

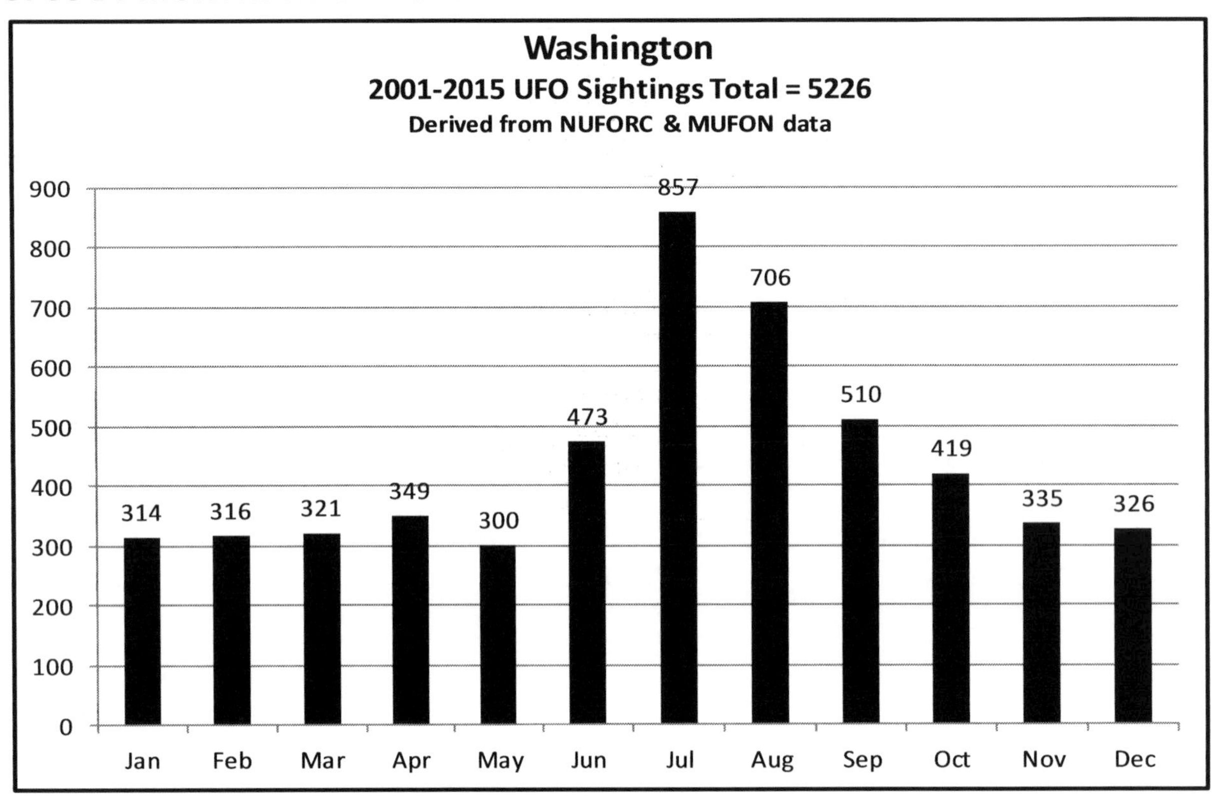

Year	Jan	Feb	Mar	Apr	May	Jun	Jul	Aug	Sep	Oct	Nov	Dec	Total
2001	18	16	25	12	10	27	16	40	22	20	18	8	232
2002	4	13	6	12	19	23	15	40	19	38	21	15	225
2003	13	21	9	12	13	14	46	38	46	26	13	15	266
2004	13	16	22	25	15	39	32	35	20	16	14	12	259
2005	16	26	18	7	12	17	39	22	25	12	11	13	218
2006	8	10	13	23	14	18	26	36	19	28	21	2	218
2007	35	11	25	27	10	24	40	27	16	19	15	11	260
2008	15	24	15	23	25	31	35	32	21	30	22	26	299
2009	19	20	23	22	39	19	76	45	58	12	9	17	359
2010	10	14	19	20	13	29	106	63	24	33	17	26	374
2011	15	33	18	28	22	33	60	62	36	38	31	47	423
2012	30	42	27	36	27	58	125	104	47	31	43	38	608
2013	29	14	34	23	24	39	96	78	43	50	38	33	501
2014	60	24	31	48	28	52	83	57	62	37	31	43	556
2015	29	32	36	31	29	50	62	27	52	29	31	20	428
Total	**314**	**316**	**321**	**349**	**300**	**473**	**857**	**706**	**510**	**419**	**335**	**326**	**5226**

Distribution of Sightings between Databases: Washington

Database	Count	Percentage
MUFON	1362	26.06%
NUFORC	3864	73.94%
Total	5226	100.00%

State Demographic Information: Washington

2010 US Census Statistics	
Population	6,724,540.00
Area in Square Miles	71,297 .95
Land Area Sq. Miles	66,455 .52
Population/Square mile	101 .2

WEST VIRGINIA UFO RANK 39/51

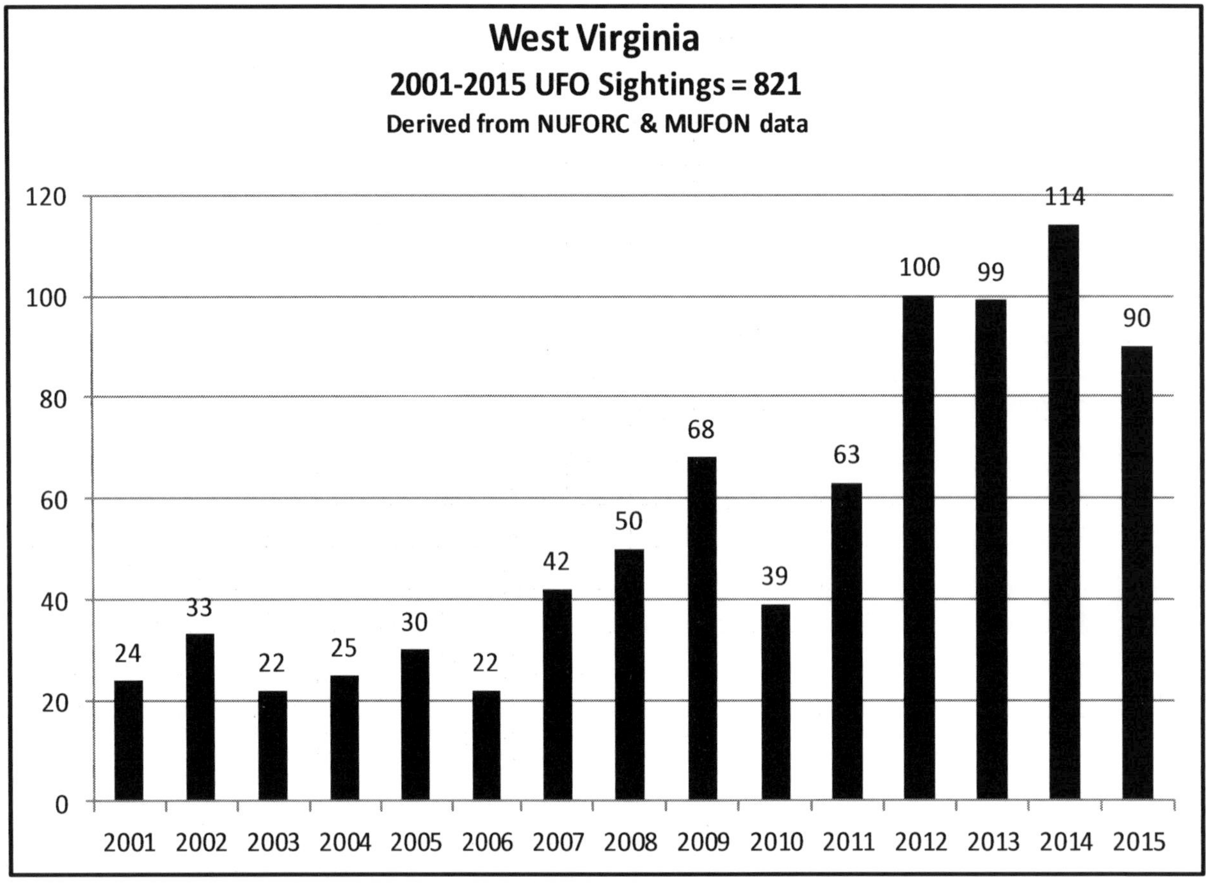

TOP TEN COUNTIES		RANK	TOP TEN SHAPES		
Kanawha	75	1	Light	112	13.64%
Cabell	72	2	Circle	104	12.67%
Berkeley	54	3	Unknown	88	10.72%
Monongalia	46	4	Triangle	84	10.23%
Harrison	36	5	Sphere	69	8.40%
Wood	36	6	Other	60	7.31%
Fayette	34	7	Fireball	51	6.21%
Mercer	31	8	Oval	40	4.87%
Marion	29	9	Cigar	34	4.14%
Jefferson	27	10	Star-like	30	3.65%

UFO SHAPES: WEST VIRGINIA

UFO Shapes	2001	2002	2003	2004	2005	2006	2007	2008	2009	2010	2011	2012	2013	2014	2015	Total
Blimp									1			2				3
Boomerang				1								2			2	5
Bullet/Missile										1						1
Changing		2		2		1	1				1		2			9
Chevron					1			1	1			1	3	1	1	9
Cigar	2		1		1	1	3	1		6	7	4	4	3	1	34
Circle	1	2	5	4	5	3	6	9	10	3	11	12	15	14	4	104
Cone							2								1	3
Cross										1		1	2			4
Cylinder		3	3	1		1		2	2			4	1	8	1	26
Diamond	1						1		1	1	1			2	3	10
Disc			1					1			2		6	1	2	13
Disk	3	1	3		1		2	1	1		1	2	1	3	3	22
Egg	1	1	1				1						1		2	7
Fireball	2	2			1	4			5	2	3	5	9	11	7	51
Flash						1		1	2	1		4	1			10
Formation						1	2	1	1		2	2	1	3	2	15
Light	4	5	1	5	5	4	5	12	12	7	8	14	11	10	9	112
N/A								1								1
Other	3	6	2	5	4	1	1	2	4	4	4	2	5	11	6	60
Oval					1		2	3	3	1	6	10	4	4	6	40
Rectangle			1								1	1	1	1	1	6
Sphere	2	1		1	1	2	3	7	6	2	5	7	8	9	15	69
Sq/Rect															1	1
Star-like					1		2	2	5	1	3	3	3	7	3	30
Teardrop							1			1	1	1				4
Triangle	1	4	2	2	3	2	7	3	5	1	4	12	12	14	12	84
Unknown	4	6	2	4	6	1	3	3	9	7	3	11	9	12	8	88
Total	**24**	**33**	**22**	**25**	**30**	**22**	**42**	**50**	**68**	**39**	**63**	**100**	**99**	**114**	**90**	**821**

UFOS BY COUNTY: WEST VIRGINIA

Counties	2001	2002	2003	2004	2005	2006	2007	2008	2009	2010	2011	2012	2013	2014	2015	Total
Barbour								2	2			2			2	8
Berkeley	1	2		3	3		2	4	4	3	4	8	2	5	13	54
Boone								1				1	1	1	1	5
Braxton					1			1			1	2	1	2	1	9
Brooke	1				1	1	1			1				1	1	7
Cabell	5	4	3	5	1	2	6	6	4	3	7	3	8	11	4	72
Clay											1					1
Doddridge				1									1	3		5
Fayette	1	3			1		2	2	1	4	2	5	6	4	3	34
Gilmer								1	1							2
Grant		2				1										3
Greenbrier	1		1						1			2		5	3	13
Hampshire							2				1	2	1	1	1	8
Hancock					1			1	3		1	4		3	4	17
Hardy		1			1			1					2			5
Harrison		2				1	3	1	4	2	2	2	7	5	7	36
Jackson	1	1	1		1		1	1				2	2	1	1	12
Jefferson		4	1					2	3	1	1	5	5	2	3	27
Kanawha	2	2	1		1	1	2	3	4	7	5	11	12	14	10	75
Lewis								1			2	1	1		1	6
Lincoln						2					1	1	1			5
Logan		1	2			1	1	1				2	1	2	1	12
Marion	1	1						1	2	2	4	5	6	4	3	29
Marshall					1		2	2	2	3	1	1	1		2	15
Mason					1			3	3	2		2	1	2	2	16
MacDowell									1				1	2		4
Mercer		2			1	4	6	1	1		3		7	5	1	31
Mineral			1				1			2			3	1	3	11
Mingo								2			2	2	1	1		8
Monongalia	1	2		4	4	1	2		4	4	2	10	1	10	1	46
Monroe												1	1	1	1	4
Morgan	2								3	1	1	3	2			12
Nicholas					1	3	1	1	2		1	3	1	2	1	16
Ohio			1	5			3				2	2	2		1	16
Pendleton	1									1			1	1		4
Pleasants					1			2			1					4
Pocahontas		1						1	1		3	1				7

Counties	2001	2002	2003	2004	2005	2006	2007	2008	2009	2010	2011	2012	2013	2014	2015	Total
Preston							1		3		2		1		1	8
Putnam		2										1	2	2	4	11
Raleigh	2		2	5	3	1	1	1	1		2	1		6	1	26
Randolph		1	1	1			1	2	1	1	3		4	4	1	20
Ritchie	1				2			1				1				5
Roane							2	1			1	1			1	6
Summers									1						1	2
Taylor									5			1		1		7
Tucker									2				1		1	4
Tyler			1			1		1	1	1		2				7
Unknown		1	2		1			1	1		4	3	3	7	3	26
Upshur						1						2	2			5
Wayne	1								4				1		4	10
Webster												1				1
Wetzel			1									1			1	3
Wirt							1							2		3
Wood	3	1	3	1	4	2	1	2	3	1	3	3	5	3	1	36
Wyoming			1										1			2
Total	**24**	**33**	**22**	**25**	**30**	**22**	**42**	**50**	**68**	**39**	**63**	**100**	**99**	**114**	**90**	**821**

If a county is missing from the list, it's because no UFO sightings were logged in either the NUFORC or MUFON databases for the 2001-2015 sample period.

UFOS BY MONTH: WEST VIRGINIA

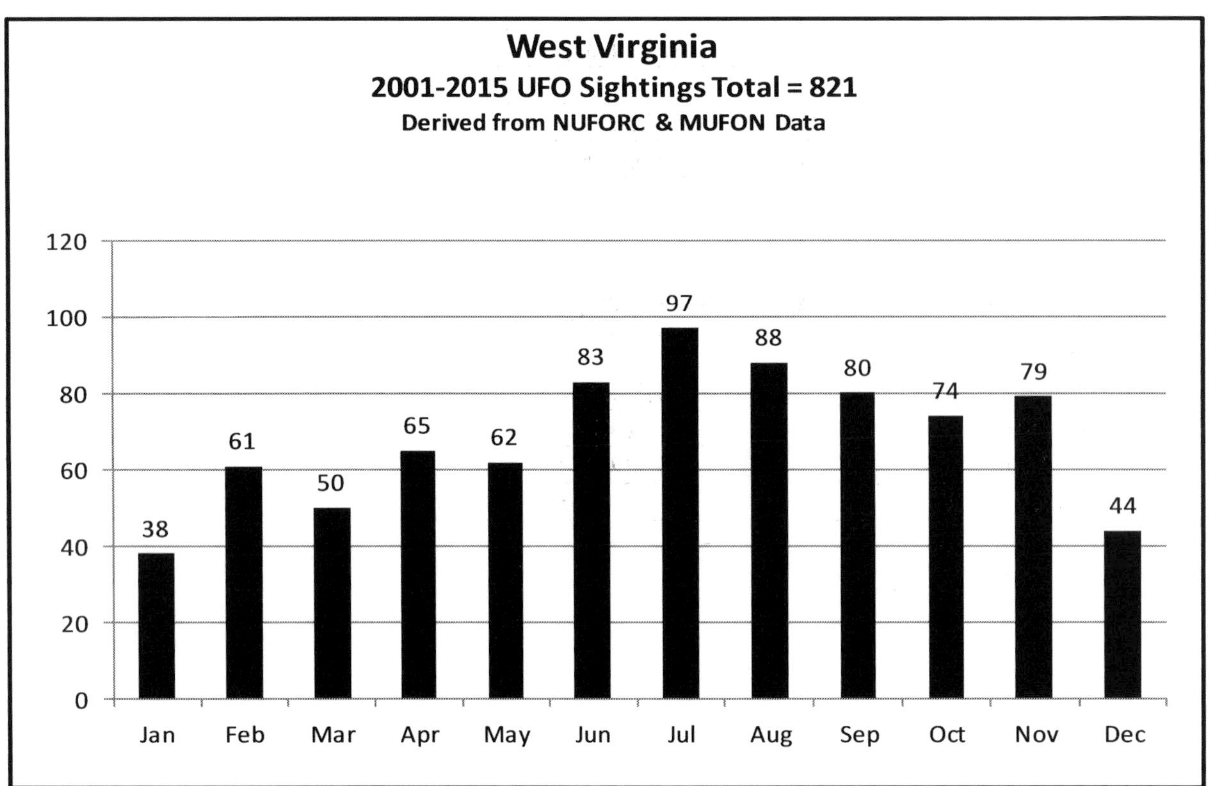

Year	Jan	Feb	Mar	Apr	May	Jun	Jul	Aug	Sep	Oct	Nov	Dec	Total
2001			2	3	1	2	2	3	3	5	3		24
2002	1	1			3	8	7	2	1	2	4	4	33
2003	1	1	1	1	2	1	1	3	2	4	2	3	22
2004		1	1		4	4	4	5		5	1		25
2005	1	4	3	3	2		3	2	5	2	4	1	30
2006	2		3	3	1	1	2	3	1	3	2	1	22
2007	4	6	4	6	3	2	1	4	4	2	2	4	42
2008	2	8	6	5	1	4	8	5	5	3	1	2	50
2009	1	4	7	4	6	5	15	2	10	7	7		68
2010	2	1	1	4	1	4	6	7	4	6	3		39
2011	1	4	4	5	7	8	9	5	3	2	6	9	63
2012	4	10	5	8	7	11	7	12	13	5	13	5	100
2013	5	1	5	5	10	9	12	13	9	9	12	9	99
2014	6	11	4	10	7	15	10	9	13	14	11	4	114
2015	8	9	4	8	7	9	10	13	7	5	8	2	90
Total	**38**	**61**	**50**	**65**	**62**	**83**	**97**	**88**	**80**	**74**	**79**	**44**	**821**

Distribution of Sightings between Databases: West Virginia

Database	Count	Percentage
MUFON	320	39.98%
NUFORC	501	61.02%
Total	821	100.00%

State Demographic Information: West Virginia

2010 US Census Statistics	
Population	1,852,994.00
Area in Square Miles	24,230 .04
Land Area Sq. Miles	24,038 .21
Population/Square mile	77 .1

WISCONSIN — UFO RANK 21/51

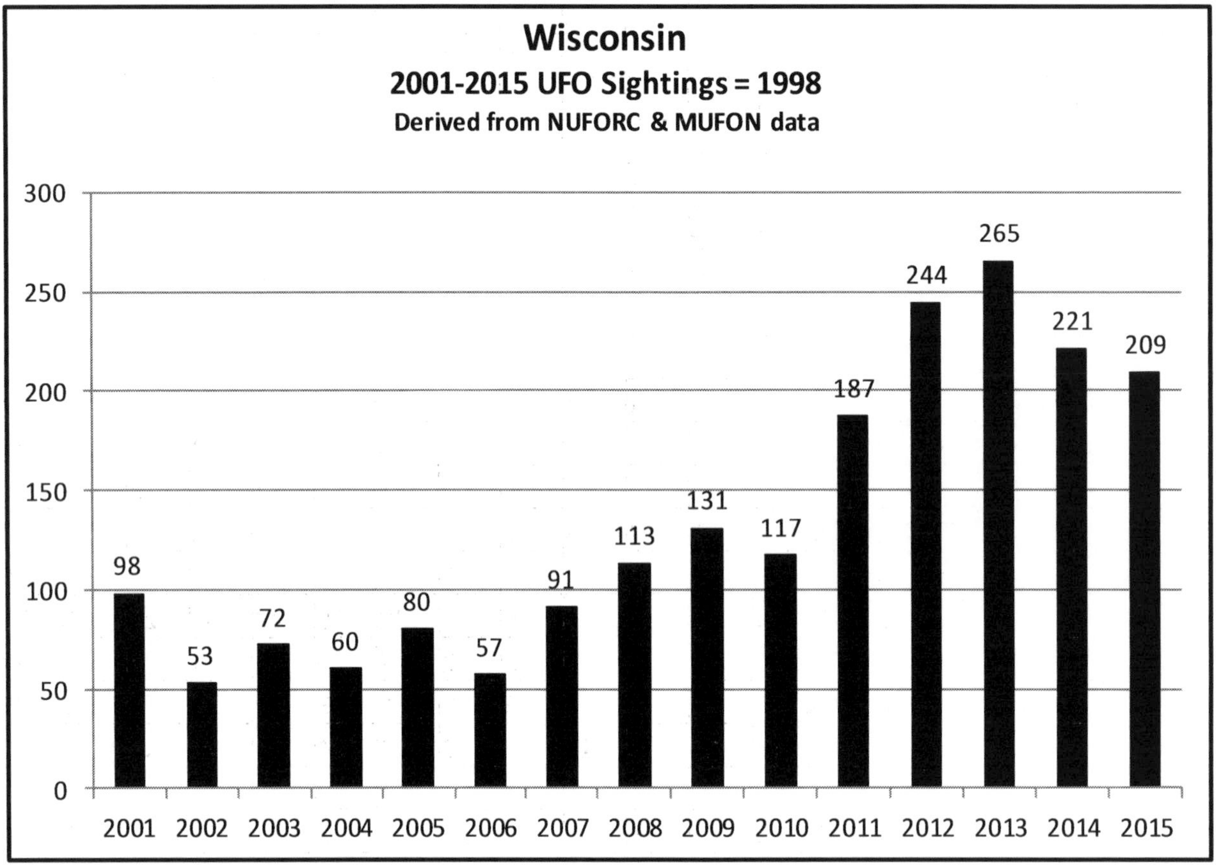

TOP TEN COUNTIES		RANK	TOP TEN SHAPES		
Milwaukee	188	1	Light	324	16.22%
Dane	164	2	Unknown	220	11.01%
Waukesha	147	3	Circle	216	10.81%
Kenosha	72	4	Sphere	195	9.76%
Brown	67	5	Triangle	177	8.86%
Outagamie	61	6	Fireball	170	8.51%
Racine	58	7	Other	124	6.21%
Winnebago	58	8	Oval	78	3.90%
Walworth	56	9	Star-like	75	3.75%
Columbia	46	10	Disk	71	3.55%

UFO SHAPES: WISCONSIN

UFO Shapes	2001	2002	2003	2004	2005	2006	2007	2008	2009	2010	2011	2012	2013	2014	2015	Total
Blimp					1		1						1		1	4
Boomerang							1	1	3	1	3	1	1	2		13
Bullet/Missile				1					1	2	1	2	2	1		10
Changing	1	2	2	1	3		1		1		3	6	1		5	26
Chevron		1	1			1		1	2			1	2	3	4	16
Cigar	3		1	3	4	1	3	1	3	2	3	1	5	4	5	39
Circle	10	5	7	5	6	3	15	12	14	16	18	30	34	23	18	216
Cone			1				1	1				3	2			8
Cross									1				1			2
Cylinder	1	1			1	1	2	1	3		4	2	2	7	2	27
Diamond			1	1	2		3	3	3	3	2	5	4	2	7	36
Disc			1								1	1		2		5
Disk	5	2	7	2	7	4	4	6	3	2	6	3	8	6	6	71
Egg	2	3			1	3		2	3						1	15
Fireball	2	1	5	4	2	3	6	4	4	10	20	39	30	23	17	170
Flash	4	3	1	2	1	1	1	5	2	7	6	3	5	2	4	47
Formation	3	1	3	5	7	1	2	6	2	1	3	7	11	6	1	59
Light	26	9	17	16	15	8	13	19	22	14	24	27	40	45	29	324
N/A											1			2	1	4
Other	8	4	5	3	2	3	6	8	13	11	9	14	15	11	12	124
Oval	4		3	3	3	4	4	5	5	5	5	8	9	8	12	78
Rectangle			1	1			1			2	1	1	6	2	1	16
Saturn-like								1			1					2
Sphere	8	2	4	3	5	6	10	10	9	8	21	26	30	19	34	195
Sq/Rect															2	2
Star-like					2	2	3	6	10	10	12	5	11	7	7	75
Teardrop	1		2	2		1	1	2	1		1		1	1	4	17
Triangle	5	13		3	6	8	6	9	9	7	19	30	19	26	17	177
Unknown	15	6	10	5	12	7	7	10	17	16	23	29	25	19	19	220
Total	**98**	**53**	**72**	**60**	**80**	**57**	**91**	**113**	**131**	**117**	**187**	**244**	**265**	**221**	**209**	**1998**

UFOS BY COUNTY: WISCONSIN

Counties	2001	2002	2003	2004	2005	2006	2007	2008	2009	2010	2011	2012	2013	2014	2015	Total
Adams	2	1	1		1		1	3	2	2	4	3	1	2	3	26
Ashland	1	2				1	1	2	1				1	1		10
Barron	1	1						2		1	1	4	2	1	2	15
Bayfield							1	2		1	1		2		1	8
Brown	4	3	2	2		2	3	2	5	3	2	9	8	15	7	67
Buffalo											2					2
Burnett			2			1							4		2	9
Burnette							1									1
Calumet						2	2	1						2	1	8
Chippewa	1			1			3	1	4	4	2		1	2	2	21
Clark			2	2	1		1		1		1	1	2		2	13
Columbia	2	1	4	3	3	2		3	1	1	9		8	7	2	46
Crawford	2		1			2	1				1	3	1	4		15
Dane	14	6	4	6	5	6	13	15	13	6	9	13	23	19	12	164
Dodge		1		1	2	1	2		3	2	4	1	2	2	1	22
Door	2	1	2			1	2		2	1	1	3	1	1	5	22
Douglas		2	1	1	2		1		1		2	6		1	2	19
Dunn							2	1	6	1	2	3	2			17
Eau Claire	1	1	1		1	1	1	1	4		1	2	5		1	20
Florence													1			1
Fond Du Lac			1				1	2	4	5	9	9	4	6	2	43
Forest			1	1								1		1		4
Grant		1		1	1		1			4		3	3		2	16
Green	1	1			1				1		1	1		2	1	9
Green Lake	4		1	1	1		1	1		1	1		5	2	1	19
Iowa							1	1	1		1	1	3	3	1	12
Iron	1			1							1	2		1	1	7
Jackson	2		1					1			2		2	2		10
Jefferson	3		2		1			1	1	2			8	5	2	25
Juneau	1	1			1	1					2	1	3	4	2	16
Kenosha	2	2	3	1	2	1	5	2	2	7	5	11	12	8	9	72
Kewaunee										1	2	1	2		1	7
La Crosse	1		1	2	1	2	1	3	5	3	5	4	6	4	2	40
Lafayette							1				2				2	5
Langlade		1		2						2	1				1	7
Lincoln			1	1	3	2		1	2	1	2	1			1	15
Manitowoc	1	1	3		1	1	1	2	1	1	2		5	3	8	30
Marathon	5	1		1	1	1	1	4	2	3	1	4	3	3	6	36

Counties	2001	2002	2003	2004	2005	2006	2007	2008	2009	2010	2011	2012	2013	2014	2015	Total
Marinette	2					1		1	2	1	1	1	4	2	3	18
Marquette								1						4	1	6
Menominee							1									1
Milwaukee	11	3	6	5	12	9	10	11	8	9	9	23	22	18	32	188
Monroe		3	2	1			1	3	3	1	2	3	1		2	22
Oconto	1					1	1		1		1	1	1	1		8
Oneida		1	1	1	2				1	2		3		1	4	16
Outagamie	3		1			1	2	3	3	5	5	9	15	3	11	61
Ozaukee	1				1	1	1	2		4	6	10			2	28
Pepin	5	1				2								1		9
Pierce		1	2	2	1	1	1		1	1	1	1	3	2		17
Polk	2			1	1		1	1	3		2	1	6	1	2	21
Portage	2		4	3	4		1	4	2		3	5	4	2		34
Price	1				1								1	1	1	5
Racine	1	2	2	3	2		2	3		4	4	8	8	8	11	58
Richland			1											1	1	3
Rock	2	2	1		2	1		1	1	2	6	7	8	9	4	46
Rusk	1						1			1	1	1		1	1	7
Saint Croix	3		1		2	1	6	1	2		3	8	2	3	6	38
Sauk			1				1	1	3		3	3	2		2	16
Sawyer		1	1		2			1	2	3	3	2		2		17
Shawano	1		1		1					1		2	3	2		11
Sheboygan	2	2	1	2	1	1		1	2	1	3	8	2	1	2	29
Taylor										1					1	2
Trempealeau		1			2				2		1	1				7
Unknown				2	1	1	2	2	4	4	6	4	6	8	6	46
Vernon		1						1				1	2	5		10
Vilas			2				2	1		2			1	3		11
Walworth					3		1	2	3	4	5	7	9	11	11	56
Washburn			1				1		2		5		1			10
Washington	1		2	1	1	1	2	4	4	2	3	9	7	7	2	46
Waukesha	2	6	5	5	6	3	4	5	12	9	19	19	22	16	14	147
Waupaca	2		1	1		1			3	3	2	5	1	2		21
Waushara		1		1	2	1	1	2			3	2	1		1	15
Winnebago	1		1	2	2	2	1	10	5	2	7	9	11	3	2	58
Wood	3	1	1	3	3	2		1		3	4	4	2	2	2	31
Total	**98**	**53**	**72**	**60**	**80**	**57**	**91**	**113**	**131**	**117**	**187**	**244**	**265**	**221**	**209**	**1998**

If a county is missing from the list, it's because no UFO sightings were logged in either the NUFORC or MUFON databases for the 2001-2015 sample period.

UFOS BY MONTH: WISCONSIN

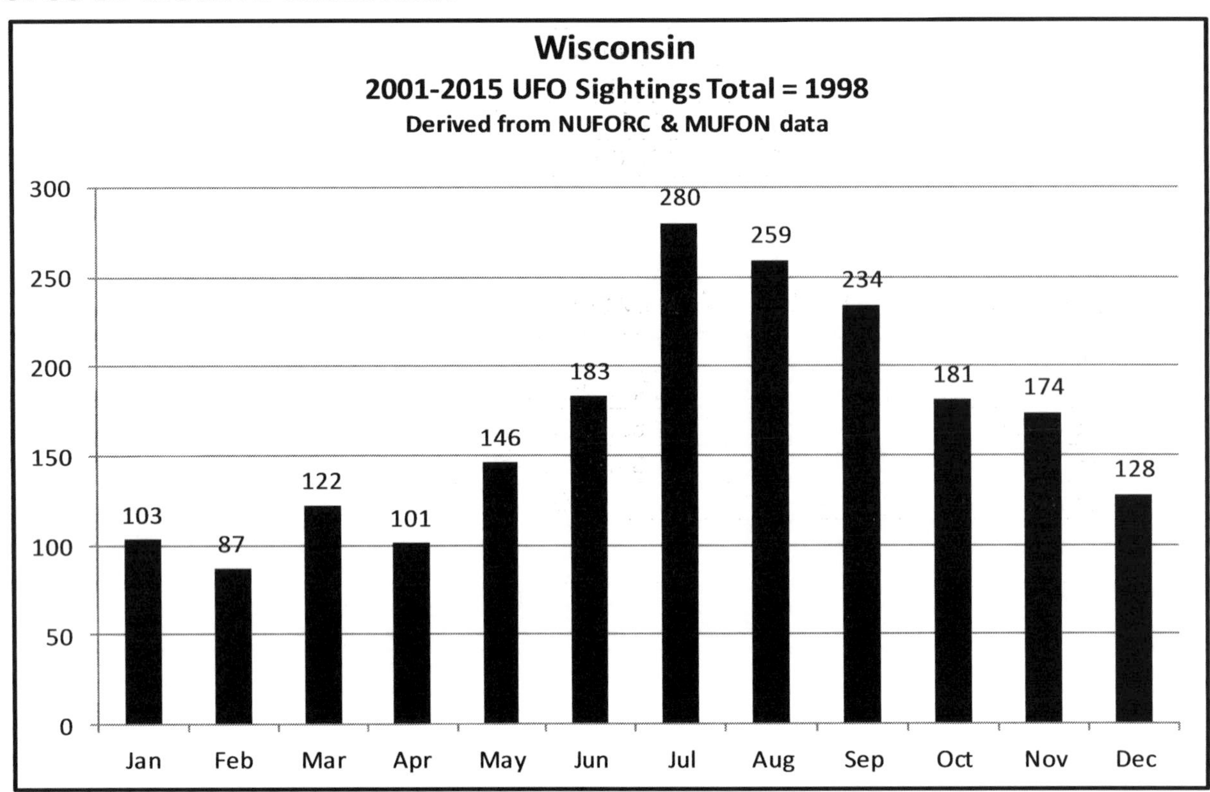

Year	Jan	Feb	Mar	Apr	May	Jun	Jul	Aug	Sep	Oct	Nov	Dec	Total
2001	7	4	16	6	4	5	26	13	8	7		2	98
2002		5		6	3	4	8	5	12	2	3	5	53
2003	10	5	2	5	5	6	6	10	1	7	9	6	72
2004	2		2	1	8	5	10	5	15	5	6	1	60
2005	8	7	8	5	1	5	7	5	15	12	4	3	80
2006	2	2	5	2	3	9	14	4	4	5	3	4	57
2007	3	7	5	7	9	5	12	14	9	11	7	2	91
2008	4	3	5	5	11	14	19	15	7	12	10	8	113
2009	7	10	5	6	13	8	22	13	22	8	13	4	131
2010	11	4	9	12	11	9	15	13	11	11	4	7	117
2011	7	12	10	2	8	14	34	18	19	24	30	9	187
2012	13	6	25	11	23	25	19	38	37	19	14	14	244
2013	9	6	6	5	15	29	36	48	28	30	36	17	265
2014	11	10	4	15	21	20	15	38	26	15	15	31	221
2015	9	6	20	13	11	25	37	20	20	13	20	15	209
Total	**103**	**87**	**122**	**101**	**146**	**183**	**280**	**259**	**234**	**181**	**174**	**128**	**1998**

Distribution of Sightings between Databases: Wisconsin

Database	Count	Percentage
MUFON	673	33.68%
NUFORC	1325	66.32%
Total	1998	100.00%

State Demographic Information: Wisconsin

2010 US Census Statistics	
Population	5,686,986.00
Area in Square Miles	65,496 .38
Land Area Sq. Miles	54,157 .80
Population/Square mile	105 .0

WYOMING

UFO RANK 47/51

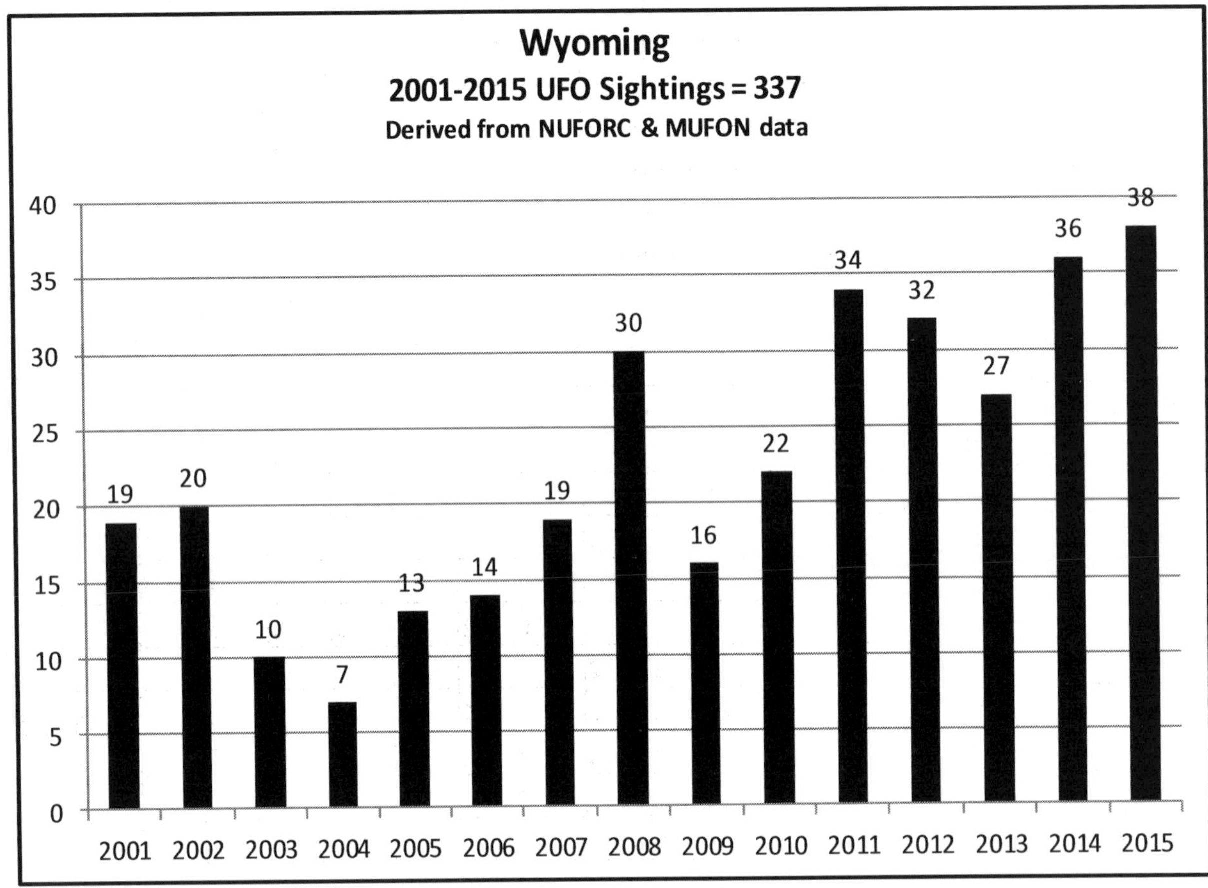

TOP TEN COUNTIES		RANK	TOP TEN SHAPES		
Laramie	46	1	Light	54	16.02%
Park	39	2	Sphere	40	11.87%
Natrona	37	3	Other	32	9.50%
Albany	31	4	Circle	30	8.90%
Sweetwater	29	5	Unknown	30	8.90%
Unknown	20	6	Triangle	26	7.72%
Campbell	19	7	Fireball	17	5.04%
Fremont	17	8	Star-like	15	4.45%
Uinta	16	9	Oval	12	3.56%
Teton	15	10	Disc	11	3.26%

UFO SHAPES: WYOMING

UFO Shapes	2001	2002	2003	2004	2005	2006	2007	2008	2009	2010	2011	2012	2013	2014	2015	Total
Blimp									1							1
Boomerang										1		1		1	1	4
Changing	1	1									2					4
Chevron			1						1			1	2		1	6
Cigar								3			1		1	1	1	7
Circle		1		1					5	1	6	9	3	2	2	30
Cone														1		1
Cross												1				1
Cylinder				1			1	1			3		1	1		8
Diamond				1									1			2
Disc						1		3	2		2	1	1		1	11
Disk		1						1		1		1			1	5
Egg	1	1					1	1						1		5
Fireball	5	4	1							2	1	1	1		2	17
Flash								3	1	1	1	1	1			8
Formation						1	2			1					3	7
Light	4	1	4	1	4	5	2		1	4	8	5	6	5	4	54
Other	2	1		2	2	1	5	2	1	2	2	1	3	5	3	32
Oval	2	3			1		1	3	1						1	12
Rectangle					1	1										2
Sphere		3	1		3	1	1	2		1	4	5	4	7	8	40
Star-like								3		3	1	2		2	4	15
Teardrop			1					1				1		1		4
Triangle	3	1	1	1		3	1	1		2	2	1	2	6	2	26
Unknown	1	3	1		2	1	4	5	3	3	1	1	1	3	1	30
Bullet							1	1							1	3
Square															2	2
Total	**19**	**20**	**10**	**7**	**13**	**14**	**19**	**30**	**16**	**22**	**34**	**32**	**27**	**36**	**38**	**337**

UFOS BY COUNTY: WYOMING

Counties	2001	2002	2003	2004	2005	2006	2007	2008	2009	2010	2011	2012	2013	2014	2015	Total
Albany	7	4			2	2	3	3	2		2	1	2	2	1	31
Campbell	2	3				1		2	1	3		2	3	1	1	19
Carbon	1	1		1	1	3				1	1		1		2	12
Converse				1			3	2			1	2				9
Crook								1			1	1	2	1	1	7
Fremont	2	1		1		1		3		1		1		4	3	17
Goshen	1										1				4	6
Hot Springs							1							2		3
Johnson										1			1			2
Laramie	3	3	2	1	2			1	3	8	3	5	2	8	5	46
Lincoln							1			2	1	1				5
Natrona				2	4	1	1	1	2	1	8	5	3	3	6	37
Park	1	1	2		1	1	4	3	4	1	9		5	4	3	39
Platte	1								1						2	4
Sheridan		2		1		3		1		1		1		3	1	13
Sublette						1		1								2
Sweetwater		1	1				1	1	2	1	4	11	3	3	1	29
Teton			2		1		1	3			2	1	3		2	15
Uinta	1	3			2	1	1	1			1	1	1	3	1	16
Unknown		1	1				3	5	1	1			1	2	5	20
Washakie			2					2								4
Wyoming										1						1
Total	**19**	**20**	**10**	**7**	**13**	**14**	**19**	**30**	**16**	**22**	**34**	**32**	**27**	**36**	**38**	**337**

If a county is missing from the list, it's because no UFO sightings were logged in either the NUFORC or MUFON databases for the 2001-2015 sample period.

UFOS BY MONTH: WYOMING

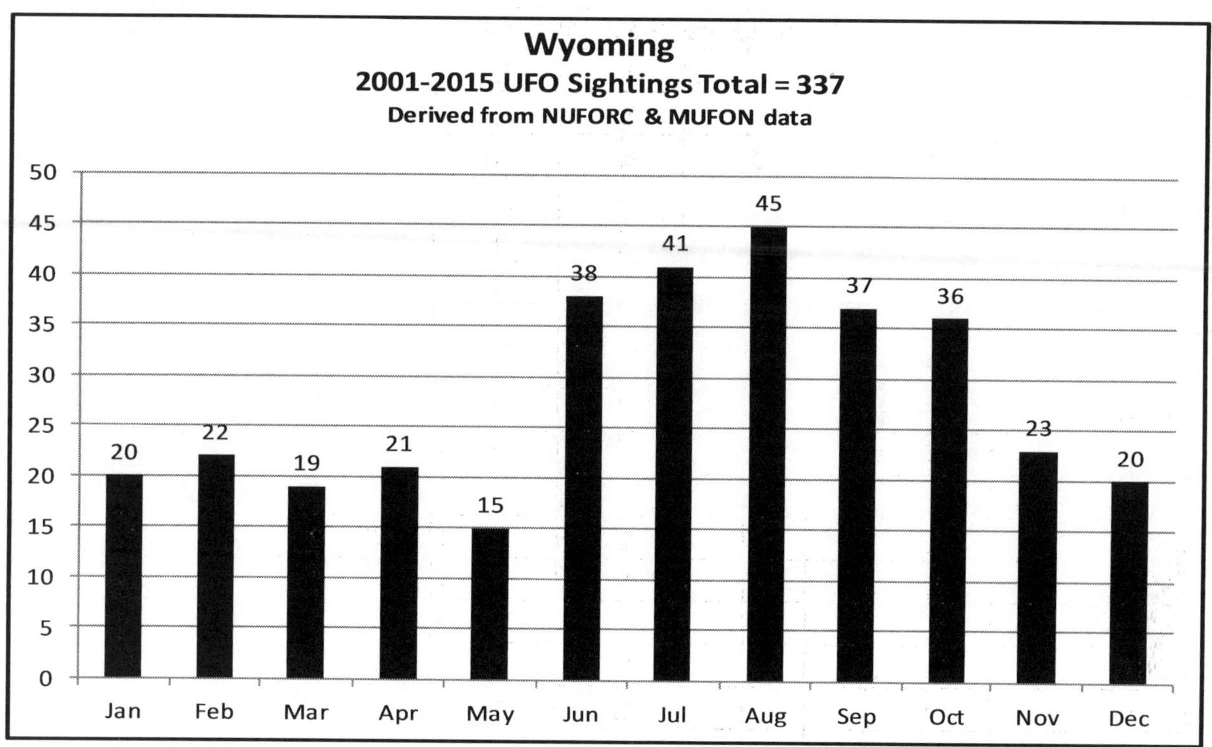

Year	Jan	Feb	Mar	Apr	May	Jun	Jul	Aug	Sep	Oct	Nov	Dec	Total
2001	2	1	1	1			3	6	1	3	1		19
2002		1	1	3	1	1	2	1	7	2	1		20
2003	2		1			1	2		2	1	1		10
2004		2	1	1	1	1				1			7
2005		2			1	1	1	1	2	1	1	3	13
2006			1	1		3	2	3		1	2	1	14
2007	1	1				6	3	1	3	2	1	1	19
2008	2	1	1	1		2	6	4	3	6	2	2	30
2009	4	3				2	3		2	1	1		16
2010				4	2	2	2	2	3	3		4	22
2011	1	3		2	1	4	4	6	5	4	2	2	34
2012	1	1	7	2	3	5	2	5	2	1	2	1	32
2013		2	3	1	3	3	3	3	2	2	2	3	27
2014	1	3	2	2	2	2	5	7	2	4	4	2	36
2015	6	2	1	3	1	5	3	6	3	4	3	1	38
Total	**20**	**22**	**19**	**21**	**15**	**38**	**41**	**45**	**37**	**36**	**23**	**20**	**337**

Distribution of Sightings between Databases: Wyoming

Database	Count	Percentage
MUFON	142	42.14%
NUFORC	195	57.86%
Total	337	100.00%

State Demographic Information: Wyoming

2010 US Census Statistics	
Population	563,626.00
Area in Square Miles	97,813 .01
Land Area Sq. Miles	97,093 .14
Population/Square mile	5 .8

ABOUT THE AUTHORS

Cheryl Costa is an upstate New York resident and a NY native, who saw her first UFO at age twelve. A military veteran, she's a retired Information Security professional from the Aerospace Industry. She's been a speaker at the International UFO Congress IUFOC and at the MUFON Symposium. Cheryl writes the wildly popular UFO column "New York Skies" for SyracuseNewTimes.com. Besides being a journalist she's also a published playwright. She holds a Bachelor of Arts degree from the State University of New York at Empire State College in Entertainment Writing.

***Linda Miller Costa*, M.L.S.** has a B.A. in Psychology from Case Western Reserve University and a Library Science masters from the University of Maryland, College Park. After a career in scientific research publishing institutions and libraries in Washington, D.C., she is currently at Le Moyne College Library in Syracuse, New York.

48398422R00209

Made in the USA
San Bernardino, CA
24 April 2017